CAPITALISM AND DEVELOPMENT

The book seeks to clarify the histories and theories of capitalist development. It provides an introduction to the main theories of capitalist development and critiques of the main problems that capitalist development still has to solve around the world. These critiques are grounded in studies of key sectors of capitalist development – electronics, automobiles, agribusiness, apparel, tourism and the cross-cutting areas of commodity chains and women's work. These chapters ask if capitalism cannot 'develop the Third World' through these industries, then how can it do so at all?

The contributors argue that not even the most enthusiastic proponents of the capitalist road to development would argue that capitalism has solved all its problems in the Third World. The book will interest students in Social Science, development and international business studies courses; the public interested in 'Third World' issues; and people working in development agencies of various types.

Leslie Sklair is Reader in Sociology at the London School of Economics. He has been a consultant for the United Nations Centre on Transnational Corporations, the UN Commission on Latin America, the ILO and the Office of Technology Assessment, US Congress.

Contributors: Henry Bernstein; Richard Child Hill; Mahmoud Dhaouadi; Diane Elson; Gary Gereffi; David Harrison; Jeffrey Henderson; Rhys Jenkins; Yong Joo Lee; Kyong-Dong Kim; Philip McMichael; Maria Mies; Ronaldo Munck; Ruth Pearson; Laura Raynolds; Michael Redclift; Leslie Sklair; Immanuel Wallerstein.

CAPITALISM AND DEVELOPMENT

Edited by Leslie Sklair

London and New York

First published 1994
by Routledge
11 New Fetter Lane, London EC4P 4EE

Simultaneously published in the USA and Canada
by Routledge
29 West 35th Street, New York, NY 10001

Typeset in Baskerville by LaserScript, Mitcham, Surrey
Printed and bound in Great Britain by
Mackays of Chatham PLC, Chatham, Kent

British Library Cataloguing in Publication Data
A catalogue record for this book is available from the British Library.

Library of Congress Cataloging in Publication Data
Capitalism and development/edited by Leslie Sklair.
p. cm.
Includes bibliographical references and index.
ISBN 0–415–07546–7 ISBN 0–415–07547–5 (pbk)
1. Capitalism – History. 2. Capitalism – Developing countries.
3. Economic development. 4. Developing countries – Industries.
I. Sklair, Leslie.
HB501.C24226   1994
330.12′2–dc20   93-49038
CIP

ISBN 0–415–07546–7 (hbk)   ISBN 0–415–07547–5 (pbk)

CONTENTS

v

CONTENTS

vi

FIGURES

vii

TABLES

CONTRIBUTORS

Henry Bernstein, Institute for Development Policy and Management, University of Manchester, Manchester M13 9QS, UK.

Mahmoud Dhaouadi, Faculté des Sciences Humaines et Sociales, Université des Lettres Arts et Sciences Humaines, 94 Boulevard 9 Avril 1938, Tunis 1997, Tunisia.

Diane Elson, Department of Economics, University of Manchester, Manchester M13 9PL, UK.

Gary Gereffi, Department of Sociology, Duke University, Durham, NC 27708-0088, USA.

David Harrison, School of Cultural and Community Studies, University of Sussex, Brighton BN1 9QN.

Jeffrey Henderson, Manchester Business School, University of Manchester M15 6PB, UK.

Richard Child Hill, Department of Sociology, Michigan State University, East Lansing, MI 48824-1111, USA.

Rhys Jenkins, School of Development Studies, University of East Anglia, Norwich NR4 7TJ, UK.

Kim Kyong-Dong, College of Social Sciences, Seoul National University, Seoul 151-742, Korea.

Yong Joo Lee, Department of Sociology, Michigan State University, East Lansing, MI 48824-1111, USA.

Philip McMichael, Department of Rural Sociology, Cornell University, Ithaca, NY 14853-8701, USA.

Maria Mies, Cologne, Germany.

ix

Ronaldo Munck, Faculty of Social and Health Sciences, University of Ulster, Co. Londonderry BT52 1SA, Northern Ireland.

Ruth Pearson, School of Development Studies, University of East Anglia, Norwich NR4 7TJ, UK.

Laura T. Raynolds, Department of Rural Sociology, Cornell University, Ithaca, NY 14853-8701, USA.

Michael Redclift, Wye College, University of London, Ashford, Kent TN25 5AH, UK.

Leslie Sklair, Department of Sociology, London School of Economics and Political Science, London WC2A 2AE, UK.

Immanuel Wallerstein, Braudel Center, State University of New York, Binghamton, NY 13902-6000, USA.

PREFACE

The contributors to this book were asked to address the questions: can capitalism develop the Third World? If yes, then how does it? If not, why not? Leaving aside the commonly agreed propositions that the very idea of the 'Third World' has become less and less useful in recent decades and that whatever use it retains is of an heuristic rather than an analytical kind, there is also to be found in these chapters a certain unease with the very concept of *development.*

Some of the authors approached the questions fairly directly, in terms of a particular component of development or in terms of an industrial sector. Others approached the question in a rather more indirect manner. Some chose to call the concept of 'development' itself directly into question. So, there are many points of view represented in this volume as there are in 'Development Studies' in general and in the 'Sociology of Development' in particular.

Nevertheless, despite the essentially contested nature of concepts like 'capitalism' and 'development', most of us know more or less what is being said when someone argues that 'capitalism, and only capitalism, can develop the Third World' (leaving other worlds aside for the moment) or when someone else argues that 'capitalism not only cannot develop the Third World, but actively underdevelops the Third World'. While academic theorists and researchers have long since dispensed with modernization and dependency theories (though they often lurk beneath the surface of some of their most virulent opponents' demolitions), out there in the field, in the planning agencies, in the corporate boardrooms, in the political circles, even in the classrooms, versions of these theories still provide much of the cognitive dynamic and moral passion for the thriving debate around development issues today. We hope that this collection will provide a solid base for understanding these issues and indicate some plausible answers to the central questions posed.

The division between Part I and Part II is deliberate rather than simply one of convenience. The chapters in Part I, 'Histories and theories of capitalist development', are intended to serve both as clarifying analyses of the main concepts of what is generally regarded as capitalist theory (or theories) of development and as a series of critiques of the main problems that capitalist development still has to solve around the world. These chapters, therefore, should be read as guides to their literatures and as open-ended engagements with unresolved problems. I suspect that not even the most enthusiastic proponents of the capitalist road to development (some of whom were invited to contribute to the volume but declined for their own good reasons) would argue that capitalism has solved all its problems in the Third World. The contributors to this book, to varying degrees, are sceptical of the development claims of local and/or global capitalists.

The chapters that make up Part II, 'Sectoral studies', are also in their own ways 'histories and theories of capitalist development', but focused on specific industrial sectors or groups of them. These sectors have not been chosen at random. They have been chosen deliberately to test out the claims of the main theories of capitalist industrialization at their strongest points. The logic of this argument is that if capitalism cannot 'develop the Third World' through these industries, then how can it do so at all?

It is worth briefly explaining why some very important issues are not addressed in this volume. One potential contributor declined on the grounds that there were other paths to 'development' than capitalism. Quite so! I flirted with the idea of some chapters on Eastern Europe and the 'communist Third World', but abandoned it early on. The reason for these omissions here is, precisely, that in this time of capitalist triumphalism there is a pressing need to pose the direct question 'Can *capitalism* develop the Third World?' without the distractions (which, surely, have to be faced sooner rather than later) of the viability of other roads to other kinds of development. If capitalism can develop, we are bound to ask: what types of 'development' result? The chapters in this book indicate the complexity of this apparently straightforward question and the possible answers.

If capitalism cannot produce viable development on a global scale, then we can start to draw our own conclusions about the future of the world in general, and the scramble to 'develop' what remains of the communist Third World and Eastern Europe on one or other version of the capitalist model, in particular. But these are the subjects of other books. For the moment, the large questions posed here are quite enough for this one book.

I have been very much helped in the tasks of editing this book by a generally very cooperative and efficient group of contributors and the difficulties of bringing together chapters from four continents have been simplified by their efforts. Seeta Persaud at LSE has carried out all her tasks with good humour and accuracy. At Routledge, Chris Rojek and Anne Gee deserve thanks for their encouragement of the project and professional skills.

Leslie Sklair
London
June 1993

Part I

HISTORIES AND THEORIES OF CAPITALIST DEVELOPMENT

1

DEVELOPMENT

Lodestar or illusion?

Immanuel Wallerstein

There is perhaps no social objective that can find as nearly unanimous acceptance today as that of economic development. I doubt that there has been a single government anywhere in the last 30 years that has not asserted it was pursuing this objective, at least for its own country. Everywhere in the world today, what divides left and right, however defined, is not whether or not to develop, but which policies are presumed to offer most hope that this objective will be achieved. We are told that socialism is the road to development. We are told that *laissez-faire* is the road to development. We are told that a break with tradition is the road to development. We are told that a revitalized tradition is the road to development. We are told that industrialization is the road to development. We are told that increased agricultural productivity is the road to development. We are told that delinking is the road to development. We are told that an increased opening to the world market (export-oriented growth) is the road to development. Above all, we are told that development is possible, if only we do the right thing.

But what is this right thing? There is of course no shortage of people who will respond to this query, and respond vigorously, even passionately. If there are protracted revolutionary movements in the world, the underlying drive is to end an oppressive situation. But the other drive that sustains the revolutionaries is the expectation that their victory at the state level will open the door at last to the real development of their country.

At the same time, there has been considerable disillusionment of late with the fruits of past development policies. In China, they talk about the ways in which the Cultural Revolution is said to have blocked for a decade, and so set back, development. In the Soviet Union, they talked about the ways in which bureaucratic rigidities and political errors have changed the economy, and they called for a *perestroika*. In Africa, they debate what explains the serious worsening of their economic situation since independence and following a 'decade', in fact several decades, of efforts to develop. In the United States and Western Europe, they talk about how too

3

large or too inappropriate government involvement in the economic process has hampered initiative and therefore has created a less desirable economic situation than these countries presumably enjoyed previously, or would presumably otherwise enjoy. In all of this grumbling, virtually no one in China or the former Soviet Union or Africa or the United States or Western Europe has challenged either the desirability or the viability of development as an objective. The critics or reformers or whatever they call themselves have merely argued that new and different policies must be adopted to replace those which they assert have failed.

We think of economic development as a post-1945 concept. And it is certainly true that most of our current language, as used by politicians and intellectuals, is a product of the geopolitics of the post-1945 era in the world-system. And it is certainly also true that since 1945 the concept as doctrine has been applied more widely and with greater social legitimation than ever before. But of course the basic idea has much older roots. It seems in fact that its history is concurrent with the history of the capitalist world economy itself. Full-fledged intellectual debates about how countries might be developed were occurring at least as early as the seventeenth century. What else, after all, was at issue in the proposed policies we group together today under the heading of mercantilism?

I should like therefore to review what we know of the history of this capitalist world-economy in order to address five questions:

1 Development is the development of what?
2 Who or what has in fact developed?
3 What is the demand behind the demand for development?
4 How can such development occur?
5 What are the political implications of the answers to the first four questions?

Then, and only then, will I come to the question in my title: is development a lodestar or an illusion?

Development is a word that has two different connotations. One is the reference to the processes of a biological organism. From little acorns do giant oaks grow. All organic phenomena have lives or natural histories. Somehow they begin; then they grow or develop; eventually they die. But, since they also reproduce, the death of a single organism is never the death of the species.

The presumed socioeconomic analogy is clear. Nations or states or societies somehow (and somewhere) begin; then they grow or develop. The rest of the analogy, however, is rarely pursued. There are few discussions of the likelihood that these entities will eventually die, or that the species will survive via a process of reproduction. We might wonder why the analogy is not pursued to its fullest, and why all our attention is concentrated on what

4

are taken to be the normalities or abnormalities of the middle segment of the sequence, the presumed growth process.

One reason may be that development has a second connotation, more arithmetic than biological. Development often means simply 'more'. In this case, we are making an analogy not to an organic cycle but to a linear, or at least monotonic, projection. And of course linear projections go to infinity. Now, infinity is far away. But it is there, and it is always possible to imagine more of something. This is clearly very encouraging as a social possibility. Whatever we now have some of, we might have more of tomorrow.

Of course, infinity is also quite terrifying. Infinity is in a very real sense a void. Endlessness is not everyone's cup of tea. There is an entire literature of clinical psychology about the ways in which human beings need to bound their universes, to create an environment of manageable scale, one which therefore offers a reasonable possibility that it is somewhat controllable. Durkheim's discussion of anomie is another version of the same argument.

Here, however, we come immediately upon a social relativity. In a set of groups which are located on a scale in terms of quantity of possessions, and which are all seeking more, those groups at the top end of the scale have only the void before them, whereas groups who are at the bottom are bounded by groups above them. So while some may face the uncharted prospects of seeming endlessness, others are clearly facing primarily the more manageable project of 'catching up' those who already have more.

There is a further element in the picture, as we all know. There are good times and there are bad times, periods of boom and periods of bust or at least of stagnation. The social interpretation of good and bad times tends to be quite straightforwardly relational. Good times are those moments in which we think we have more than previously. Bad times are those in which we think or fear we have less. If then we distinguish between groups at the high end of the scale of possessions and those at the low end, economic expansion and contraction present different pictures. Those at the high end to be sure have the comfort of being at the high end. They may however in times of expansion fear the void and in times of contraction fear that they will no longer be at the high end. Those at the low end start from the base knowledge of their relatively low level of material reward. Expansion then may open up the optimistic hope of immediate absolute improvement and relative middle-term catching up. Contraction offers on the other hand the gloom of decline from an already low level.

It seems to me therefore not hard to understand why people feel so passionately about development and oscillate so rapidly among alternative schemata for realizing development. Development as the achievement of 'more' is the Promethean myth. It is the realization of all our libidinal desires. It is pleasure and power combined, or rather fused. The desire lies within all of us. What the capitalist world-economy as an historical system has done is to make these desires for the first time socially legitimate.

'Accumulate, accumulate!' is the leitmotiv of capitalism. And in fact, the scientific-technological output of this capitalist system has created some widely visible spectacles of significant accumulation, and an impressive consumption level for about 10 to 20 per cent of the world's population. In short, the realization of the dream of endless accumulation has come to be not merely legitimate but to seem in some sense plausible.

At the same time, as living beings, we are all too conscious of the problem of death, and suffering. We are all aware that if some consume much, most do not. We are all equally aware that consumption is a present-oriented activity, and that in the future we shall not be there to consume. Those who consume well tend to draw the organismic implication that not only they as individuals but the groups of which they are a part will one day 'decline'. In short, they are faced with 'civilization and its discontents'.

However, although the controversies concerning development have deep resonances in the collective social psychologies (or mentalities) bred by historical capitalism, the basic issue is not psychological but social. The fact is that historical capitalism has been up to now a system of very differential rewards, in both class and geographic terms. As an empirical fact, this seems to me uncontestable, whether or not we think it theoretically inevitable or historically enduring.

Yet it is also the case that if we look at the various geographical-juridical zones that are today sovereign or potentially sovereign states, some are uncontestably better off than they were at previous moments in the history of the capitalist world-economy, whether the comparison is made between a given state today and that same state (more or less) 50 or 100 or 300 years ago, or the comparison is made between a given state's ordinal ranking in GNP per capita and the ordinal interstate rank level of the same state 50 or 100 or 300 years ago. This is usually what we mean when we say that a given state, say the United States or Sweden, has 'developed'. It is 'better off' materially and (many would argue) politically (expansion of civil rights etc.).

Who then has really developed in this sense? At one level the answer is easy. What we mean by the locutions, 'developed' and 'underdeveloped' countries, as they have come to be used in the last 30 years, is precisely the list of those who have 'developed' (or not) in either or both senses I spelled out above over the past 50 to 300 years. Generally speaking, we think of the countries of Western Europe plus Japan as the members of that list of 'developed' countries. We think of the so-called Third World as constituting the list of underdeveloped countries. The former socialist countries of Eastern Europe present the most controversial category in terms of either comparison: where they are today in relation to where they were; and where they stand in an ordinal ranking today compared to formerly. Analysts do not agree on what the basic economic measurements show and/or on whether these measurements are valid indicators for the socialist countries.

What then do we know of the pattern of 'national development' within the framework of the capitalist world-economy prior to 1945? I believe there are a number of things we can say today with some clarity.

One, a capitalist world-economy began to form centred on the European continent in the sixteenth century. From the beginning, this involved the establishment of integrated production processes we may call commodity chains. These commodity chains almost all tended to traverse the existing political boundaries. The total surplus extracted in these commodity chains was at no point in time distributed evenly in terms of the geographical location of the creation of the surplus, but was always concentrated to a disproportionate degree in some zones rather than in others. We mean by 'peripheries' those zones that lost out in the distribution of surplus to 'core' zones. Whereas, at the beginning of the historical process, there seemed little difference in the economic wealth of the different geographical areas, a mere one century's flow of surplus was enough to create a visible distinction between core and periphery in terms of three criteria: the accumulation of capital; the social organization of local production processes; the political organization of the state structures in creation.

Thus, by 1600 we could already say three things about the emergent peripheral zones (such as East Central Europe and Hispanic America) compared with the emergent core zones in Northwest Europe. The per capita consumption was lower. The local production processes used labour that was more coerced and received less real income. (This was of course a major reason why per capita consumption was lower.) The state structures were less centralized internally and weaker externally. It is crucial to note that while all three statements were true by 1600, none had been true as of 1450. The three empirical truths were the consequence of the operation of the capitalist world-economy.

Second, the mode of obtaining a larger proportion of the surplus was the relative monopolization of some segment of the commodity chain. The monopolization could occur because of some technological or organizational advantage which some segment of the producers had or because of some politically enforced restriction of the market. Whatever was the source of monopolistic advantage, it was inherently vulnerable. Others could over time try to 'copy' in one way or another the technological or organizational advantage or try to undermine the politically enforced restrictions of the market. This of course was the constant desire of producers who received less than others of the overall created surplus.

The vulnerability of historically temporary monopolizations was real. The advantages were constantly under attack – within states and between states. The eighteenth-century concern with the 'wealth of nations' was simply one ideological expression of the interest that producers had in maintaining or creating their own monopolistic advantages and undermining those of others. What we call mercantilism was simply one organized method of this struggle, in which producers whose abilities to corner surplus were somewhere in the middle rank sought to use the state structures in which they were influential to undermine economically stronger rivals, located in other state structures.

The recurring problem of 'overproduction' relative to any existing market, which regularly led to stagnations in the world-economy, was similarly the result of new producers jumping on a bandwagon of highly profitable goods and undermining monopolistic advantage by the expansion of total production. Whereas mercantilist policies sought to overturn existing advantage through political mechanisms, entry into production undermined advantage via the market. The net result could be the same, and neither method excluded the other.

When one kind of monopoly in the commodity chains was undermined, producers sought to create other new kinds of monopolistic advantages, since this was the only viable mechanism of cornering a large (as well as disproportionate) share of the capital accumulated through market-oriented production. What we call technological advances simply reflect this search for new monopolistic advantages. Often entirely new commodity chains were established. Certainly old ones were constantly reorganized.

Since locational rent is a relatively rare (and in the long run economically minor) phenomenon, the only reason why some geographic areas have been better off than others in terms of capital accumulation, the only reason that is why some are more central and others more peripheral at any given time, is their immediate past history within the operation of the world economy. That a given geographical zone occupies a given role is far from immutable. Indeed, every time a major monopoly has been undermined, the pattern of geographical locations of advantage has been subject to reorganization. In our discussion, we tend to ignore the relationships involved and instead summarize such phenomena in terms of the juridical units we call states. Hence we observe interstate 'mobility'. Some states 'rise'. Of course, this means, this must mean, that other states 'decline'. It must mean this, as long as surplus is accumulated unevenly and we therefore can rank geographical-juridical zones ordinally.

Third, the frontiers of this capitalist world-economy which was originally located in Europe were expanded over the subsequent three centuries. The explanation of why these frontiers expanded lies in processes internal to its changing structure. The fundamental process may be described as a sequence. The exhaustion of 'leading' monopolies led to periodic economic stagnations in the world-economy (so-called Kondratieff B-phases). Each economic stagnation led to a whole series of changes designed to restore the overall rate of profit in the world-economy as a whole and to ensure its

8

continued uneven distribution: reduction of costs of production by reduction of wage costs (both by the further mechanization of production
and by site relocation); creation of new monopolized leading products via
innovation; expansion of effective demand by further proletarianization of
segments of the workforce.

The last change however entailed on balance a rise in real income for
those segments, and hence was in partial contradiction with the objective
of increasing the global rate of profit. It is here that expansion of the
boundaries of the world-economy entered, as a mode of incorporating new
low-cost labour which would in effect compensate for the increases in real
wages elsewhere and thereby keep down the global average. Of course,
global averages were of no concern to individual capitalists. The uneven
distribution of profit remained crucial. But the path to this objective lay in
part through expansion of the reach of the capitalist world-economy.

The fact that the dominant forces in the capitalist world-economy sought
at various moments to expand its boundaries did not mean necessarily that
they could. Peoples everywhere offered resistances, of varying efficacity, to
the process of incorporation into the world-economy, especially given the
fact that incorporation was so unattractive a proposition in terms both of
immediate material interests and the cultural values of those being incorporated. Here, however, the capitalist world-economy benefited from the
advantages of its internal mechanisms. The constant reward for innovation
had the effect, among other things, of technological advances in armaments and therefore a steadily growing disparity in the control of military
force between the core states of the capitalist world-economy and those
political structures outside the world-economy. Conquest, even the
conquest of bureaucratically organized world empires or at least their
piecemeal dismemberment, became more and more possible.

It is quite clear now what the process of incorporation involved when it
occurred. On the one hand, it meant the transformation of a certain
number of production processes in these areas such that they were integrated into the commodity chains of the world-economy. Initially the
incorporated zones fit in at one of three points in the chain: production of
a 'raw material' – a cash crop (including food crops) or mineral product –
involved in some manufacturing process in core areas; production of
additional food crops to feed the workforce in peripheral zones producing
the raw materials; use of local surplus to sustain a workforce that would
migrate for specified periods to work in the production of raw materials or
of the food crops needed to sustain the producers of raw materials.

The second transformation that occurred in the incorporation process
was the reconstruction of existing political structures into states operating
within the interstate system of the capitalist world-economy. This involved
sometimes the remoulding of existing political structures, sometimes their
dismemberment, sometimes the fusion of several, and sometimes the creation

9

of entirely new and quite arbitrarily delimited structures. Whatever the case, the crucial element was that the resulting 'states' (sometimes they were those non-sovereign 'states' called 'colonies') had to operate within the rules of the interstate system. They had to maintain a certain degree of effective internal control which would permit the flows necessary to the operation of the commodity chains. But they could not be so strong *vis-à-vis* the states in the core zone of the world-economy that they could effectively threaten the interests of the major existing monopolizers.

The multiple expansions of the capitalist world-economy occurred sporadically but continually from the seventeenth through the nineteenth centuries. By the late nineteenth century, there were no areas left on the globe outside the operations of its interstate system. If there were still geographical zones not involved in any of the commodity chains that made up the functioning of the capitalist world economy, they were not many, and by and large the remaining few non-involved loci came to be involved by the time of the Second World War.

The fourth observation has to do with overall growth in the forces of production and levels of wealth. Though it is logically irrefutable that, in an ordinal ranking, if some rise others must fall, it might still be possible that either or both of the following could be also and simultaneously true: (a) all or most states have 'risen' on some absolute measurement of 'development'; (b) the dispersion of the absolute measures has diminished. Indeed, the main argument of liberal developmentalists has been that this could be true, and many of them would argue further that it has been in fact historically true.

I think it is unquestionable that for 10 to 20 per cent of the world's population at the top in terms of income, the absolute level of consumable wealth has risen over the past 400 years, and risen considerably. Furthermore, since this 10 to 20 per cent of whom I speak are unevenly distributed across the globe, it is certain that for a majority of the population of the core zones the statement is true. If therefore we utilize state-level measures like GNP per capita we will find such an increase, even when we control for price inflation.

The question is not whether the extraordinary expansion in accumulated physical plant and real wealth due to the transformation of the forces of production has occurred or not. Of course it has. Nor is it whether this expansion has not benefited the world's so-called middle strata, or cadres. Of course it has. The question is primarily whether it has meant any rise in real well-being for the large majority of the world's population. Certainly, up to 1945, when this majority was still largely rural, it is quite dubious that it did. If anything, in terms of absolute income, these populations were probably worse off than their ancestors had been. The gap between their incomes and those of the top tenth or top seventh of the world's population had certainly grown enormously over the previous four centuries.

We thus come to the point in time with which we began the discussion –
1945. The transformation of the capitalist world-economy since 1945 has
been remarkable in two regards. The absolute expansion of the world-
economy – in population, in value produced, in accumulated wealth – has
probably been as great as in the entire period 1500–1945. The political
strength of anti-systemic forces has been incredibly greater than before
1945. These two facts, taken together, provide the explanation of why
'development' has become so central an ideological theme and field of
combat since then. When the United Nations proclaimed the 1970s the
'Decade of Development', the combination of material growth and growth
in anti-systemic forces was thought by many to herald a fundamental
transformation of the pre-1945 structure of the world-economy. The
heralded transformation did not occur. And today, less than 20 years later,
the debate largely centres around why it has not occurred.

What then did occur since 1945 so far as the structure of the capitalist
world-economy is concerned? Two things, mainly. The absolute development of the forces of production has meant a massive reduction of the
percentage of the world population engaged in producing primary goods,
including food goods. The absolute growth of the manufacturing sectors
and the absolute and relative growth of the tertiary sectors have led to a
runaway 'urbanization' of the world which is still going on at a reckless
pace. In the process we have gone a considerable distance towards exhausting the pools of low-cost labour which have hitherto existed. The
boundary limits are being reached. Virtually all households are at least
semi-proletarianized. And economic stagnations continue to have the
consequence of transforming segments of these semi-proletarianized
households into proletarianized ones. Both leading and lagging profit
margins must as a consequence now decline.

Of course, efforts may be made by firms and state agencies to try to fight
back by constantly attempting to 'marginalize' some formerly proletarianized households. And there is much evidence that this occurs. Indeed, a
good deal of the neo-liberal governmental policies undertaken in many
countries during the 1980s represented attempts to do just this. For
example, the frequent proposals in the United States and Western Europe
to allow individuals to opt out of collective social insurance schemes would,
if adopted, have this effect. The resistance has been great. And I think the
evidence of the next 30 years will show conclusively that it is politically more
difficult for capital to 'marginalize' proletarianized populations than it is
for segments of the working class to 'proletarianize' themselves. Thus, the
net movement will in all likelihood remain in the direction of full proletarianization of households, which means higher-cost wage-labour. If this is
true, then capital is faced with an increasing squeeze.

The second main transformation of the post-1945 period has been the
remarkable series of triumphs of all the branches of the worldwide family

of anti-systemic movements. One manifestation has been the creation of a series of countries we call 'socialist countries', meaning that they claim the heritage in one way or another of the Third International. To be sure, some of these triumphs were due primarily to the military prowess of the USSR, but a significant number were the result of internal revolutionary forces – notably China, Korea, Vietnam, Yugoslavia, Albania and (with a somewhat special history) Cuba.

A second manifestation of this was the triumph of national liberation movements in a number of countries of the Third World. In many cases this too was the outcome of a significant popular struggle. The process, of course, varied considerably from country to country, but a minimal list of countries where a significant popular struggle took place might include India and Indonesia, Ghana and Algeria, Angola and Mozambique, Nicaragua and Zimbabwe.

A third manifestation of this has been the coming to power after 1945 of labour and/or social-democratic parties in the western world and the institutionalization of a 'welfare state' in most of these countries.

I am not arguing that the coming to power of Marxist-Leninist parties in the socialist bloc, of national liberation movements in the Third World, and of social-democratic parties in the OECD countries were the same thing. But there were none the less three elements they shared in common. First, each was the result of the upsurge of popular forces in their countries, forces which saw their victories as in some sense being antisystemic. (You and I may or may not agree with this conceptualization; I merely at this point suggest that it was a widespread self-image.) Second, each involved parties or movements that had been in political opposition (and frequently illegality) assuming governmental office. Third, and most relevant to our present discussion, in each case the groups in power set themselves the double policy objective of economic growth and greater internal equality. I said they shared three things in common. In fact, of late, there is a fourth. Each type of movement in power has come under internal criticism from within their countries, and often even from within the movements in power, for their failures to achieve, or to achieve to a sufficient degree, these goals – economic growth and greater internal equality. This is the source of the disillusionment to which I referred at the outset.

This then brings us to the third question that I said I would address: what is the demand for development about? The twin goals indicate the double answer. On the one hand, development was supposed to mean greater internal equality, that is, fundamental social (or socialist) transformation. On the other hand, development was supposed to mean economic growth which involved 'catching up' with the leader. For everyone this meant catching up, somewhere down the line, with the United States. This was the objective even for the USSR, as was made notorious in Khrushchev's prediction that the USSR would 'overtake' the United States by the year 2000.

But social transformation and catching up are seriously different objectives. They are not necessarily correlative with each other. They may even be in contradiction with each other. This latter, it seems to me, is the heart of what Mao Zedong was arguing in the 1960s. In any case, it should be clear by now that we have to analyse these objectives separately and cannot continue blithely to assume their pairing, which developmentalists, both liberal and Marxist, as well as many of their conservative opponents, have for the most part done for the past 150 years.

I say that both liberals and Marxists have blithely assumed that growth leading to catching up and an increase in egalitarian distribution are parallel vectors, if not obverse sides of the same coin, over the long run. What I really mean is that the ideological statements of both groups have asserted this. The question remains however as to which of the two objectives, derived from the two different connotations of the concept of development, has been the driving force of the political thrust towards development. To put it bluntly, which of the two objectives did people, do people really care about? To which did they give priority?

The answer has to be that the states have always given their priority to catching up and that the movements have been split on this issue. Indeed the split goes back to the very beginning of their individual and collective histories. The movements brought together under one organizational roof those who wished to have more, to catch up to (and implicitly to surpass) some others, and those who have searched for equality. The ideological belief that the two objectives were correlative served initially as organizational cement. This cement often took the form of the assertion that it was through economic growth (the end of scarcity) that equality would be made possible. However, the coming to power of the movements has forced them to operationalize their priorities, which has unglued, at least partially, the ideological coating. Hence the disillusionment, or at least the confusion and discontent.

This was scarcely a problem before 1945, for two reasons. First, the capitalist world-economy was still in secular expansion. As long as that was true, the prospects of a growing pie were there to ensure that everyone could hope for more. Those who could hope for more in a near future usually supported the system outright. Those whose hopes for more seemed more distant usually formed the social base of the anti-systemic movements, one of whose principal attractions was that they seemed to offer a political route to speeding up the realization of the hope for more.

Second, as long as the capitalist world-economy was in secular expansion, the antisystemic movements remained politically weak. Though the movements claimed to represent the popular classes and hence the overwhelming majority of the population, their support was always being eroded at both ends of their sociological spectrum. On the one hand, at the top end, for those popular strata that were relatively better off, the lure of individual mobility, perfectly rational in a system in secular expansion, undid their sense of collective solidarity in the struggle. And at the low end, those strata that were worst off (the semi-proletarianized households) were often defeated, hard to organize, or simply scrambling for subsistence. Some too were rendered docile by the prospect of full-time employment, which constituted significant upward mobility, not of course into the bourgeoisie but into the proletariat. This was plausible only for a few, but it was never certain which few this was. And hence it seemed a plausible prospect to many. This double 'defection' is of course the explanation of why the traditional nineteenth-century scenario of a workers' revolution has never really occurred thus far.

Paradoxically, the political weakness of the antisystemic movements prior to 1945 was their strength. Because they could never be in power, they could maintain untouched their unifying if contradictory ideology and hence they could survive, and survive quite well, as movements. It was the weakening of the political carapace of capitalism which, by allowing the antisystemic movements to arrive at state power in large numbers, exposed the deep internal cleavage of these movements, the rift between those who sought upward mobility and those who sought equality.

The answer, then, to the question of what the demand for development is about, is that there is no single coherent answer to that question to be gained through historical analysis. The slogan has masked a contradiction that is deep and enduring. What has happened since 1945, and especially since the 1970s, is that this contradiction is now a glaring one, and we are collectively being required to make political choices that are quite difficult and quite large.

Before, however, we can deal with the political choices, we must clear up one more historical question, how in fact 'national development' did occur where it occurred, or at least where it is claimed that it has occurred – more or less in the OECD countries.

The usual picture that has been painted is that between, say, 1750 and 1950, a number of countries have successively 'developed' or 'industrialized', the latter term usually taken as a synonym or indicator of development. The tale is usually told this way. First, England developed, then perhaps some other western countries, finally the whole list (plus Japan). This version of historical events takes us down to say 1950. At that juncture, the more conservative and more radical versions differ. The more conservative scenario is that the process is still continuing since 1950, with some countries like the Republic of Korea demonstrating this fact. The more radical version is that while such development did occur in the nineteenth century, the conditions are now entirely different and the obstacles to national

14

'capitalist' development far greater. Hence today the only alternative is said to be a radically new path of total rupture with the system.

But before examining the export-oriented model vs. the delinking model, let us first ask whether this scenario in fact reflects accurately what occurred? There is another way of reading world history for the period 1750–1950. Instead of seeing it as the story of a succession of successful national development efforts, we could see it as the story of the secular expansion of the world-economy as a whole. I remind you of two aspects of this structure we discussed: the polarization of zones which has been accentuated over time, and the constant expansion of the outer boundaries of the system. What has been happening seems to me quite simple. The increase of the geographical scope of operations led to an increase in the populations included in the world-economy. They were added in order to create low-cost, surplus-creating but not surplus-retaining segments of the worldwide commodity chains. As such segments grew absolutely, it had to mean that there was parallel growth of other segments of these commodity chains. And if the first segments were low on the retention of surplus, that of course meant that the others were higher. If core zones had not grown in size (and therefore in geography) at the same time as peripheral zones, the system would no longer have been a capitalist one.

The fact that, in 1950, many more geographical loci seemed to be 'developed' than in 1750 was not the consequence of the fact that a dozen or two dozen states had 'developed' their 'national' economies. It was that a dozen or two came to enclose the principal fruits of the expansion and development of the capitalist world economy as a whole. The OECD states did not 'achieve' their 'national development'; they had it 'thrust upon them'. What developed was the capitalist world-economy. It was as though there were an expanding inkspill of accumulated surplus which spread to the near parts of the blotter. That it was registered in the national accounts of one country rather than another was not necessarily or primarily the result of the policies of that country.

The situation has indeed changed today. The geography of the whole system can no longer expand. *Ergo*, the geographic reach of the core can no longer expand. If there is to be any significant change in which geographical areas are core-like, this is *more than ever* a zero sum game. If a new area comes in, an old area must go out. This was always partially true, but only partially, because of the overall expansion of the system. Now it is entirely true. If in the next 30 years China or India or Brazil were in a true sense to 'catch up', a significant segment of the world's population elsewhere in this world-system would have to decline as a locus of capital accumulation. This will be true whether China or India or Brazil 'catches up' via delinking or via export-orientation or by any other method. This will be true as long as states, separate states, are each searching for ways to develop themselves. Catching up implies competition, and competition

15

means that one country's development will be at someone else's expense ultimately.

We therefore arrive at the issue everyone really cares about: what shall be done? What political implications shall we draw from this analysis? The first one I draw is the most radical. National development may well be a pernicious policy objective. This is so for two reasons. For most states, it is unrealizable, whatever the method adopted. And for those few states which may still realize it, that is transmute radically the location of world-scale production and thereby their location on the interstate ordinal scale, their benefits will perforce be at the expense of some other zone. This has always been true up to a point. It is more true than ever today.

I hear the shouts of all those who are suffering by the current unequal allocation of the world's created surplus. What then shall we do? Surely you do not expect us to do nothing. And my answer is: surely not.

At this point I must make an assumption. The assumption is that the objective is truly an egalitarian, democratic world, and not simply a reversal of fortunes inside our present inegalitarian, undemocratic world-system. If this is the objective, what is the route? In the late nineteenth and early twentieth centuries the dominant view was that the route was via nationally organized working-class movements. In the period since 1945 this view has evolved *de facto* into a somewhat different one: that the route is via popularly organized national movements.

But will popularly organized national movements in fact achieve greater equality and democracy? I have become increasingly sceptical of this, as have many others. I think popularly organized national movements have found themselves in a dilemma for which there is no easy solution and which has contributed strongly to the sense of impasse and frustration that has been growing of late.

The great argument in favour of state-organized attempts to retain surplus created within the frontiers is that the state is the only agency potentially capable of going against the strong currents of unequal exchange flows structurally central to the functioning of the capitalist world economy. This is a very strong argument and has secured wide support. The great negative however of that argument is that the state as an agency requires decision-making actors, those who occupy the key political and bureaucratic posts. And these persons have a direct interest as a subgroup in the choice of priority between an emphasis on growth/catching up and equality. It is clear that economic self-interest pushes them towards the goal growth and 'catching up', and the consequences for the popular strata tend to be in the middle run usually at best no change for the better, sometimes even a worsening of their condition. As long as solutions are framed and sought at the national level, the dilemma will remain, and states governed by erstwhile anti-systemic movements will remain repressive of their own popular strata and at best only partial winners of the catching-up game, to the primary benefit of the cadres.

Is not another strategy available for the movements? I am not referring to a world-level strategy, if by that one means a strategy that requires implementation by a world-level movement. Such an alternative is unrealistic, at least presently. World revolution or even coordinated worldwide political struggle remains a rhetorical flourish for the most part. I am thinking rather of attacking the flows of surplus at another point, at the point of their production. Suppose that anti-systemic movements concentrated their energies everywhere – in the OECD countries, in the Third World countries, and yes in the socialist countries as well – on efforts defined as retaining most of the surplus created. One obvious way would be to seek to increase the price of labour or the price of sale by the direct producers. These prices, like most prices, are controlled by market considerations, but market considerations *within parameters established by political struggle*. These parameters are subject to change, and change constantly. This is exactly what capitalists know. They spend a considerable amount of their worldwide political energy on the politics of pricing.

The OPEC oil price rise was a marvellous instance of this. It was clearly a consciously political struggle, and the OPEC countries initially did very well for themselves. No doubt you may retort, look at them now. Without going into the details of the anti-OPEC counteroffensive which did over a decade force OPEC to retreat, the retreat illuminates all the pitfalls of national-level development strategies. When the OPEC countries retained after 1973 a larger percentage of the flow of surplus, it was the states who retained this. It was then up to the states to redistribute this – to the cadres, to the creation of infrastructure, to the workers, etc. The pressures were obvious and so were the vulnerabilities.

If the start of the process had been a rise in the price of labour on OPEC oilfields, the impact might have been less dramatic, but it might also have been considerably more difficult to reverse. If the struggle had been a workers' struggle within the OPEC states and not an OPEC state struggle against the world powers-that-be, the politics would have been quite different. A steady politically induced rise in surplus retention would be unlikely to lead to serious losses in the world market. That is, if tomorrow, in all the NICs, textile workers were paid 20 per cent more, the choice facing the purchasers of such textiles might only be to turn to other equally expensive zones. They might do this in part. Or they might look for new NICs. The battle would have its ups and downs. But, and this is the crucial point, in a world-economy that is in the process of exhausting its reserve labour forces, such a battle would have far more ups than downs.

In a sense what I am calling for is a return of the pendulum. The first great strategy in the fight against inequality involved the so-called class struggle. In the nineteenth century this struggle was fought both in the workplace (via the construction of trade unions) and in the political arena (via the construction of socialist parties). Capitalists fought back in two main ways. They used the state to repress such movements. And they recruited new workers from the national and worldwide pool of reserve (semi-proletarianized) households.

Since the distribution of proletarian and semi-proletarian households was not random but stratified nationally, ethnically, racially, it was clear that a political strategy that focused on proletarian households missed a good half of the battle. Thus we got the swing, ever more sharply in the twentieth century, to what might be called an 'anti-imperialist' focus. The struggle now emphasized *national* liberation and national development of the national economy, and within the OECD states the emphasis shifted to the anti-racist struggle, an equivalent shift in emphasis.

Meanwhile, however, the inexorable drive of capitalism for the accumulation of capital has been undermining its ability to command access to a *de facto* unlimited, reserve labour force. This has now become quite limited. The strategy of capitalists has thus shifted. The OPEC-type battle in fact serves them quite well. None of the Seven Sisters suffered from the OPEC price rise. Quite the contrary! As long as the focus is on national distribution of the accumulated surplus value, capitalists can relocate the locus of their capital without necessarily losing long-run control over it.

On the other hand, capitalists are now vulnerable to the original strategy of a 'class' struggle as they were not before because of the fact that the world-economy has reached its geographic limits. But this then requires a reorganization of the emphasis of the movements. The movements cannot afford their close links to the states, even to the regimes they have struggled to bring to power. Their concern must be how at each point on very long commodity chains a greater percentage of the surplus can be retained. Such a strategy would tend over time to 'overload' the system, reducing global rates of profit significantly and evening out distribution. Such a strategy might also be able to mobilize the efforts of all the many varieties of new social movements, all of which are oriented in one way or another more to equality than to growth.

This is not a new Fabian strategy. We will not inch our way to world equality. Rather it is premised on the belief that global rates of profit are quite open to political attack at a local level. And, as the local victories cumulate, a significant cave-in of political support for the system will occur. For it will force the greedy to fall out among themselves, and to try to eat into the portion of the surplus they apportion to their agents and intermediaries. But that of course would be collectively suicidal, since an underfed 'army' tends to refuse to fight, and without an 'army' to protect the capitalists (that is, an extensive political and ideological apparatus), the capitalist world-economy has no secure way to survive.

Well, then – development: lodestar or illusion? I hope by now my answer is obvious. National development is today an illusion, whatever the method advocated and used. If all our energies are turned in that direction, then capitalism may have the 200 extra years Schumpeter hoped it could create for itself. And with the 200 extra years, the privileged strata of the world may be able to manage a transition to a completely different but similarly inegalitarian world-system.

But development can be a lodestar. We can try to force the pace on the secular trends of the capitalist world-economy, exactly what capitalists fear most. The local and localized demands for greater participation and higher real income, that is, worldwide unruliness by producers in the loci of production (using this term in its broadest sense) is politically mobilizing and economically redistributive. It also disarms the tenants of the status quo of some of their best weapons: the political divisions between proletarian and semi-proletarian households (nationally and worldwide); and the appeal to sacrifice (of the surplus each produces) on behalf of the state.

This strategy is less obvious than one thinks. None of the traditional or erstwhile anti-systemic movements – the Social Democrats in the West, the Communist parties of the world, the national liberation movements – is preaching it, even secondarily, in any serious way. And few of the newer anti-systemic movements that have arisen in the last 20 to 30 years are doing so either, or at least they are not doing so with the kind of conscious intent to overload the system I am advocating. The movements still have too much faith in equality via growth; what they need seriously to envisage is growth through equality. But it cannot be an egalitarianism that turns its back on individual realization and social variation. Equality is not in competition with liberty. They are intimately linked. When an attempt is made to keep these objectives separate – as happened in the Cultural Revolution – it fails to achieve either.

The weakness of the capitalist world-economy is in its self-fulfilment. As it becomes more and more commodified, it undermines its ability to maldistribute surplus and hence to concentrate its accumulation. But it is far from enough to say more commodification is the route to the undoing of the system. For, left to themselves, the dominant forces will seek to slow down the pace. The efforts of national development have been traditionally seen as something that has speeded up the pace. I suggest that they should be seen instead as substitutes for other policies that would have, can still, speed up the pace far more and far faster.

An emphasis on surplus retention by the producers, that is an emphasis on greater equality and democratic participation, far from being Utopian, could be devastatingly effective. The great barrier to that today is less the large-scale capitalists than the anti-systemic movements themselves. They must become aware of their historic ambivalence about the two meanings of development – more, and more equal. And they must opt for the latter.

In such an option, the state is not irrelevant. There are many ways in which the state apparatuses can abet this programme. But if the state apparatuses are the motor, then development will be an illusion and not a lodestar.[1]

NOTE

1 This is a slightly revised version of a talk, Distinguished Speaker series, Center for Advanced Study of International Development, Michigan State University, 22 October 1987. I am grateful for the astute comments, as usual, of Terence K. Hopkins, and for the continuing intellectual discussions with him and with Giovanni Arrighi.

2

DEMOCRACY AND DEVELOPMENT

Deconstruction and debates

Ronaldo Munck

For Francis Fukuyama, new guru of the right and scourge of the left: 'There is an unquestionable relationship between economic development and liberal democracy, which one can observe simply by looking around the world' (Fukuyama 1992: 125). Before launching into a tirade about crass empiricism and naive optimism, we must note that Fukuyama goes on to state that this relationship is more complicated than it first appears, and that the logic of development does not necessarily lead to democratization. In brief, in spite of the observed relationship between democracy and development across the globe, and Fukuyama's conservative Hegelian quest for a 'Mechanism' underlying history, he can only conclude lamely that 'there does not appear to be a *necessary* connection between the two' (Fukuyama 1992: 125). This can be a useful starting point for my own attempt to explore the relationship between democracy and capitalist development, in general theoretical terms and through a schematic case study of Latin American history in this regard. The first task is to deconstruct the two terms – democracy and development – so as to understand better the possible relationship(s) between the two phenomena.

DEMOCRACY

Democracy can be labelled bourgeois, liberal, national, radical, pseudo, empowered or even socialist. We are all for it, but we find it difficult to define. It is a universal good, except when it is given an epithet of 'western' or 'bourgeois' or 'populist'. One place to start would be with the minimalist definition of Schumpeter for whom: 'the democratic method is that institutional arrangement for arriving at political decisions in which individuals acquire the power to decide by means of a competitive struggle for the people's vote' (Schumpeter 1962: 269). For Schumpeter, democracy was government by politician and not by the people. Following in this tradition, the early work of Dahl referred to democracy as government

21

by minorities, adding however, the need for a normative consensus behind these minorities (see Dahl 1956). Yet there is another tradition, including C. B. Macpherson and Norberto Bobbio, for which democracy is above all about popular participation, and argues that the principles of democracy need to be extended to the economic sphere if its objectives are to be attained (see Macpherson 1973; Bobbio 1987). Thus, in the Latin American debate on the transition to democracy Amparo Menendez Carrion writes categorically that: 'We cannot speak of democracy as such . . . straightforward democracy does not exist. We prefer to label the so-called "actually existing democracies", civilian governments or civilian regimes of an electoral type' (Menendez Carrion 1991: 76). So, we can have a restricted definition of democracy or a broader, dynamic concept of considerable flexibility.

An advantage of a restricted definition of democracy is that it allows us more easily to make cross-cultural comparisons. Certainly, democratization is a dynamic process and not a simple linear progression. We may also wish to define citizenship, following T. H. Marshall, as civil (the prerequisites for individual freedom), political (participation in the exercise of political power) and social, defined as 'the right to a modicum of economic welfare and security' (Marshall 1973: 72). We may also note that the long-term consolidation of representative democracy, for example in Latin America, will require an extension of participation beyond the electoral act, for example, to determine the development model, the definition of basic needs, etc. What does not seem particularly fruitful in terms of analysis, is to *define* democracy in broad, ultimately Utopian terms and then judge reality against this model. Political democracy begins then to appear as an inadequate temporary way-point on the road to 'real' democracy. As Daniel Levine points out: 'Political arrangements need not be wholly egalitarian or completely participatory to merit the term "democracy"' (Levine 1988: 383). Rather than 'overload' the term democracy, in terms of substantive equality, we may take as a working model a political system characterized by free and open elections, competing electoral states, civil liberties, and equity in political procedures.

DEVELOPMENT

Development is another term with multiple meanings or usages: human, grassroots, economic, social, capitalist, organic, uneven, sustainable or socialist amongst others. It used to be assumed also that it was a 'good thing' although some now argue that 'The metaphor of development gave global hegemony to a purely Western genealogy of history, robbing peoples of different cultures of the opportunity to define the forms of their social life' (Esteva 1992: 9). A development discourse has now emerged which can mean everything and nothing. Development implies progress from backwardness to modernity, from a simple to a complex society, from bad to good ultimately. As with democracy, development can be given a minimalist definition. In this case, it is usually equated with economic growth or, more precisely, gross national product per capita. More ambitiously, however, the United Nations Development Programme in its 1990 Human Development Report defines 'human development' as a process involving 'the enlargement of relevant human choices' (UNDP 1991: 2). Other UN bodies have referred variously to 'endogenous development' which rejected the ethnocentric modernization model of old, and 'sustainable development', which presented a green and democratic development model for the post-communist era. This proliferation of meanings causes problems for analysis, because we can always define 'true' development in ways which disqualify most actual situations.

We could simply accept the judgement by Wolfgang Sachs that 'development was a misconceived enterprise from the beginning' and that this catch-all concept, hailed alike 'by revolutionaries carrying their guns as well as field experts carrying their Samsonites', is virtually meaningless (Sachs 1992: 4). However, while we can agree that the development discourse is profoundly contradictory, it is hard to see how the West 'invented' underdevelopment (as social reality rather than concept). It does not take a Fukuyama to agree with the World Bank's truism that 'Development is the most important challenge facing the human race' (World Bank 1991). Again, following the demon Bank, 'The challenge of development, in the broadest sense, is to improve the quality of life' (World Bank 1991: 4). This is defined in ways which go beyond growth in per capita incomes to the reduction of poverty and greater equity, to progress in education, health and nutrition, and to the protection of the environment. While we need to deconstruct the development discourse and explore its contradictions and silences, it is naive to think that we can somehow refuse this terrain altogether. Again, separating normative stances where we can 'define' democracy and development in as broad and radical terms as we wish, for the purposes of comparative and quantitative analysis, a minimalist definition may be most useful.

DEMOCRACY AND DEVELOPMENT: THE RECORD

In moving beyond the task of deconstruction we can start to clarify the conceptual profusion, not to say confusion, of the terms by adopting 'minimal' or restricted definitions in the first instance. Thus democracy is basically taken to be a political system with free elections and the prevalence of civil liberties. And development can be defined primarily in terms of economic growth measured conventionally as gross national product per capita. We may then proceed, as a first step, to a general quantitative survey of the relationship between the two phenomena.

A broad cross-cultural survey carried out in 1990 by Partha Dasgupta concluded that 'political and civil rights are positively and significantly correlated with real national income per head and its growth' (Dasgupta 1990: 28). At the very least most studies conclude that liberties do not hold growth back. A typical phrasing is that of Atul Kohli for whom 'Third World democracies clearly are capable of generating and sustaining moderate but satisfactory growth rates' (Kohli 1988: 160). An implicit assumption is that authoritarianism, by controlling labour and incomes generally, can provide higher growth rates. Yet there is a counterargument that, put crudely, democracy 'is good for business' in the sense that constitutional political environments and respect for individual liberties are part of the essential framework for entrepreneurial economic achievements (Munck 1993).

Before we can conclude on how strong the relationship between democracy and capitalist development is, we need to examine the actual record in more detail. Gunder Frank expressed a common view amongst radicals in the 1970s in arguing that the systematic violation of political, civil and human rights in many Third World countries was neither accidental nor merely ideologically motivated: 'Rather it is a necessary concomitant of economic exploitation' (Frank 1981: 88). The evidence gathered for this statement was rather impressionistic although Frank does cite in his favour: 'The correlation between repressive "sociopolitical measures and invest-ment climate" in the Third World . . . documented from a Japanese point of view in a "risk table" published by Nikkei Business, Japan's leading business magazine' (Frank 1981: 228). So in 1977 Japanese capital thought the 'investment climate' was better in (repressive) South Korea than in (relatively democratic) India, and the Shah's Iran rates higher than Mexico. But perhaps a more salient fact is that in the double A category, amongst the Swedens and Netherlands only the solitary (and exceptional) case of Saudi Arabia bears out the thesis that the denial of democracy is economically necessary. The point is that one cannot declare a priori that this or that political system is *necessary* to capitalist development. There is no obvious way in which we can deduce that capitalist development will lead inevitably either to democracy or to dictatorship. Certainly we cannot do this on the basis of a sketchy, impressionistic tour of capitalist 'horror stories' in a particular phase of the world economy.

A broad survey of 115 capitalist countries between 1960 and 1980 was carried out by Gerald Scully which compared growth rates with measures of political, civil and economic liberty:

It was found that the choice of the institutional framework has profound consequences on the efficiency and growth of economies. Politically open societies, which bind themselves to the rule of law, to private property, and to the market allocation of resources, grow

24

at three times the rate and are two and one-half times as efficient as societies in which these freedoms are circumscribed or proscribed.

(Scully 1988: 652)

Leaving aside the point about private property (obviously its 'respect' is essential to capitalism) the gist of the argument is clear. Likewise, Grier and Tullock in a similarly broad survey find that 'political repression is negatively correlated with growth in Africa and Central and South America' (Grier and Tullock 1989: 259). Certainly all these measurements are fairly crude and cannot sustain firm conclusions. There are also studies pointing in the opposite direction that there is an ineluctable 'cruel choice' between development and democracy (see, for example, Marsh 1979; Adelman and Morris 1967). However, as the World Bank notes: 'Dictatorships have proven disastrous for development in many economies' (World Bank 1991: 33). This led, in part, to a growing number of democratic regimes in the 1980s. This does not mean, of course, that democratic regimes would do any better at meeting the 'development challenge' of the 1990s. Nor is the trend towards democratization as universal as some thought in 1988–9, as a cursory look at the conflicts created or exacerbated as a result of the end of the Cold War would demonstrate.

In general we can conclude that recent studies correlating democracy and development tend to find a certain 'elective affinity' between them. Yet we must beware of what Guillermo O'Donnell has called the 'universalistic fallacy' according to which: 'Since some positive correlation between socio-economic development and political democracy can be found, it may be concluded that this relationship holds for all the units (say, regions) included in that set' (O'Donnell 1973: 6). Not only is this logically erroneous but we can point to a very clear negative correlation between levels of development and the prevalence of democratic regimes in Latin America during the 1970s for example. More generally, the quantitative approach misses the precise historical context of the relationships between democracy and development across time and across regions. Nor can these studies tell us much about the 'quality' of either democracy or development in a particular situation. So, while we must perforce accept the empirical generalization that democracy and development go hand in hand, the relationship between these two phenomena remains a 'black box' as Rueschemeyer, Stephens and Stephens (1992: 32) put it. The precise explanation of this apparently causal relationship is not clear, beyond the glib generalizations of modernization theory.

It is thus necessary to move on to the various theoretical accounts (often contradictory) which seek to make sense of the 'black box' which mediates the relation between development and democracy.

DEMOCRACY AND DEVELOPMENT: THE DEBATES

If a quantitative approach to the relationship between democracy and development has its limitations, the qualitative debates are not devoid of confusion. We are told by serious analysts that (capitalist) development leads to democracy while others argue that it leads inevitably to authoritarianism. We are told that democracy is 'the best possible shell' for capitalist development and, conversely, that it is a dangerous source of instability for that system.

For S. M. Lipset, 'The more well-to-do a nation, the greater the chances that it will sustain democracy' (Lipset 1963: 48). Guillermo O'Donnell translates this into an 'optimistic equation' whereby 'More socioeconomic development = likelihood of political democracy' (O'Donnell 1973: 4) to which he counterposes a less optimistic equation in which 'More socioeconomic development = more political pluralisation = less likelihood of political democracy' (O'Donnell 1973: 9). It must be said that whereas O'Donnell's model of the bureaucratic state has been seriously undermined by subsequent criticism (see Collier 1978) there has been little challenge to his earlier conclusion that political authoritarianism – and not political democracy – was the more likely concomitant of higher levels of modernization. Certainly, the history of Latin America in the 1970s clearly supports his argument that there is a weak correlation between modernization and democracy. Coulter's study supports this view in so far as the strong global correlation between development and democracy could not be sustained for Latin America (Coulter 1975). Today we could argue that while democracy can withstand bad economic performance, there is certainly a positive benefit to democracy from buoyant economic conditions.

For Lenin, 'a democratic republic is the best possible political shell for capitalism' (Lenin 1918: 296). To this view we can contrast that of Samuel Huntingdon who, in his report to the Trilateral Commission, argued that 'threats to democracy arise ineluctably from the inherent workings of the [capitalist] system itself' (Crozier, Huntingdon and Watanaki 1975: 8). From this position sprang the concern with the 'crisis of governability' in modern democracies. In the Marxist tradition there was, for a period, a concerted effort to 'derive' the form of the state from the nature of capital itself. This experiment in alchemy inevitably failed and we are left with no necessary relationship between democracy and capitalism. As Bob Jessop pointed out: 'if there is no one-to-one correlation between capitalism and democracy in specific societies, it is clear that the relation between them must be contingent rather than a relation of logical entailment' (Jessop 1978: 19). The way this side of the debate (democracy is good or bad for capitalist development) is played out today is slightly different. It is now very common to hear in the Latin American context that 'no one can deny that democracy is the only path to modernity' (Weffort 1990: 39). From a discussion of whether development led to democracy or not, the debate has now shifted to a consideration of democracy as a prerequisite for the development or modernization process (cf. Nun 1991). While no 'iron rules' can be discerned, there is now a clear vision of a 'virtuous circle' involving democracy and development.

It should be clear by now that all these debates on the causal relationship between democracy and development (albeit simplified somewhat) work with a limited two-dimensional view of political development: either democracy or non-democracy. As Chai-Anan Samudavanija notes, this preoccupation reflects a certain poverty of ideas in western political science, and fails to grasp that 'Third World states encompass within themselves *contradictory* characteristics and structures, for example those of development and underdevelopment, democracy and authoritarianism, civilian and military rule, *at the same time*' (Samudavanija 1991). The simple dichotomies of the democracy/development debate and their unilinear, often teleological nature, lead invariably to theoretical cul de sacs.

One option would be to adopt the 'absolute historicism' of Antonio Gramsci which rejects the transformation of principle into a dogmatic ideology which pretends to unlock the secrets of history, or the temptation to seek 'general laws' of historical development. Another important direction of clarification is to understand that the meaning of a word does not exist 'in itself' (i.e. in its transparent relation to the literal character of the signifier) but is determined by the ideological positions brought into play in the sociohistorical process in which words, expressions and propositions are re/produced (Pecheux 1982: 11). Thus, the 'words' development and democracy can be seen to take on different meanings in conflicting discourses. These 'words' are also, clearly, the site of an 'ambiguity', part of a decisive battle on the possible futures of humankind. From a broader post-modernist perspective, we can argue further that 'all privileged points of view have been annulled, along with the dominant position which allowed the establishment of hierarchies of interpretation' (Richard 1993: 467). So, not only must we refuse the notion that democracy and development are terms which possess a single, simple and definitive meaning, but we must now question whether they point in a politically and historically determined direction. The very idea of development is suffused by the universalizing model, or ethic, of modernity as rationalization. As to democracy, we need to challenge the security of this supposedly univalent sign, noting the profoundly contradictory nature of the present world, where the disorder of the economy (or market) is only partly balanced by a political order which is increasingly dissociated from social structures.

APARTHEID AND CAPITALISM

What might appear as a diversion from our main object of enquiry may in fact help clarify the debate considerably. For in South Africa we see many of the debates mentioned above played out in a particularly dramatic political context. Was apartheid (a denial of democracy if ever there was one) a brake on the development of capitalism or a necessary condition for its survival? Is democratization occurring now in South Africa to facilitate capitalist development, or simply because of the success of a national liberation movement?

Amalgamating the various strands within the 'liberal' school, we find the argument that apartheid is a retarding factor on capitalist development. An extreme formulation is that of O'Dowd who argued in the mid 1960s that growth would eventually bring about the end of apartheid (O'Dowd 1974). For economic liberalism, apartheid, like other forms of state intervention, restricted the free operation of the market. It was often argued that capitalists were opposed to the institutions of apartheid, but lacked the power to rid South Africa of this unfortunate market distortion. Although the positive effects for capital of cheap labour (as produced by apartheid's mechanisms) were sometimes recognized, on the whole it was argued that 'the *net* effect of the major political policies of the post-war period has been to slow economic growth below its achievable level' (Bromberg and Hughes 1987: 223).

The radical critique of the liberal views tended to stress the functional nature of apartheid for capitalist development in South Africa. Thus Frank Johnstone argued that the dynamic economic development of South Africa under the allegedly dysfunctional system of apartheid 'suggest[s] very strongly that there has been something highly functional and causally significant about the relationship between the economic system and the system of racial domination' (Johnstone 1976: 215). Apartheid is thus seen as generated and, in the strong sense, determined by capitalist development in South Africa. Increasingly, the interests of individual capitalists, the capitalist system, and the apartheid state, were viewed as identical, thus foreclosing any possibility of conflict within apartheid capitalism. As Nicoli Natrass puts it, in a useful overview of this whole debate, 'The determinants of racial policies were seen as ultimately rooted in the requirements of the economy. If a system could be shown to be functional to capitalism, then it was assumed that it must have arisen for those purposes' (Natrass 1991: 667). From specific relations between apartheid and capital at given points of time, and for certain capitalist sectors, there is a slide to a seamless ahistorical picture of elective affinity between apartheid and capitalism. Recent developments in South Africa are sufficient testimony to the crudeness of this conclusion.

It is not possible here to examine in detail whether apartheid (as denial of democracy) has passed from being a boost to a brake on capitalist development in South Africa. In methodological terms we now find earlier proponents of the radical-functionalist view such as Harold Wolpe, arguing that the relationship between apartheid and capitalism is 'historically contingent' and also 'Janus faced, being simultaneously functional and contradictory' (Wolpe 1988: 8). We can thus move beyond the earlier, somewhat sterile counterposition between apartheid as either 'good' or 'bad' for capitalist development. The relationship between development and its political context is too complex and mediated for us to isolate particular factors and establish a clear-cut correlation between them. The empirical studies which have been carried out into the 'booster to brake' thesis on apartheid's relation to capitalism tend to reject the radical theory (see Moll 1990). This does not mean that class and power can be seen as mere 'distortions' to the market as in the liberal analysis. From crass functionalism and deep-structure analysis, we need not jump to a naive faith in the efficiency of the market and its supposed affinity with democracy. We do, however, need to go beyond a static analysis which was also so heavily overdetermined politically, that the lines between analysis and polemic were at times somewhat blurred.

In general terms, the conclusion we can draw from the South African debate is that no necessary or permanent relationship exists between democracy and development. That relationship is necessarily contingent and historically bound. As Unger argues, against all 'false necessity' approaches, we need to develop 'an antinecessitarian approach to social and historical explanation' (Unger 1987: 5). We need to question accounts which emphasize any lawlike necessities, and examine the real nature of connections and the complexity of their genealogy. The turn to empirical sources is necessary but not sufficient for this. Because, as Natrass argues in relation to the South African case: 'no precise figure can be placed on the 'corrosive effect' upon growth of distortions in the labour market, nor on the importance of apartheid repression to political stability and hence as a stimulus to investment and growth' (Natrass 1991: 660). If there is no quantitative panacea we can, at least, direct our attention to a more deconstructed analysis. The actual question we are addressing – whether economic growth shores up or erodes apartheid – is, as Merle Lipton notes, 'too crude and needs reformulation' (Lipton 1986: 9). Economic growth can have different labour and market requirements over time which can make apartheid or a non-racial democracy, more or less attractive to capital in general and capitalists in particular.

LATIN AMERICA: THE MAKING OF DEMOCRACY

The development of democracy in Latin America was both slow and uneven. There are no clear-cut patterns of an evolutionary type which could lead us to conclude that (capitalist) development leads inevitably to democracy (see Therborn 1979). Not only was the emergence of democracy uneven, but it was also characterized by serious reverses. There is certainly nothing in this story to support the Marxist modernization theory of Bill Warren for whom 'Capitalism and democracy are . . . linked virtually as Siamese twins' (Warren 1980: 28).

Democratic norms had emerged in only a few of the agrarian or mineral export-based oligarchies before the crisis of 1929. Only Argentina and Uruguay achieved a level of democratization prior to 1929, based on an exceptional level of urbanization and development of working and middle classes. The agrarian economies were not highly labour intensive which would have prompted a much stronger anti-democratic tendency amongst landowners. In a sense then landowners could afford a certain level of liberalization of the political regime. As to the social forces behind the drive towards democratization, we note the middle classes (state employees, artisans, urban professionals, etc.) and the working class, which in Argentina reached an exceptional level of political mobilization.

The world economic crisis of 1929 shattered the relative stability and coherence of the agro-export social and political order. The new post-1930 political regimes tended towards a more interventionist state and the development (albeit uneven and, in some cases, very delayed) of import-substitution industrialization policies. The working class generated by industrialization posed a potential problem for the dominant classes and this encouraged moves towards political institutionalization and inclusion. The social differentiation which resulted from industrialization and urbanization moved the centre of gravity of society away from the hacienda, the plantation and the mine. The new dominant discourse replacing economic liberalism was 'developmentalism' (*desarollismo*) which combined Keynesian economic policies, a pronounced statism and varying degrees of populism. This discourse promoted the idea that social development depended on industrialization, and saw the state as at once generator of order and agent of social integrations. This was a conservative modernization from above, or, to use Gramsci's phrase, a form of 'passive revolution'. This 'transformism' incorporated industrialists and the urban middle class into the power structures of most countries, but was not always so successful with the working classes. As Rueschemeyer, Stephens and Stephens (1991: 181) note, in Latin America, 'as in Europe, the bourgeoisie was nowhere the driving force behind democratization'.

When Lipset carried out his analysis of economic development and democracy in 1959, he found that the various 'indices' of development – wealth, industrialization, urbanization and education – were higher in the Latin American democracies than in the Latin American dictatorships (Lipset 1963: 50). The obvious conclusion was that (capitalist) economic development created better conditions for democracy. At least, this was obvious from within the modernization paradigm, which posited a uni-linear and teleological view of history where development and (a particular version of) democracy acted in a virtuous circle. Yet in most of Latin America in the late 1950s political regimes were at best restricted de-mocracies and there was a high propensity towards military intervention. If the usage of 'democracy' was quite uncritical and un-deconstructed the same could be said of the notion of 'development' deployed. Coarse statistical indicators tell us nothing about the nature of development in Latin America, characterized by its uneven and dependent nature. And if class and class struggle is not exactly absent from Lipset, it takes a strange Manichean form of considering the relationship between development and the Communist threat to democracy. Other writers sharing the moderniz-ation paradigm took an even more simplistic view of the 'elective affinity' between democracy and development in Latin America based on a quite conscious support for the current US strategy in the region through the Alliance for Progress.

Development – in the broad sense of industrialization, social differ-entiation and urbanization – created the potential for democratization in Latin America. This was not a direct one-to-one relation, however, and was mediated through the emergence of civil society and the consequent pressures for political inclusion. As Rueschemeyer, Stephens and Stephens conclude: 'The timing of the first significant growth in industrialization and urbanization . . . shaped the emergence of pressures for democratiz-ation from the middle and working classes . . . *in so far as* these two processes strengthened civil society' (Rueschmeyer, Stephens and Stephens 1991:86, emphasis added). So, if capitalist development is associated with democracy it is not through some unilinear, magic-like 'elective affinity'. Rather, it must be traced through the transformations of the class structure it causes, in particular, the weakening of the landlord class in socio-economic terms and, conversely, the strengthening of the working and middle classes. The other crucial intervening factor is the emergence of a stable political party system able to mediate conflicting class interests, and to accommodate the underlying interests of the dominant classes in the midst of social transformation. A strong civil society is necessary for democ-racy to emerge, as is also the consolidation of two or more political parties able to express diverse social interests, including those of the dominant classes.

LATIN AMERICA: DEMOCRACY DENIED

Brazil 1964, Chile 1973 and Argentina 1966 and 1976, mark the end of a democratic era in Latin America and the start of what seemed a very long night of dictatorship in the region. The exhaustion of 'easy' import-substi-tution industrialization and the dissolution of the populist-developmentalist coalition set the scene for this change. The delayed, dependent indust-rialization since 1929 had reached an impasse, with chronic inflation and economic instability, a decline in local and foreign investment, and a fiscal crisis of the state. To this potential crisis of accumulation one can add the equally threatening crisis of political hegemony which was caused by, and in turn led to, increased political activity by hitherto quiescent layers of the urban and rural working classes. O'Donnell's analysis of this transition period could quite easily find evidence to overturn Lipset's optimistic equation between economic development and political democracy. In fact, everything pointed towards a correlation between high levels of moderniz-ation (e.g. Argentina and Uruguay) and a propensity towards military intervention and the inauguration of a new bureaucratic-authoritarian state form. However, as O'Donnell himself recognized (O'Donnell 1973: 113), both schemas operated with a unidimensional view of economic development and political democracy, stressing the unilinear effects of the first on the latter.

One of the most noticeable effects of the military era on political discourse was the revalorization of democracy. It was to be valued not just as a stepping stone towards socialism, or for the promise of development, but in its own right. A new democratic ideology was to emerge based on the following principles (Flisfisch 1984: 12):

1 the diffusion and consolidation of effective practices of *self-government*;
2 a process of expansion of the spheres of life subject to *personal control*;
3 the need for a process of fragmentation or *socialization of power*;
4 the restitution of the collectivity of *personal capabilities and potential.*

This new democratic discourse was clearly anti-statist; it rejected the con-centration of power in the hands of the state, which it would see dissolved into civil society. It is hostile towards all forms of bureaucracy, and the spurious legitimacy of the expert. It seeks to de-professionalize politics and move towards its definitive socialization. If these themes are those of a libertarian or radical democracy, others are more akin to the neo-liberalism of Milton Friedman. Thus there is a great stress on personal freedoms and potentials, which are seen as being hitherto subsumed under the weight of the state and social structures. The military era thus shifted the terrain of debate on democracy and development and made it imposs-ible to return to the old statist and populist models of economy and polity.

The military regimes responded to the crisis of development with a new economic model. The new economic liberalism argued that the market, functioning freely without state intervention, is the most efficient allocator of resources in society. The main source of economic problems was seen to be the 'bloated' public sector and the distortion of relative prices intro-duced by an 'artificial' industrialization policy. There was a felicitous blend between global economic transformations – the era of finance capital hegemony – and the internal class struggle which had thrown up a decisive bourgeois leadership committed to ending the populist cycle and reasserting a new order to rival the pre-1929 'golden era' of the agro-export-based oligarchy. The destruction of the old order – the developmental compromise state – was carried out quite effectively but political reformation and construction of a new stable order was less successful (with the partial exception of Chile). As the logic of war gave way to a political logic, the military regimes found themselves plagued by the same contradictions of dependent development faced by the previous democracies. We certainly saw disproved in practice the notion that the bureaucratic-authoritarian state was now the 'natural' political form for the Third World bourgeoisie. Political process and not inexorable logic led to the rise of military dictatorships and also to their demise (Munck 1989).

All the bureaucratic-authoritarian states were eventually to enter a period of liberalization and democratization. Why that happened is of considerable interest to the democracy-development debate. First, we can note that a prime factor was often the failure of the authoritarian regimes to deal with the economic crisis. Thus the new democracies were to inherit a heavy development legacy. Second, we saw in many cases a profound reactivation of civil society with the actions of old social movements (neighbourhood associations and, above all, the trade unions) and new social movements (women, ecology and, above all, human rights) playing a key part in rolling back the military state. It is in keeping with Warren's 'optimistic' view of development and democracy that in some countries (e.g. Brazil) it was capitalist expansion which created a qualitatively more decisive working class which was to be a prime actor in the democratization process. Finally, we witness the bourgeoisie, and primarily industrialists, turning against the military state, thus recalling the classic statement of Barrington Moore: 'No bourgeoisie, no democracy' (Moore 1966: 148). For the Brazilian case, Cardoso notes how criticism of the military regime by industrialists began with specific points about economic policy but broadened out to 'a sort of general acceptance of the opposition's standpoint in terms of the social and political distortions of the prevailing "development model" . . . [and] . . . the reiteration of the importance of democracy' (Cardoso 1986: 144). The increasing role of the state and the often erratic and non-institutionalized nature of economic decision-making under the military regimes, led the bourgeoisie back towards democracy as, what we might call, a 'less bad political shell' for capitalist development.

LATIN AMERICA: DEMOCRACY REGAINED

The 1980s was the decade of democracy reborn in Latin America with 1989 marking a watershed every bit as significant as in Eastern Europe. Scott

Mainwaring notes the tragic paradox for Latin America in the 1990s, namely, that 'the period of most dismal economic results the region has experienced this century has also been the most democratic decade ever' (Mainwaring 1992: 312). Clearly, as all theorists of democracy have recognized, economic stagnation or decline places severe constraints on the prospects for democratic consolidation. Certainly there is no inexorable law in this regard and some countries (e.g. Venezuela) have withstood severe economic difficulties in the last decade. Some of the new democracies (e.g. Uruguay) have, to some extent, managed to overcome the economic legacy of authoritarian rule. Yet Argentina stands as a warning of the intense difficulties faced by the new democracies when confronted with disinvestment and high inflation with the attendant social and political costs (see Munck 1992). However, we need to reject any Manichean view that 'the new civilian rulers are "fall guys" whose allotted task is to take primary responsibility for assured economic failures' (Herman and Petras 1985: 9). Instead we must recognize that the development record of democracy is mediated through popular perceptions and evaluations which have created considerable 'political space' for drastic economic measures. The new realism this signals is not, of course, divorced from the perceived lack of alternatives in global historical terms.

The new democracies in Latin America assumed office just when the international turn to 'structural adjustment' began in earnest. The new watchwords were deregulation (of prices), de-statization and the elimination of protectionism. The objectives were economic stabilization and efficiency, along with solvency of the state sector. Democratic politicians – along with most of the left – had turned decisively away from the state as the agent of development to embrace the market wholeheartedly. Indeed, the legitimacy of these regimes (at least in the short term) allowed for a more decisive implementation of these measures than had been possible under the military state. Economic rationality – through the market – and political democracy were now to go hand in hand. So radical has been the shift in the dominant political economy that Przeworski needs to remind us that:

> the very term 'reform' has in the last few years become synonymous with a transition from an administered to a market economy. Twenty years ago this term conjured up distribution of land to peasants in Latin America or tinkering with the planning system in Eastern Europe. Today it is tantamount to the reign of markets.
>
> (Przeworski 1991: 58)

It is this reality, and the impossibility of returning to the *status quo ante*, that lies behind the triumphal optimism of the neo-liberal discourse. Whether this new phase of capitalist development will create the conditions for a durable democratic outcome is, of course, another matter.

There now appears in Latin America to be a consensus that the consolidation of stable democratic systems passes through the implementation of the neo-liberal free-market policies. The alternatives are seen to be a return to military rule or a collapse into populist chaos. Of course, the structural adjustment plans of the International Monetary Fund tend to preclude, or at least do not facilitate, some of the essential characteristics of democracy such as popular participation and the full citizenship rights T. H. Marshall spoke of. As Laurence Whitehead's sombre conclusion puts it: 'The choice would be between a stunted version of liberal democracy that works, or a generous vision of social democracy that remains a mirage (the Chilean Constitution of 1980 versus the Brazilian Constitution of 1988)' (Whitehead 1992: 154). Recent elections in Latin America point to the emergence of a neo-populism (except that there is little to redistribute) with volatile, inorganic electorates and labile political identities. There appears to be a profound disjuncture between the uncontrolled economic processes consequent on the neo-liberal reforms, and the need for some form of rationality of the political process. Old identities melt away and, with a lack of real political options, electoral results take on the same disorder as the market.

Whatever the eventual outcome for the fragile democracies in Latin America, in methodological terms, the democracy-development debate has been transformed. The original debate on the effects of economic transformation in the political sphere was premised on the primacy of the state's role. Now, the discussion is about the potential benefits of democracy for the development process, partly due to the now dominant role of the market. The neo-liberal conception of freedom virtually equates political democracy and the 'free' market. In more general terms, we see a shift from a structural class-analytic focus to an emphasis on the autonomy of political processes. Rather than examine the 'conditioning' influence of socioeconomic factors in the political arena, analysis now tends to focus on political institutions, civic culture and, even, political leadership. As Mainwaring remarks: 'the dependency and bureaucratic-authoritarian paradigms . . . both saw politics primarily as derivative, i.e., they saw politics as primarily determined by the socioeconomic system and by international variables' (Mainwaring 1992: 326). Whereas now there is a healthy emphasis on the autonomy of political processes, on the nature of a democratic compromise and the importance of stable political institutions, the overall framework seems to be an implicit version of the old modernization paradigm, with all its evolutionary baggage.

BEYOND METANARRATIVES

The postmodern distrust of metanarratives is as good a place as any to start on our conclusions. It is impossible today to sustain a 'master' narrative based on the idea of a homogeneous, universal history. These totalizing narratives, predicting the evolution of the Absolute Spirit, the Proletariat, Democracy or Development, are all equally normative and coercive, and, ultimately, untenable. Democracy has been, for too long, an abstract western ideal inextricably bound up with a particular notion of (capitalist) development. Whatever the contingent relationships between them we cannot simply conflate democracy and development. We need also to question the logic of foundations prevalent in western thought, and in particular, the logocentric tendency to see all human action as grounded in some unproblematic principle of interpretation. As Edgar Ruiz argues, 'what is notable about this logocentric disposition is its celebration not only of dichotomous thinking . . . but its privileging of one term over another' (Ruiz 1991: 173). We have noted in our own narrative how democracy and development suffer from this type of dichotomous thinking and a tendency to privilege one above the other in a somewhat arbitrary manner.

We began this chapter by looking at the proliferation of meanings lying behind the terms 'development' and 'democracy'. That both are floating signifiers should be both clear and not a cause for intellectual/political alarm. Because, as Laclau writes, 'The ambiguity of the signifier "democracy" is a direct consequence of its discursive centrality; only those signifiers around which important social practices take place are subject to this systematic effect of ambiguity' (Laclau 1993: 342). Our analysis confirms precisely that the 'identity' of development or democracy is both ambiguous and lacks fixity. That we began by fixing a minimalist meaning to them was for purposes of cross-cultural analysis and as a starting point only. It does not mean that we can still indulge in the fantasy that words have a simple and definitive meaning, or that there is a privileged vantage point standing above these debates. There is now a fairly global crisis of transformative projects, but these debates are still crucial sites of struggle. We know that the future is open and 'irreducible to a coherent and harmonious design' and that 'our dreams are necessarily inconclusive, always being reformulated' (Lechner 1991: 14). We no longer have the blueprint for an (impossible) alternative society, but we do still need to explore the contradictory meanings of those two vital, sought after but never achieved states, namely, development and democracy. One response to the Panglossian acceptance of the 'end of ideology' and 'end of history' theses is to refuse their very terminology. Thus Thomas Docherty writes of how: '"Democracy", after all, is a term so abused as to have become trivial . . . democracy now means increasingly the freedom to make a small hieroglyphic mark on a piece of paper on some twenty occasions in a normal human lifetime' (Docherty 1993: 319). Trivialized or not in some contexts, democracy and democratization are not terrains that can be ceded through a glib nihilistic sleight of hand. Many analysts now talk about democracy as a new 'global revolution' (Rustow 1990). What we lack though is a debate on what vision of liberal democracy, social democracy or another, might be viable in those parts of the globe with a less than democratic history. We still need to explore further what conditions or factors facilitate or hinder the development of democracy. We have mainly focused in this chapter on the relative importance of socioeconomic or structural factors, but the strictly political factors are certainly just as important. Democracy in the so-called 'Third World' means essentially a national democracy (Ruiz 1991). What are its prerequisites, and how might they relate to the current debate on 'radical democracy' (Mouffe 1992)? These are all questions which take us beyond the present chapter but are, at the same time, an integral part of its theme.

With 'development' too we find an increasing reaction of simple refusal of the traditional agenda. Thus Sachs introduces a de-mistifying volume on development concepts noting that: 'By now development has become an amoeba-like concept, shapeless but ineradicable. Its contours are so blurred that it denotes nothing' (Sachs 1992: 4). This may be true, but it does not invalidate what used to be called the 'development imperative' or the need to overcome poverty and hunger worldwide. Rejecting an all-embracing metadiscourse does not necessarily entail making all norms relative. The disenchantment with modernization – as technocratic/managerial/ bureaucratic development politics – is not necessarily a disenchantment with modernity. The flourishing debate on post-modernism in the advanced industrial societies has not meant a completion of the modernity agenda in the Third World. While we may perfectly well understand the postmodern lecture about 'the heterogeneity, plurality or contradictory nature of Latin American space', we need not accept that the most relevant or pressing conclusion is that this 'produced the effect of postmodernism prior to its descriptions in European discourse' (Docherty 1993: 446). The relationship between democracy and development – albeit contingent and historically bound – remains on the agenda for most of the people in this world.

REFERENCES

Adelman, I. and Morris, C. (1967) *Society, Politics and Economic Development,* Baltimore: John Hopkins University Press.

Bobbio, N. (1987) *The Future of Democracy,* Oxford, Polity Press.

Bromberg, N. and Hughes, K. (1987) 'Capitalism and underdevelopment in South Africa', in J. Butler, R. Elphick and D. Welsh (eds) *Democratic Liberalism in South Africa,* Cape Town: David Philip.

Cardoso, F. H. (1986) 'Entrepreneurs and the transition process: the Brazilian case', in G. O'Donnell, P. Schmitter and L. Whitehead (eds) *Transitions from Authoritarian Rule. Prospects for Democracy,* Baltimore: John Hopkins University Press.

Collier, D. (ed.) (1978) *The New Authoritarianism in Latin America,* Princeton NJ: Princeton University Press.

Coulter, P. (1975) *Social Mobilization and Liberal Democracy*, Lexington: Heath.

Crozier, M., Huntingdon, S. and Watanaki, S. (1975) *The Crisis of Democracy*, New York: New York University Press.

Dahl, R. (1956) *A Preface to Democratic Theory*, Chicago: University of Chicago Press.

Dasgupta, P. (1990) 'Well-being and the extent of its realisation in poor countries', *The Economic Journal* 100: 1–32.

Docherty, T. (ed.) (1993) *Postmodernism. A Reader*, London: Harvester Wheatsheaf.

Esteva, G. (1992) 'Development', in G. Sachs (ed.) *The Development Dictionary. A Guide to Knowledge and Power*, London: Zed Books.

Flisfisch, A. (1984) 'El surgimiento de una nueva ideologia democratica en America Latina', *Critica y Utopia* 2: 10–22.

Frank, A. G. (1981) *Crisis In the Third World*, London: Heineman.

Fukuyama, T. (1992) *The End of History and the Last Man*, London: Hamish Hamilton.

Grier, K. and Tullock, G. (1989) 'An empirical analysis of cross-national economic growth, 1951–80', *Journal of Monetary Economics* 24: 259–76.

Herman, E. and Petras, J. (1985) 'Resurgent democracy: rhetoric and reality', *New Left Review* 154: 74–88.

Jessop, B. (1978) 'Capitalism and democracy: the best possible political shell?', in G. Littlejohn, B. Smart, J. Wakeford and N. Yuval-Davis (eds) *Power and the State*, London: Croom Helm.

Johnstone, F. (1976) *Race, Class and Gold*, London: Routledge.

Kohli, A. (1988) 'Democracy and development', in J. Lewis (ed.) *Development Strategies Reconsidered*, Washington DC: Overseas Development Council.

Laclau, E. (1993) 'Politics and the limits of modernity', in Docherty 1993.

Lechner, N. (1991) *Los Patios Interiores de La Democracia. Subjetividad y Politica*, Chile: Fondo de Cultura Economica.

Lenin, V. I. (1918) 'State and revolution', in *Selected Works Vol. I*, Moscow: Progress Publishers, 1963.

Levine, D. (1988) 'Paradigm lost: dependence to democracy', *World Politics* 40, 3: 377–94.

Lipset, S. (1963) *Political Man*, London: Mercury.

Lipton, M. (1986) *Capitalism and Apartheid. South Africa, 1910–1986*, Aldershot: Wildwood House.

Macpherson, C. B. (1973) *Democratic Theory: Essays in Retrieval*, Oxford: Oxford University Press.

Mainwaring, S. (1992) 'Transitions to democracy and democratic consolidation: theoretical and comparative issues', in S. Mainwaring, G. O'Donnell and J. Samuel Valenzuela (eds) *Issues in Democratic Consolidation: The New South American Democracies in Comparative Perpsective*, Notre Dame: University of Notre Dame Press.

Marsh, R. (1979) 'Does democracy hinder economic development in the latecomer developing nations?', *Comparative Social Research* 2: 220–45.

Marshall, T. H. (1973) *Class, Citizenship and Social Development*, Westport: Greenwood Press.

Menendez Carrion, A. (1991) 'Democracias pendientes y representacion politica en America Latina: algunas ideas en voz alta', in M. Lopez Maya (ed.) *Desarollo y Democracia*, Caracas: Editorial Nueva Sociedad.

Moll, T. (1990) 'From booster to brake? Apartheid and economic growth in comparative perspective', in N. Nattrass and E. Ardington (eds) *The Political Economy of South Africa*, Cape Town: Oxford University Press.

Moore, B. (1966) *The Social Origins of Dictatorship and Democracy*, Boston, Beacon Press.

Mouffe, C. (ed.) (1992) *Dimensions of Radical Democracy. Pluralism, Citizenship, Community*, London: Verso.

Munck, R. (1989) *Latin America: The Transition to Democracy*, London: Zed Books.

—— (1992) 'The democratic decade: Argentina since Malvinas', *Bulletin of Latin American Research* 11, 2: 205–16.

—— (1993) 'Political programmes and development: the transformative potential of democracy', in F. Schuurman (ed.) *Beyond the Impasse: Development Theory in the 1990's*, London: Zed Books.

Nattrass, N. (1991) 'Controversies about capitalism and apartheid in South Africa: an economic perspective', *Journal of Southern African Studies* 17, 4: 654–77.

Nun, J. (1991) 'La democracia y la modernizacion: treinta anos despues', *Desarollo Economico* 31, 123: 375–93.

O'Donnell, G. (1973) *Modernization and Bureaucratic-Authoritarianism. Studies in South American Politics*, Berkeley: Institute of International Studies, University of California.

O'Dowd, M. (1974) 'South Africa in the light of stages of economic growth', in A. Leftwich (ed.) *South Africa. Economic Growth and Political Change*, London, Allison and Busby.

Pecheux, M. (1982) *Language, Semantics and Ideology. Stating the Obvious*, London: Macmillan.

Przeworski, A. (1991) *Democracy and the Market. Political and Economic Reforms in Eastern Europe and Latin America*, Cambridge, Cambridge University Press.

Richard, N. (1993) 'Postmodernism and periphery', in Docherty 1993.

Rueschmeyer, D., Stephens, E. and Stephens, D. (1992) *Capitalist Development and Democracy*, Cambridge: Polity Press.

Ruiz, L. E. (1991) 'After national democracy: radical democratic politics at the edge of modernity', *Alternatives* 10: 161–95.

Rustow, D. (1990) 'Democracy: a global revolution?', *Foreign Affairs* 69, 4: 75–91.

Sachs, W. (ed.) (1992) *The Development Dictionary. A Guide to Knowledge and Power*, London: Zed Books.

Samudavanija, C. A. (1991) 'The three-dimensional state', in J. Manor (ed.) *Rethinking Third World Politics*, London: Longman.

Schumpeter, J. (1962) *Capitalism, Socialism and Democracy*, New York: Harper and Row.

Scully, G. (1988) 'The institutional framework and economic development', *Journal of Political Economy* 96, 3: 652–62.

Therborn, G. (1979) 'The travail of Latin American democracy', *New Left Review* 113–14: 71–110.

UNDP (United Nations Development Programme) (1991) *Human Development Report 1991*, New York: Oxford University Press.

Unger, R. M. (1987) *False Necessity. Anti-Necessitarian Social Theory in the Service of Radical Democracy*, Cambridge: Cambridge University Press.

Warren, B. (1980) *Imperialism: Pioneer of Capitalism*, London: Verso.

Weffort, P. (1990) 'A America errada', *Lua Nova* 21: 5–40.

Whitehead, L. (1992) 'The alternatives to "liberal democracy": a Latin American perspective', *Political Studies* XL (special issue): 146–59.

Wolpe, H. (1988) *Race, Class and the Apartheid State*, London: James Currey.

World Bank (1991) *World Development Report 1991. The Challenge of Development*, New York: Oxford University Press.

3

AGRARIAN CLASSES IN CAPITALIST DEVELOPMENT

Henry Bernstein

THEMES AND QUESTIONS

In the new capital-intensive agricultural strategy, introduced into the provinces in the late 1960s, the Congress government had the means to realize the imperial dream: progressive farming amongst the gentry. Within a year or two of the programme's inception, virtually every district could field a fine crop of demonstration ex-*zamindars* – the Rai Sahibs with their 30-, 40-, 50-, 100-acre holdings, their multiplication farms of the latest Mexican wheat and Philippines paddy, their tube-wells gushing out 16,000 gallons an hour, much of it on highly profitable hire, their tractors, their godowns stacked with fertilizer, their cold-stores . . . in short, a tenth of the *zamindari*, but ten times the income.

(Whitcombe 1980: 179)

Sharecropping is not much better. I do all the work, and then at harvest time Mahmud Haji takes half the crop. When I work for wages, at least I bring home rice every night, even if it's not enough. But when I work on my sharecropped land, I have to wait until the harvest. In the meantime I have no rice in the house, so what are we to eat? Since I have no cow or plough, I have to rent them from a neighbour. The price is high – I plough his land for two days in return for one day's use of his cattle. In this country, a man's labour is worth half as much as the labour of a pair of cows!

(Landless villager quoted in Hartmann and Boyce 1983: 163)

Women weed the coffee, they pick coffee, pound it and spread it to dry. They pack and weigh it. But when the crop gets a good price, the husband takes all the money. He gives each of his wives 200 shillings and climbs on a bus the next morning . . . most go to town and stay in a boarding house until they are broke. Then they return and attack

their wives, saying 'why haven't you weeded the coffee?'. This is the
big slavery. Work has no boundaries. It is endless.

(Rural woman activist quoted in Mbilinyi 1990: 120–1)

The reason for all this was land speculation: two thousand hectares of
virgin forest would be cleared, a thousand turned over to pasture, and
then rubber tappers were deprived of their livelihood . . . From this
developed the struggle for extractive resources in Amazonia, which is
also a tribal area. The Indians did not want to be like colonists, they
wanted to hold the land in common, and the rubber tappers con-
curred with this view. We do not want private property rights to land,
we want it to belong to the Union and rubber tappers to enjoy
usufruct rights. This appealed to the Indians, who were starting to
mobilize . . . In 1980, Wilson Pinheiro, a very important leader who
headed all the movements in Amazonia, was murdered. The landowners . . . had him killed. Seven days later the workers took their
revenge and murdered a landowner. This is the way justice operates.

(Mendes 1992: 162, 168; interview published after Mendes' murder
on 22 December 1988)

These four vignettes – from northern India, Bangladesh, Tanzania and
Brazil – point to the immense variety of agrarian social forms, of farming
systems and environmental conditions, in the contemporary Third World.
The variety defies empirical generalization. None the less, these few vignettes, in all their specific detail, resonate broad themes of agrarian change
in capitalism:

- class and gender differentiation in the countryside;
- divisions of access to land, of labour, of the fruits of labour;
- property and livelihood, affluence and poverty;
- colonial legacies and the activities of states;
- paths of agricultural development and international markets (for
  technology, for finance, for commodities from Tanzanian coffee to
  Amazonian beef supplying the American appetite for hamburgers);
- relations of power and inequality, their contestation and the violence
  (from domestic violence to organized class violence) often deployed to
  maintain them.

Within present limits it is impossible to treat these themes adequately, but
this chapter attempts to map their terrain in relation to some key questions
about agricultural development:

1 How can the growth of production and productivity in farming be
  achieved?
2 What paths of agrarian change are characteristic of capitalism?
3 What are their effects for accumulation by agrarian classes?

4 What are their effects for livelihoods in the countryside?

To these we should add a fifth question: what are the effects of different paths of (capitalist) agrarian change for accumulation and livelihoods in economic development more generally?

The following discussion moves between the conditions and forms of capitalist agriculture in 'North' and 'South' within a broad periodization of capitalist development on a world scale. The ideas it presents suggest a framework, albeit schematically outlined, that draws on a very large body of theoretical and empirical work that is (inevitably) both complex and hotly debated. Here it is possible only to provide signposts to some of the key areas of contestation, rather than to elaborate them. The usefulness of the framework (as any other) can only be tested by 'putting it to work' in seeking answers to questions like those above, in a range of contexts. Its distinctive features are its central emphasis on social relations and dynamics, and especially those of *class relations*, in capitalist agrarian change, and its aspiration to connect 'very general themes' of capitalist development with the 'complex variations' that particular histories weave of them (to borrow, from a different context, the formulation of Gilsenan 1982: 51).

LANDED PROPERTY AND LABOUR

In the celebrated eighth part of volume 1 of *Capital*, Marx (1976) analysed 'so-called *primitive accumulation*' in the transition to capitalism. This is the process, typically protracted and violent, of the formation of the definitive social classes of the capitalist mode of production: the class of capital owning the means of production, and the class of labour 'freed' from access to means of production (dispossessed), hence 'free' (obliged by 'the dull compulsion of economic forces') to sell the single commodity it possesses – labour power – to capital in order to acquire the means of subsistence. Marx's rich historical analysis of primitive accumulation drew on the transition from feudalism to capitalism in Western Europe and especially Britain, where the breakdown of feudalism and disappearance of serfdom occurred much earlier than elsewhere.

This transition entailed the transformation of feudal landed property into capitalist landed property, and the dispossession of the feudal peasantry to form the proletariat, the source of wage-labour for capitalist agriculture and subsequently for capitalist industry and other non-agricultural sectors as well. Capitalist landed property is constituted by its use in capitalist production, whether undertaken by owners of land themselves or by capitalist tenant farmers who rent it from them, the latter being a distinctive feature of the British 'path' of capitalist development (Byres 1991: 12–22).[1]

Marx's analysis, and its particular historical reference point, was extended by Lenin (1973a) who suggested two further paths of capitalist agrarian transition: the Junker or Prussian path in which feudal landowners convert themselves into capitalist farmers (often with coercive labour regimes on their farms), and the American path in which independent petty commodity producers ('family farmers') are differentiated over time into classes of capitalist farmers and wage workers. The Prussian path is associated with a transition to capitalism unmarked by a successful bourgeois (political) revolution; the American path in the 'New World' had the appeal of avoiding the long gestation and violent upheavals of European transitions from feudalism to capitalism, as well as providing the first major example of mechanized agriculture in the development of the prairies as the national 'granary' (and soon a global granary – Friedmann 1978a, 1982b).[2] Lenin's preference for the American path had an explicit and strong political rationale: it was more conducive to the formation and functioning of bourgeois democracy as a stage in the struggle for socialism.

In transitions from feudalism to capitalism, therefore, a more progressive resolution of the agrarian question (in both economic and political terms) is to establish the conditions of development of the American path by land reforms that abolish feudal landed property and distribute land to now independent agricultural petty commodity producers, who are then subject to class differentiation through the normal competitive processes of capitalism. Such land reforms (exemplified in the slogan 'land to the tiller') have been pursued by various means in a number of societies marked by feudal (or feudal-'like') circumstances of a dependent and oppressed peasantry, in various historical conjunctures – of revolutionary upheaval in France, Russia, Mexico, China, Vietnam, Ethiopia; of decolonization in South Korea, Taiwan, India, Egypt; of 'modernization' under the Alliance for Progress in parts of Latin America in the 1960s following the 'warning' of the Cuban revolution.

For Marx, and even more for later Marxists, the capitalist transformation of agriculture is also crucial in terms of how it contributes to *industrialization*. The subtitle of Lenin's *The Development of Capitalism in Russia* (1973a) is 'The process of the formation of a home market for large-scale industry'. Following the October revolution of 1917 the Bolsheviks confronted the question of how to industrialize on the basis of a 'backward' (as well as war-ravaged) agriculture and peasantry. In a notable contribution to the Soviet debates of the 1920s, Preobrazhensky (1965) considered how to achieve 'socialist primitive accumulation' in order to industrialize, and in doing so broadened Marx's analysis to encompass mechanisms of capitalist primitive accumulation involving appropriation from *non*-capitalist formations:

> Another form of plundering which was of very great importance was the colonial policy of the world-trading countries . . . plundering in

the form of taxes on the natives, seizure of their property, their cattle and land, their stores of precious metals, the conversion of conquered people into slaves, the infinitely varied system of crude cheating, and so on. To this category also belonged all methods of compulsion and plundering in relation to the peasant population of the metropolitan countries . . . The most typical methods were, first, plundering of the serf peasants by their lords and sharing of the plunder with merchant capital, and, second, crushing taxation of the peasantry by the state and transformation of part of the means so obtained into capital.

(Preobrazhensky 1965: 85)

In this view, then, outright dispossession of pre-capitalist peasantries is the *final* moment of capitalist primitive accumulation. Until that moment, *reproduction* of such peasantries and their exploitation by means of rent ('feudal', 'semi-feudal' landed property), unequal exchange (merchant capital), debt (moneylending capital) and taxation (the state), contribute to capital accumulation *elsewhere* than in agriculture (including spatially in the imperialist countries, sectorally in industry). This idea retains a vivid resonance in views of 'continuing' primitive accumulation as explaining the 'backwardness' of much agriculture in the Third World today, which we shall come back to.[3]

AGRARIAN TRANSITIONS/COLONIAL TRAJECTORIES

In a seminal essay, Byres (1991) follows the logic of the 'very general themes' of capitalist development as presented by Marxism, but also shows how 'particular histories have woven [more] complex histories' from them than the few 'paths' suggested by Marx and Lenin. For purposes of illustration, table 3.1 summarizes some of the central features of Byres' comparative analysis of successful capitalist agrarian transitions by (a) their pre-capitalist agrarian structures; (b) the class character of transition and the social forms of agricultural production it generated; (c) how agricultural productivity increased (investment in farming); and (d) how agricultural development contributed to industrialization (intersectoral links), which is the criterion of successful transition. The table also gives several examples of ways in which states played a key role in these transitions.

Primitive accumulation in the form of (intensified) exploitation of the peasantry rather than its dispossession appears most evident in the East Asian cases of Japan, Taiwan and Korea. Japan's post-war industrial reconstruction and its success, and especially the spectacular industrialization of Taiwan and (South) Korea, have led to celebrations of the 'small farmer' path of agrarian transition they are held to exemplify. Facile generalization and recommendation of their experience, however, ignores its special historical conditions, including highly (yield) productive irrigated rice cultivation, the investment in and close regulation of agriculture by the Japanese colonial state, and the transfer of agricultural surplus to 'feed' (literally and metaphorically) industrial accumulation, first in Japan from the late nineteenth century and after 1945 in its former colonies.

If Taiwan and Korea experienced 'a highly exploitative, but also highly developmental form' of colonialism that increased the productivity of land and labour, providing favourable conditions for their post-war industraliz-ation, the same does not apply to the vast regions colonized by European overseas expansion (Saith 1990: 206–7). This expansion first contributed to British and other Western European capitalist transition by plunder, slavery, and trade in luxury goods, and to their subsequent capitalist development by different and more systematic forms of control over the conditions of production and exchange in colonial agriculture. The last three decades of the nineteenth century marked a turning point in the development of global capitalism as western countries entered their 'Second Industrial Revolution' (Barraclough 1964: ch. 4; Hobsbawm 1987: ch. 3), generating demand for ever-increasing quantities of tropical agricultural commodities (as well as minerals) for processing and manufacturing. This was also a period of increasing overseas investment in extractive sectors (plantation agriculture, mining) and their transport links to world markets (railways, bulk shipping), of the final great wave of colonial imperialism (above all in Africa and in Southeast Asia), of increasing exposure of British industry to competition from the 'newly industralizing countries' of the time (Germany, the United States), and of the emergence of Japan as the first non-western industrial power.[4]

For the agrarian economies of the Third World this new period was marked by three broad types of change. One was the emergence of the 'industrial plantation' (Courtenay 1965: ch. 3), distinguished by:

> the *connection* between its organization of production [labour pro-cesses, technologies, management structures and imperatives], its character as [part of] corporate capitalist enterprise, and the new, more highly integrated, conditions of its world market location, in-volving linkages with finance capital, shipping, industrial processing and manufacturing – aspects of that late nineteenth century develop-ment aptly described [by Stoler 1985: 17] as a 'worldwide shift towards agribusiness'.
>
> (Brass and Bernstein 1992: 4)

The 'industrial plantation' replaced earlier types of plantation in Asia, the Caribbean, and parts of Latin America, generated new plantation 'frontiers' (in Indo-China, Malaya, Sumatra), and greatly enlarged the scale and

Table 3.1 Paths of agrarian transition

	Peasants	Landlords	Form of production	Investment in farming	Intersectoral links	Character of transition
1 The English path. (15C.-19C.)	From serfs to tenants (14C., 15C.). Gradual differentiation of peasantry	From feudal lords to private landowners (Enclosures (16C.-19C.)	'Trinity of landowners-tenant (capitalist) farmers-wage workers (16C.-19C.)	Rents held in check. To some extent 'improving landlords' 'Agricultural revolution' of 18C.	1846 repeal of Corn Laws mark dominance of industrial capital (cheap food)	'Classical' model of transition to capitalist farming; special features include an accommodating vs. obstructive landowner class
2 The Prussian path (16C.-19C.)	Enserfment of a free peasantry 16C. Abolition of serfdom 1807	Called Junkers: (commercial) manorial production - *Grundherrschaft*	Junker transition to estate economy - *Gutswirtschaft* with mostly tied labour (former serfs) From 1870s increasingly (migrant) wage labour			'Internal metamorphosis of feudal landlord economy', capitalism from above (Lenin) *Contrast* south and west of Germany: no Junkers, differentiation of peasantry, emergence of capitalist farming
3 The American path (second half of 19C.)	No feudalism	—	Rise and consolidation of family farming from 1860s, especially with settlement of internal land frontier west of Mississippi Relative absence (and high costs) of wage labour	Extensive cultivation of vast land frontier Mechanization from 1870s (Friedmann 1978a)	State support of (a) colonization of prairies (19C.); (b) family farming (subsidies), 1920s on	'Petty' commodity production from below (Byres 1991)

Table 3.1 Continued

Peasants	Landlords	Form of production	Investment in farming	Intersectoral links	Character of transition
4 The French path (15C.–20C.) From serfs to tenants (by 15C.) Strong resistance by village community Very limited differentiation	From feudal property to purely *rentier* landlords (Vs. England, Prussia)	Post 1789: family farming (including share-cropping) in central and southern France 1840s development of capitalist farming in northern France	—	—	Protracted transition after 1789, marked by tenacity of small peasantry (and its political weight)
5 The Japanese path (second half of 19C.–20C.) Tenancy central (increased 1860s–1945)	Mostly resident in countryside (vs. France) (To post-1945 land reform: owner cultivators)	Landlord–tenant family farming Strong interest of landlords in improvement	Extreme labour intensity Very heavy rents in kind (rice)	Heavy state taxation of peasantry Problem of cheap food supply and colonial policies (see below)	Primitive accumulation borne by peasantry ('semi-feudalism'?) Key role of state in (a) securing conditions of 'high rent landlordism'; (b) taxing peasantry; (c) controlling peasantry
6 The Taiwanese/South Korean path **(a) Japanese colonial period (first half of 20C.)** Tenancy central (as Japan)	Japanese as well as indigenous (colonial system)	Landlord–tenant family farming	Extreme labour intensity Heavy rents and taxes on peasantry Investment by landlords/ state	Cheap food for Japanese industrialization	Colonial ('and 'semi-feudal'?) exploitation of peasantry
(b) 1950s, 1960s Land reforms	—	Owner-cultivation of very small farms	Extreme labour intensity	Substantial net capital transfers through heavy taxation, especially intersectoral terms of trade	State 'substitutes' for landlords: primitive accumulation for industrialization with 'self exploitative peasantry' and 'super exploitative state' (Amsden 1979)

Note: The blank spaces are areas missing from Byres' account in terms of categories I have used to summarize it – this should be remedied in the book he is now writing on paths of agrarian transition.

volume of this kind of highly specialized world-market production of such commodities as rubber, oil palm, sisal, sugar, cocoa, tea and bananas (Daniel, Bernstein and Brass 1992).

A second type of pervasive change, especially in Asia and Africa, was the increased incorporation (in scale and intensity) of colonial peasantries in capitalist economy as producers of export crops (cotton, oil palm, coffee, cocoa, tobacco, groundnuts), of food staples for domestic markets, and of labour power, via migrant labour systems (including indentured and *corvée* labour), to build the railways and roads, to work in the plantations, mines and ports.

A third, and contrasting, type of change occurred in Latin America, most of which was independent of colonial rule several generations before most of Africa was colonized (and, significantly, before the international hegemony of industrial capital; at the same time, the industrialization of Northern Europe contributed to the increasingly 'backward' status within Europe of Spain and Portugal). The early colonization of Spanish America had established a form of extensive landed property, the *hacienda* or *latifundia*, akin to the manorial domain of feudal Europe (Kay 1974; while Portuguese Brazil was a pioneer of plantation slavery). Together with the 'industrial plantation', Latin America's massive agricultural export boom from the 1870s – 'a virtually unique combination in the nineteenth century of political independence and primary commodity led incorporation into the international capitalist economy' (Archetti, Cammack and Roberts 1987: xvi) – took place on the basis of a new phase of commercialization of the *hacienda*, involving further land grabbing from peasant communities and the expansion of a captive labour force.

These three broad types of change in Third World agrarian economy are familiar, at least in their narrative outline, from such influential accounts of the formation of global capitalism as Gunder Frank's (1969) 'development of underdevelopment', Amin's (1974) 'accumulation on a world scale', and Wallerstein's (1979) 'world-system' analysis. Beyond this act of recognition, however, some difficult and contested theoretical issues have to be acknowledged. One set of issues concerns the important differences of agrarian structure of the range of pre-capitalist societies incorporated in an evolving global capitalism, the important differences of the *timing* of their incorporation (as against Gunder Frank's seamless 'continuity' of world capitalism since 1492), and the *effects* of such differences for subsequent paths of development.

Without being able to pursue these issues here, some remarks may at least highlight their salience for transformations of the uses of land and agrarian labour in colonial economies. The organization of the initially feudal Spanish American *hacienda* in its epoch of world-market commercialization from the second half of the nineteenth century suggests a transition resembling the Prussian path, as outlined above (see de Janvry

1981). In Asia and Africa, with the exception of areas of European settler farming (especially in parts of North, East, Central and Southern Africa) and of plantation zones (especially in parts of South and Southeast Asia), colonization did not entail such extensive land grabbing and/or dispossession of existing agrarian classes (controllers as well as cultivators of land). Peasantries in most of Asia and Africa were incorporated in colonial capitalism in the ways noted earlier, with the ruling groups of pre-capitalist formations (landlords, aristocrats, military castes, chiefs) often reconstituted within colonial economy and polity as subordinate (and sometimes uneasy) partners of the imperial order. For example, in much of northern India the 'Permanent Settlement' reconstituted Mughal *zamindars* as landlords-cum-revenue collectors of the British Raj; in British Africa, 'indirect rule' operated via the establishment of 'Native Authorities' (and in British India in another version, that of the 600 or so 'princely states'). The overall effect of colonial agrarian economy in India has been stated succinctly by Barrington Moore (1966: 344):

> the [land] settlements were the starting point of a whole process of rural change whereby the imposition of law and order and associated rights of property greatly intensified the problem of parasitic landlordism. More significantly still, they formed the basis of a political and economic system in which the foreigner, the landlord, and the money-lender took the economic surplus away from the peasantry, failed to invest it in industrial growth [that is, in India] and thus ruled out the possibility of repeating Japan's way of entering the modern era.

Thus a colonialism that was highly exploitative without being 'developmental' (for the colonies concerned). The most pervasive thread of such exploitation was the *forcible commercialization* (Bharadwaj 1985) of peasant production, whether inflected through 'parasitic landlordism' as in India, or in conditions (as in most of Africa) without pre-capitalist classes of landed property or 'land settlements' of the Indian colonial type. Forcible commercialization denotes the initially coercive integration of peasant farmers into (capitalist) commodity production to obtain the money income to pay taxes, and to meet other legally and politically imposed obligations.

There was a great variety of forms of land tenure and differential access to land, reflecting both diverse pre-colonial histories and the complex ways in which colonial rule and commoditization incorporated and changed them. Patterns of ownership and/or control of land were combined with a variety of labour regimes in colonial agriculture (as well as affecting the recruitment of labour for mining). Table 3.2 sketches those labour regimes in terms of Marx's criteria of primitive accumulation noted earlier: the 'freeing' of pre-capitalist producers from access to means of production (that is, the means to produce their subsistence), and their 'freedom' to exchange their labour power under 'the dull compulsion of economic forces' (rather than extra-economic coercion). Conditions of wage labour that include less than complete separation from the means of production and/or direct coercion, are termed 'transitional' in table 3.2 in a conceptual sense rather than an historical one – such types of labour regime are not necessarily transitory (and may indeed be structural features of certain kinds of capitalism).

Table 3.2 suggests that the labour regimes of primitive accumulation (in the second sense noted earlier) were increasingly replaced in the twentieth century by labour regimes of semi-proletarian, proletarian and household labour (petty-commodity production) that, it is argued below, are generated by the class relations of capitalism, rather than capital continuing to fix on pre-existing forms, or to create new forms, of non-capitalist production as the basis of exploitation. Before pursuing the issues this raises concerning the fate(s) of peasants in the Third World today, in the historical tracks of their colonial trajectories, it is worth making some observations about capitalist farming and capitalist agriculture.

CAPITALIST FARMING/CAPITALIST AGRICULTURE

A common view, inherited from classical political economy (and its roots in the British 'path'), is that the capitalist agricultural enterprise – the farm – is homologous with the capitalist *mode of production*, that is, that it necessarily consists of capitalists and 'free' wage workers. Further, and by analogy with the development of capitalist industry, this conception anticipates that capitalist farming will increase the scale of its enterprises (concentration of capital), the division of labour within enterprises (the 'collective worker', as Marx termed it), and its productivity through technical innovation (revolutionizing 'the productive forces'), in accordance with the 'laws of motion' of capitalism.

Already in the late nineteenth century, the strong 'persistence' of small-scale and household farming into the era of industrial capitalism was noted and debated. In much of Europe the 'peasantry', with its historical provenance in feudalism, survived on a scale and in ways that contrasted with the fate of pre-industrial artisans and craft producers. In the United States, the development of mechanized grain cultivation in the prairies occurred on the basis of 'family farms' rather than capitalist (wage labour) farms.

Commoditization is always an uneven process, but seems to be particularly so in agricultural transition in capitalism. Attempts to explain this in general terms have started from the conditions of transforming nature peculiar to agriculture, and their implications. While industrial production transforms materials already appropriated from nature by prior extractive

Table 3.2 Labour regimes in colonial economies

Labour regime	Separation of producers from means of production	Extra-economic coercion	'Free' wage labour	Examples
1 Forced labour				
Slavery	Complete	Yes	No	Caribbean, Brazil, southern USA, 16C.–19C.
Tribute, tax in kind	No	Yes	No	Spanish America, 16C.–17C.; Africa 19C. to early 20C.
Labour service	Partial	Yes	No	Spanish America, 16C.–18C.; Africa, Asia, 19C. to early 20C.
Indenture	Complete	Partial	'Transitional'	Caribbean, East Africa, Malaysia, Mauritius, Fiji, 19C.–20C.
'Forcible commercialization'	No	Yes	No	India, 19C.–20C.; Africa, late 19C.–20C.
2 Semi-proletarian labour				
Debt bondage	Partial or complete	Possible	'Transitional'	Spanish America, 18C.–20C.; Asia, 19C.–20C.
Periodic labour migration	Partial	Possible	'Transitional'	Africa and Third World generally, 20C.
3 Petty commodity production	No	No	No	India and Africa, 19C.; throughout Third World, 20C.
4 Proletarianization	Complete	No	Yes	Some sectors of colonial economies: from 18C. (Latin America), 19C. (India), 20C. (Africa)

Source: Adapted from Bernstein 1988b

processes, agriculture only transforms nature through the very activity of appropriating it. Farming thus confronts the uncertainties of natural environments and processes, and their effects for the growth of plant and animal organisms.

Accordingly it has been suggested that capital is often inhibited from investing directly in farming for several reasons. One is that such investment tends to be more risky than investment in other branches of activity: the 'normal' risks of market competition are compounded by the risks inherent in the uncertain natural conditions of farming. A second explanation focuses on the non-identity of labour time and production time in farming (by contrast with their convergence in industrial production). In agriculture production time is greater than labour time because of the growth cycle of plants (and livestock), during which capital is 'tied up' and unable to realize profits – the value created by labour is not released until crops are harvested (Mann and Dickinson 1978). A third explanation is that it is much more difficult, hence costly, to supervise and control the pace and quality of (hired) labour in the field than it is in the factory.

These are, of course, very general reasons advanced to explain a tendency, the accentuated unevenness of capitalist transformation of farming, not the impossibility or improbability of such transformation; they are not intended to apply to all cases at all times in the history of capitalism. In fact, a central aspect of the dynamic of technical innovation in capitalist agriculture is to standardize its conditions of production: to reduce the variations, obstacles and uncertainties of natural environments to bring farming closer to the ideal of control exercised in industrial manufacturing, to produce yields that are as predictable as well as large (and fast maturing) as possible – by acting on soils (through drainage, fertilizers), climate (irrigation, greenhouses), crop and livestock attributes (selective breeding, improved varieties, and now genetic engineering), plant parasites and diseases (pesticides and other chemicals), weed growth (herbicides), and so on.

None the less, it remains the case that farming enterprises across the world of contemporary capitalism (and *within* as well as across both 'North' and 'South') exhibit great diversity in their social organization (forms – and combinations – of family labour, free and unfree wage labour), the distribution and degree of concentration of capital in them, their size and scale, extent of mechanization, their modes of integration in markets for means of production (land, labour, machinery, seeds and chemicals, credit) and output markets, and the ways in which they are affected by (and might influence) state policies and practices.

This diversity of types of farming in capitalism is much greater than that of the branches of production to which farming links backwards and forwards. The former, 'upstream' of farming, consist of capital in input production (above all chemical companies, also farm-machinery manufacturers), and the latter, 'downstream' of farming, consist of food-industry capital in processing and distribution. These upstream and downstream corporate capitals tend to be more concentrated the more 'developed' the agricultural sector (and economy in which it is located), and likewise tend to play a greater role in shaping and regulating the agricultural sector, relative to farming and its interests. Of course, agribusiness capital may invest directly in farming (crop, animal, timber production) as well, but typically as part of a larger and vertically integrated corporate structure (as the industrial plantation mentioned in the previous section).

In short, it is useful to distinguish farming and agriculture in capitalism, or, more precisely, *farming* and 'the *agricultural sector*' (in national economies, international divisions of labour and markets) whose structuring by agribusiness capital (at least partly) determines the conditions and prospects of different types of farming. Also implicit in this view is that capitalist farming need not consist exclusively of capitalist *farms* (whether operated by corporate or individual capitals), in the sense of enterprises comprising capitalist owners (and managers) and hired wage workers. In effect, we have returned to the question of the 'family' or 'household' farm (in its many shapes and forms).

In a seminal theoretical paper, reflecting on the historical trajectory of American grain cultivation, Harriet Friedmann (1980) argued that family farming in western capitalism exemplifies a distinctive form of household production, namely *simple commodity production* (SCP). It is distinctive in that it is a 'family labour' enterprise whose conditions of existence are satisfied only by developed capitalist economy, formulated by Friedmann as complete market integration for all 'factors of production', including labour power (on which see Friedmann 1978b). Because of such market integration, even simple reproduction of family farming enterprises requires high levels of competitiveness, hence continuous technical innovation and productivity growth. This means higher levels of capitalization over time which, in turn, implies increasing the scale of operation of the farm. The latter may include extending the area of land worked (farm size), as with family grain farming in the United States in the twentieth century, but not necessarily so. In other branches of capitalist farming, containing both SCP and wage labour enterprises, increasing scale (of capital and output) can be achieved through technologies that are highly land (or space) intensive, such as drip irrigation, greenhouses, feedlots, and the 'factory' production of eggs, poultry and pigs.

Thus family farming can be as characteristic of capitalist agriculture as the capitalist (wage labour) farm 'proper'. But what of 'peasant' farming – and capitalist agricultural development – in the Third World today?

FATE(S) OF THE PEASANTRY

Friedmann (1980) contrasted SCP, constituted exclusively within capitalism, with peasant farming in the Third World that is not fully integrated in capitalist markets for two types of reasons. The first is when (some) conditions of agricultural production (and appropriation of the product) are secured through non-market relations and mechanisms, whether of a class kind (landlordism, sharecropping and other forms of tenancy/labour involving relations of personal dependence) or a non-class kind (communal land tenures, kin relations). The second reason is when farming is directed towards 'subsistence' (self-consumption) as well as market exchange.

By inference, to the extent that peasant farming fails to qualify as capitalist, the less likely it is to exhibit the dynamic attributes of SCP: technical innovation, productivity growth, and capitalization (in short, 'development').

Both reasons link with other views of the non-capitalist nature of peasant farming. The first resonates arguments that exploitation of the peasantry through persisting 'pre-capitalist' class relations (landlordism, usury, dominance of merchant capital) 'blocks' the transition to capitalist agriculture and its anticipated fruits of productivity growth and productive (versus 'parasitic') accumulation. Such arguments have featured strongly in India around the notion of 'semi-feudalism' (Bhaduri 1983) and in the Indian 'mode of production debate' (Patnaik 1990). The second argument, from household 'subsistence' production, appears and reappears in a variety of theoretical and ideological guises – in populist celebrations of peasant 'resistance' to commoditization (e.g. Richards 1983, on Africa; and for a similar position with respect to some European family farmers, van der Ploeg 1990), as explicable in terms of the 'functions' of (non-capitalist) household production for capitalism in both articulation theory (Wolpe 1980) and 'world-system' analysis (Smith, Wallerstein and Evers 1984), and not least (together with kinship organization of economic activity) as generating peasant 'backwardness' and the obstacle it presents to development (Hyden 1983).

These various views, including Friedmann's, contain some or other notion of the intrinsically non-capitalist nature of peasant farming in terms of its social basis, its 'internal' relations, and/or its subsistence 'logic'. They do not deny that peasants are incorporated in capitalism, but suggest that they are not constituted through capitalist relations of production. Hence there remains some element of contradiction between peasant farming and capitalist development (whether bemoaned by those advocating such development, or celebrated in anti-capitalist, anti-developmental, versions of populism). An alternative to the theoretical basis of such views, and their applications to empirical trends, can be assessed against the Marxist concept of petty commodity production (PCP) in capitalism. The theory of PCP focuses on three related themes: the social relations of PCP within capitalism; how PCP is both destroyed and generated in capitalist development; and the tendency of PCP to class differentiation.[5]

The concept of PCP specifies a form of small-scale (usually 'household' or 'family') enterprise in capitalism engaged in more or less specialized commodity production, and which combines the class places of capital and labour. The agents of this form of enterprise (petty commodity producers) are capitalists and workers at the same time: capitalists because they own or have access to means of production (unlike landless or otherwise propertyless workers, that is, proletarians), and workers because they use their own labour (unlike those capitalists who employ the labour power of others). In short, they are capitalists who employ (hence exploit) themselves.[6]

54

Peasants become petty commodity producers in this sense when they are unable to reproduce themselves outside the relations and processes of capitalist commodity production, when the latter come to constitute the conditions of existence of peasant farming and are internalized in its organization and activity. This historical moment is satisfied when 'forcible commercialization' gives way to commoditization under 'the dull compulsion of economic forces' (albeit shaped by political class struggle and its outcomes), in order to acquire the necessities of life. As Gibbon and Neocosmos (1985: 169) put it:

> to suggest that a social formation is capitalist by virtue of being founded on the contradiction between wage-labour and capital is not to assert that all – or even the majority of – enterprises in this social formation will conform to a 'type' in which capitalists and wage-labourers are present . . . what makes enterprises, and more generally social formation, capitalist or not, is . . . *the relations which structurally and historically explain their existence* . . . what has to be shown in order to 'prove' the capitalist nature of such social formations is that the social entities and differences which form the social division of labour in such formations are only explicable in terms of the wage-labour/ capital relation.

In effect, capitalist relations of production – the *structural* conditions of existence of PCP (including peasant farming) – are not exclusively or necessarily manifested in (full) market integration (*pace* Friedmann 1980), any more than capitalist farming consists exclusively or necessarily of enterprises 'in which capitalists and wage-labourers are present'. The extent to which, and ways in which, peasants are integrated in different markets (and indeed the class, gender, and institutional characteristics, and power relations, of particular markets – see Mackintosh 1990) are matters of *historical* investigation, including that of various colonial trajectories and their legacies.

The second theme in theorizing PCP concerns its continuous destruction and (re)creation in processes of capitalist development. An exclusive focus on the former, and the expectation of the inevitable demise of all small-scale production within capitalism, are characteristic features of mechanical Marxism. Evidently certain types of small-scale production disappear in the development of the capitalist social division of labour (for example, the emblematic fate of hand-loom weavers in early nineteenth-century Britain, and later in colonial India, in the face of factory-produced textiles), but the dynamics of such development – stemming from the law of value in capitalist competition, accumulation and concentration (including technical change) – also continuously create new spaces for PCP in the social division of labour: 'A number of "new middle strata" are inevitably brought into existence again and again by capitalism' (Lenin 1973b: 39; see also Gibbon and Neocosmos 1985: 178–80).

The (re)creation of PCP is an *effect* of capitalist development, as distinct from explaining the 'persistence' of peasant (and more generally household) production by its 'functions' for capitalist accumulation (as in much articulation and 'world-system' analysis). Furthermore, the (re)creation of particular 'spaces' for family farming (in both 'North' and 'South') is also an effect of the accentuated unevenness of capitalist development specific to farming, and the increasing subordination of farming over time to agribusiness capital that organizes the 'agricultural sector' (as outlined in the previous section; see also below on contract farming).

Finally, one must distinguish between the destruction of particular *branches* of production characterized by PCP, and the demise of *individual enterprises* as the effect of competition between petty commodity producers (just as between capitalists). This last point links to the third theme of the tendency to class differentiation of peasants and other petty commodity producers.

The tendency to class differentiation arises from the peculiar combination of the class places of capital and labour in PCP, hence its 'special exaggerated form of instability' (Gibbon and Neocosmos 1985: 177). As petty commodity producers, peasants have to reproduce both their means of production (as capitalists) and their labour (as workers) in circumstances of greater or lesser risk or opportunity, whether exerted by:

1 conditions of access to key resources (land, credit) and to markets, and relations with powerful groups and individuals (landowners, merchants, agrarian and industrial capitalists, state officials);
2 nature (climatic uncertainty, ecological degradation on one hand; the availability of land and labour-enhancing technologies on the other hand);
3 markets (the relative prices, or terms of trade, of what they need to buy and what they need to sell to purchase necessities);
4 government policies (affecting their economic conditions, as (1) to (3), and access to public goods such as health care, clean water, and education, which affect the reproduction of labour).

The pressures of reproduction as both capital and labour, and the degree to which peasants succeed in dealing with them, can be charted in their class differentiation. *Poor peasants* are subject to a simple reproduction 'squeeze' on their capital or labour, or both. Their poverty and depressed levels of consumption (reproduction of labour) are often the result of intense struggles to maintain their means of production (reproduction of capital). If the latter is a losing battle, poor peasants become semi-proletarianized or proletarianized, that is, securing their subsistence by working largely or wholly for others.

Middle peasants are those able to meet the demands of simple reproduction: maintaining their means of production and raising the next generation of labour to work with them; while *rich peasants* are able to engage in expanded reproduction: to increase the land and/or other means of production at their disposal beyond the capacity of family labour. They then start to employ the labour of others, and may undergo a transition from better-off petty commodity producers to capitalist farmers.

It is my contention that the vast majority of those termed 'peasants' were constituted as petty commodity producers within capitalism, in the sense just explained, by the end of the colonial era in Asia and Africa. That is to say, they had completed the transition from 'forcible commercialization' to commodity production under 'the dull compulsion of economic forces'. This also implies that (capitalist) class differentiation of the peasantry, by various means and to varying degrees, had taken root in the colonial period, even if limited or circumscribed in many cases by the appropriation of surplus from peasant farming by landowners, moneylenders, merchants, and colonial states.

The categories of rent, interest, commercial profit, and taxation, evidently exist in capitalism no less than in some pre-capitalist modes of production, albeit constituted on a different social basis. To paraphrase Gibbon and Neocosmos (1985: 169) as quoted earlier: 'what makes rent, interest, commercial profit, and taxation, capitalist or not, is the relations which structurally and historically explain their existence'. Such relations are the object of investigation, which may show that in particular circumstances certain types of rent, interest, commercial profit, and taxation, represent more or less progressive forms of capitalist social relations, rather than signalling the (residually) 'pre-capitalist' or 'semi-feudal' as the only possible sources of agrarian 'backwardness'.[7]

If the vast majority of peasants in Asia and Africa were (differentiated) agricultural petty commodity producers by the end of the colonial era, processes of capitalist agrarian change since then have also been structured by the policies and practices of developmental states (Lea and Chaudhri 1983; Mkandawire and Bourenane 1987), by aid agencies such as the World Bank (Heyer, Roberts and Williams 1981), by the agricultural, trade, and aid policies of the United States and European Community (Raikes 1988; Friedmann 1982a, 1990), and, probably above all, by how agribusiness capital (re)shapes international division of labour and global trade in agricultural technologies and commodities (Friedmann 1993; Chapter 15, this volume). The effects of these encompassing and powerful forces can only be illustrated selectively in the rest of this discussion which elaborates commoditization and differentiation as they bear on the fate(s) of peasants today.

First, it must be emphasized that differentiation of the peasantry is a *tendency* in capitalism, rather than a uniform empirical trend observable in all places at all times. Differentiation proceeds by different routes, and to different degrees, that are shaped in complex ways by particular conditions of competition and struggle between peasants (over land, labour, credit, access to markets, etc.) and between peasants and other social forces (landowners, merchants, agribusiness capital, the state). The depredations, actual or threatened, of the latter frequently generate solidary ideologies of 'community' or 'tradition' that both serve as a means of peasant mobilization and defence, *and* obscure patterns of class differentiation of the peasantry and their effects. Thus it is common to find the 'peasant interest' or 'agrarian interest' articulated by rich peasants and even petty capitalist farmers, who provide the leadership of peasant political action. The objectives of such action typically reflect farming interests in capitalism (also familiar from US and EC agricultural politics) of higher crop prices and subsidies, lower input prices and interest rates, and protectionism, however these demands are wrapped up in the moral(istic) discourses of agrarian populism.[8] Of course, for poor and middle peasants, these types of demands bear on their survival (simple reproduction) as agricultural, petty commodity producers, while for rich peasants (and some better-off middle peasants) they bear on the opportunities of accumulation (expanded reproduction).

Class differentiation of the peasantry can be obscured in other ways too. For example, ostensibly 'traditional' forms of access to land (communal tenure) and labour (through cooperative work parties to clear/plant/harvest land, 'sharing' of the tasks of cattle herding and grazing, recruitment of additional 'family' labour by fictive kinship) can conceal underlying patterns of differentiation – how such practices transfer resources and value from poorer to richer, from female to male, peasant farmers – and relations of capital and labour within as well as between households.[9]

Differentiation also varies with particular patterns of commoditization (although there is no single correlation between intensified commoditization and accelerated differentiation). Markets for crops and for basic consumption goods often develop before markets in land, in other means of production, and in labour (Bharadwaj 1985). An important stage of commoditization is reached when farmers have to purchase means of production such as tools, seeds and fertilizers, as commodities, rather than produce them themselves. For example, peasant farmers have to purchase hybrid high yielding variety (HYV) seeds each season because the grains they harvest from them (wheat in India and Latin America, rice in South, Southeast and East Asia, maize in much of Africa and Latin America) cannot be used as seed for future planting. (By contrast, the ex-*zamindar* capitalist farmers of northern India described at the beginning of this chapter operate their own HYV seed multiplication farms.) In addition, to realize the yield potential of HYVs requires buying an accompanying 'package' of complementary inputs – chemical fertilizers, pesticides, irrigation pumps or water.

Such biochemical innovations – of very recent provenance in staple food crops in the Third World compared with tropical export crops like sugar, rubber and cotton (Evenson 1984) – entail both increased opportunities and increased risks. Evidently opportunities and risks are not distributed equally across a farming population differentiated by class and gender relations, as Green Revolution experiences demonstrate. In parts of northern India, capitalist farmers (whether emerging from the ranks of former landlords or the rich peasantry) quickly became the dominant class of the Green Revolution (Byres and Crow 1988). Rice-growing areas in South India where many small farmers adopted the new biochemical technology, and a middle peasantry appears to reproduce itself over time, illustrate a different aspect of differentiation. In a village studied over a long period by John Harriss (1987), this relatively stable middle peasantry comprises only half the households, those whose principal income comes from their own farming. A third of the households are landless, deriving their livelihoods from a combination of local farm labouring, periodic labour migration, and petty craft production. This suggests several further sets of issues and themes concerning patterns of commoditization and differentiation.

One theme is implicit in what was said earlier about intensifying commoditization, namely that the levels of capitalization required for higher-productivity, agricultural, petty commodity production – its 'entry costs', to use the jargon of economics – increase, along with opportunities and risks (just as in Friedmann's analysis of SCP in western family farming).[10] The effect can be that while this may provide the basis for a relatively stable middle peasantry, the latter establishes and reproduces itself at the expense of poorer peasants who are unable to afford such entry or reproduction costs.

This is an important point, and all the more so for being frequently neglected or confused.[This oversight or confusion is partly because agrarian populism views middle peasants as 'the backbone of the peasantry' (Williams 1976), as exemplifying a somehow 'natural' condition which is subverted by the intrusion of capitalism, a force *external* to peasant society or community that sows the poisonous seeds of differentiation and division within it. This view, of course, conflicts with the position argued here that peasants are petty commodity producers constituted by capitalist relations of production, whose contradictory tendencies are *internal* to the social relations, organization and practices of peasant farming. In short, therefore, when and where relatively stable middle peasantries are generated by capitalist development, their particular conditions of existence require explanation, just as situations which manifest different patterns of differentiation. These conditions of existence include the relations of middle peasants with other agrarian and non-agrarian classes, with the state, and not least, in many instances with agricultural (wage) labour.[11]

Another broad theme, glimpsed in the South Indian village cited above, is that many (my 'guesstimate' is most) agricultural, petty commodity producers in the Third World today pursue a variety of income-generating activities besides farming, both in the countryside and in towns and cities. The patterns of this diversification are likewise marked by class and gender differentiation (Berry 1980; Agarwal 1990). For poor peasants, and especially those sliding into (semi-)proletarianization, diversification of income sources from (casual) wage labour, petty trade and craft production, and the harvesting of common property resources, is necessary for survival. For middle peasants, wage or salaried labour and other 'off farm' activity may be necessary to secure savings against bad harvests, and/or to gain the additional income to invest in improved technologies (as above). For rich peasants, investment in crop trading and processing, retail trade, transport, machinery rental, education for their sons and political connections, provides a more diverse portfolio than farming as the source of current and future accumulation and/or additional income to capitalize further their farming operations.

Diversification can also obscure class differentiation, which is not necessarily manifested in (growing) inequality of landholding (the single most widely used indicator of peasant differentiation). The scale of farming can be increased by capital-intensive rather than land-extensive means (as noted earlier, and especially where irrigation is used). Also rich peasants often augment the area they farm by renting in land from poorer peasants who lack the capital to work it themselves, and so on (a practice noted by Lenin (1973a), in late nineteenth-century Russia). Accordingly, studies of differentiation processes have to combine landholding/farm-size criteria with others such as the 'labour exploitation criterion' (Patnaik 1987) and the combined 'portfolio' of farming and other commodity enterprises (Neocosmos 1987).

State policies and development schemes, and the strategies and practices of agribusiness, intensify commoditization by promoting and 'delivering' to Third World farmers new technologies, services and market possibilities, typically in ways that lock them into particular (increased opportunity/risk) patterns of commodity production. Farmers may be controlled directly by specifying obligatory crops and cultivation practices, and/or less directly by the use of credit, monopoly purchasing arrangements (whether by state or private trading enterprises) and quality controls. More extreme versions of state-managed (but foreign-aid funded and designed) schemes of this kind in Africa have provoked the suggestion that they create 'state peasantries' (Barker 1989: 182). An agribusiness version of locking farmers into more intensive and specialized forms of commodity production is contract farming (Clapp 1988; Watts 1990).

Interestingly, while it has a number of colonial antecedents in the compulsory cultivation of certain crops (e.g. cotton in Tanzania and Mozambique, indigo in Bihar, India – see Gandhi 1982: 370–84), in the massive 'tenant farmer' Gezira scheme (irrigated cotton) in the Sudan (Barnett 1977; Barnett and Abdelkarim 1991), and in 'outgrower' contracts with plantations (sugar, sisal, rubber), much contract farming in the Third World today represents the extension of an organizational 'model' pioneered in US agriculture, and then 'transferred' by international agribusiness. It comprises both 'exotic' vegetables, fruits and flowers, air freighted to the supermarkets of Europe and North America (where so much of global 'effective demand' is concentrated)[12], and the contracted production of commodities for food industry companies, transnational and national, to supply domestic markets (e.g. milk for industrial dairies, grains for breweries; this seems to be more the case in Latin America, generally the most developed and highest income region of the Third World, than elsewhere).

The intensified commoditization stimulated or imposed, directly or indirectly, by the activities of developmental states, aid agencies, and agribusiness, has complex effects for class differentiation. In terms of the processes outlined above, their overall effect is probably towards greater differentiation, albeit in different forms according to circumstances. In the context of the Green Revolution in India, Rao (1975) made an important distinction between 'scale neutrality' and 'resource neutrality'. The new biochemical (HYV) package was designed to be 'scale neutral', meaning that it could be adopted by, and yield its benefits of increased productivity and income to, those farming on any scale.[13] However, it proved not to be 'resource neutral' in that the risks attached to the new opportunities it offers are affordable only by (relatively) richer farmers, who can also fund the entry costs and tend to have privileged access to supplies of inputs and credit, and to crop markets. Somewhat similarly, while contract farming is often depicted as 'exploiting the peasantry' (unspecified as to its class and gender differentiation), the entry costs and other requirements of its arrangements frequently mean that its participants are richer peasants and indeed capitalist farmers. On the other hand, a very widespread finding concerning state-promoted schemes is that richer peasants are able to secure a disproportionate share of the resources they provide, due to their local political connections and influence (Heyer, Roberts and Williams 1981; Barker 1984).

This section has tried to explain and illustrate some of the reasons why there are multiple fates of the Third World peasantry towards the end of the twentieth century (as there are of 'family farmers' in the European Community, the United States, Japan). This is what should be expected if we grasp the extensive class differentiation of the peasantry, and its ubiquitous (if not uniform) gender differentiation, and the diverse trajectories of agrarian change within capitalism. The fate of most poor peasants today is their *marginalization* as agricultural, petty commodity producers: even if they retain access to some land, the major part of their livelihood has to be gained from activities other than farming on their own account. Middle peasants make up the most heterogeneous category, subject to pressures of downward mobility (if they cannot reproduce themselves as capital) or possibilities of upward mobility (through accumulation), according to the particular conditions of commoditization and differentiation they confront. These conditions also bear on the prospects of relatively stable reproduction of middle peasants, which include, as we have seen, their ability to increase levels of capitalization to survive as petty commodity producers, and the likely necessity of (adequate) 'off-farm' income to achieve this. Rich peasants may also be subject to downward mobility (like any enterprise in capitalism), as well as the possibility of becoming capitalist farmers. The latter is not an inevitable outcome: for a variety of reasons (unfavourable climatic or market trends, the pressures of class and popular struggle), rich peasants may pursue accumulation through a portfolio of diverse investments rather than expanding their agricultural enterprises.

AGRARIAN TRANSITIONS AND CLASS STRUGGLE

Agriculture in the Third World displays a great variety of forms of capitalist and petty commodity production. The former includes industrial plantations, ranches, and timber resources, owned by, or linked into, international agribusiness capital, as is a range of types of contract farming; it also includes corporate and individual capitals from the vast expanses of sugar estates and soya farms, and ranches eating into the Amazonian forests, in Brazil, to the 'Rai Sahibs' of the Punjab, powerfully established on irrigated wheat and rice farms from 12 hectares upwards. Petty commodity production includes a prodigious variety of forms of peasant farming linked into local, national and international markets, as well as 'capitalized family farms' (first cousins of Friedmann's American 'simple commodity producers'), especially in the more developed regions of the Third World (Keyder 1983, on Turkey; Llambi 1987, on Latin America).

This chapter has focused on some of the 'general themes' of capitalist development, its processes of agrarian class formation and accumulation, rather than the 'complex variations' they generate. In doing so, it has suggested that these themes and processes are common to agriculture in both 'North' and 'South'. What makes agriculture different – and produces complex variations – in the various regions and economies of capitalism is their different historical conditions and trajectories, not any essential difference of their underlying social relations, processes or 'logics'. Those regions and economies are, moreover, connected in the 'uneven and combined development' – manifested through international divisions of labour and markets, global patterns of investment and demand – characteristic of imperialism.

Also common to the forms of agricultural capitalist and petty commodity production listed, is that they entail capitalist landed *property*, albeit in a variety of legal, institutional and ideological forms, and despite the 'persistence' of apparently 'pre-capitalist' means of allocating and working land in some instances (communal tenures, sharecropping, etc.). This, I would suggest, is the principal reason why (bourgeois) land reform has virtually disappeared from the agenda of agricultural 'development policy' issues compared with its prominence in the 1950s and 1960s.[14] The implication is that agrarian classes established on the basis of capitalist landed property, *including* the different classes of the peasantry, confront *wage labour* in the definitive contradiction of capitalism. The classes of wage labour in the countryside comprise tens of millions of landless, propertyless people, with rural (and urban) labour markets further augmented by those peasants semi-proletarianized by their impoverishment and marginalization as agricultural, petty commodity producers (and who experience the contradiction of capital and wage labour within their own person as failed peasants, as well as in relation to those who purchase labour power).

In a theoretical sense, as noted earlier, petty commodity production presupposes the existence of a class of wage labour; empirically, a great deal of peasant production, including middle-peasant production, depends on the employment of casual and seasonal wage labour. It can be further suggested that class struggle between capitalist landed property and wage labour, compounded by the difficulties and costs of close supervision of hired field labour and by the weapons at its disposal (e.g. striking at the time of harvest), is one of the principal factors in the mechanization of agricultural labour processes, even in countries with a vast rural labour 'surplus' like India.[15]

Ironically, diminishing employment in agriculture – in relative and (sooner or later) absolute terms – is a characteristic feature of agrarian transition. In some 'classical' models, it was even emphasized as a principal 'function' of transition, namely releasing labour from farming to meet the demand for workers of industrialization. The reduction of employment opportunities in agriculture would not be a problem if there were enough productive, and adequately paid, jobs available elsewhere in the economy (Ghosh and Bharadwaj 1992). This would satisfy the meaning of development as overcoming poverty, and simultaneously its meaning as accumulation centred on the growth of the domestic market ('the formation of a home market for large-scale industry' as Lenin, cited earlier, put it), especially for commodities of mass consumption or 'wage goods' (emphasized by structuralist economists like Amin (1974) and de Janvry (1981).

While this benevolent scenario seems almost incapable of realization in the conditions of contemporary capitalism in the Third World (and as far as full employment is concerned, maybe anywhere in the capitalist world), the countries of the Third World exhibit a great range of 'levels', as well as paths, of capitalist development. The powerful forces of international capital (including agribusiness), and its regulatory agencies like the IMF and World Bank, provide one side of the equation of the development processes and prospects of Third World economies, including their differential positions within global capitalist economy (imperialism). The other side of the equation is how they have been shaped historically (if not immutably) by their colonial trajectories, and how their modes of incorporation in world economy are mediated and influenced by their processes of internal class formation and struggle.

The political course of class and popular struggle can generate more progressive forms of agrarian relations and change within capitalism, in three areas implied in this chapter. A first area is the organization of agricultural wage workers to fight for better conditions of work and payment, for the acceptance of basic democratic rights, and to defend themselves against the class violence inflicted on them. This includes fighting against all forms of 'tied' labour arrangements based in personal dependence, debt bondage, patronage, etc. – in short, 'deproletarianization' (Brass 1986b, 1990; Brass and Bernstein 1992) which denotes the denial or loss of the one positive 'freedom' of the proletarian condition in face of 'the dull compulsion of economic forces', namely workers' mobility within labour markets.

A second area is establishing the conditions of 'accumulation from below' by agricultural, petty commodity producers in situations of national and/or authoritarian class oppression (Neocosmos 1993). 'Accumulation from below' confronts 'parasitic' appropriation by landlordism and merchant capital (on the latter see Harriss 1990), and/or by states that (variously) support individual accumulation by 'bureaucrat capital' (Mamdani 1987, on Africa), or privileged sectors of capitalist farming at the expense of petty producers (de Janvry 1981, on Latin America; Gibbon 1992, on Africa). The third area concerns accumulation by dominant agrarian classes at the expense of industrial accumulation and development, hence the interests of the working class (Mitra 1977, and Byres 1979 on India).

Such struggles and how they shape processes of capitalist development, are, in the nature of the beast, highly ambiguous. The first touches on the fundamental contradiction between all forms of capital, including petty commodity production, and wage labour. Conditions of employment on middle and rich peasant farms may be as bad or worse, and the conflicts they generate as or more violent, than on capitalist farms (forcefully stated for India by Banaji (1990)); in addition, the effectiveness of worker resistance and organization is a principal factor stimulating mechanization and the reduction of (especially permanent) wage employment in farming (see n. 15 on India; de Janvry, Sadoulet and Wilcox Young 1989, on Latin America).

64

With respect to the second area, 'the agrarian interest' (as noted
is often constituted under the leadership of rich peasants an
capitalist farmers pursuing advantages for themselves, that may be
at the expense of both poorer peasants and agricultural labourers.

Concerning the third area, the tension between agrarian accumulation
(to develop the productive forces in farming) and the accumulation needs
of industrialization, is the definitive tension of agrarian transition. Its 'worst
case' manifestation is when agrarian accumulation is depressed without any
significant industrial accumulation taking place, as sub-Saharan Africa
seems to exemplify most readily.[16]

Awareness of these ambiguities, tensions and contradictions (qualities
intrinsic to *all* processes of capitalist development), is key to effective
knowledge, and contrasts with the technicist 'blueprints' for development
familiar from economics textbooks and the framework of contemporary
'structural adjustment' (Bernstein 1990; Gibbon 1992). Using such awareness and knowledge to inform analysis and political strategy appropriate to
specific conjunctions of struggle, is necessary for moving from less to more
progressive forms of capitalist social relations, whether one believes that
capitalism represents 'the end of history', or that it may eventually be
replaced by a type of society that offers more to the exploited and oppressed majority of the world's population, both rural and urban, of both
'South' and 'North'.

NOTES

1 The tension between theoretical abbreviation and historical specificity and
complexity, unavoidable in a discussion of this kind, starts here. Controversy
over the transition to agrarian capitalism in Western Europe has been revived
by the work of Robert Brenner – see Aston and Philpin 1985; Albritton 1993;
on the persistence of small-scale farming in England in the nineteenth and
twentieth centuries, see Reed 1986; and Donajgrodzki 1989.

2 The characteristic image of mechanization – of combine harvesters moving in
formation across the prairies (and the steppes) – had a particular fascination
for what Corrigan, Ramsay and Sayer (1978) called the 'Bolshevik problematic',
to which it provided the agricultural equivalent of the industrial labour process,
indeed the 'industrialization of agriculture'. Of course, post-bellum development in the United States included the dispossession of native Americans on
the frontier as well as the legacies of plantation slavery in the South.

3 The most sophisticated arguments for 'continuing' primitive accumulation as
a structural necessity of capitalism, influenced by the theory of imperialism of
Rosa Luxemburg (1963), are those of the French 'articulation of modes of
production' theorists, notably Rey (1973, 1976) and Meillassoux (1981), see
also Wolpe (1980); on the other hand, the voracious appetite of the 'world-
systems' approach swallows this idea undigested, along with almost everything
else.

4 The rest of this section plunders elements of Bernstein (1988b, 1992a, b, c),
and the next section Bernstein (1990).

5 My debt to the paper of Peter Gibbon and Michael Neocosmos (1985) should

be evident, a debt which extends to their other work, to that of my co-editors of the *Journal of Peasant Studies*, Tom Brass and T. J. Byres, and, theoretical differences notwithstanding, to that of Harriet Friedmann. This section draws on ideas presented in Bernstein (1986, 1988a), Berstein, Crow and Johnson (1992: 30-3).

6 This does not mean that petty commodity production represents a homogeneous or egalitarian combination of 'collective' capitalist and worker. Typically these class places are distributed unequally *within* peasant households, above all through the structures and practices of gender relations. Feminist scholarship (e.g. Guyer 1981, 1984; Whitehead 1990) has demonstrated that notions of 'self-exploitation', with peasant and other petty commodity enterprises treated as a collective 'self', are problematic and have to be investigated in terms of gender relations within households as well as more widely.

7 On the theory of rent in the context of capitalist landed property, see Neocosmos 1986.

8 Brass 1991 provides an encompassing and provocative critique of the principal intellectual strands of agrarian populism, while Brass 1989 explores the contradictions of a peasant movement in Peru. Byres 1988 is a fascinating essay on the writings and long career of Charan Singh, 'a true organic intellectual of the rich and middle peasantry' who was briefly prime minister of India. Mamdani (1987) distinguishes peasant politics organized 'from below' and 'from above' (i.e. by rich peasants).

9 See the powerful essays by Brass 1986a and Mamdani 1987, also see note 6 above.

10 Friedmann's apparent lack of interest in differentiation is probably due to the relatively stable reproduction of SCP as the characteristic enterprise in American wheat farming. However, the emergence of capitalist (wage labour) farms from family farms is not the only pattern of differentiation: while SCP has persisted in American wheat growing it has done so through the tendency to fewer and bigger family farms (growth of scale and levels of capitalization).

11 A fine example of careful investigation and explanation of specific conditions of middle-peasant reproduction is Michael Cowen's research on Central Province, Kenya (1981a, b).

12 A pioneering work, with the evocative title of 'strawberry imperialism', is Feder's (1977) study of Mexico. Mackintosh (1989) provides a case study of an international agribusiness venture with a profound and precise analysis of its impact on peasant communities in Senegal. The World Bank (1989: 92) reports that horticultural products became Kenya's third most important agricultural foreign-exchange earner during the 1980s, including flowers (especially roses, orchids, carnations) of which Kenya is the world's fourth largest exporter.

13 This was the policy makers' (both Indian and international) dream scenario: an apparent alternative to radical land reform, and radical political change more generally, provided by technology, i.e. Green vs. 'Red' Revolution. Williams (1981) argues that the World Bank's shift towards 'reaching the (rural) poorest' in the 1970s expressed its reading of the 'lessons' of why 'Vietnam was lost'.

14 The symptomatic exception is the World Bank's 1989 current interest in replacing 'indigenous' land tenure in Africa with individual private property rights in land. A range of studies, from Lenin 1973a on the Russian peasant commune or *mir* to Barrows and Roth 1990 on contemporary Africa, show that communal land tenure is no obstacle to land accumulation and peasant differentiation in processes of commoditization. Mackenzie 1990 is an illuminating account of gender as well as class conflict over 'customary' access to land in

Kenya; MacWilliam 1988 is an interesting attempt to theorize the 'hidden' commoditization of land within communal tenure in Papua New Guinea.

15 Mechanization started soon after the introduction of the Green Revolution in the Punjab in the 1960s, in the face of struggles with agricultural labour (Frankel 1971; Byres 1972). Trends in rural labour markets and labour regimes in Indian peasant farming are analysed by Brass (1986b, 1990) and John Harriss (1992), and in terms of gender patterns of employment and payment by Agarwal (1986) and Kapadia (1993). The mechanization of rice harvesting by combine, which is just starting in India (Peter Mollinga, personal communication), will have serious effects for a major source of agricultural wage employment.

16 Recalling the (anonymous) response to the aphorism attributed to Stalin that 'You can't make an omelette without breaking eggs', namely that 'You can, however, break eggs without getting an omelette from them.'

REFERENCES

Agarwal, B. (1986) 'Women, poverty and agricultural growth in India', *Journal of Peasant Studies* 13(4).

—— (1990) 'Social security and the family in rural India: coping with seasonality and calamity', *Journal of Peasant Studies* 17(3).

Albritton, R. (1993) 'Did agrarian capitalism exist?' *Journal of Peasant Studies* 20(3).

Amin, S. (1974) *Accumulation on a World Scale*, New York: Monthly Review Press.

Amsden, A. (1979) 'Taiwan's economic history: a case of etatisme and a challenge to dependency theory', *Modern China* 5(3).

Archetti, E. P., Cammack, P. and Roberts, B. (eds) (1987) *Sociology of 'Developing Societies': Latin America*, London: Macmillan.

Aston, T. H. and Philpin, C. H. E. (ed.) (1985) *The Brenner Debate. Agrarian Class Structure and Economic Development in Pre-Industrial Europe*, Cambridge: Cambridge University Press.

Banaji, J. (1990) 'Illusions about the peasantry: Karl Kautsky and the agrarian question', *Journal of Peasant Studies* 17(2).

Barker, J. (ed.) (1984) *The Politics of Agriculture in Tropical Africa*, Beverly Hills, CA: Sage.

—— (1989) *Rural Communities Under Stress. Peasant Farmers and the State in Africa*, Cambridge: Cambridge University Press.

Barnett, T. (1977) *The Gezira Scheme: An Illusion of Development*, London: Frank Cass.

Barnett, T. and Abdelkarim, A. (1991) *Sudan: The Gezira Scheme and Agricultural Transition*, London: Frank Cass.

Barraclough, G. (1964) *An Introduction to Contemporary History*, London: Watts.

Barrows, R. and Roth, M. (1990) 'Land tenure and investments in African agriculture: theory and evidence', *Journal of Modern African Studies* 28(2).

Bernstein, H. (1986) 'Capitalism and petty commodity production', in Scott 1986.

—— (1988a) 'Capitalism and petty-bourgeois production: class relations and divisions of labour', *Journal of Peasant Studies* 15(2).

—— (1988b) 'Labour regimes and social change under colonialism', in Crow *et al.* 1988.

—— (1990) 'Agricultural "modernization" and the era of structural adjustment', *Journal of Peasant Studies* 18(1).

—— (1992a) 'Agrarian structures and change: Latin America', in Bernstein *et al.* 1992.

—— (1992b) 'Agrarian structures and change: India', in Bernstein *et al.* 1992.

—— (1992c) 'Agrarian structures and change: Sub-Saharan Africa', in Bernstein *et al.* 1992.

Bernstein, H., Crow, B. and Johnson, H. (eds) (1992) *Rural Livelihoods. Crises and Responses*, Oxford: Oxford University Press in association with The Open University.

Bernstein, H., Crow, B., Mackintosh, M. and Martin, C. (eds) (1990) *The Food Question*, London: Earthscan.

Berry, S. (1980) 'Rural class formation in West Africa', in R. H. Bates and M. Lofchie (eds) *Agricultural Development in Africa: Issues of Public Policy*, New York: Praeger.

Bhaduri, A. (1983) *Economic Structure of Backward Agriculture*, London: Academic Press.

Bharadwaj, K. (1985) 'A view on commercialization in Indian agriculture and the development of capitalism', *Journal of Peasant Studies* 12(4).

Brass, T. (1986a) 'The elementary strictures of kinship: unfree relations and the production of commodities', in Scott 1986.

—— (1986b) 'Unfree labour and capitalist restructuring in the agrarian sector: Peru and India', *Journal of Peasant Studies* 14(1).

—— (1989) 'Trotskyism, Hugo Blanco and the ideology of a Peruvian peasant movement', *Journal of Peasant Studies* 16(2).

—— (1990) 'Class struggle and the deproletarianization of agricultural labour in Haryana (India)', *Journal of Peasant Studies* 18(1).

—— (1991) 'Moral economists, subalterns, new social movements, and the (re)emergence of a (post)modernist (middle)peasant', *Journal of Peasant Studies* 18(2).

Brass, T. and Bernstein, H. (1992) 'Introduction: proletarianization and deproletarianization on the colonial plantation', in Daniel, Berstein and Brass 1992.

Byres, T. J. (1972) 'The dialectic of India's green revolution', *South Asian Review* 5(2).

—— (1979) 'Of neo-populist pipe dreams: Daedalus in the Third World and the myth of urban bias', *Journal of Peasant Studies* 6(2).

—— (1988) 'Charan Singh (1902–87): an assessment', *Journal of Peasant Studies* 15(2).

—— (1991) 'The agrarian question and differing forms of capitalist agrarian transition: an essay with reference to Asia', in J. Breman and S. Mundle (eds) *Rural Transformation in Asia*, Delhi: Oxford University Press.

Byres, T. J. and Crow, B. (1988) 'New technology and new masters for the Indian countryside', in Crow *et al.* 1988.

Clapp, R. A. J. (1988) 'Representing reciprocity, reproducing domination: ideology and the labour process in Latin American contract farming', *Journal of Peasant Studies* 16(1).

Corrigan, P., Ramsay, H. and Sayer, D. (1978) *Socialist Construction and Marxist Theory. Bolshevism and its Critique*, London: Macmillan.

Courtenay, P. P. (1965) *Plantation Agriculture*, London: Bell.

Cowen, M. P. (1981a) 'The agrarian problem', *Review of African Political Economy* 20.

—— (1981b) 'Commodity production in Kenya's central province', in Heyer, Roberts and Williams 1981.

Crow, B., Thorpe, M., *et al.* (1988) *Survival and Change in the Third World*, Cambridge: Polity Press.

Daniel, V. E., Bernstein, H. and Brass, T. (eds) (1992) *Plantations, Peasants and Proletarians in Colonial Asia*, special issue of *Journal of Peasant Studies* 19(3–4).

de Janvry, A. (1981) *The Agrarian Question and Reformism in Latin America*, Baltimore: Johns Hopkins.

de Janvry, A., Sadoulet, E. and Wilcox Young, E. (1989) 'Land and labour in Latin American Agriculture from the 1950s to the 1980s', *Journal of Peasant Studies* 16(3).

Donajgrodzki, A. P. (1989) 'Twentieth-century rural England: a case for "peasant studies"?' *Journal of Peasant Studies* 16(3).

Evenson, R. E. (1984) 'Benefits and obstacles in developing appropriate agricultural technology', in C. K. Eicher and J. M. Staatz (eds) *Agricultural Development in the Third World*, Baltimore: Johns Hopkins.

Feder, E. (1977) *Strawberry Imperialism. An Enquiry into the Mechanisms of Dependency in Mexican Agriculture*, The Hague: Institute of Social Studies.

Frank, A. G. (1969) *Capitalism and Underdevelopment in Latin America*, New York: Monthly Review Press.

Frankel, F. R. (1971) *India's Green Revolution: Economic Gains and Political Costs*, Princeton NJ: Princeton University Press.

Friedmann, H. (1978a) 'World market, state, and family farm: social bases of household production in the era of wage labour', *Comparative Studies in Society and History* 20(4).

—— (1978b) 'Simple commodity production and wage labour in the American plains', *Journal of Peasant Studies* 6(1).

—— (1980) 'Household production and the national economy: concepts for the analysis of agrarian formations', *Journal of Peasant Studies* 7(2).

—— (1982a) 'The political economy of food: the rise and fall of the post-war international food order', *American Journal of Sociology* 88 (supplement).

—— (1982b) 'State policy and world commerce: the case of wheat, 1815 to the present', in P. McGowan and C. W. Kegley (eds) *Foreign Policy and the Modern World System*, Beverly Hills CA: Sage.

—— (1990) 'The origins of Third World food dependence', in Bernstein *et al.* 1990.

—— (1993) 'The political economy of food: a global crisis', *New Left Review* 197.

Gandhi, M. K. (1982) *An Autobiography*, London: Penguin (first published 1927).

Ghosh, J. and Bharadwaj, K. (1992) 'Poverty and employment in India', in Bernstein, Crow and Johnston 1992.

Gibbon, P. (1992) 'A failed agenda? African agriculture under structural adjustment with special reference to Kenya and Ghana', *Journal of Peasant Studies* 20(1).

Gibbon, P. and Neocosmos, M. (1985) 'Some problems in the political economy of "African Socialism"', in H. Bernstein and B. K. Campbell (eds) *Contradictions of Accumulation in Africa. Studies in Economy and State*, Beverley Hills CA: Sage.

Gilsenan, M. (1982) *Recognizing Islam*, London: Croom Helm.

Guyer, J. (1981) 'Household and community in African studies', *African Studies Review* 24(2–3).

—— (1984) 'Naturalism in models of African production', *Man* (NS) 19.

Harriss, B. (1990) 'Another awkward class: merchants and agrarian change in India', in Bernstein *et al.* 1990.

Harriss, J. (1987) 'Capitalism and peasant production: the Green Revolution in India', in T. Shanin (ed.) *Peasants and Peasant Societies*, 2nd edn, Oxford: Blackwell.

—— (1992) 'Does the "depressor" still work? Agrarian structure and development in India: a review of evidence and argument', *Journal of Peasant Studies* 19(2).

Hartmann, B. and Boyce, J. K. (1983) *A Quiet Violence: View from a Bangladesh Village*, London: Zed Books.

Heyer, J., Roberts, P. and Williams, G. (eds) (1981) *Rural Development in Tropical Africa*, London: Macmillan.

Hobsbawm, E. J. (1987) *The Age of Empire, 1875–1914*, London: Weidenfeld and Nicholson.

Hyden, G. (1983) *No Short-Cuts to Progress*, London: Heinemann.

Kapadia, K. (1993) 'Mutuality and competition: female landless labour and wage rates in Tamil Nadu', *Journal of Peasant Studies* 20(2).

Kay, C. (1974) 'Comparative development of the European manorial system and the Latin American hacienda system', *Journal of Peasant Studies* 2(1).

Keyder, C. (1983) 'Paths of rural transformation in Turkey', *Journal of Peasant Studies* 11(1).

Lea, D. A. M. and Chaudhri, D. P. (eds) (1983) *Rural Development and the State*, London: Methuen.

Lenin, V. I. (1973a) *The Development of Capitalism in Russia*, vol. 3 of *Collected Works*, Moscow: Progress Publishers (first published 1899).

—— (1973b) *Marxism and Revisionism*, vol. 15 of *Collected Works*, Moscow: Progress Publishers (first published 1908).

Llambi, L. (1987) 'Emergence of capitalized family farms in Latin America', *Comparative Studies in Society and History* 31(4).

Luxemburg, R. (1963) *The Accumulation of Capital*, London: Routledge and Kegan Paul (first published 1913).

Mackenzie, F. (1990) 'Gender and land rights in Murang'a District, Kenya', *Journal of Peasant Studies* 17(4).

Mackintosh, M. (1989) *Gender, Class and Rural Transition: Agribusiness and the Food Crisis in Senegal*, London: Zed Books.

—— (1990) 'Abstract markets and real needs', in Bernstein *et al.* 1990.

MacWilliam, S. (1988) 'Smallholdings, land law and the politics of land tenure in Papua New Guinea', *Journal of Peasant Studies* 16(1).

Mamdani, M. (1987) 'Extreme but not exceptional: towards an analysis of the agragrian question in Uganda', *Journal of Peasant Studies* 14(2).

Mann, S. A. and Dickinson, J. A. (1978) 'Obstacles to the development of a capitalist agriculture', *Journal of Peasant Studies* 5(4).

Marx, K. (1976) *Capital*, vol. I, Harmondsworth: Penguin (first published 1867).

Mbilinyi, M. (1990) 'Structural adjustment, agribusiness and rural women in Tanzania', in Bernstein *et al.* 1990.

Meillassoux, C. (1981) *Maidens, Meal and Money: Capitalism and the Domestic Community*, Cambridge: Cambridge University Press.

Mendes, C. (1992) 'The defence of life', *Journal of Peasant Studies* 20(1).

Mitra, A. (1977) *Terms of Trade and Class Relations*, London: Frank Cass.

Mkandawire, T. and Bourename, N. (eds) (1987) *The State and Agriculture in Africa*, Dakar and London: CODESRIA.

Moore, B. (1966) *Social Origins of Dictatorship and Democracy*, Boston: Beacon Press.

Neocosmos, M. (1986) 'Marx's third class: capitalist landed property and capitalist development', *Journal of Peasant Studies* 13(3).

—— (1987) 'Homogeneity and differences on Swazi Nation land', in M. Neocosmos (ed.) *Social Relations in Rural Swaziland. Critical Analyses*, Kwaluseni: University of Swaziland, Social Science Research Unit.

—— (1993) *The Agrarian Question in Southern Africa and 'Accumulation from Below'*, Uppsala: Scandinavian Institute of African Studies.

Patnaik, U. (1987) *Peasant Class Differentiation. A Study in Method with Reference to Haryana*, Delhi: Oxford University Press.

—— (ed.) (1990) *Agrarian Relations and Accumulation. The 'Mode of Production' Debate in India*, Delhi: Oxford University Press.

Preobrazhensky, E. A. (1965) *The New Economics*, Oxford: Clarendon Press (first published 1926).

Raikes, P. (1988) *Modernizing Hunger. Famine, Food Surplus and Farm Policy in the EEC and Africa*, London: James Currey.

Rao, C. H. H. (1975) *Technological Change and Distribution of Gains in Indian Agriculture*, Delhi: Macmillan.

Reed, M. (1986) 'Nineteenth-century rural England: a case for "Peasant Studies"?' *Journal of Peasant Studies* 14(1).

Rey, P.-P. (1973) *Les Alliances de classes*, Paris: Maspero.

—— (1976) *Capitalisme négrier*, Paris: Maspero.

Richards, P. (1983) 'Ecological change and the politics of African land use', *African Studies Review* 26(2).

Saith, A. (1990) 'Development strategies and the rural poor', *Journal of Peasant Studies* 17(2).

Scott, A. M. (ed.) (1986) *Rethinking Petty Commodity Production*. Special issue series of *Social Analysis* 20.

Smith, J., Wallerstein, I. and Evers, H.-D. (eds) (1984) *Households and the World Economy*, Beverly Hills CA: Sage.

Stoler, A. L. (1985) *Capitalism and Confrontation in Sumatra's Plantation Belt, 1870-1979*, New Haven CT: Yale University Press.

van der Ploeg, J. D. (1990) *Labor, Markets and Agricultural Production*, Boulder CO: Westview.

Wallerstein, I. (1979) *The Capitalist World-Economy*, Cambridge: Cambridge University Press.

Watts, M. (1990) 'Peasants under contract: agro-food complexes in the Third World', in Bernstein *et al.* 1990.

Whitcombe, E. (1980) 'Whatever happened to the Zamindars?' in E. J. Hobsbawm, W. Kula, A. Mitra, K. N. Raj and I. Sachs (eds) *Peasants in History: Essays in Honour of Daniel Thorner*, Calcutta: Oxford University Press.

Whitehead, A. (1990) 'Food crisis and gender conflict in the African countryside', in Bernstein *et al.* 1990.

Williams, G. (1976) 'Taking the part of peasants', in P. Gutkind, and I. Wallerstein (eds) *The Political Economy of Contemporary Africa*, Beverly Hills CA: Sage.

—— (1981) 'The World Bank and the peasant problem', in Heyer, Roberts and Williams 1981.

Wolpe, H. (ed.) (1980) *The Articulation of Modes of Production*, London: Routledge.

World Bank (1989) *Sub-Saharan Africa from Crisis to Sustainable Growth. A Long-Term Perspective Study*, Washington DC: World Bank.

4

CAPITALIST DEVELOPMENT IN THE NICs

Rhys Jenkins

INTRODUCTION

The discussion of capitalist development in the Third World has often been divided between 'impossibilists' and 'inevitabilists' (Hamilton 1983). The former regard the world economy as permanently divided between a developed centre and a subordinate periphery. They believe that the countries of the periphery are condemned to underdevelopment or at best can aspire to rise to an intermediate or semi-peripheral status. However no peripheral economy has ever made the transition from periphery to centre.

The 'inevitabilists' on the other hand contend that extensive capitalist development is in fact occurring as market forces spread from the developed countries to the Third World. This comes in both a Marxist version (Warren 1980) and a neo-classical version which emphasizes 'doing what comes naturally' (Riedel 1988).

DEVELOPMENT IN THE NICs

A small group of newly industrializing countries (NICs) provide a test case of the propositions of development theories concerning capitalist development. These countries include the four East Asian 'tigers' or 'dragons', South Korea, Taiwan, Hong Kong and Singapore, and the two most industrialized Latin American countries, Brazil and Mexico. Sometimes the grouping is extended to include Argentina and India in view of their considerable industrial development, and some southern European countries. In this chapter however the term will be used to refer to the first six countries mentioned.

The East Asian NICs particularly have experienced spectacular economic growth over the past three decades as can be seen from table 4.1. If successful capitalist development is taking place anywhere in the Third World, it is here. Growth has been reflected in a rapid ascent of these countries in the hierarchy of nations ranked by GNP per capita. South Korea which in 1962 was ranked ninety-ninth, below Sudan, has climbed to twenty-seventh in 1990. Taiwan has gone from eighty-fifth, behind Zaire, to twenty-fourth. Hong Kong and Singapore which were more favourably placed in 1962 in fortieth and thirty-eighth place have also managed to rise to nineteenth and twentieth respectively (table 4.1 and Wade 1990: table 2.1). As a result, Hong Kong and Singapore are now classified as high-income economies by the World Bank, while GNP per capita in South Korea and Taiwan is comparable to those of the poorer European countries such as Greece and Portugal.[1]

Although both Brazil and Mexico experienced substantial economic growth in the 1960s and 1970s, the debt crisis and the lost decade of the 1980s has meant that the Latin American NICs have lagged behind their East Asian counterparts. They have been overtaken by South Korea and Taiwan in terms of GNP per capita and their ascent in the international hierarchy has been much less marked, from sixty-seventh to thirty-sixth for Brazil and fifty-first to fortieth for Mexico between 1962 and 1990 (table 4.1 and Wade 1990: table 2.1).

All six NICs have broken with the traditional role of the periphery in the world economy of supplying raw materials and agricultural products to the centre. Manufactures now account for more than half of total exports in all countries (except Mexico where because of oil exports it is just under half) and for over 90 per cent in Hong Kong, South Korea and Taiwan. The competitiveness of their manufactured exports are indicated by the increased share of world exports of manufactures accounted for by each country since the mid-1960s (OECD 1988: table 1.4).

Table 4.1 Indicators of GNP per capita for six NICs

	GNP per capita growth 1965–90 (%)	GNP per capita, 1990 ($)	Ranking by GNP per capita
Hong Kong	6.2	11,490	19
Singapore	6.5	11,160	20
Taiwan	6.9[a]	7,761[b]	24
South Korea	7.1	5,400	27
Brazil	3.3	2,680	36
Mexico	2.8	2,490	40
Low and middle income countries	2.5	840	

Sources: World Bank 1992: table 1; Council for Economic Planning and Development (1987: table 3.3); Directorate-General of Budget, Accounting and Statistics (1991: table 39)

Notes: (a) 1965–86; (b) GDP per capita

Moreover these exports are not confined to low-tech, labour-intensive products or simple offshore assembly operations. There has been a substantial 'deepening' of the manufacturing sector reflected in the increasing share of value added accounted for by heavy industry. This has been accompanied by growing technological mastery on the part of producers (Lall 1990). South Korea, Mexico and Brazil are major exporters of steel and motor vehicles, Taiwan of machine tools, personal computers and electronic products, Hong Kong of radios, watches and clocks and Singapore of petroleum products, electronic components and telecommunications equipment.

Various social indicators show that rapid economic growth has been associated with a wide distribution of benefits, at least in the case of the East Asian NICs, refuting the notion that there has been growth without development (see table 4.2). Taiwan and South Korea both have relatively equitable income distribution compared to other Third World countries, a position which they have maintained despite periods during which inequality increased. Hong Kong and Singapore have greater inequality than the two larger East Asian NICs, but not the extremely unequal distribution that characterizes the Latin American NICs.

Table 4.2 Social indicators for six NICs, 1990

	Hong Kong	Singapore	Taiwan	S. Korea	Brazil	Mexico	LDCs	DCs
HDI	0.913	0.848	n. a.	0.871	0.739	0.804	n. a.	n. a.
Life expectancy[a]	77.3	74.0	73.8	70.1	65.6	69.7	62.8	74.5
Infant mortality[b]	7	7	6	17	57	39	63	8
Literacy[c]	90	88	92	96	79	85	60	96
Gini coefficient[d]	0.45	0.47	0.32	0.36	0.57	0.58	n. a.	n. a.

Sources: UNDP (1992); World Bank (1992); Haggard (1990: table 9.1); Directorate-General of Budget, Accounting and Statistics (1991: tables, 13, 14 and 110)

Notes: (a) Life expectancy at birth in years; (b) Infant mortality per thousand; (c) Literacy as percentage of population over 15; (d) Gini coefficient – low value indicates a more equitable distribution. Figures refer to 1985

All six countries have achieved substantial improvements in life expectancy, infant mortality and literacy over the past two or three decades. In terms of life expectancy and infant mortality, the East Asian city states and Taiwan have already attained the levels achieved in the developed countries, while South Korea is not far behind (table 4.2). Looking at literacy levels, South Korea has comparable levels to those of the developed countries, while those of Taiwan and the city states are slightly lower. On all these indicators, the Latin American NICs are some way behind with Mexico performing better than Brazil.

This pattern is broadly born out by the UN Human Development Index, a composite based on a longevity variable, a knowledge variable and an income variable (UNDP 1992). Hong Kong is the leading country of this group, ranked twenty-fourth in the world just behind Spain. South Korea is thirty-fourth behind the former USSR, followed by Singapore. The Latin American NICs are in forty-sixth (Mexico) and fifty-ninth place (Brazil).

The success of the East Asian NICs in achieving rapid economic growth and improvements in the standard of living of the mass of the population has led to their advocacy as models of development for other Third World countries. However the development pattern of the NICs also has its critics, and it is to these that we now turn.

CRITICS OF THE NIC MODEL

Rapid economic growth in the NICs has undoubtedly had its costs and these have been highlighted by the critics of the NIC model.[2] The critics imply either that the costs are so high as to render the model unattractive, or unsustainable in the long run, or both.

Superexploitation

A central plank in the argument is that the NIC development strategy has been based on superexploitation of the labour force, exemplified by low wages, long hours of work and a high level of industrial accidents (Frank 1981: ch. 5). This has been made possible by repression of the working class and either low levels of unionization or government control of official trade unions.

There is some evidence, particularly in South Korea and Brazil, that industrial development has given rise to more combative independent unions which have begun to question the model of superexploitation. The 'docile' labour of the past is fast disappearing, as is reflected by the increased number of labour disputes (Bello and Rosenfeld 1992: tables 1.4 and 13.1). However, it is not certain that this will go so far as to undermine the entire model.

Although initially the industrial success of the NICs was facilitated by cheap labour, rapid productivity growth has meant that continued success has been compatible with rising real wages in the four East Asian countries (Haggard 1990: table 9.3; Deyo 1990: table 7.2). In Brazil and Mexico the trend for wages to rise was reversed with the economic crisis of the 1980s. Thus the threat that increasing real wages will compromise international competitiveness is less serious than the critics suggest.

Sacrificing agriculture

A new line of criticism is that, 'The subordination of agriculture to export-oriented industrialization in Taiwan and South Korea led to the serious erosion of the agrarian base of these economies' (Bello and Rosenfeld 1992: 11). This is somewhat surprising since many of the advocates of the East Asian model claim that it has avoided the extremes of 'urban bias' which characterize other development strategies.

It is true that in the early years of rapid industrialization, the state in South Korea and Taiwan succeeded in transferring surplus from agriculture to support the industrialization drive. Given that agriculture was the largest sector, there was probably little alternative. However land reform and rapid increases in yields meant that this did not lead to impoverishment of the rural population, and the gap between rural and urban incomes was much less than in other Third World countries.[3]

Other evidence quoted to illustrate the way in which agriculture has been sacrificed is not convincing. The fact that the proportion of the population living in rural areas is declining, is hardly surprising in view of the rapid growth of manufacturing employment in both South Korea and Taiwan. Despite the fact that both countries are relatively small and densely populated, until the 1980s they had a surprisingly large rural population (Amsden 1989: 203).

Finally, the protests by South Korean and Taiwanese farmers at policies to open up their domestic markets have parallels in the developed world, particularly France. This suggests that the protests are not an indication of development failure at the periphery.

The argument that agriculture has been subordinated to industry with negative consequences for development is more plausible for the Latin American NICs (de Janvry 1981). The erosion of the agrarian base is far more marked in Brazil and Mexico where increases in agricultural productivity have lagged behind those achieved in South Korea and Taiwan (Jenkins 1991: table 2) and rural–urban differentials are far greater in Latin America.

Environmental destruction

Rapid industrialization has also had substantial environmental costs (Bello and Rosenfeld 1992: chs 5 and 12). Air and water pollution is widespread in industrial areas. Moreover both South Korea and Taiwan have invested heavily in nuclear energy, with concomitant environmental risks and safety hazards. In Taiwan particularly, an active environmental movement has developed in response to the threat posed by industrialization, which has succeeded in blocking some proposed projects on environmental grounds.

In Latin America too, major industrial centres such as Mexico City and the industrial belt around São Paulo suffer from serious environmental problems. Cubãtao near São Paulo has one of worst levels of industrial pollution anywhere in the world and is referred to as 'the Valley of Death' by many Brazilians (Faber 1992).

As in the case of agriculture, however, the environmental problems which the NICs face, particularly in East Asia, have more in common with those that give rise to concern in the advanced capitalist countries, than with the typical environmental problems of the Third World such as desertification and soil erosion.

Authoritarianism

The political regimes of all six NICs have fallen well short of western democratic standards throughout most of the last three decades. Democratic and other human rights have often been violated, opposition groups repressed and elections (when they have been held) rigged.[4] This is indeed a major limitation of the development model. However, despite ideological claims to the contrary, democracy and human rights have never been an essential part of capitalist development. These rights have been won through democratic and popular struggles. In this respect there are encouraging signs of a move away from authoritarianism in most of the NICs in recent years.

Vulnerability

The final element of the critics' picture of growth in the NICs is to stress the fragility of the development that has taken place. The East Asian NICs particularly are seen as being highly dependent on external markets, foreign technology and in the case of Singapore, foreign capital. They are threatened by protectionism in the developed countries, competition from countries which enjoy even lower labour costs, and increasing domestic tensions and contradictions. As a result it is more likely that individual NICs will fall back to the periphery, than advance to join the countries of the centre (see a CIA study quoted approvingly by Bello and Rosenfeld 1992: 16).

We will return to the question of the prospects for further development in the NICs later in this chapter. The critics have rightly stressed some of the costs of capitalist development in the NICs, an aspect which is often forgotten or ignored amid the enthusiasm for the model. However none of these costs contradicts the claim that substantial capitalist development has occurred in these countries. Many of the costs have historically been part and parcel of capitalist development wherever and whenever it has taken place. Indeed the absence of industrial pollution or declining rural population would probably indicate a lack of capitalist development.

THE BASES OF CAPITALIST DEVELOPMENT IN THE EAST ASIAN NICs

Why then has capitalism successfully developed the East Asian NICs? Other parts of the Third World have not been so lucky, and the economic decline of much of sub-Saharan Africa over the last two decades has in some ways made notions of the 'development of underdevelopment' more plausible than they were when first propounded in the mid-1960s. Even amongst the NICs, the evidence of successful capitalist development is far more compelling in the East Asian countries than in their Latin American counterparts.

Land reform

Virtually all successful cases of capitalist industrialization have been preceded or accompanied by a process of agricultural modernization (Senghaas 1985: 46–54). As city states, neither Hong Kong nor Singapore had a significant agricultural sector to modernize. However both Taiwan and South Korea did, so that land reform in the late 1940s and early 1950s played a key role in providing the bases for capitalist development.

The land reform effectively destroyed the local landlord class which had been weakened in South Korea by its collaboration with the Japanese, and which was made up of native Taiwanese in Taiwan (Hamilton 1983: 153–6). Thus a potential obstacle to capitalist development was removed as a political force in both countries. The virtual total elimination of tenancy in both countries where owner-cultivators accounted for 90 per cent of the labour force after the land reform, was followed by rapid increases in both land and labour productivity in agriculture during the 1960s and early 1970s (Jenkins 1991: table 2). As indicated above, this enabled the state to extract a substantial surplus from agriculture without depressing income levels in the rural areas.

Primitive accumulation

The destruction (in South Korea and Taiwan) or absence (in Hong Kong and Singapore) of a feudal landowning class was no guarantee of successful capitalist development. It merely removed one potential obstacle to such development. It did however also facilitate the process of 'primitive' or 'original' accumulation of capital. In South Korea expropriated landlords were compensated in government bonds which could be exchanged for industrial property. Many of these bonds were bought up by entrepreneurs at a substantial discount, but there is also evidence that landowning families moved into industry (Hamilton 1986: 31). In Taiwan large landowners were compensated with shares in four big state enterprises in cement, paper, mineral and forestry products (Bello and Rosenfeld 1992: 237).

Moreover the state was able to extract a substantial surplus from agriculture through compulsory grain purchases in South Korea and the manipulation of the barter ratio between fertilizer and rice in Taiwan. In the latter case it has been estimated that the net capital outflow from agriculture increased at a rate of 10 per cent per annum during the 1950s (Amsden 1985: 85).

In addition the substantial inflows of US aid to both countries in the 1950s and the early 1960s also provided resources for original accumulation. The largest business group in Taiwan, Formosa Plastic, began by producing PVC in a plant set up by USAID, and aid funds helped promote other industries such as glass and synthetic fibres (Bello and Rosenfeld 1992: 237–8). In South Korea too US aid during the 1950s contributed to the emergence of the *chaebols*, the diversified business groups which now dominate Korean industry (Amsden 1989: 38–41).

A further factor that contributed to the process of primitive accumulation in East Asia was the Vietnam War, which led to substantial US purchases, contracts for local firms and spending for 'rest and recreation'. South Korea's construction giants such as Hyundai and Daewoo first began working overseas for the US military in Vietnam. Hong Kong and Singapore had long played a significant role in entrepôt trade, which had given them a substantially higher level of per capita income in 1950 than South Korea or Taiwan (Papanek 1988: table 3.1). In both the city states therefore the resources for industrial accumulation came from trade rather than from agriculture.

In Hong Kong the loss of the Chinese market after the US ban of 1950 and the UN embargo of 1951 forced local firms to start local manufacture to increase value added (Hamilton 1983: 153). In Singapore too, a similar shift from commerce to manufacturing took place, although here foreign capital played the major role.

Role of the state

Concentration of capital in the hands of private entrepreneurs (or the state) is a necessary but not a sufficient condition for capitalist development. Resources must also be invested productively, not dissipated in grandiose projects or channelled into real estate or financial speculation. This in turn requires a commitment to development objectives on the part of the state and an ability to discipline private capital.

A number of authors writing about the East Asian NICs have commented on the high degree of autonomy of the state from classes and class fractions, and the way in which state structures in these countries have insulated economic policy-making from direct political pressures by vested interests (see for example Hamilton 1984; Haggard 1988; White and Wade 1988). More specifically the ability of the state to block the major channels for unproductive money-making, through land reform, controls on real estate and over finance in the East Asian NICs have been well documented (Harris 1987: ch. 2; Hamilton 1983). Moreover, particularly in South Korea and Taiwan, the state has also been able to set performance targets for private capital and to punish non-compliance (Amsden 1989; Wade 1990).[5]

Wage labour

In the advanced capitalist countries, a crucial factor in the development of capitalism was the creation of free wage labour, with nothing to sell except its labour power. The problem in the periphery is not so much the freeing of labour, which is readily available amongst the unemployed and under-employed, but rather the creation of a disciplined labour force with a sufficient level of education for industrial employment.

As indicated above, the state in the East Asian NICs succeeded in creating an apparently docile labour force through a combination of repression and other strategies (see Deyo 1987 for a discussion of the different labour control strategies followed in the four East Asian NICs). The state has also invested heavily in education. In 1990, adult literacy was 96 per cent in South Korea, 92 per cent in Taiwan, 90 per cent in Hong Kong and 88 per cent in Singapore (see table 4.2 above). Enrolment ratios in secondary schools were also high (UNDP 1991: table 14).

In South Korea, Singapore and Taiwan especially, education has been tailored towards the needs of the economy, particularly at the higher levels where there has been a heavy emphasis on engineering (Wade 1990: 65; Amsden 1989: table 9.2). This is reflected in the high level of engineers per person employed in manufacturing in the three countries (Wade 1990: 65).

Wages and productivity

Sustained capitalist development has nowhere been maintained on the basis of cheap labour in the long term. In the advanced capitalist countries, increased productivity has been accompanied by rising wages which has provided a market for expanded production. For some this is what distinguishes capitalism at the centre from peripheral capitalism which is characterized by disarticulation and heterogeneity.[6] In the advanced capitalist countries, rising real wages was made possible by the elimination of the large industrial reserve army of labour and the growth of trade-union organization. In most Third World countries large-scale un- and under-employment mean that this is a long way off, particularly when the large potential labour force of the rural areas is taken into account.

In the East Asian NICs, rapid growth has been accompanied by a fast growth of industrial employment and a substantial reduction in un- and underemployment (see Haggard 1990: table 9.7 for data on the growth of manufacturing employment). High unemployment characterized Hong Kong when it began to industrialize but most of the labour surplus had been eliminated by the early 1960s (Pang Eng Fong 1988: 223). Unemployment in Taiwan was under 2 per cent in virtually every year between 1968 and 1982 (Wade 1990: 38). In South Korea the unemployment rate fell from 9.5 per cent in 1963 to virtually full employment by 1980 (van Liemt 1988: 70), and in Singapore from 9 per cent in 1966 to full employment by the early 1970s (ibid.: 68).

It is not surprising therefore to find that real wages have increased significantly in the East Asian NICs.[7] The upward trend in wages began around 1960 in Taiwan and Hong Kong, the mid-1960s in South Korea, and around 1970 in Singapore (Haggard 1990: table 9.3; van Liemt 1988: table 16). This has contributed to the development of the domestic market, so that particularly in the larger countries, domestic demand has made an important contribution to economic growth (see Chenery 1988: table 2.3).

Thus there is some evidence to support the view that capitalist development in the East Asian NICs has many of the characteristics of capitalist development at the centre, rather than the supposed disarticulated model of peripheral capitalism.

OBSTACLES TO CAPITALIST DEVELOPMENT

The discussion of the factors which have contributed to successful capitalist development in the East Asian NICs can be reinforced by considering the obstacles to such a development in other parts of the Third World.

First, the continued existence of pre-capitalist classes with substantial political power, at least to block major reforms, is a problem in many countries. Even in the Latin American NICs, landed interests have considerable influence and this is a factor in the less successful development experience of these two countries (Jenkins 1991). While this has made it difficult to extract surplus from agriculture as effectively elsewhere as in East Asia, the absence of sources of primitive accumulation has not presented itself as a problem. Although aid accounted for 6 per cent of GNP in Taiwan in the 1950s and 8 per cent in South Korea in the period up to 1965, other countries, particularly in Africa, have also benefited from substantial inflows.

A more significant obstacle has been the failure of the state in many Third World countries to create the conditions under which resources will be channelled into productive investment. This occurs both where the state itself absorbs substantial resources unproductively through a large and inefficient bureaucracy and grandiose projects, and where the private sector finds it more profitable to invest in real estate, engage in financial speculation or to send flight capital abroad, than to invest productively.

These state failures often reflect the weakness of the state which is either used to advance particularistic interests of small groups, or is internally divided so that it cannot pursue a coherent economic strategy at all. Such 'weak' states are much more common in the Third World than the autonomous states found in East Asia.

As far as labour is concerned, the most striking distinguishing factor of the East Asian NICs is the relatively high level of education and literacy of the labour force compared to many Third World countries. Compared to Latin America, the labour force was also relatively quiescent during the 1960s and early 1970s (Jenkins 1991) although as noted above the incidence of labour disputes has increased significantly in South Korea and Taiwan since the mid-1970s.

However labour repression was by no means unique to the East Asian NICs and this factor alone cannot account for the success of capitalist development in these countries. Indeed in recent years it is the success of labour in obtaining higher wages and the fact that these are not obtained at the expense of other sectors of the population which indicates the success of capitalist development in the East Asian NICs. This is in sharp contrast to most other developing countries where a large mass of labour in low productivity services and agriculture exercises downward pressure on real wages, and where if industrial workers do obtain higher wages, this only serves to accentuate the differences in income and productivity levels between different sectors. This is illustrated by the situation in the Latin American NICs where a substantial proportion of the labour force continues to work in low-productivity services and agriculture. In Brazil underemployment in the mid-1970s was estimated at more than 35 per cent, while in Mexico unemployment and underemployment together were close to 50 per cent of the labour force (van Liemt 1988: 70–1).

It is not surprising therefore that increases in real wages in these countries have been short lived and that by the mid-1980s they had increased little, or even fallen, compared to the early 1960s (van Liemt 1988: table 16). As a result the domestic market in these countries lacks dynamism and occasional spurts of growth do not give rise to a self-sustaining development process.

THE PROSPECTS FOR CAPITALIST DEVELOPMENT IN THE THIRD WORLD

The first question that needs to be addressed here is whether, as was mentioned above, the development of the NICs can be sustained, or whether they are more likely in the future to return to the ranks of the periphery. As was pointed out earlier, GNP per capita in Hong Kong and Singapore is already comparable to that of some countries in Western Europe. At present rates of growth Taiwan will have caught up with the per capita income of Britain or Italy by the end of the century (Wade 1990: 38) and South Korea will not be far behind.

There are those who predict that the East Asian NICs are now facing a serious crisis (most notably Bello and Rosenfeld 1992). However the above analysis suggests that they are over pessimistic. All four countries have moved beyond the stage of exports based on cheap, unskilled labour.

This was brought home recently in Britain by the announcement of a joint venture between British Aerospace and Taiwan Aerospace to produce the BAe 146 in Taiwan and the elimination of half of BAe's current 146 production capacity in the UK (Henderson 1992). The Taiwanese, and the South Koreans particularly, have the skilled labour and are developing the technological capability to upgrade production when faced by competition from other countries with lower wage levels.[8] They have also reached levels of income at which the growth of the domestic market can provide a significant impetus to further expansion.

Perhaps one of the most striking indicators of the extent to which capitalism has developed in the NICs is the international expansion of firms of East Asian origin. This is not to say that they will continue to grow at the same spectacular rates as they have over the past three decades. As the gap between them and the advanced capitalist countries narrows, it is only to be expected that the rate of growth will slow down since their industrial development has been based largely on imitation and learning (see Amsden 1989). However there is no reason to suppose that they will fall back to the level of the rest of the Third World.

It is not unprecedented for countries which have apparently joined the developed countries in terms of per capita income to find themselves back amongst the less developed countries. Argentina is a case in point. In 1929 Argentina's per capita national income was similar to that of France and substantially higher than that of Austria or Italy (Balassa et al. 1986: table 1.2). By 1962 it had fallen back to thirty-first place in the world ranking behind Japan and by 1986 it was forty-fifth behind South Korea (Wade 1990: table 2.1). However high income levels in Argentina in the 1920s were based on its natural-resource wealth and favourable international markets for its agricultural exports. It never achieved the dynamic interaction of rising industrial productivity and wages which has characterized the NICs in recent years.

The second issue which must be considered is whether or not successful capitalist development in the NICs can be emulated in the Third World generally. If South Korea with income levels similar to that of Sudan in 1962 could do it, why could not Sudan replicate its achievement? It clearly does not follow that if some peripheral countries can develop then any must be able to do so. As this chapter has shown, there were very specific conditions which were themselves the result of a complex historical process which enabled the East Asian NICs to achieve capitalist development. To suppose that capitalism could achieve the same results elsewhere would be to ignore these factors. The 'fallacy of composition' argument also applies here. Even if it were possible to replicate the conditions of the East Asian NICs elsewhere, it does not follow that all Third World countries could achieve the same type of capitalist development. The success of the East Asian NICs was based on their ability to expand their shares of international markets. However in aggregate these shares remain relatively small. If all Third World countries were to attempt to do this they would run up against the limited absorptive capacity of existing markets (Cline 1982).

In conclusion then, while the case of the East Asian NICs shows that capitalist development in the periphery is possible and that countries can still aspire to leave their peripheral position, it does not support the inevitabilist position. In fact capitalist development is not something that comes naturally in all circumstances. There are substantial obstacles to such development and only under very specific circumstances can they be overcome.

NOTES

1 If comparisons of income are made on the basis of purchasing power parities rather than official exchange rates, the position of Hong Kong and Singapore is even more favourable, coming eighth and fifteenth in the world rankings. This puts Hong Kong just behind West Germany and ahead of Australia and Sweden in terms of real GDP per capita, and Singapore just behind the United Kingdom and ahead of the Netherlands and Italy (World Bank 1992: table 30).

2 An up-to-date critical account of the development experience of South Korea, Taiwan and Singapore is given by Bello and Rosenfeld (1992) from whose study many of the criticisms discussed below are drawn.

3 In the mid-1980s the average income of a rural family in South Korea was reported in fact to be higher than that of an urban family (Amsden 1989: 202).

4 Out of forty indicators of human freedom identified by Humana, Hong Kong recognized 26, Brazil 18, Mexico 15, South Korea 14, Singapore 11 and Taiwan 10 in the mid-1980s (UNDP 1991: box 1.2; Humana 1986).

5 Hong Kong is a partial exception to these generalizations about the role of the state in the East Asian NICs, but it is by no means the totally *laissez-faire* state which is often portrayed. It has also been argued that its economic performance is not as impressive as that of the other three East Asian NICs (See Wade 1990: 331–3; Harris 1987: 54–60).

6 Heterogeneity refers to the very large differences in productivity between different sectors of the peripheral capitalist economy. Disarticulation refers to the lack of an integrated economic structure which means that the impetus from increased income leaks out of the economy rather than leading to a cumulative process of increased demand, investment and growth. (For further elaboration see Amin 1976; and de Janvry 1981: ch. 1.)

7 The growth in employment is not the only factor accounting for rising wages in the East Asian NICs, and as Amsden has emphasized institutions and history are also important in explaining wage trends (Amsden 1989: ch. 8).

8 These points relate more to South Korea and Taiwan than to the city states. The

future development of Hong Kong depends on political decisions since it will revert to China in 1997. Singapore is moving away from manufacturing to becoming a financial and service centre for the Far East.

REFERENCES

Amin, S. (1976) *Unequal Development*, Hassocks: Harvester.

Amsden, A. (1985) 'The state and Taiwan's economic development', in P. Evans, D. Rueschemeyer and T. Skocpol (eds) *Bringing the State Back In*, Cambridge: Cambridge University Press.

—— (1989) *Asia's Next Giant: South Korea and Late Industrialization*, Oxford: Oxford University Press.

Balassa, B., Bueno, G., Kuczynski, P. and Simonsen, M. (1986) *Towards Renewed Economic Growth in Latin America*, Washington DC: Institute for International Economics.

Bello, W. and Rosenfeld, S. (1992) *Dragons in Distress: Asia's Miracle Economies in Crisis*, Harmondsworth: Penguin.

Chenery, H. (1988) 'Industrialization and growth: alternative views of East Asia', in H. Hughes (ed.) *Achieving Industrialization in East Asia*, Cambridge: Cambridge University Press.

Cline, W. (1982) 'Can the East Asian model of development be generalized?', *World Development*, 10 2: 81–90.

Council for Economic Planning and Development (1987) *Taiwan Statistical Data Book, 1987*, Taipei.

de Janvry, A. (1981) *The Agrarian Question and Reformism in Latin America*, Baltimore: Johns Hopkins University Press.

Deyo, F. (1987) 'State and labor: modes of political exclusion in East Asian development', in F. Deyo (ed.) *The Political Economy of the New Asian Industrialism*, Ithaca, NY: Cornell University Press.

—— (1990) 'Economic policy and the popular sector', in G. Gereffi and D. Wyman (eds) *Manufacturing Miracles: Paths of Industrialization in Latin America and East Asia*, Princeton NJ: Princeton University Press.

Directorate-General of Budget, Accounting and Statistics (1991) *Statistical Yearbook of the Republic of China, 1991*, Taipei.

Faber, D. (1992) 'The ecological crisis of Latin America: a theoretical introduction', *Latin American Perspectives* 19, 1.

Frank, A. G. (1981) *Crisis in the Third World*, London: Heinemann.

Haggard, S. (1988) 'The politics of industrialization in the Republic of Korea and Taiwan', in H. Hughes (ed.) *Achieving Industrialization in East Asia*, Cambridge: Cambridge University Press.

—— (1990) *Pathways from the Periphery: The Politics of Growth in the Newly Industrializing Countries*, Ithaca NY: Cornell University Press.

Hamilton, C. (1983) 'Capitalist industrialization in the four little tigers of East Asia', in P. Limqueco and B. McFarlane (eds) *Neo-Marxist Theories of Development*, London: Croom Helm.

—— (1984) 'Class, state and industrialization in South Korea', *IDS Bulletin* 15, 2: 38–43.

—— (1986) *Capitalist Industrialization in Korea*, Boulder CO: Westview Press.

Harris, N. (1987) *The End of the Third World*, Harmondsworth: Penguin.

Henderson, J. (1992) 'Time for Britain to halt decline by taking leaf from East Asia's Book', *The Guardian*, 14 December 1992.

Humana, C. (1986) *World Human Rights Guide*, London: Pan.

Jenkins, R. (1991) 'The political economy of industrialization: a comparison of Latin American and East Asian newly industrializing countries', *Development and Change* 22: 197–231.

Lall, S. (1990) *Building Industrial Competitiveness in Developing Countries*, Paris: OECD.

OECD (1988) *The Newly Industrialising Countries: Challenge and Opportunity for OECD Industries*, Paris: OECD.

Pang Eng Fong (1988) 'The distinctive features of two city-states' development: Hong Kong and Singapore', in P. Berger and H. Hsiao (eds) *In Search of an East Asian Development Model*, New Brunswick: Transaction Books.

Papanek, G. (1988) 'The new Asian capitalism: an economic portrait', in P. Berger and H. Hsiao (eds) *In Search of an East Asian Development Model*, New Brunswick: Transaction Books.

Riedel, J. (1988) 'Economic development in East Asia: doing what comes naturally?', in H. Hughes (ed.) *Achieving Industrialization in East Asia*, Cambridge: Cambridge University Press.

Senghaas, D. (1985) *The European Experience: A Historical Critique of Development Theory*, Leamington Spa: Berg Publishers.

UNDP (1991) *Human Development Report, 1991*, Oxford: Oxford University Press.

—— (1992) *Human Development Report, 1992*, Oxford: Oxford University Press.

van Liemt, G. (1988) *Bridging the Gap: Four Newly Industrialising Countries and the Changing International Division of Labour*, Geneva: ILO.

Wade, R. (1990) *Governing the Market: Economic Theory and the Role of Government in East Asian Industrialization*, Princeton NJ: Princeton University Press.

Warren, B. (1980) *Imperialism: Pioneer of Capitalism*, London: Verso.

White, G. and Wade, R. (1988) 'Developmental states and markets in East Asia: an introduction', in G. White (ed.) *Developmental States in East Asia*, London: Macmillan.

World Bank (1992) *World Development Report, 1992*, Oxford: Oxford University Press.

5

CONFUCIANISM AND CAPITALIST DEVELOPMENT IN EAST ASIA

Kim Kyong-Dong

INTRODUCTION

The recent high-speed economic growth being achieved by some of the non-Confucian NICs in Southeast Asia, notably Indonesia, Malaysia and Thailand, makes one wonder if the heyday may soon be over for the so-called 'post-Confucian hypothesis'. No doubt, this does not necessarily shut out the theoretical relevance of what is known as the 'culturalist' argument much in the tradition of the Weberian 'Protestant ethic analogies', for one may still want to pursue the search for some cultural equivalents of the Protestant ethic or, for that matter, that of the Confucian work ethic, even in the case of these non-Confucian Asian Dragons.

In a way, therefore, we have not yet lost the ghost of Max Weber reappearing whenever this controversy erupts, either to be supported, refuted or re-examined (Eisenstadt 1968). In the process, however, Weber has never been either fully supported or completely repudiated. As Berger (1988: 7) has aptly put it, while it may no longer be 'terribly interesting' to declare that Weber was wrong, his original questions still remain important.

As a matter of fact, Weber may not have been entirely wrong in his conclusion that Confucianism was not conducive to a capitalist development in modern China. Not only his conclusion became 'obsolete' after Sinic East Asia succeeded in capitalist development in the latter half of the twentieth century. More importantly, in view of the more recent developments in most of Asia, his approach may have become less fruitful. Now it may be high time to break with Weber's ghost in order to find a more reasonable way of dealing with the issue on hand.

In order to come up with this new approach, one may not have to discard outright the culturalist position and jump to the opposite extreme held by the institutionalists (Berger 1988: 9–10). The real problem is not which of these two positions is right, but a 'methodological' one of how we can

87

KIM KYONG-DONG

identify the precise nature of the linkage between, say, Confucianism (or Confucian tradition, legacy or heritage) and capitalist development (or even socialist development) in East Asia. And the real question one may want to raise seems to be 'How do societies with different cultures accomplish similar economic goals by means of different strategies, relying upon whatever resources available, cultural or otherwise?'

In dealing with the issue of Confucianism and capitalist development in East Asian countries, including Japan, South Korea, Taiwan, Hong Kong and Singapore, some have done an admirable job of identifying certain attitudinal-behavioural tendencies they claim to be Confucian in origin, and then linking them to the capitalist development in these societies, as the functional equivalents of the Protestant work ethic (Bellah 1968, 1970; MacFarquhar 1980; Morishima 1982; Tu 1989a, b). Still, however, it is not clear if these elements can really be located exactly in *the* Confucian portion of the culture.

To begin with, as Berger (1988: 8–9) has already pointed out, these cultures have contained much more than just Confucian heritage, and these other elements too must have contributed to the kind of work ethic under consideration. Moreover, one still is left with the thorny methodological problem of the nature of the 'linkage'. Are they causally related, and if so in which direction? Are they functionally linked, and if so in what manner? Do they happen to be interwoven by some historical accident, and if so under what conditions? It may be difficult to answer them, but they are the kind of essential questions that need to be tackled squarely to handle the issue adequately.

My strategy, therefore, is to work within a moderately general theoretical-conceptual framework to map out carefully, with the aid of historical and empirical evidence, the probable processes of change involving East Asian capitalism, with a view to locating the possibly Confucian element within the historical dynamics. For this purpose, I am using a modified modernization theory proposed in my earlier work (Kim 1985, 1990, 1991a).

A MODIFIED THEORY OF MODERNIZATION

The reason why I rely upon a modernization theory rather than any other perspective for present purposes, is simply that 'capitalist' development in East Asia has its origin in a global process of modernization, which started in the West and which has subsequently expanded worldwide. My theory, however, departs from the earlier 'classical' modernization theories by placing greater emphasis on the global nature of the process, on the one hand, and by providing a more complex scheme for the analysis of dynamic interplay of the internal and external forces in the transformation of societies and cultures, on the other (Harrison 1988; So 1990).

In a way, it views the process of modernization from the purview of the

88

societies on the receiving end of international acculturation initiated by western modernization, stressing the importance of the initial effort to adapt to the changing global environment. Also, it tries to view the process from a more comprehensive societal and cultural perspective. Within this broad scheme then one could examine more concrete processes of change in different sectors and aspects of society and locate the essential factors in such change processes. Let me now briefly go over the gist of the theory.

I take the historical fact for granted, that the 'modernization' as we know it today was originated in the West around the turn of the sixteenth century. And it is duly recognized that the inherently expansionist orientation of modern western capitalism has led western capitalism to 'invade' other parts of the globe, spreading the modernization process all over the world (Wallerstein 1979; Chirot 1986). Thus far, however, much less emphasis has been accorded to the fact that due to this intrusion, other non-western societies, at one point of modern history or another, have had to make some form of indigenous effort to adapt to the changing situation.

As the dependency and world-system theories have rightly indicated, the nature of this interaction between the modernizing capitalist West and the traditional non-West (or the so-called Third World) has been largely one-sided and asymmetrical. The economic, technological and military power of the western capitalist-imperialist forces has pressured in various forms the societies they came into contact with to 'receive' the values, institutions and whatever societal-cultural stocks these powers have brought with them to the strange land (Chirot 1977). This may be characterized as a process of 'tilted acculturation', cultures of the stronger societies flowing down, so to speak, into the weaker societies (Kim 1985).

Quite naturally, the response from the contacted societies varied. Some indigenous assessment of the situation must have been made before any reaction came forth. The level of information about the foreign intruders and the level of preparedness to understand them are extremely important in determining how they respond. This I call the element of 'cultural preparedness'.

On the basis of its own comprehension and definition of the situation, the receiving society now has to make up its mind as to how to respond. More often than not, the traditional Third World societies have put up rather adamant resistance against any foreign intrusion, owing to the lack of adequate understanding of the intruders, because of certain cultural orientations, or internal power struggles. The nature of this response thus largely depends upon the degree of cultural and structural flexibility of the society. The more flexible the social structure and culture are, the more feasible adaptive change would be, with less friction and sacrifice on either side, according to this principle of 'flexibility'.

Once the encounter is made and the response is put forward, the relative strength of the societies in contact, in terms of economic wealth, technical

89

know-how, military prowess, national integration and the like, determines the consequence, especially with respect to the relative degree of autonomy and independence the receiving society or the weaker society can retain. Complete subjugation, colonization, temporary occupation, establishment of diplomatic relations, and other forms of relationship can ensue. One may call this the principle of 'relative strengths'.

In the process of acculturation, nevertheless, some degree of selective adaptation always takes place. This selection is made in the cultural realm, for each culture may have some selective affinity with some of the incoming cultural elements (the principle of 'cultural selectivity'). If the culture of the receiving society is flexible enough, it may absorb whatever elements come in without much restraint, but it still requires some selectivity, adopting some rather than others.

Selectivity also occurs in the political arena because some decisions have to be made regarding what kind of adaptive response, in what manner, and how much of assimilation, is to be forthcoming in the face of the surge of external cultures (the principle of 'political selectivity'). And it is quite possible that these two forms of selectivity interact in such a way that, while political decisions regulate cultural selectivity, often taking advantage of the existing social arrangements, value orientations or behavioural tendencies, cultural selection may already be embedded and effectively operate in the process of political decision-making, generally unwittingly, of course. In consequence, such cultural and political selection now determines the nature of adaptive change and the extent to which it may contribute to the survival or demise, or even development of the society.

Needless to say, in the course of making adaptive change, various social forces and groupings, such as status groups, social classes, interest groups of occupational, political and cultural nature, and the like come to be engaged in diverse forms of struggle to win an upper hand in the unfoldings of adaptive modernization. Now, it is the characteristics and orientations of the winning forces that largely would determine the course of modernization in the 'receiving' Third World societies.

One has to come back, though, to the global context once again, to finalize this modified modernization theory. No matter which forces win the struggle for control of the destiny of the nation in these late-comer societies, they still have to work within the constraints of the global conditions, in the economic, military, political and other spheres. And their relative position in the general world system of cross-national interrelatedness or interdependence necessarily poses a fundamental limit within which they must find room for their own manoeuvrability. This is the kind of condition under which each nation constantly has to make whatever necessary adaptation to survive and thrive as a wholesome entity, in the on-going process of modernization which will end only when the world can find and create an entirely different politico-economic order on this planet, beyond the world system that has emerged and flourished ever since its inception around the sixteenth century in the western hemisphere.

CAPITALIST DEVELOPMENT IN EAST ASIA

Modernization viewed in this light has as its central feature the capitalist development accompanied by other social, political and cultural alterations. Although there emerged exceptions in the case of some late-comer societies which adopted and experimented with socialist modes of production and distribution, these may still be regarded as part of the capitalist world economic system when viewed from the global standpoint (Chase-Dunn 1982). I return to this issue later.

Since, however, our main subject is capitalism and Confucianism, let me first consider the basic features of the capitalist development in East Asia, from a historical perspective. This I have to do in two parts, one briefly reviewing the incipient modernization of China, Korea and Japan, in the nineteenth and early twentieth centuries, and the other focusing on the later experiences of economic growth by Japan and the Four Little Dragons in the latter half of the present century. Basic ideas proposed above in the summary of a modified theory of modernization will be reflected in this necessarily synoptic analysis.

The rough road to modernization: historical overview

Seclusion, challenge and response may most appropriately represent the salient features of the initial modernization of East Asia, covering the Chinese continent, the Korean peninsula protruding from it, and the Japanese archipelago off the Sea of Korea. Although China had already established some contact with the West in the thirteenth century, the tide of modernization reached this part of the world in the 1500s. The first Europeans to arrive in China and Japan were Portuguese Jesuits and traders, followed by the Spanish, the Dutch, the British and the French who later even crossed the borders from China into Korea (see Koh 1984; Worden, Savada and Dolan 1988; Dolan and Worden 1992; and Savada and Shaw 1992; Clyde and Beers 1971; Reischauer and Fairbank 1958; for a summary of the historical overview presented here).

When these 'barbarians' from the western lands appeared on their shores or their soil, these three countries had been maintaining a policy of seclusion vis-à-vis the outside world, since the fourteenth century in China and Korea which later even came to be accorded the infamous label of 'a Hermit Nation' by visiting westerners and, since the seventeenth century, in Japan. This particular policy was adopted in all three states after each had established a strong centralized dynasty, the Ming (1368–1644) in China, the Choson (1392–1910) in Korea and the Tokugawa regime (1600–1867) in Japan.

While limited trade under strict state control was permitted and Christianity was largely prohibited and at times persecuted, still some religious beliefs and practices, ideas of scientific and technical nature, and other kinds of practical knowledge, together with a variety of goods, seeped into these societies to a limited segment of the population, on a very selective basis. In general, however, the closed-door policy was successful enough to keep the foreign influence to a minimum.

This high and stiff wall of isolation was not to withstand the mounting physical and diplomatic pressure from the western imperialists forever, for by the mid-nineteenth century this pressure came in the form of armed threats. And the most symbolic of this kind of threat and actual conflict incurred in the course of interaction are the Opium War of 1839–42 in China, Commodore Perry's 'Black Ships' appearing in Edo (Tokyo) Bay in 1853, and the repeated conflicts involving American warships along the Korean coasts in 1866 and 1871. Eventually, all three countries had to succumb to the imperial pressure to sign a series of unequal treaties with the major western powers, one after another in the ensuing decades of the nineteenth century.

However, there appeared a slight twist in the interrelationship of the three countries. Soon after Japan had embarked on her own modernization under the impact from the outside, she began to imitate the western imperialists in encroaching on her two neighbours; forced China to cede Taiwan to Japan in 1895, and colonized Korea in 1910. In meeting the challenge from the outside, all three countries underwent a series of political and ideological struggles among the major power groups, often engulfed by violent armed conflicts. In their fight over the control of the nation, the issue of isolation itself became one of the central targets of controversy. Depending upon which force won over and the capability of that force, the results diverged in the three countries.

In China, the internal conflicts brought an end to the Ch'ing Dynasty (1644–1912), ushering in the era of final shoot-out among the ultra-conservatives, nationalists and communists. In Korea, while the strifes between conservatives and reformists were intermittently complicated by internal mass revolts and external encroachments, the national energy completely went down the drain, only to be taken over by Japan. Japan also went through waves of power struggle among different factions, but the elite force that came out triumphant, the Meiji regime, was able at the turn of the century to adopt selectively western technology and know-how in order to develop her political economy sufficiently for her to emerge as a new small imperialist power and the dominant nation in East Asia.

In all three countries, in the meantime, the economy had been growing, with agriculture at the hub of the economy. The limited yet useful information introduced from the West gradually was put to use to enhance agricultural production, industries and commerce, but very little 'capitalist' development was achieved until they were exposed to the international acculturation. It all came too late for the economy to be able to take care of the livelihood of the already impoverished nation. The only country that emerged as a new capitalist industrial state in this incipient period of modernization was Japan.

In the following paragraphs one finds a nice summary of the typical explanations for the divergent developments of these three Asian nations. In the case of China typically, and perhaps also for Korea, '[T]he empire's inability to evaluate correctly the nature of the new challenge or to respond flexibly to it resulted in the demise of the Qing and the collapse of the entire millennia-old framework of dynastic rule' (Worden, Savada and Dolan 1988: 20).

In contrast, the Japanese experience is depicted as follows:

> Since the mid-nineteenth century, when the Tokugawa government first opened the country to Western commerce and influence, Japan has gone through two periods of economic development . . . The first began in 1854 and extended through the Second World War; the second began in 1945 and continued into the early 1990s. In both periods, the Japanese opened themselves to Western ideas and influence . . . the Japanese government encouraged economic change by fostering a national revolution from above, planning and advising in every aspect of society. The national goal each time was to make Japan so powerful and wealthy that its independence would never again be threatened.
>
> (Dolan and Worden, 1992: 198)

No doubt, the actual historical unfoldings were much more complex and dynamic than what is summarized here, but it pretty much represents the essence of the historical experiences of the three traditional East Asian dynasties in their struggle to respond to the challenge of modernization as secluded nations.

Capitalist development after the end of the Second World War

The lengthy quotation above was intentional; it not only suggests the contrasting developments between Japan and the other two countries during the period of early modernization, but it also anticipates the nature of development in the Four Dragons in the post-Second World War era. Still, certain similarities and distinctions are important to note among them.

To begin with Japan, the defeat of militarists in the Pacific War and the occupation by the US military authorities provided an entirely new setting for Japan to start the second wave of modernization. Many of the internal problems involving different political factions and labour movements with various ideological strains, and large-scale monopoly industrial conglomerates, have been relatively smoothly ironed out under the safe umbrella of the US occupation authorities which also have carried out, partly on behalf of the Japanese, necessary reforms without too much cost. On top of that, the Korean War in the early 1950s greatly helped Japan to reconstruct her war-devastated economy under the auspices of the US protection. The rest of the success story is well known.

Of course, Japan's pre-war conditions and experiences provided useful legacies, but more important was the level and quality of investment in the post-war period, especially in capital equipment and techologies to develop the industrial base. They first improved the industrial base through tech-nology licensing, patent purchases, and the imitation and improvement of foreign inventions, and then beginning in the 1980s industries stepped up their research and development to be able to make innovations on their own. In the process of industrialization and rapid economic growth, government played a central role, by helping provide economic conditions in which business could flourish. Government was to be the guide, and business the producer, and government became the chief promoter of private enterprise in the process (Papaneck 1988; Dolan and Worden 1992: 198–9; 201–2).

In principle, however, Japan's economic growth was pursued in the capitalist mode. Even though the level and nature of government intervention may have been higher and more direct than one could find in the classical capitalist development in the West, entrepreneurs, whether collectively or individually, produced for a market with the purpose of making a profit, the essential ingredients of capitalism (Berger 1986: 19). What is most important for our purpose is that such capitalist development, in part, came about as an historical accident introduced by the western imperial intruders and, in part, was a result of careful selective adaptation made by the Japanese in response to the external challenge.

Conditions for other Asian nations were not as amenable as was the case for Japan. Because the historical circumstances and the timing of capitalist development rather neatly separate South Korea and Taiwan, on the one hand, and Hong Kong and Singapore, on the other, these two pairs will be compared separately.

After 1945, China still was embroiled in factional strifes to be finally seized by the Communists, forcing the Nationalists (Kuomintang, KMT) under the leadership of Chiang Kai-shek to flee to Taiwan. Since mainland China now began on a path to socialism, our focus is on Taiwan. At the end of the Second World War, the Korean peninsula suddenly was divided into North and South, by the unilateral decisions made by the triumphant allied forces, with little input from the Korean people. Much like the case of China, North Korea came under the control of communists, leaving us to concentrate on South Korea, in a comparison with the Taiwanese experi-ence of development.

While Taiwan and South Korea of course have trodden divergent historical paths, there are sufficiently comparable experiences shared by them to warrant a summary characterization of their common features as follows (for this summary see Berger 1986; Gold 1986; Hsiao 1988; Kim 1988a; Papanek 1988; Wu 1988; Savada and Shaw 1992).

Up to 1945, both Taiwan and Korea were colonies of Japan and they went through similar colonial distortions imposed by the Japanese in their political economy as a whole. As distorted and as limited as it was, this period also provided some essential physical and institutional infrastructure useful for later capitalist development in both states. In a negative way, their colonial experience had inculcated in the heart of the people in Taiwan and Korea (both North and South in this case) quite strong nationalist sentiments which in due course turned out to be a central psychological impetus for the economic miracles the two countries achieved.

In the immediate post-war period, both Taiwan and South Korea underwent some sort of 'military invasion'. In February 1947, in what is now known as '2–28 (meaning 28 February) incident', Taiwan was terrorized by the KMT troops for political reasons, and in 1950 the KMT finally 'conquered' Taiwan (taking refuge from the defeat on the mainland), making Taiwan the territory for the Republic of China. In Korea, the North invaded the South in a surprise attack on Sunday 25 June 1950, which became the start of a three-year full-fledged warfare involving the United Nations forces, and devastating the whole country as a result. The KMT's defeat and escape to Taiwan and the Korean War symbolically represent the beginning of the Cold War era which has created a global atmosphere within which both Taiwan and South Korea felt constant threat and therefore required a tight security umbrella and economic aid provided by the United States. This was to give a significant edge to these two countries to make the economic take-off in the 1960s.

The world economy in the 1960s was favourable for the East Asian latecomers to start their journey into rapid economic growth by export-led industrialization programmes. Technical and managerial know-how as well as capital and other resources needed for such programmes were readily available, through the generosity of the western industrial allies for security reasons, if not otherwise. Internally, the fairly well organized state sector with a strong authoritarian grip over the entire society was able to provide guidance and support for the active economic activities by the private sector with entrepreneurial zeal and managerial skill learned from both Japan and the West, mostly the United States. Here, too, the basic orientation was capitalist, even with extensive state intervention (Johnson 1987).

Both Hong Kong and Singapore also share certain important features. (For this, see Berger 1986; Pang 1988; Papanek 1988; So 1990). They were created as city states by immigration, no doubt under different historical circumstances, with the majority of the population being Chinese; had been under British influence in one form or another; and experienced threatening external relationships which also have prompted them, at least in part, to pursue economic growth. It is said that Hong Kong Chinese who had limited opportunities for political involvement under the relatively effective British administration had very little to do but to work hard for economic success, individually or in combines. The government with its basically *laissez-faire* orientation helped the private sector to flourish by various provisions. In Singapore, government wielded much greater power over the political life of the people but in providing a free environment for economic activities may be matched with that of Hong Kong. Perhaps, in this sense, the capitalist features are relatively more apparent in these two city states.

To offer any further detail of the economic strategies of these 'four dragons' is beyond the scope of this chapter: the above summary is sufficient for our purpose. But to recapitulate the most essential ingredients of East Asian capitalist development, one finds certain common threads in all five countries under consideration. The global conditions were conducive to development; to a certain degree, all faced some external threats, instigating strong nationalistic reaction; the sense of insecurity and the urge to survive as an integral entity provided an unusually strong psychological motive to perform well economically; the state was in good control of the internal stability needed for the economic push and was manned by sufficiently trained and disciplined bureaucracy to formulate selective strategies and provide necessary guidance; and the private sector was full of entrepreneurial zeal and energy, and equipped with reasonable managerial skill, was able to perform well in close cooperation with the state.

CONFUCIANISM IN EAST ASIAN CAPITALIST DEVELOPMENT

Now, turning to the issue of Confucianism in this development, above all, one cannot overemphasize the simple historical fact that Confucianism from its inception in ancient China has undergone enormous change over time and has evolved into diverse versions in different societies (Chan 1973; Fung 1983; Tu 1989a). In other words, Confucianism has many faces, and for the kind of analysis undertaken here, therefore, it is necessary to clearly delimit which version of Confucianism one deals with (Kim 1990, 1991a). For the present purpose, we shall not go beyond the modern era and touch upon only the Neo-Confucian and Practical Learning schools.

These, however, still represent what is called the 'high' Confucianism of the elite, mostly the literati class, which is basically of a philosophical nature, providing the ideological-normative foundation for statecraft and govern- ance, social control and individual self-discipline. How much of these philosophical preachings have been practised by the literati themselves must be carefully scrutinized, but a more important and interesting question would be how much such teachings were adopted and practised among the non-literati, before and after the modern era began in this part of the world. Thus, for our exercise, kinds of vulgarized or secularized Confucian heritage should be identified. It is such legacies in contemporary East Asia that are in fact the subject for the post-Confucian arguments.

Confucianism and the early modernization in East Asia

Before the first wave of modernization in East Asia, neo-Confucianism of Chu Hsi school developed during the Sung period (960–1279) was predominant, attaining orthdoxy in the Choson Dynasty, and in Ming and in Ch'ing China. By some account, the state itself was at once the church or the 'body' of neo-Confucian civil religion that permeated throughout the society, and this was most pronounced in the Choson which in fact was created by the neo-Confucians with a vision of achieving an ideal Confucian society in Korea (Cho 1989).

In the Tokugawa Japan, while neo-Confucianism was also adopted by the court of the military regime and preached to the warrior class (*samurai*) mostly as a system of ethical codes, the ruling elite was not the Confucian literati like in the other two societies; the warrior class was in control and Buddhism still was the most influential religion (Dolan and Worden 1992).

Risking an oversimplification, as far as modernization is concerned, however, this version of neo-Confucianism cannot be said to have been conducive to an early transition to modernity. It was the very neo-Confucian elites who were responsible for the seclusion policy resisting the tide of international acculturation until they were virtually forced to open doors to the outside world, in the nineteenth century. They viewed western ideas, particularly Christianity, as heretical, threatening the legitimacy of the Confucian orthodoxy.

Internally, while economic conditions did improve and commerce also flourished in limited urban areas, partly thanks to the western influence, these were not sufficient for indigenous capitalist development. Under the Confucian status system, the literati (or warrior) occupied the top echelon of the hierarchy, followed by three layers of commoners in the strict order of peasants, craftsmen and merchants. The last two were despised occupations. Commerce and industry were not encouraged by the ruling elite, but rather, were strictly controlled by the state, primarily for the purpose of revenue. In addition to this, the mass of peasantry became further impoverished, largely due to the depravity and exploitation of the ruling elite, and frequent uprisings ensued.

Upon exposure to the outside world, and concerned about the worsening conditions since the seventeenth century, movements arose within

Confucianism to reform the overly metaphysical and impractical theories and rigid norms of neo-Confucianism. One such faction is known as the School of Practical Learning, advocating a wide range of sociopolitical and economic reforms. In China and Korea, particularly in Korea, this school was largely condemned and persecuted as heretical, and hence had little chance to implement their innovative ideas (De Bary and Bloom 1979; Kim 1988b; Worden, Savada and Dolan 1988).

In short, Confucianism of any kind, whether orthodox or reform-minded, historically was not the spiritual or ideological source of inspiration or impetus for indigenous transformation to capitalist development in the initial stage of East Asian modernization. This does not imply that neo-Confucianism, for example, did not stress in its ethical teachings such norms and virtues as frugality, diligence, hard work, self-sacrifice, discipline, or even some form of rationality, which are often singled out as the ingredients of capitalist spirit. It may be true that merchants even in those days did indeed adhere to these norms in their everyday economic pursuits (Tu 1989a). And yet, the conditions were not sufficiently amenable to modern capitalist development, and the dominant Confucian systems of ideas and norms were not conducive to it.

Basically, it was the impact of western modernization that provided the impetus for change. The transition was made possible when the leading elite who gained political control in the turbulent struggle opted for absorption of certain selective ideas and practices from the West for the radical institutional changes needed for rudimentary capitalist development. And if there was a single most important ideological factor that actually helped these leaders in pushing for such reforms, it was certainly not Confucianism but a form of extremely strong 'nationalism' that was outstanding in all three East Asian countries.

In fact, this first phase of modernization around the turn of the century has meant an abrupt break with the Confucian orthodoxy in terms of official state ideology and formal social institutions. These now were essentially formulated and instituted in the western moulds. Confucianism now had to go 'secularized' (without any formal institutional basis, or 'church') and go underground beneath the facade of modernized (meaning 'westernized') polity, economy, society and culture. If, for instance, the Meiji reformers turned to some Confucian legacy for the purpose of promoting national integration or social order, it certainly was not any wholesome version of Confucian ethics but highly selective segments of some vulgarized version (Kim 1964). It would be far fetched to claim it was a Confucian capitalism.

Confucianism and industrial East Asia today

For the decades following the end of the Second World War, then, there was no such thing as an integrated system of 'Confucian' ideology intact in the official statecraft or purely 'Confucian' ethic operative in the secular world of everyday life among the general populace. There is no denying that despite the coexistence of many other religions Confucianism was the pervasive ideological-ethical system prior to the nineteenth-century modernization in all East Asian societies. Some legacy of Confucianism must have been retained so that part of it may be selectively retrieved when needed, or must have been exerting some influence in the attitudes and behaviour of the ordinary people, largely on the less conscious level. It is to this layer of the Confucian legacy our discussion is directed.

As has been pointed out earlier, the 'High Confucianism' of the ruling elite is *passé*; what is under scrutiny is 'Low Confucianism' (Wang 1988), 'bourgeois Confucianism' (Bellah in Berger 1988: 7), the 'Confucian-derived values in the lives of ordinary people (Berger 1988: 7), or the Confucian 'habits of the heart' (Tu 1989a: 15). This is the secularized version of Confucianism in contemporary East Asia that the 'post-Confucian' hypothesis is interested in tapping.

A detailed discussion is impossible here, but the following are the most often mentioned items (MacFarquhar 1980; Berger 1988: 7–8; Tu 1989b: 16): a generally this-worldy orientation, including a positive attitude to the affairs of this world and faith in the transformability and perfectibility of the human condition, self as a centre of an ever-expanding stream of relationships and interconnectedness, the importance of self-cultivation, the sustained lifestyle of discipline and the desirability of hard work and frugality as social discipline, duty-consciousness in the form of reciprocity of respect for authority and public accountability of the authority, the centrality of, or at least an overriding concern for, the family in social harmony and stability, the primacy of education, the political order as a moral community, the necessity of government leadership, the aversion of self-centredness or group-orientation, and the disinclination for civil litigation.

My immediate reaction to this kind of list is that many of these items may be elements of the old Confucianism in the 'High' tradition, already defunct and inoperative in the contemporary context. Furthermore, the extent to which each of these elements is practised in each of the East Asian societies today must vary to an extensive degree. Each society must have selectively discarded, modified, or at least downplayed some of these while retaining others in the process of absorbing and assimilating western cultures. Furthermore, one cannot be totally sure that even these items on the list are 'purely' Confucian, until very careful research provides reasonable evidence to that effect. Syncretic tendency of East Asian religions including Confucianism itself is so outstanding that the task of delineating the differential input of various religions is not going to be easy (Berger 1988: 8–9; Kim 1988a).

For the sake of brevity, let us sample a few of the elements on the list to examine their implications for the subject under consideration.

Take the case of 'this-worldliness' of the East Asian mentality as a cultural equivalent of that of the Protestant ethic, supposedly a basic ingredient of the spirit of capitalism. While Confucianism indeed is very much oriented to this world, the same holds for folk Taoism, shamanism, Shintoism, or even Mahayana Buddhism. Thus, to attribute it to the Confucian background alone would be incorrect (Berger 1988; Kim 1988a).

Another distinctive feature of East Asian capitalist development as a most interesting case of deviation from the original *laissez-faire* model of western capitalism is the central role played by the government and its authoritarian principle of organization. Although it is hard to pin down the logically necessary connection between strong state intervention and capitalist development, one is easily tempted to trace the 'cultural' root of this feature to the apparently Confucian belief placing an importance on the government and respect for authority.

Without denying this, one is reminded that there are other societies where strong and perhaps benevolent central government exists without Confucian background or capitalist development. More careful examination of the historical dynamics may soon reveal that the source of the modern version of, say, the East Asian 'authoritarian-bureaucratic statism' actually lies in a much more complex mixture of factors and forces than meets the eye.

To begin with, in Confucianism, the true meaning of respect for authority centres around the idea of righteous interpersonal relationships between people in various positions in the social hierarchy. Due to this vertical element, later versions of Confucianism were adopted by the strong centralized dynastic rulers as the principle of organization to legitimize their authoritarian rule. It should be emphatically repeated that in the nineteenth century, the neo-Confucian statehood was officially abolished in East Asia to be replaced by some western form of modern nation-state.

Interestingly enough, the Meiji oligarchy, when they aggressively sought to emulate the West, opted for the Prussian style under the strong man, Bismarck, rejecting the British and American form of government. Then, they instituted a much more autocratic state in Korea and Taiwan when they colonized them. The reformers in China learned either from Japan or from the Soviet Union. Even after the end of the Second World War, despite the western-style democracy these countries prima facie had adopted, the majority of leaders in the top political and government positions were those with a background of Japanese training or influence. Working for them were technocrats who in large part had some education or training in the United States (Kim and Lee 1987, for the Korean example). Considering all this, it would be hard to assert that they were substantially influenced by the Confucian legacy.

Probably in the face of great historical exigencies, without much experience of liberal democracy anyhow, these countries must have chosen the already familiar model of strong central government with an authoritarian principle of organization in their hurried pursuit of nation-building and economic growth. In the process, though, one could still retrieve and even extol some select part of the Confucian heritage, already dim in the minds of the ordinary people, in an effort to exhort them to respond to the call for national mobilization, as was the case was with Emperor Meiji, President Park Chung-Hee or Senior Minister Lee Kwan Yew. Even so, it may not have been the Confucian heritage that made these people respond positively to achieve the goal. Other, self-interested, motivations may have been more immediate than such a remote cultural legacy already eroded or affected by many other religious and ethical factors on the way.

One could even argue that authoritarianism may have had a rather negative effect, by discouraging creative thinking and innovative action on the part of individuals. Today, then, people in the same 'Confucian' states have started reacting against the authoritarian government and principle of social organization itself, by demanding political democratization, societal liberalization, loosening of the vertical order in interpersonal relations, especially among the younger generation for whom the Confucian heritage may be much more irrelevant.

The strong group orientation in the form of familism and collectivism, for instance, also has intrigued many observers who have been so used to the almost ineluctable linkage between individualism and capitalism in the West. Confucian norms do emphasize human-relatedness, stable family life, and loyalty to kinship and communal collectivities. But there are other pertinent considerations requiring due attention.

For instance, if 'familism' manifested in the form of relentless family entrepreneurship has been useful for capitalist economic growth, the same 'familism' has also hindered much needed individual initiative. That is, the level of individuation releasing the individual from the collectivity may have advanced much further, say, in Korea where the colonial policy of 'divide-and-rule' must have contributed to the atomization of individuals, while in Japan the societal incentive systems may have kept the collectivistic orientation pretty much intact. How many of such variations may be attributed to the Confucian legacy is still unclear.

Modernization at some point requires a sense of identity on the national level, commitment to the nation-state as the largest unit of collectivity. While all East Asian societies are not void of unusually strong 'nationalistic' sentiments in the emotional dimension, a more sophisticated sense of identity with the nation-state as an interest group, so to speak, is less apparent. And one of the factors inimical to the development of such a sense happens to be rather crude loyalty to much smaller, limited units of collectivity, particularly the nuclear family, kinship group, locality of origin, school attended, and the like. In Korea, for one thing, what is called the 'family egoism', or 'community self-interest' affects the achievement of badly needed national consensus related to certain crucial issues of modernization (Kim 1991b).

Before I close, let me just single out one such cultural factor that has eluded the attention of most authors in the post-Confucian camp. Because it is familiar, and because too it may be less relevant to the cases of China and Japan, I will confine the discussion to the case of Korea. And I am referring to the so-called 'status orientation'. My hypothesis in this connection is that one of the most resilient and important factors motivating the Korean people to achieve economic growth has been this strong interest in status attainment, not the kind of need-Achievement proposed by McClelland and others.

In the pre-modern society under the Confucian reign, achieving an official status by competitive examination given by the state was the central goal in life for the aspiring youth. They were tested for depth and breadth of knowledge and understanding of Confucian classics. And in accordance with the Confucian values, achieving a high official status was not for personal glory but for the sake of the family and kinship group. The central importance of education, therefore, was conceived in terms of its role as the channel for status attainment and upward mobility.

This tradition has survived even the colonial rule which ironically reinforced it by a discriminatory policy excluding the Koreans from opportunities for education and status achievement. And in the process of capitalist development, afterwards, it was not the need-Achievement or the pecuniary rewards as such that pushed the ordinary Korean people to be actively involved in capitalistic behaviour, but largely this status-achievement motive, inherited from the Confucian tradition. The same status motive, however, may also have exerted negative influence on economic development by leading many of the more able individuals to pursue non-business careers in the legal, medical and other professional fields, which in a sense reflects the Confucian heritage of emphasizing literati career, too.

And in the process of capitalist development, afterwards, the most salient motivational factor that pushed the Korean people to be actively involved in capitalist behaviour must have been this status-achievement motive inherited from the Confucian tradition. Even if immediate pecuniary incentives certainly had played a part, the accumulation of wealth was largely viewed as a means to bring some social status. The sort of need-Achievement for the sake of the pleasure of achievement itself, said to have been effective in the western capitalist development, for instance, may not have been the principal motivating forces in the case of the Koreans (Kim 1992).

In short, these select examples are intended to demonstrate that the apparently Confucian legacies may no longer have been 'purely' Confucian in the contemporary context, and that, even if they are Confucian in origin, their actual effect may have been attenuated by the workings of other cultural and non-cultural factors in connection with the capitalist development in East Asia. In addition, even the same Confucian element may be either conducive or inimical to capitalist activity, depending on the context and the mechanism of interaction among various forces.

CONCLUSION

In exploring the possible linkage between Confucianism and capitalist development in East Asia, one may well acknowledge that 'the opening of Japanese and NIE's economies to the outside world and their subsequent subjection to the rigorous competitive pressure of the international market economy, have undeniably contributed to their economic dynamism' (Tan 1989: 11). In my modified modernization theory, as well, the impact of the international acculturation has been duly emphasized. To stop at that, however, is unwarrantedly one-sided. The adaptive effort on the part of the indigenous forces, too, should be recognized and taken into account.

In the process, then, one has to look into the dynamic interaction among the many political, economic, social and cultural factors; the selective adoption, absorption and assimilation of some foreign elements; and the selective abandonment, modification and utilization of others. As suggested earlier, the selectivity can occur through the culture or through political decisions.

My overall assessment of the place of the Confucian heritage in East Asian capitalist development may be summarized as follows: it had initially hindered the process; then by becoming a dormant force under the impact of international acculturation it may have exerted not direct but passive influence as a sort of cultural basin from which the elite could retrieve some useful elements in the first wave of modernization.

By the time the second wave was beginning, the Confucian heritage had already been tainted and modified by the influx of other cultures, and if still left lingering on in the minds of the general populace, it may have contributed to the kind of work ethic required for the economic take-off, not necessarily as the sole source of such cultural input but as an intermixed part of the whole cultural stock. At most, it may sometimes have been referred to as the cultural legacy by the development elite for the purpose of attaining legitimacy or of stimulating the people.

It is true that East Asians are very much Confucian in many aspects; they are very much something else as well. If one attributes everything to the Confucian origin because Confucianism once was so pervasive in these societies, one does not really explain anything. Just for the sake of argument, compare today's China and North Korea. Both having isolated themselves for a fair amount of time, they have in fact manifested much stronger Confucian tendencies in many respects than either Taiwan or South Korea, which have been extensively exposed to American influence since 1945. And despite the fact that both have taken the socialist path, their present position is vastly different from each other. 'What has their Confucian heritage done to these two societies?', one might ask.

Of course, one cannot simply dismiss the argument that cultural factors affect economic activities. My major concern here has been with the methodological difficulties of identifying such effects. My modified theory of modernization is meant to ease, if not resolve, this problem, by suggesting an analytic framework which enables one to view the cultural factors in perspective and to trace their effect in the complex dynamics of historical transformation. The significance of the East Asian model of capitalist development in contrast to that of the West may lie in that cultural differences can produce similar results by providing a context in which the society could choose different strategies in achieving the same goals.

Looking to the future, now, one still might want to listen to some of the pro-Confucian advocates whose views suggest a different but extremely important kind of linkage between Confucianism and capitalism. Their voice clearly reflects some of the most serious problems encountered by the entire humanity today, owing to the general technological and economic development related to capitalism (De Bary 1989; Tu 1989a). Even if we are left with no other option but capitalism at the moment after the absurd failure of the grand social experiment on the part of the communist zealots, we are not unaware of the shortcomings and pitfalls of capitalism. Pernicious effects of capitalist development have been pointed out over and over again by many critics. And they include among others the problem of environmental costs of the greedy pursuit of material comfort, societal deterioration owing to the extreme individualism fostered by capitalism, and the overemphasis on the material to the detriment of the spiritual and moral. It is in this respect that the relevant wisdom provided in the great East Asian thoughts, particularly Confucianism, can be of enormous value to help save humankind from disastrous consequences of misguided capitalist development.

REFERENCES

Bellah, R. (1968) 'Reflections of the Protestant Ethic analogy in Asia', in S. N. Eisenstadt (ed.) *The Protestant Ethic and Modernization: A Comparative View*, New York: Basic Books.
—— (1970) *Beyond Beliefs: Essays on Religion in a Post-Traditional World*, New York: Harper & Row.
Berger, P. L. (1986) *The Capitalist Revolution: Fifty Propositions about Prosperity, Equality, and Liberty*, New York: Basic Books.

—— (1988) 'An East Asian development model?' in P. L. Berger and H. H. M. Hsiao (eds) *In Search of an East Asian Development Model*, New Brunswick and Oxford: Transaction Books.

Chan Wing-Tsit (1973) *A Source Book in Chinese Philosophy*, Princeton, NJ: Princeton University Press.

Chase-Dunn, C. (1982) *Socialist States in the World System*, Beverly Hills, CA: Sage.

Chirot, D. (1977) *Social Change in the Twentieth Century*, New York: Harcourt Brace Jovanovich.

—— (1986) *Social Change in the Modern Era*, New York: Harcourt Brace Jovanovich.

Cho Hein (1989) 'Secularization of neo-Confucianism and industrialization of Korea: a study of counter-secularization', unpublished Ph. D. dissertation, University of Pennsylvania.

Clyde, P. H. and Beers, B. F. (1971) *The Far East: A History of the Western Impact and the Eastern Response (1830–1970)*, 5th edn, Englewood Cliffs, NJ: Prentice-Hall.

De Bary, W. T. (1989) 'Encounter between East and West and the creation of global culture', in Christian Academy (ed.) *The World Community in Post-Industrial Society*, vol. V, Seoul: Wooseok.

De Bary, W. T. and Bloom, I. (eds) (1979) *Principle and Practicality: Essays in Neo-Confucianism and Practical Learning*, New York: Columbia University Press.

Dolan, R. E. and Worden, R. L. (eds) (1992) *Japan: A Country Study*, Washington, DC: Library of Congress.

Eisenstadt, S. N. (1968) 'The Protestant thesis in an analytical and comparative framework', in S. N. Eisenstadt (ed.) *The Protestant Ethnic and Modernization: A Comparative View*, New York: Basic Books.

Fung Yu-lan (1983) *A History of Chinese Philosophy*, 2 vols, trans. D. Bodde, Princeton, NJ: Princeton University Press.

Gold, T. B. (1986) *State and Society in the Taiwan Miracle*, New York: M. E. Sharpe.

Harrison, D. (1988) *The Sociology of Modernization and Development*, London and Boston: Unwin Hyman.

Hsiao, H. H. M. (1988) 'An East Asian development model: empirical explorations', in P. L. Berger and H. H. M. Hsiao (eds) *In Search of an East Asian Development Model*, New Brunswick and Oxford: Transaction Books.

Johnson, C. (1987) 'Political institutions and economic performance: the government-business relationship in Japan, South Korea, and Taiwan', in F. C. Deyo (ed.) *The Political Economy of the New Asian Industrialism*, Ithaca, NY: Cornell University Press.

Kim Kyong-Dong (1964) 'Confucian values in Korea: analysis of children's moral education textbooks', in *Collection of Articles in Commemoration Dr. Prof. Sang Beck Lee on His Sixtieth Birthday* (in Korean), Seoul: Ulyoo Publishers.

—— (1985) *Rethinking Development: Theories and Experiences*, Seoul: Seoul National University Press.

—— (1988a) 'The distinctive features of South Korea's development', in P. L. Berger and H. H. M. Hsiao (eds) *In Search of an East Asian Development Model*, New Brunswick and Oxford: Transaction Books.

—— (1988b) 'The aborted Confucian Reformation in Korea's incipient modernization: the case of Tasan, Chong Yag-yong', *Seoul Journal of Economics* 1: 313–56.

—— (1990) 'Development, modernization, and Confucianism', in *Report: International Conference on Culture and Development in Asia and the Pacific*, sponsored by United Nations University, Fukuoka, Japan, 5–7 March 1990.

—— (1991a) 'Confucianisme introuvable, confucianisme retrouve', *Espace-Temps* 45/46: 62–72, trans. L. Husson.

—— (1991b) 'Radioactive waste disposal as a social issue', *Korea Journal of Population and Development* 20(2): 49–57.

—— (1992) *Values and Social Attitudes of the Korean People* (in Korean), Seoul: Pakyongsa.

Kim Kyong-Dong and Lee On-Jook (1987) 'Educational background of the Korean elite: the influence of the United States and Japan', in Kyong-Dong Kim (ed.) *Dependency Issues in Korean Development: Comparative Perspectives*, Seoul: Seoul National University Press.

Koh Byong-ik (1984) *Tradition and Modern History of East Asia* (in Korean), Seoul: Samjiwon.

MacFarquhar, R. (1980) 'The post-Confucian challenge', *The Economist* 9: 67–72.

Morishima, Michio (1982) *Why has Japan Succeeded? Western Technology and the Japanese Ethos*, Cambridge: Cambridge University Press.

Pang Eng Fong (1988) 'The distinctive feature of two city-states' development: Hong Kong and Singapore', in P. L. Berger and H. H. M. Hsiao (eds) *In Search of an East Asian Development Model*, New Brunswick and Oxford: Transaction Books.

Papanek, G. (1988) 'The new Asian capitalism: an economic portrait', in P. L. Berger and H. H. M. Hsiao (eds) *In Search of an East Asian Development Model*, New Brunswick and Oxford: Transaction Books.

Reischauer, E. and Fairbank, J. K. (1958) *East Asia: The Great Tradition*, Boston: Houghton Mifflin.

Savada, A. M. and Shaw, W. (1992) *South Korea: A Country Study*, Washington, DC: Library of Congress.

So, A. Y. (1990) *Social Change and Development: Modernization, Dependency, and World System Theories*, Newbury Park and London: Sage.

Tan Kong Yam (1989) 'Pattern of Asia Pacific economic growth and implications for China', mimeo paper presented at the Symposium on Economic and Trade Co-Operation between China and Asian Pacific Region, Beijing, China, 28–31 October 1989.

Tu Wei-ming (1989a) 'The Confucian dimension in the East Asian development model', mimeo paper presented at the Chinese Institute for Economic Research, Taipei, Taiwan, June 1989.

—— (1989b) 'The rise of industrial East Asia: the role of Confucian values', mimeo paper presented at the Centre for East Asian Studies, University of Copenhagen, May 1989.

Wallerstein, I. (1979) *The Capitalist World-Economy*, New York and Cambridge: Cambridge University Press.

Wang, Gungwu (1988) 'Trade and cultural values: Australia and the Four Dragons', *Current Issues in Asian Studies Series* No. 1, Victoria, Australia: The Asian Studies Association of Australia.

Worden, R. L., Savada, A. M. and Dolan, R. E. (eds) (1988) *China: A Country Study*, Washington, DC: Library of Congress.

Wu, Rong-I (1988) 'The distinctive features of Taiwan's development', in P. L. Berger and H. H. M. Hsiao (eds) *In Search of an East Asian Development Model*, New Brunswick and Oxford: Transaction Books.

6

'GENDER' AND GLOBAL CAPITALISM

Maria Mies

INTRODUCTION

Before analysing the relationship between global capitalism and what has been coined as 'gender' I want to spell out my critique regarding the use of certain concepts in this chapter. The first focuses on the concept 'development' which is used as a key concept in the title of this book. The second critique deals with the concept of gender, used since the early 1970s.

CRITIQUE OF THE DEVELOPMENT DISCOURSE

After several unsuccessful 'development decades' and a growing body of critical literature on the concept of development itself, the paradigm of development and the ideology of development, it is no longer possible, in my view, to continue to use this concept in the same naive way as is usually done and is also expressed in the title of this book. This title suggests that 'development' is something desirable and independent from capitalism, and that capitalism either promotes or hinders development.

'Development' as reality, concept and Utopia has been criticized by a variety of people, ranging from grassroots movements in the South against the construction of big dams, against the destruction of the rainforests in the name of development, against the felling of trees, like the Chipko movement in India, against tourism, as in Ladakh, to a number of disillusioned groups and individuals both in the South and in the North (Alvares 1992). This critique has been voiced in recent years by Third World feminist networks like DAWN, by people like Brigitte Erler (Germany), Vandana Shiva (India), Gustavo Esteva (Mexico), Thierry G. Verhelst (Belgium), Trainer and Lummis (UK), C. v. Werlhof, V. Bennholdt-Thomsen and myself (Germany). Wolfgang Sachs has collected a number of these dissident voices in his *Development Dictionary* (1992). Whereas the earlier critique of the development process focused rather on the inter-

107

dependence of development and underdevelopment (Frank 1969; Amin 1974), the later critics look at this process and its results more from the perspective of the victims: nature, women and colonized people in the South.

Some of these critics, like Esteva, have traced the history of this concept and have shown that it was introduced by President Truman in his inaugural speech in January 1949 to hail a new era of US American hegemony. A hegemony which would replace the old imperialism and colonialism, but would nevertheless serve corporate interests by a bold new programme for making the benefits of our scientific advances and industrial progress available for the improvement and growth of underdeveloped areas. 'The old imperialism – exploitation for foreign profit – has no place in our plans. What we envisage is a program of development based on the concepts of democratic fair dealing' (Esteva 1992: 6).

From then onwards, the world is dualistically divided up into 'developed' and 'underdeveloped' countries and areas. This not only suggests that the 'developed' are the image of the future, the concrete Utopia, for the 'underdeveloped' but also that the 'advancement' of the 'underdeveloped' follows a 'natural' and evolutionary process. The concept 'development' was originally coined in the eighteenth century to describe the natural growth of an organism to its maturity. This biological metaphor was later used, both by liberals and Marxists, to conceptualize the historical and social processes underway in the nineteenth and twentieth centuries. 'Historical development was the continuation of natural development' (Esteva 1992: 8). The concrete content of this 'development' was, and is, the industrial mode of production. This industrialization, also called modernization, was then declared by scientists and politicians as the universal goal of mankind, the goal of history. Science and technology were seen as the moving force for this development. But what was and still is hidden is the fact that the 'development' of Europe and of the United States was not an evolutionary, 'natural' process but was and is based on violence, on conquest, exploitation and colonization not only of foreign peoples and their lands but also of nature and of women (Esteva 1992; Mies 1991). Therefore, 'development' is always and necessarily causally linked to underdevelopment. Or in other words: development (i.e. industrialism) creates underdevelopment somewhere else (Frank 1969).

The concept 'development', like the concept 'growth' – both are borrowed from biology – is a natural metaphor meant to obscure and obfuscate the violence and crude exploitation that continue to characterize the relationship between 'development' and 'underdevelopment'.

What is particularly dangerous in this concept is the fact that it suggests that all those who were declared as 'underdeveloped' could eventually *catch up* with those who have already reached the pinnacle of the world economic social pyramid: Western Europe, North America, Japan. This myth of *catching-up development*, originally based on the theory of economic stages, developed by Rostow (1960), is not only the foundation of all political and economic strategies *vis-à-vis* the 'underdeveloped', but it has, to a large extent also captured the imaginations and shaped the expectations of the poor in the Third World. It has been proved convincingly by Trainer (1989), by Lummis (1992) and others that this catching-up development is not possible for all. The present 'development' is even unsustainable for the rich in the 'developed' countries, which make up only 20 per cent of the world's population. *Therefore this development paradigm cannot be generalized:*

> It has been estimated . . . that for the present world population to live at the per capita energy consumption level of the city of Los Angeles would require five planets. The precise figure may be dubious, but the general point remains indisputable.

> (Lummis 1992: 46)

In spite of the fact that the impossibility of catching-up development is recognized even by analysts and policy-makers, the main strategies for solving both the problems of poverty and of environmental destruction continue to propose more economic growth (World Commission On Environment And Development 1987; World Watch Institute 1992; Club of Rome 1991). The development paradigm with its inbuilt contradictions is nowhere put into question. Instead, population growth is identified as the causal factor for the present crises (Mies 1992).

But catching-up development is not only not possible for all people, sexes, countries, classes and regions, *it is also not desirable.* This is not only due to the fact that capitalist development always entails sacrifices (as the president of the World Bank, B. Conable pointed out in a reaction to the protest movement against the construction of the Narmada dams in India), but also because those who are forced to sacrifice are usually not those who reap its fruits. In view of the environmental destruction caused by development, and industrialism, not only in the underdeveloped but also in the overdeveloped world as well as globally, catching-up development can only result in local and global catastrophies. This is particularly true if one looks at this development from the perspective of its victims, the poor in the South, particularly women and children. From this perspective, development, the emulation of the capitalist–industrial mode of production and consumption can no longer be upheld as a blueprint for the future.

Critique of the 'gender discourse'

The concept 'gender' was introduced into the feminist discourse in the early 1970s. By making a conceptual distinction between 'sex', as a biological and 'gender' as a cultural (social, historical, psychological) category these feminists hoped to avoid biological determinism which was and is still used to explain the oppressive, exploitative, unequal relationship between men and women.

r This new concept was immediately accepted, not only by feminists of the English-speaking world, but also by many organizations, the media, politicians, etc. It was also introduced into the development discourse and replaced a number of concepts which irritated particular male sensitivities because they were too direct and concrete. Instead of 'sexual violence' one would talk of 'gender violence', instead of inequality between men and women one would talk of 'gender' inequality. The concept 'sexual division of labour' was replaced by 'gender division of labour'.

I have criticized the conceptual distinction between 'gender' and 'sex' already in 1986 because it reinforces the dualistic division between 'nature' and 'culture', 'matter' and 'spirit', and obscures the fact that human sex and sexuality is as much a cultural and historical category as gender is (Mies 1991: 22–3).

Today we are witnessing a worldwide and inflational use of the concept 'gender'. It has the effect of virtually excluding 'women' again from the public discourse. This was spelt out clearly by Kate Young at a conference on 'gender training' in Dhaka in September 1992. Kate Young said that this concept was introduced to avoid biological determinism. But now it makes women again invisible.

By introducing this apparently scientific concept into the development discourse, feminist scholars hoped to make research on women and development more acceptable to fund-giving organizations, to the scientific community. The term 'gender' sounds less threatening, is more abstract, does not suggest that every man has something to do with the problem of women's oppression and exploitation. It removes this problem again from a political to an academic discourse level and thus neutralizes and blunts the social movement for the abolition of capitalist patriarchy as a system.

For all these reasons I shall avoid using the concept gender in the following text.

FROM 'INTEGRATION INTO DEVELOPMENT' TO 'INVESTMENT IN WOMEN'

From stone-age economics (Sahlins 1974) up to capitalism no economy can function without women, women as procreators and women as workers. But capitalism is the first social formation which has created the notion that women are not part of the economy, not part of the public sphere, of politics, culture, science, technology and progress, but that they belong to the private, the family, the household and in the last analysis to the realm of 'nature'. It is on the backdrop of this dualistic worldview, prevalent since the eighteenth century in all 'modern' societies, that a discourse could start on 'how to integrate women into development'.

It will be remembered that the talk on Women and Development started around 1975 in the context of the International Women's Conference in Mexico. There it was admitted that women generally, but Third World women in particular 'had been left out' of the development process. This deficit had been first identified by Ester Boserup in 1970 who had empirically proved that particularly rural women in Africa, Asia and South America had not benefited from whatever development had taken place in these areas (Boserup 1970). Her findings were corroborated by many reports on the status of women, prepared by the governments of underdeveloped countries. It was found that in the course of development women's economic, educational, legal, political status had deteriorated in most poor countries. But also in the rich countries things were bad. To remedy this situation the World Plan of Action was formulated which had the main aim to 'integrate women into development'.

I want to point out, that also before the Mexico conference women were 'integrated' into the capitalist development strategy, namely as invisible and unpaid or low-paid subsistence producers and homemakers. They constituted the necessary 'underground' for the development process. Integrating women into development did not mean to question this basic sexual division of labour, or even the division of labour between over-developed and underdeveloped societies. The strategy follows the evolutionary paradigm criticized above.

It has to be further remembered that around the same time, namely the 1970s, the Globalization of Capital, or in other words, the New International Division of Labour was propagated as a new development strategy (Fröbel, Heinrichs and Kreye 1980). Also this strategy was basically not new. As Wallerstein pointed out, capitalism rose and functioned as a 'world-system' right from its beginnings in the sixteenth century (Wallerstein 1974). What was new was a restructuring of what has been called the International Division of Labour (IDL). Whereas the old International Division of Labour meant the import of cheap raw materials from the colonies and ex-colonies and the production of high-cost, machine-made goods in the industrial countries, the new IDL meant the relocation of whole factories to cheap labour countries like Sri Lanka, Tunisia, Malaysia, Thailand, Mexico, etc. This strategy, worked out by the OECD, had the aim of avoiding social upheavals in the industrialized countries where economic growth, the main dogma of capitalism, slowed down. Whole labour-cost-intensive plants like textile, electronics, toy and other industries were exported by multinational corporations of the United States, Japan, Germany to so-called world market or free production zones (FPZ).

In all these relocated or run-away industries the vast majority of the labour force was and is female. Fröbel and his colleagues estimate that women make up about 80 per cent of the workforce of the electronics industry in Southeast Asia (Fröbel, Heinrichs and Kreye 1980; Grossman 1978/9).

It is no mere coincidence that the strategy of the new globalization of capital was formulated at the same time when the strategy of 'integrating women into development' entered the public discourse. The New International Division of Labour went hand in hand with a New Sexual Division of Labour.

As far as women are concerned this new strategy of globalization of capital and of feminization of labour in the poor countries of the South takes place in four areas:

1 in the *formal sector*, in relocated large-scale manufacturing industries in free trade zones or world market factories (electronics, textiles, garments, toys, etc.);
2 in the *informal sector*, in small-scale manufacturing in cottage industries, home-working, sweat-shops, so-called income-generating activities (handicrafts, food processing, ancillary jobs for industry, garments, art objects);
3 in *agriculture*, including subsistence and cash-crop production for export, work in plantations and food processing, work as unpaid family and low-paid wage labour.
4 in the 'service sector', particularly in the sex and tourist industry (Mies 1991: 114–15).

Housewifization and accumulation

The strategy to 'integrate women into development' means mainly the following: poor women in underdeveloped societies particularly rural women who constitute the majority in the South should get more education, more access to modern technology and to '*income-generating activities*' by which they would be able to supplement the insufficient income of their husbands. It did and does not mean that their control over subsistence production is strengthened, that exploitation of their natural resources would be stopped or that their men would also be asked to share in this survival production. It means in fact to introduce women more directly to commodity production, to a market-oriented production system instead of their production for their own sustenance. It means production for *money* instead of production for *life*. Above all it does not mean that women are *defined as workers*. It is revealing that the phrase which is used does not talk of women's *labour*. By this two things are achieved: (a) women are basically *defined as housewives* who are involved in some money-earning production to supplement the male 'breadwinner's' income; (b) as women are not defined as workers there need not be any fear of their unionizing or their

112

demanding better wages; (c) what further characterizes all income-generating activities: women do not produce usually what is necessary in their local environment, but what can be sold in an external, mainly a foreign market, where the programmes are based on the production of superfluous luxury items like handicrafts, lace, flowers, exotic foods for already overconsuming western buyers.

This integration of women into the 'development process' is based on the 'social construction' of women as *housewives*, a definition which first arose in the eighteenth and nineteenth centuries in the bourgeois class, but was later extended to all women.

I have called the process by which womens' work in the production and reproduction of life – generally called housework or subsistence work – was made invisible, the *process of housewifization* (Mies 1982: 176, 1991: 100–20). This process has accompanied the process of proletarianization by which mainly men are defined as wage earners and breadwinners.

The characteristic features of housewives are the following:

- they are dependent for their livelihood on a 'breadwinner';
- their work is not remunerated by a wage;
- their work is invisible, it is not counted in the GNP or in the statistics of the economy proper (Waring 1989);
- their work is not protected by labour laws and their labour time is not limited;
- their work is not based on a labour contract;
- they are isolated and atomized, cannot easily be unionized.

These characteristics of women's housework, however, are not restricted to the housewives proper, but they are attributed practically to all women workers who are gainfully employed. The social definition of women as housewives is the secret behind the wage differences between men and women, the continuing inequality of women regarding jobs, careers, economic and political participation.

This housewifization of women and their work is also the secret behind the new discovery of women in the South by global capital. Not only in the informal sector and in income-generating activities' are women structurally defined as housewives, dependent on a 'breadwinner' but also in the relocated or runaway industries in free trade zones or world market factories, in agriculture and in the tourist and other service industries.

Women, defined as housewives and sex objects, are the optimal labour force for global capital. The new strategy of deregulation or flexibilization of labour, propagated for a few years as the new economic philosophy, finds least resistance when workers do not consider themselves as workers but as 'housewives'. I have summarized the benefits of this housewifization for global capital as follows:

1. Contrary to what is commonly accepted, women, not men, are the optimal labour force for the capitalist (and the socialist) accumulation process on a world scale. Though this has always been the case, in this phase of development of the world economy this fact is openly incorporated into the economic strategies of national and international planners.

2. Women are the optimal labour force because they are now being universally defined as 'housewives', not as workers; this means their work, whether in use value or commodity production, is obscured, does not appear as 'free wage-labour', is defined as an 'income-generating activity', and can hence be bought at a much cheaper price than male labour.

3. Moreover, by defining women universally as housewives, it is possible not only to cheapen their labour, but also to gain political and ideological control over them. Housewives are atomized and isolated, their work organization makes the awareness of common interests, of the whole process of production, very difficult. Their horizon remains limited by the family. Trade unions have never taken interest in women as housewives.

4. Due to this interest in women, and particularly in women in the colonies as the optimal labour force, we do not observe a tendency towards the generalization of the 'free' proletarian as the typical labourer, but of the marginalized, housewifized, unfree labourer, most of them women.

5. This tendency is based on an increasing convergence of the sexual and the international division of labour; a division between men and women – men defined as 'free' wage-labourers, women as non-free housewives – and a division between producers (mainly in the colonies and mainly in the countryside) and consumers (mainly in the rich countries or the cities). Within this division there is also the division between women mainly as producers – in the colonies – and as consumers – mainly in the West.

6. The overabundance of commodities in the Western supermarkets is not the result – as is mostly assumed – of the 'productivity' of work and of the workers in the industrialized countries; this 'productivity' is itself a result of the exploitation and super-exploitation of the colonies, particularly of women there.

(Mies 1991: 116)

The internationalization of the social construction of women as housewives and the strategy of 'integrating them into development' has, of course, not enabled poor women in the South to 'catch up' with the men or even with women in the North.

At the end of the International Decade for Women, 1985 in Nairobi, it again became clear, that this catching-up development, or the integration of women into development had not in the least changed the basic capitalist and patriarchal structure in which women were caught up, nor had it solved women's survival problems. On the contrary: things had become worse. Integrating women into development had only increased women's work load, but had not given them more income and more assets. Since 1980 the famous UN statement makes the round that women do two-thirds of the world's labour, get one-tenth of the world's income and possess less than one-hundredth of the world's property. A whole series of studies on the effect of development on women has meanwhile shown that almost everywhere development means for women the destruction of their independent subsistence base, ecological destruction, more work for their sheer survival, more state control over women's immediate life, particularly in the sphere of reproduction and health, and generally more violence and destruction of women's dignity and integrity (cf. Agarwal 1988; Schrijvers 1988; Ng and Mohamed 1988; Chee Heng Leng 1988; v. Werlhof 1985; Akhter 1986).

This pauperization and marginalization of women, however, is not due to some malfunctioning of the capitalist world system, it is rather a precondition for its success. Because, as Rosa Luxemburg (1923) already noticed, extended reproduction of capital or permanent growth is possible only if ever more human labour, ever more resources and ever more markets can be integrated into this process. That means, the exploitation of 'free' wage labour presupposes the exploitation of non-wage labour – mainly women and people in colonies – and of nature. Therefore, the process of 'primitive accumulation' of capital did not only precede the capitalist accumulation process, as Marx thought, it is rather its continuing precondition and basis (Mies, Bennholdt-Thomsen and v. Werlhof 1988). Without this 'ongoing primitive accumulation' the superiority of the capitalist productivity of labour would not exist.

The World Bank and women

As the global strategies of capitalist development are mainly spelt out and put into practice by the World Bank (WB) and the International Monetary Fund (IMF) it may be useful to analyse briefly the World Bank's policy with regard to women from 1975 to 1988.

In 1975 we read in a World Bank statement:

The need to recognize and support the role of women in development is an issue which the World Bank considers of great importance for itself and its member governments. The bank expects to participate to an increasing extent in the efforts of those governments to extend the benefits of development to all of their population, women as well as men, and thus ensure that so large a proportion of the world's human resources is not underutilized.

(World Bank 1975)

The WB spelt out two main goals for its women's policy: (a) to educate women in order to increase their productivity, to use their 'underutilized capacity more productively'; (b) to increase their knowledge about contraception and family planning in order to bring down the population growth rates.

The main aim of the World Bank's policy on women can thus be said to be: *to increase women's productivity and to decrease their fertility.* The World Bank put pressure on Third World governments asking for loans to take specific action to reduce fertility and to raise the status of women. These two goals are not contradictory, but are part and parcel of the same strategy of 'investing in women' as will become presently clear.

What is meant by the phrase: 'increase women's productivity'? In classical economic terms it means to use their labour for the production of exchange values, of commodities for an external market which can generate a profit. The term 'productivity of labour' is clearly related to the process of capital accumulation. It also means to increase the output of this labour in a given time and for a given cost. Hence, to increase women's productivity means above all, from the point of view of capital accumulation, to save costs and link women's labour to the money economy, to *draw them away from subsistence production* (Bennholdt-Thomsen 1988). Because as long as people only produce what they need themselves, money cannot 'breed' more money.

We may ask, why, at this present juncture, the World Bank i.e. international capital, discovers women, particularly poor Third World women? The reason is, as was said, that women are defined as housewives and mothers who are responsible for the family, the children, the old, etc., in short: *for the production of life.* That means they cannot simply go away but are forced to accept wages which are often below subsistence level. According to Claudia v. Werlhof, the women defined as housewives are the optimal labour force for capital, not the male proletarian. Therefore free wage labour has not been generalized, as Marx expected, but the definition of women as housewives has. The reason for this housewifization is, according to v. Werlhof, that the male wage labourer in the industrialized West is too expensive, works too little (due to trade-union pressure), knows too little.

He can do only what he is paid for and what has been agreed upon by contract . . . he cannot be mobilized for all purposes, as a person, a whole human being. The masculine work capacity is too inflexible and unfruitful.

(v. Werlhof 1988: 179)

This is the reason why the World Bank is not talking any longer only about 'integrating women into development' but about 'investing in women'. At the 1988 annual conference of the World Bank and the IMF in Berlin a paper was presented by Barbara Herz to the assembly which had the title: 'Briefing on Women in Development'. Barbara Herz is the head of the newly created World Bank division: Women in Development which was set up by the president of the World Bank, Mr Barber B. Conable, Jr. In this paper the main points of the new strategy of 'investing in women' are clearly spelt out. The paper starts with the well-known facts that women worldwide are already doing most of the work, not only in the household (in 'reproduction') but also in food production and also in industry. It is also admitted that all this labour, in spite of its important contribution to the society, is not adequately remunerated. The reason for this situation, however, is not seen in the sexual division of labour, in exploitation and in the capitalist world-market system as such but in 'women's low productivity', which on its part is attributed to lack of education and training, and non-modern or patriarchal traditions:

> But women lack the means to work at full or even moderate levels of productivity. Their capacity to contribute is specially constrained by tradition, sometimes codified into law or policy that limits their access to information and technology, to education and training, to credit and resources and to markets.
>
> (Herz 1988: 2)

The message is clear: women are poor because they are not sufficiently linked to the money economy and the market system. The strategy following from this analysis is obvious: *'Investing in women can make development programmes more productive'* (Herz 1988: 2, emphasis in the original). As women do already a lot of the work in agriculture it would lower the costs of development programmes considerably if governments would 'invest in women'.

The case of the Kenyan government is cited where extension agents now mainly choose women agriculturists for their programmes. The government hopes that thus extension could be doubled and costs reduced. 'The result would be greater food security for rural families, greater food supplies in town, and greater export earnings' (Herz 1988: 2). The paper addresses these women in agriculture now no longer as subsistence farmers but as 'entrepreneurs':

> As a general proposition, it makes sense to allow women, like other entrepreneurs, an expanded range of economic opportunities and let them weigh market potential and family concerns rather than assuming they 'should' stay in certain lines of activity. Culture may limit the scope and pace of such expansion, but the economic virtue of deregulation ought to be clear.
>
> (Herz 1988: 2)

It is interesting to note the shift in terminology. Up to recently we heard the talk of 'income-generating *activities*' – not of work. Now women are called *entrepreneurs*, but unlike male entrepreneurs they have to combine and 'weigh' family concerns and market production. The strategic aim of this new terminology is to hide from the women themselves that they are exploited for the world market and the production of export crops. It also hides that these women, most probably, will never be able to accumulate capital, unlike real entrepreneurs. Other beneficial effects expected from 'investing in women' are the following:

1 *To help poor women to get access to credit*: as success stories the Grameen Bank in Bangladesh and SEWA in India are mentioned. It is emphasized that these assetless women in Bangladesh – 250,000 have received bank loans – have shown a much better payback record than most credit programmes.

2 *To help poor women to get access to more and better education and training*, particularly with regard to income earning.

3 *To promote more effective and sustainable use of food, water and other natural resources*: the World Bank paper recognizes that women and not men in most underdeveloped countries are responsible for fuel, water, food, sanitation, etc. It repeats the well-known myth that due to this responsibility women are the ones to be blamed for environmental destruction, particularly their search for fuel wood. The big dams, timber companies who export exotic timber, the big national and transnational corporations are not mentioned among the destroyers of the environment. Women's survival struggles for the maintenance of their forest, water and soil resources against these corporate interests are not mentioned (Shiva 1988). The fact that they have to go ever further up in the hills to find fuel wood is attributed to their outmoded farming methods: 'women are also likely to lack access to improved environmentally sound farming methods. They often get stuck with outmoded technology that may be more conducive to misuse of land as population density rises' (Herz 1988: 3).

It seems the author(s) of this paper are deliberately twisting the facts, namely that the environmental destruction, as is well known, is due solely to 'improved farming methods', of which none is really ecologically sound so far, either in the North or in the South. On the other hand the 'outmoded technologies' of the women have never destroyed the environment provided their territory was not invaded and exploited by colonial interests. Before that, shifting cultivation has never destroyed the forests (Shiva 1987a). As a remedy for the environmental damages women are called upon to join the World Bank's Social Forestry Programme.

And it is again their responsibility for the family which makes them also the optimal partners for the World Bank's environmental strategy:

Because women must supply the family, they often have more incentive to make these programs work. Including women more effectively in such natural resouce management programs can contribute to solutions to some of the most pressing environmental threats, including the recent catastrophic flooding and soil erosion in South Asia and the widespread decline in forest cover.

(Herz 1988: 3)

This reminds me of the German *Trümmerfrauen* after the Second World War who had to clear up the ruins in the bombed cities to make Germany habitable again. Men make war against other peoples and nature and women have to clear up the mess afterwards. No mention in this passage that those corporate interests who have caused and are still causing the environmental catastrophies, should stop this war, because these are the same interests which the World Bank represents on a world scale (Shiva 1987a, 1988). It is much easier to blame the poor victims and their 'reckless breeding' for environmental destruction. This then is also the last and in my view main argument why the World Bank is interested in 'investing in women', namely:

4 *To slow down population growth*: this was already one of the two main objectives of the World Bank's policy for women in 1975: to increase women's productive labour and to decrease women's fertility. Poor women in underdeveloped societies are wanted as cheap producers, but not as reproducers of more of their kind and as consumers (Mies 1991).

To implement the anti-fertility part of this strategy a new programme was launched, the Safe Motherhood Initiative (SMI) which combines measures to reduce maternal mortality with birth control: 'President Conable announced that the Bank would double its population, health and nutrition lending over the next several years and give much more attention to safe motherhood dimension' (Herz 1988: 6).

If I try to compare this policy statement with earlier ones I cannot discover much that is new. It is rather more of the same with a more outspoken terminology, however. 'Investing in women' places development programmes for women more clearly into a capitalist market strategy than the discourse on 'integrating women into development'. It is, however, based on the same philosophy, which attributes poverty to the lack of money, of modern technology and education, and of capital growth. As the main cause for this lack of growth the 'population explosion' in the poor South is identified. It does not draw a lesson from the available evidence which shows that it was precisely this development, this integration of women into the market economy and into export production which has destroyed women's control over their independent subsistence base and eventually increased their poverty. It also does not take into account that this development, as Bina Agarwal and Farida Akhter point out, everywhere

119

means an increased coercive state intervention in women's lives and bodies, particularly through population control measures (Agarwal 1988; Akhter 1986).

What I have described before about the changing strategy of the World Bank with regard to women and development is not at all new. Already in 1980 Veronika Bennholdt-Thomsen analysed the World Bank's policy with regard to the poor in the underdeveloped world which was already in 1974 called 'investment in the poor' by World Bank experts. From 1973 onwards the president of the World Bank, McNamara, promoted the Small Farmers Development Programme, ostensibly meant to help the poorest in the Third World. In reality its aim was to use the poor peasants' assets and labour 'productively' and to give them access to small credits and above all: 'to draw farmers from subsistence to commercial agriculture' (World Bank 1975: 20, quoted in Bennholdt-Thomsen 1988: 58).

In the context of the UNCED, the role of poor women as breeders of too many people has been even more emphasized than before. As the World Bank cannot offer another development paradigm than an economy based on the capitalist principle of permanent growth it can only propose measures to the poor and indebted countries of the South, measures euphemistically called 'structural adjustment' which necessarily lead to more poverty, more misery, less health and educational services, particularly for poor women. Utsa Patnaik has given us a clear analysis of the consequences of this policy (Patnaik 1993). In spite of all rhetoric on women and development it has become clear by now that capitalism is not capable of solving the problems of women generally, particularly not of poor women in the poor South.

Given this situation, it is now time to ask whether we should continue to use such phrases as 'investing in women' and to adopt uncritically such a strategy as proposed by the World Bank. Would it not be better, as Claude Alvares suggests (Alvares 1988) to stop this development as soon as possible and allow poor people in general and poor women in particular to keep control over their material base of existence and to work for their own subsistence instead of for export and capital growth. The Chipko women have shown, as Vandana Shiva has reported, that they do not want this modernization, this industry, this development, this wage labour which they know will be possible only at the expense of their water, soil and forest resources which are the basis of their sustenance, life and culture. They know that the integration of their men and of their own resource base into the capitalist money economy, into development, will throw them into poverty and dependence. The women of Nahi Kala in the Doon Valley who fought for the closing of a chalk mine in their area put it thus, when asked what were the three most important things in life which they want to conserve:

Our freedom, forests and food ... With our own food production we are prosperous. We don't need jobs, either from businessmen or the government. We have our own livelihood. We even produce crops for sale, like rajma and ginger (1 quintal for Rs 1000 to Rs 1200). Two quintals of ginger can take care of all our needs.

(reported by Shiva 1987b)

I think it is important to reflect upon which of the two ways should be pursued: the one proposed by the World Bank and followed by a number of states and NGOs, namely 'investing in women' or the path proposed by the Doon Valley and Chipko women, namely to *strengthen women's control over their subsistence base* and their independence from the market economy, from external economies and external commercial interests, who treat women and the natural environment only as 'resources'. Such a goal is diametrically opposed to the way development and progress are defined by multinational corporate interests, the World Bank, most international organizations and many NGOs. This is, in Magda Renner's words: 'What is technically feasible and economically rewarding to the entrepreneurs today, is propagated as progress and development' (Renner, quoted in Shiva 1987a: 11).

REFERENCES

Agarwal, B. (ed.) (1988) *Structures of Patriarchy: State, Community and Household in Modernizing Asia*, New Dehli: Kali for Women.

Akhter, F. (1986) *Depopulating Bangladesh: A Brief History of the External Intervention into the Reproductive Behaviour of a Society*, Dhaka: UBINIG.

Alvares, C. (1988) 'Development as plunder', paper presented at the conference 'Die Subsistenzperspektive, ein Weg ins Freie', Bad Boll, Germany.

—— (1992) 'Science', in Sachs 1992.

Amin, S. (1974) *Accumulation on a World Scale. A Critique of the Theory of Underdevelopment*, New York: Monthly Review Press.

Bennholdt-Thomsen, V. (1988) 'Investment in the Poor: An Analysis of World Bank Policy', in Mies, Bennholdt-Thomsen and v. Werlhof 1988.

Boserup, E. (1970) *Women's Role in Economic Development*, New York: St Martin's Press.

Chee, H. L. (1988) *Babies to Order: Recent Population Policies in Malaysia and Singapore*, in Agarwal 1988.

Club of Rome (1991) *The First Global Revolution*, Hamburg: Spiegel Spezial No. 2.

Erler, B. (1985) *Tödliche Hilfe. Bericht von meiner letzten Dienstreise in Sachen Entwicklungshilfe*, Freiburg: Dreisam Verlag.

Esteva, G. (1992) 'Development', in Sachs 1992.

Frank, A. G. (1969) *Capitalism and Underdevelopment in Latin America*, New York: Monthly Review Press.

Fröbel, F., Heinrichs, O. and Kreye, J. (1980) *The New International Division of Labour*, Cambridge: Cambridge University Press.

Grossman, R. (1978/9) 'Women's place in the integrated circuit', *Pacific Research* 9 (5–6).

Herz, B. (1988) 'Briefing on women in development', paper presented at World Bank/IMF Annual Meetings, Berlin.

Lummis, D. C. (1992) 'Equality', in Sachs 1992.

Luxemburg, R. (1923) *Die Akkumulation des Kapitals*, Berlin: Vereinigung Internationaler Verlagsanstalten.

Mies, M. (1982) *The Lacemakers of Narsapur. Indian Housewives Produce for the World Market*, London: Zed Books.

—— (1991) *Patriarchy and Accumulation on a World Scale: Women in the International Division of Labour*, London: Zed Books.

—— (1992) 'Consumption patterns of the North – the cause of environmental destruction and poverty in the South', paper presented at 'Women and Children First', symposium on the impact of environmental degradation and poverty on women and children, UNCED, Geneva, 27–30 May 1991.

Mies, M., Bennholdt-Thomsen, V. and v. Werlhof, C. (1988) *Women, the Last Colony*, London: Zed Books.

Ng, C. and Mohamed, M. (1988) *Primary but Subordinated: Changing Class and Gender Relations in Rural Malaysia*, in Agarwal 1988.

Patnaik, U. (1993) 'The likely impact of economic liberalization and structural adjustment on the food security system in India', paper given at ILO Workshop on Employment, Equality and Impact of Economic Reform for Women, India, 27–9 January.

Rostow, W. W. (1960) *The Stages of Economic Growth: A Non-Communist Manifesto*, Cambridge: Cambridge University Press.

Sachs, W. (ed.) (1992) *The Development Dictionary: A Guide to Knowledge and Power*, London: Zed Books.

Sahlins, M. (1974) *Stone Age Economics*, London: Tavistock Publications.

Schrijvers, J. (1988) 'Blueprint for undernourishment: the Mahaveli River development scheme in Sri Lanka', in Agarwal 1988.

Shiva, V. (1987a) *Forestry Crisis and Forestry Myths: A Critical Review of Tropical Forests: A Call for Action*, Penang, Malaysia: World Rainforest Movement.

—— (1987b) 'Fight for survival. Interview with Chamun Devi and Itwari Devi', in *Illustrated Weekly of India*, 15 November.

—— (1988) *Staying Alive. Women Ecology and Survival in India*, New Dehli: Kali for Women.

Trainer, T.F. (1989) *Developed to Death. Rethinking Third World Development*, London: Green Print.

Verhelst, Thierry G. (1990) *No Life Without Roots: Culture and Development*, London: Zed Books.

v. Werlhof, C. (1988) 'The Proletarian is dead. Long live the Housewife!', in Mies, Bennholdt-Thomsen and v. Werlhof 1988.

Wallerstein, I. (1974) *The Modern World System: Capitalist Agriculture and the Origins of the European World Economy in the Sixteenth Century*, New York, San Francisco, London: Academic Press.

Waring, M. (1989) *If Women Counted: A New Feminist Economics*, London: Macmillan.

World Bank (1975) *Integrating Women into Development*, New York: World Bank.

World Commission On Environment And Development (Brundtland Commission) (1987) *Our Common Future*, Oxford, New York: Oxford University Press.

World Watch Institute (1992) *The State of the World 1992*, New Dehli: Horizon India Books.

7

DEVELOPMENT AND THE ENVIRONMENT

Managing the contradictions?

Michael Redclift

INTRODUCTION

From the perspective of the 1990s it seems extraordinary that the environment should have been so neglected by political economists. Who would have imagined, even five years ago, that a United Nations' conference on the *environment* would attempt to set the agenda for *development* into the next century? The United Nations Conference on Environment and Development (UNCED) meeting in Rio de Janeiro in 1992 illustrated more effectively than anything else, the enormous rift that has appeared between North and South. Not only is the *agenda* of the North different from that of the South, as I have argued elsewhere (Redclift 1992a, b) but the language, the discourse, is different. This chapter was conceived as a contribution to the new discourse on development and the environment which is being constructed in the developing world, in the wake of the 1992 Earth Summit. It consists of an exploration of the divergence between North and South in terms of the limited northern perspective represented by 'environmental managerialism'.

In the North the virtual collapse of radical, distributive politics has left a vacuum which will be difficult to fill. Some sociologists, such as Ulrich Beck (1987, 1992) have argued that this marks an important social transition, away from distributional politics and towards the 'risk society'. If we take a closer look at environmental concerns, and politics, in the South as well as the North, it becomes clear how partial and Eurocentric is this position. The failure to grasp the global nature of environmental issues lies at the heart of the problem for radical scholarship. To some extent this omission is being made good (McCormick 1989; King 1991; Durning 1992; Leyshon 1992). However, few writers have attempted to integrate the environment within a political economy framework (Vitale 1983; Smith 1984; Blaikie 1984; Galtung 1985; Blaikie and Brookfield 1987). It is interesting that the most effective assaults on neo-classical environmental economics have come

123

not from Marxists, but from institutionalists (Jacobs 1991), Green theorists (Ekins 1992; Ekins and Max-Neef 1992) and iconoclasts (Martinez-Alier 1987).

What Humphrey and Buttel (1982) described as 'their collective celebration of Western social institutions' has caused most sociologists to regard 'energy-intensive industrial development [as] the natural end point of a universal process of social evolution and modernisation'. If it *is* the end point, then, this paper argues, we are certainly witnessing a crisis, since the inability of international capitalism to regulate the world economy successfully has been eclipsed by its inability to regulate the environmental consequences of this 'development'. This paper addresses itself to the neglect of the environment in social science theory. As such it is partly the product of an increasingly challenging and provocative literature debate among those interested in 'development' (McNeely and Pitt 1984; Conway 1984; Goodland 1983; Blaikie 1984; Saint 1982; Norgaard 1984). Not for the first time theoretical discussion has failed to cross the North/South divide. Reassessments of theory and conceptual adequacy would benefit, in my judgement, from a more systematic attempt to relate environmental change in the North to structural development processes in the South and vice versa. This absence of an international and historical dimension is apparent wherever social scientists meet together to discuss environmental issues.

The objectives of this chapter are as follows:

1 to review existing perspectives on environmental change under capitalism;
2 to locate our conception of the 'environment' within a broader historical and comparative framework, one which distinguishes the historical role of the environment at different stages of capitalist development;
3 to identify common elements in a political economy of the environment in which changes in the natural environment are analytically related to 'superstructural' factors, such as ideology and policy, and at different levels of political complexity.

It will be apparent that I have set myself a daunting task. Furthermore it is one which grows in urgency, as what I term 'managerialist' solutions to environmental problems fail to address the causes of the problems.

THE ENVIRONMENT WITHOUT THE MARKET

Much of the environmental debate has been conducted with only fleeting references to the development of capitalism. Different theoretical currents can be distinguished.

One current of opinion has its root in Herbert Spencer and has sought to explain human behaviour as the 'internalization' of Nature. The premise is that a biological basis exists for social action and behaviour: biological determinism. This approach seeks to explain social institutions like property in terms of their biological 'roots' and nationalism in terms of territoriality. But the writing of Robert Adrey and Desmond Morris is illustrative of a broader and more academically respectable perspective: which includes ethology and, most recently, sociobiology. For sociologists whose training has taught them to distance themselves from the evolutionary perspectives derived from nineteenth-century natural science, such perspectives are irrelevant if not potentially dangerous (Buttel 1983).

Another approach, which has proved to be more insistent and more capable of generating widespread intellectual support during recent years can be described as 'neo-Malthusian'. In essence it rests on the Malthusian principle that population cannot exceed resources without famine or disease providing 'natural checks' on population growth. In the view of neo-Malthusians' recent successes in reducing mortality rates, especially dramatic in many Third World countries, have given added importance to the Malthusian edict. In the influential 'tragedy of the Commons' discussion Hardin (1968) argued that people are incapable of putting 'collective' interests before 'private' ones. Hence the resource base was constantly under threat from behaviour which, at a disaggregated level, was logical. In later writing Hardin and others have argued that pre-emptive, even coercive, action is needed to control population and conserve resources. As technological society progresses, the scarcity-induced control mechanisms which formed an important part of Malthus' argument, fail to work as expected. One dimension that has been explored by Commoner (1971), Ehrlich (1974) and Myers (1979) is the political impasse. Social and political institutions change too slowly, and are unable to accommodate the realities of new resource pressures.

There are a number of objections to the 'neo-Malthusian' position and its variants. Marx's original strictures about Malthus' writing are still one source of criticism. The neo-Malthusians do not address distributive issues with the urgency they require. Marx put it more bluntly, arguing that the Malthusians of his own time emphasized the 'limits of nature' for ideological reasons – it justified them in the view that nothing could be done about poverty.

Neo-Malthusians also meet objections from a geopolitical standpoint. From the perspective of a less developed country the emphasis on population and 'global' solutions looks suspiciously like an attempt to evade the issue of the role of international economy in structural underdevelopment. The developed countries have an interest, it is claimed, in drawing attention to resource scarcities, since they imperil *their* economic development. They have much less interest in a fundamental restructuring of the international economy, which might relieve many of the resource pressures experienced by societies in the South.

Another, equally forceful, approach corresponds with O'Riordan's (1981) 'ecocentric' category. Deriving advantage from the 'limits to growth' discussion of the 1970s (Meadows *et al.* 1972), it is argued that the problem is *not* the balance between population and resources but the *ends* to which resources are put in the pursuit of economic growth. In the process of 'development' we, in the industrialized countries, have lost our 'respect' for Nature, and with it our margin of freedom to proceed by trial and error (Dasmann 1975: 19). The ecocentric perspective takes issue with the objectives of development as well as the means. In this respect, at least, it represents a more radical break with orthodoxy than other ideological/paradigmatic positions.

One of the features of the last few years is the way in which the ecocentric approach has become much more concerned with structural factors in both developed and less developed countries (LDCs). Within a 'Green' perspective the implications of radical action must, ultimately, bear on 'us' as well as 'them'. International food policy and international trade increase the economic dependence of LDCs and reduce the sustainability of their environments. The question we need to pose is that raised almost ten years ago, in the British response to the World Conservation Strategy (WCS-UK 1983): what does sustainability imply for *our* development?

The ecocentric approach has assumed maturity, then, but in doing so has proved to be increasingly heterogeneous. In LDCs 'ecocentric' positions seek to rediscover what existed before the colonial embrace distorted their development process (Gonzalez 1979). It implies building 'bridges to the past'. In developed countries the emphasis is rather on what we usually term 'post-industrial' society, and what this implies for work, leisure and culture (Gorz 1980; Bahro 1982; Williams 1984).

Neither neo-Malthusianism nor the ecocentric perspective gives much emphasis to the way in which capitalist development *makes use* of the environment. The ecological crisis is depicted as larger than politics, larger even than capitalism – tempting some towards a position which Pepper (1984) sees as 'ecofascism'. Certainly both approaches disavow conflict in the Marxian sense, of a historical and necessary source of change and liberation. The appeal to balance, to good husbandry, to the defence of the species, appears to put Nature before people; but it does so in a way that reduces the role of human beings in their own development. There are objections to the market as a principle of economic organization, notably from the ecocentric perspective, but little interest in exploring how the market works, historically. The commitment to 'stable-state' resource allocation, and to a 'zero-growth' position, in which use values are substituted for exchange values, precedes any systematic attempt to establish how these new goals can be legitimized or brought nearer under capitalism. Sustainable development is the objective of many perspectives on the environment, but the role of the market in defining its various historical stages remains obscure.

THE PROBLEM-CENTRED SOLUTION:
ENVIRONMENTAL MANAGERIALISM

The strength of 'holistic' approaches to the environment is that they regard the interrelationship of environmental variables as of primary concern. They are explicitly anti-reductionist, and attribute many of the problems of environmental degradation to the paradigm within which environmental 'problems' are understood. Environmental Managerialism begins with the 'problems' and attempts to resolve them in a more *ad hoc*, piecemeal fashion. The paradigm is a positivist one, that assumes responsibility for resolving issues with whatever technical means are at our disposal. Thus the armoury of Environmental Managerialism consists of different methodological techniques, each of which enables the environment to be better 'managed'. This is the shallow end of the 'deep' ecological swimming pool (Sylvan 1985b: 12).

The first technique is that of land-use planning. Land-capability studies are undertaken so that certain economic activities can be confined to the most appropriate places. In the case of the 'biosphere reserves' that have been established throughout the globe by UNESCO's Man and the Biosphere Programme (MAB), 'zoning' activities correspond to the priority attached to conservation in different spatial settings. Some areas within 'biosphere reserves' and 'core areas'; others are 'buffer zones' or 'zones of influence' (Batisse 1985). The idea is that ecosystems can be protected and their value enhanced, through the example of good conservation as well as exclusion from market influences. Planning controls seek to protect an ecosystem, or a species/habitat, by removing land from cultivation or ensuring that it remains 'outside' the development process.

Knowing what needs to be conserved also requires careful attention to procedures for cataloguing and surveying protected environments: species lists, soil surveys, etc. The objective is to establish conservation priorities which can be given added authority by planning controls. Often this implies developing production technologies for agriculture which incorporate conservation goals, or reducing the harmful environmental effects of using existing technologies. The second process is much more common. Despite interesting attempts to develop agricultural technologies which are more sensitive to ecological (and social) factors, those judging performance in agricultural development seldom give as much weight to 'sustainability' and 'equity' considerations as they do to 'productivity' alone (Conway 1984).

Environmental management makes increasing use of techniques to evaluate the 'environmental' impact of development. The costing of environmental losses over an extended period enables calculations to be made about the weight to be attached to 'non-economic' factors, notably the maintenance of ecological diversity. Similarly, the social impact of

127

environmental change can be assessed, in the case, for example, of resettlement programmes. Legal regulations are another dimension of the socio-economic package which usually forms part of those large-scale development projects which are admitted to have substantial environmental impacts.[1] The emphasis throughout the project cycle is on measurability and quantification.

Environmental Managerialism rests on a set of assumptions, although these assumptions are rarely the subject of explicit discussion. The underlying belief is that there is an optimum balance of natural-resource uses, which can combine sustainability in agriculture and forestry. The object of policy is to determine where this optimum lies and to use the machinery of planning and political persuasion to help bring it about. Environmental conservation is not seen as a binding constraint on development, except in a few designated areas such as 'biosphere reserves'. Normally conservation objectives can be incorporated within the development policy package.

It is also an assumption of this approach that long-term interests in the environment are convergent, however much short-term interests might diverge. In the long term, securing environmental goals is the only guarantee of survival. In the short term the means of resolving short-term interests have to be negotiated. Environmental Managerialism is heavily prescriptive and unanalytical. When the objectives are 'agreed' and evaluation confined to the means at our disposal, there is not much room left for an analysis of conflicting outcomes or the interest of different groups in these outcomes.

THE ENVIRONMENT AND CAPITALIST DEVELOPMENT

This chapter has concentrated so far on the way that environmental issues are understood. In general little consideration is given to the impact of capitalist development on the environment in any of the perspectives discussed. The approach which probably can count upon most support – 'Environmental Managerialism' – is concerned with objectives that, until recently, appeared to lie outside the camp of market economics, such as conservation and physical planning.

Similarly no account is taken of the structural linkages which exist between economic development and the environment in the North and the South. Policies such as the disposal of food-grain surpluses from the North (US Public Law 480 in the past; EEC food 'mountains' in the present) radically affect the environment in the South. The penetration of the South by new agricultural production technologies, marketing and contract farming, have also served to shift agriculture in parts of Latin America and Africa away from traditional, environmentally sustainable, systems towards greater specialization and economic dependency. These problems are more acute when so many countries in both continents have enormous external debts, which they are urged to repay by more specialized exports of cash crops, forest products, etc. Changes in the environments of the South need to be understood, then, in terms of the international redivision of labour. These processes carry important implications, especially for 'transitional' environments, like those outlined below.

If we consider the historical role of the environment in capitalist development the relationship between the market and environmental management assumes much more importance. It is important to clarify this historical role in order to appreciate the part played by policy and planning responses such as those that figure within Environmental Managerialism, in long-term environmental change.

Three different situations can be discerned in which the environment plays a role in capitalist development today. This treatment of synchronic processes might also be extended back to the early development of capitalism, but that is a task which cannot be undertaken in this chapter. It needs to be emphasized that the three situations discussed below are *not* part of a linear progression or evolutionary framework. They each exist – and are linked – through the global development of contemporary western capitalism.

SMALL-SCALE SOCIETIES

It is not possible to talk of 'pre-capitalist' societies except in a historical sense. As Wolf (1982) demonstrates in *Europe and the People without History*, the emergence of European colonialism and, at a later stage, industrial capitalism served to obscure the history of cultures with which contact was made. Nevertheless 'capitalism did not always abrogate other modes of production, but it reached and transformed people's lives from a distance as often as it did so directly' (1982: 311). When the transformation took place at a distance, sustainable resource use was sometimes practised, despite the exigencies of the market. Sustainability of the environment in these societies is not divorced from traditional agricultural practice; it has no independent ontological status.

In these environments the effects of capital penetration are often very apparent, but they have still not been incorporated within the logic of the household production unit. As some wilderness resources are utilized by advanced capitalist economies, for their exotic species as well as their 'frontier' potential, the relations of production which maintain and 'conserve' the environment break down. But the process is not advanced. The integration of Nature and human society is most complete when it corresponds closely to 'natural economy'. Its gradual destruction raises issues for cultural identity that are *also* issues for environmental conservation: notably how indigenous people can secure their 'rights', and how we can learn from indigenous knowledge (McNeely and Pitt 1984; Parkin and Croll 1992).

129

MICHAEL REDCLIFT

POST-INDUSTRIAL ENVIRONMENTS

The historical moment to which we belong can be characterized as 'post-industrial'. The 'environment' (or 'countryside') which we know is a product of past capitalist development in our own societies. Despite this fact, there has been a tendency, until recently, to isolate 'environmental' change in 'post-industrial' societies from agricultural change in general. The environment is, in a manner of speaking, what remains when the production process in agriculture has been accounted for. Such environments have at least three characteristics.

First, post-industrial environments are ones in which food security has already been secured at the national level. This does not mean that self-sufficiency in agricultural commodities has been secured, especially at the farm level. What it does mean is that policies have been implemented which guarantee basic provisioning for the domestic market, and a role in the international division of labour which supports this agricultural specialization. Thus policies achieve food security around subsidized family production and preferential access to cheap inputs, many of them from LDCs.

Second, the class structure of agriculture in post-industrial environments is relatively 'formed' and surprisingly homogenous. Social conflicts exist, between farmers and farm workers, for example, but most conflict is institutionalized within organizations of farmers, or between the state bureaucracy and farmers' groups.

Third, the fundamental issue for such environments is what we might term *environmental* sustainability, rather than *agricultural* sustainability, which, as we have already seen, in many LDCs refers to whether agriculture can be sustained in the light of environmental degradation. The problem is how to sustain the environment in the face of agricultural production increases of an intensive kind. Ecological diversity in habitats and aesthetic considerations play a large part in determining environmental objectives. Issues of *agricultural sustainability* have also arisen, especially in those post-industrial environments (such as parts of the United States) where poor soil and water conservation actually threatens economic efficiency under the current model. Particularly where environmental amenity is geographically separated from agriculture, as it is in large parts of North America, and to a much more limited extent within capitalist agriculture in Western Europe, agricultural sustainability promises to be of increasing importance in the future.

Within post-industrial environments the conviction has grown that 'conservation' cannot be achieved simply by protecting the environment. Conservation also requires a brake on market forces. In the past the market enabled agriculture to grow, partly by removing environmental constraints on production. This was the impetus given agriculture by technical change.

Today the opposite process is observed. That is, agricultural *contraction* has to be 'managed' to maximize environmental gains and to meet budgetary constraints (in the West European case of the Common Agricultural Policy). This planned contraction also presents problems, although they are little understood. The focus tends to switch to individual farm-level decision-making, the research and policy agenda becomes more complex, and 'solutions' more situational, more uniquely defined (Potter 1985).

In developed countries, then, the changes within agriculture have served to transform the environment, and the separation between Nature and society is most complete. The environment frequently appears more important than food production itself, but is no less socially constructed. Environmental consciousness is not a necessary ingredient of successful agriculture, as in many small-scale societies, but is capable of assuming independent significance in rural planning. The 'environment' has become increasingly detached from the agricultural production process, spatially and conceptually. Policy responses underline this separation.

STRUCTURALLY TRANSFORMED ENVIRONMENTS

Most less developed country environments and some developed country environments differ from both kinds of environmental situation discussed above, in the sense that although they have been transformed by contact with the developed industrialized countries, capitalist production relations have not been universally established. There is no reason to believe that such environments will evolve as 'post-industrial' environments have done. Structurally transformed environments are ones in which the primary emphasis in development is the achievement of agricultural growth through the operation of market forces, often supported by state intervention. In some areas stimulus is provided by rapid urban growth, in others by technological breakthroughs of the 'Green Revolution' type. The development of food production is increasingly linked to transnational corporation and the agribusiness complex based in the developed countries. In many areas the environment is only beginning to be affected by these linkages. Some areas have seen the market recede, leaving a 'vacuum' which either contributes to accelerated migration (northeast Brazil) or which the state attempts to fill for political and other reasons (Yucatan Mexico).

The class structure of structurally transformed environments is formative and social conflicts are often not institutionalized. The divisions that occur within rural areas, and between the rural poor, reflect sectoral considerations ('urban bias') as well as commodity-producing interests. Class interests are frequently mediated through nationalist, tribal or other ethnic identities.

The main feature of change in structurally transformed environments is whether agriculture is developed according to a 'market logic' determined outside the region, or according to some other 'logic' with a basis in the pre-colonial history of the area. It is much more difficult than in 'post-industrial environments' to define the parameters of environmental activity. Rather like women's labour (with which it is closely linked), the 'environment' involves different 'spheres' of activity, some within the household and some outside. The environment includes the production of commodities for exchange and for use. Not all exchanges are market exchanges and not all domestic production affecting the environment (food, clothing, shelter, energy) is for the personal consumption of the family. Like women's labour the environment is both valorized and non-valorized in different structural contexts (Redclift 1985). The impact of the market in one sphere of environmental activity where exchange values prevail (e.g. cash cropping or forestry) has important implications for other spheres where use values predominate (food staples or firewood collection). In this case structurally transformed environments represent the meeting point of two 'spheres': one of which produces commodities from the application of labour to natural resources, while the other (simple reproduction) is concerned with the material and social reproduction of the household unit.

The implications of sustainable development for structurally transformed environments will vary considerably. In largely undeveloped areas, even those with fragile ecosystems like the tropical forests, sustainable development implies long-term resource efficiency for a large number of people. Most actual development in such areas involves short-term efficiency for a small number of people (Norgaard 1984). Powerful commercial interests are in a position to exploit the openness of the environment to market pressures. The relatively easy access to new land, which the 'frontier' represents, together with the social fluidity of frontier societies, means that the effort to develop sustainable agriculture is rarely worthwhile. In extreme cases the environment is 'mined' to produce the required resources: timber, minerals or exotic natural species. In general the ethic of private property and the ownership of land come to assume more importance in the process of accumulation.[2] In general, too, the interests in unsustainable production far outweigh those in conservation. This state of affairs is not a historical accident, but the result of powerful social classes acquiring ideological legitimacy from new forms of agricultural production, rather than from environmental sustainability. What we term 'the environment' is transformed in the development process from a situation in which use values predominate, through one in which exchange values assume increasing importance (structurally transformed environments) to a situation where the environment is often an area of 'collective consumption', in the public rather than the private domain (post-industrial). Of course, in most societies this process is not completed in a linear way: few 'small-scale' societies will become 'post-industrial' ones.

Nevertheless, as will be argued in the next section, the way we conceive of the environment in one setting is critical for our understanding of others.

OBJECTIONS TO ENVIRONMENTAL MANAGERIALISM

Environmental Managerialism consists of a set of responses to specific circumstances. It is the task of social science to understand how these responses arose, and to ask whether they are appropriate to very different circumstances, of time and place. Some of the perspectives on the environment discussed at the beginning of this chapter make explicit claim to be generalizable, in the current global context, as well as historically. The set of measures and techniques which are referred to as 'Environmental Managerialism' frequently make such claims. Some of the positions outlined at the beginning have paid explicit attention to the historical dimension of environmental change and, in the structuralist 'Green' position at least, to the interrelationship between development and the environment. Environmental Managerialism pays attention to neither the conceptual framework within which we understand 'environmental problems' nor the international economic framework in which these problems are manifested. Of the perspectives reviewed above Environmental Managerialism has both the greatest currency today and the narrowest historical and geographical base.

The first objection to Environmental Managerialism is that it considers the environment *after* the 'development' objectives have been set. At best it requires a modification of these objectives to take account of ecological factors. It does not propose an alternative development in which ecological factors – together with social ones – are given initial weight (Glaeser 1979; Galtung 1985; Riddell 1981). Environmental Managerialism is characterized by what Holling (1978) has called the 'protective and reactive' response.

The second objection is to the way that the environmental consequences of development are separated from the social and economic ones within the Managerialist approach. Extending protection to geographical areas on ecological grounds (meeting the first and second objectives of the World Conservation Strategy 1980) is perfectly valid. Nevertheless, ecological objectives usually imply social ones. In developed countries we are accustomed to regard access to the environment as a means of escaping social control. Indeed, this is part of the environment's ideological legitimacy in post-industrial societies. In most LDCs the people most affected by environment interventions frequently have their access to the environment reduced, through resettlement programmes, for example. Environmental management is an important means of social control available to governments and international agencies, and should be recognized as such. Once this fact is recognized the important issue is raised of who is to 'manage' the environment.

The third main objection to Environmental Managerialism is that it takes as a 'given' the distributive consequences which the market produces in the course of development. Development aid offered on a bilateral basis tends often to accelerate environmental degradation in the immediate vicinity of the urban and rural poor.[3] If environmental factors are to be given real weight in the development process then the distributive effects of development policy need to be recognized, and environmental management needs to assume redistributive functions. The emphasis needs to lie not with 'compensation' for environmental damage, as it does at present, but with establishing environmental objectives that reduce the poverty and vulnerability of the poor: whether to so-called 'natural disasters', fluctuations in market prices for their commodities, or health hazards.

Finally, the techniques which form part of the Environmental Managerialist package deflect attention away from the context of environmental degradation. As Blaikie (1984) argues 'the problems start with the context, not with the poor'. It is essential, therefore, that an alternative is posed to the reductionism of most conservation techniques applied in LDCs. Environmental Managerialism locates structural, usually international, problems in geographical space. They become synonymous with the areas where they occur. Thus, for example, four 'biosphere reserves' have been established in Mexico in fulfilment of international conservation goals. They are in remote and underpopulated areas. In areas where the environmental consequences of rapid economic growth are extremely prejudicial to the poor, such as the oil 'boom' region around Villahermosa, nothing has been done to protect the poor or their environment from contamination (Toledo 1984).

The point is that if conservation goals are pursued in protected areas it enables governments to argue, as the Mexican government has done, that they are complying with global directives, whatever the consequences of ignoring environmental factors in areas which are more important to national development policy. Environmental Managerialism does not address the gap between global conservation goals and national development policy. As the UK response to the World Conservation Strategy put it: 'any useful analysis of the reasons for natural resource-destruction would have to include questions of wealth distribution within and between nations' (WCS-UK 1983: 324).

ELEMENTS IN AN ALTERNATIVE THEORETICAL PROJECT

At this point it is necessary to return to the second and third objectives set out at the beginning of this chapter:

- to locate our conception of the 'environment' within a broader historical

and comparative framework, one which distinguishes the historical role of the environment at different stages of capitalist development;
• to identify common elements in a political economy of the environment in which changes in the natural environment are analytically related to 'superstructural' factors, such as ideology and policy, and at different levels of political complexity.

We are now in a position to relate the theoretical concern with the environment to the historical/comparative framework of capitalist development. First, it is clear that the transformation of the environment under capitalism – the 'production of Nature' (Smith 1984) – has contradictory effects. On the one hand it allows people to regulate the production of use values to meet human needs. With the development of the market, exchange values assume more importance, and benefits can be derived from the specialized production of commodities.

At the same time as societies become freer from the constraints of Nature, social control assumes more importance. Ultimately class society is created out of the differentiation of the productive process and the accompanying social differentiation. Production under capitalism produces a liberation from Nature and a transformation of the environment. Nevertheless, as labour is employed in the transformation of the environment the problem is presented of how to *sustain* development. That is, how to provide commodity production for the market and a renewal of the natural-resource base. In this case the difficulty in achieving 'sustainability' presents itself as one of the contradictions of capitalist development.

Most analysis of the development of capitalism in the productive sphere has concentrated on the use that is made of Nature. Development theory, beginning with Rosa Luxemburg (1951), has usually considered the breakdown of 'natural economy' as linked to the production of exchange values, for distant markets. Subsequently we have learnt that primitive accumulation did not disappear from underdeveloped countries, indeed it has continued to be important as a means of guaranteeing the existence of non-capitalist production within social formations dominated by capitalism.

It is increasingly clear that we need to push our analysis beyond the sphere of production alone. In considering the environment within a historical dimension we also need to consider the way that nature is transformed. This is particularly true in what I have termed structurally transformed environments. Here we can distinguish between sustainable development and the progressive depletion of resources, as reflected in the loss of soil fertility to which Marx referred in the celebrated paragraph from *Capital* (Marx 1867: 505–7). These processes, moreover, take place in a social and historical context which provides them with meaning. Hence the 'consciousness' of the environment under conditions of resource degradation is different from situations where sustainable options exist and are practised.

We can ask several questions of this process: what kinds of 'consciousness' accompany changes in the relationship between people and Nature, not simply over time (Pepper 1984: 163) but also within a spatial dimension? Are they determined largely by *the use* to which Nature is put or *the way* that Nature is transformed? The answers to these questions are important precisely because they will help us to understand the political conditions governing environmental interventions. The perceptions that are held of the environment by different classes and interests and the channels that exist for articulating these interests, are a necessary part of any alternative to Environmental Managerialism, as Blaikie (1984: 91) demonstrates.

CONCLUSION

I began by arguing that social scientists have not addressed theoretical aspects of environment change with the urgency they deserve. When market relations entered the analysis at all it was usually at an aggregated level, suggesting that 'the market' was an obstacle to the achievement of environmental solutions. In some cases (neo-Malthusianism) demographic and technical change, rather than the market, imperilled viable, resource-sustainable policies. At the same time the development of capitalism, a process which has attracted enormous theoretical interest during the last two decades, has rarely considered environmental change in a systematic, theoretical way (Redclift 1984, 1987; Smith 1984).

Most discussion of the 'environment' has more limited objectives. It concerns the ways and means by which conservation objectives can be advanced, and account taken of non-market 'externalities'. Environmental Managerialism is the term I used to describe the various techniques employed to reduce the damage to the environment of unchecked economic growth. These techniques provide more than a framework for policy interventions: they have also acquired ideological legitimacy. Environmental factors have become incorporated in the discussion of development policy, in a way which echoes the experience in developed countries. Environmental management has been advocated as a way of reaching beyond market-induced agricultural changes.

The argument of this chapter is that such an approach needs to be recognized as partial and conjunctural. Environmental change can only be separated from the development process by ignoring the historical development of capitalism, by confining to 'the market' aspects of the transformation of Nature which have much wider implications. Activities that occur within the household are often 'invisible' to environmental managers. In developing countries such activities are often critical in determining responses to 'the market' (Evans 1984). Unless we conceptualize 'the environment' in a less reductionist way, to take account of both

136

processes of production *and* reproduction our analysis will remain unsatisfactory.

Second, not only is 'the environment' a category which requires greater analytical rigour, but it is also historically constructed. In seeking to develop a political economy of the environment, we need to give more attention to the links between sustainability and the development of capitalism. Within a comparative framework 'sustainability' assumes different importance in small-scale, transitional and post-industrial environments. Policies to effect 'conservation' goals carry different implications for each context. Social and political struggles need to be understood in relation to the broader parameters of development and environmental change, not merely as ingredients in successful 'planning'. Environmental consciousness is not confined to post-industrial environments, although our awareness of it may be.

Four hundred and seventy years ago a rag bag army of *conquistadores* discovered the garden city of Tenochtitlan/Tlatelolco, a quarter of a million people whose livelihoods depended on 'raised-bed' cultivation, in what we know today as the valley of Mexico (Diaz 1963). In the half a millennium, which followed this discovery the Valley has very nearly been reduced to what one report calls a 'concrete plank' (Sanchez de Carmona 1984). If we forget that the environment is part of history, and part of the development process, we not only abdicate responsibility as social scientists, we also abdicate responsibility towards future generations . . . on *both* sides of the North/South divide.[4]

NOTES

1 Only a minority of projects in developing countries for which outside funding is obtained, are defined as *mainly* concerned with the environment. Most, of course, have environmental aspects.

2 As Robert Goodland has put it: 'The ethic of private property became enshrined in common law when the carrying capacity of the environment greatly exceeded the population and its use of resources' (1983: 30). People's use or abuse of land had little or no effect on the neighbours or their society, let alone the world in general. Although that time has ended for much of the world, the ethic of ownership of natural resources, and land in particular, has yet to be modified to stewardship (1983: 30).

3 The UK Response to the World Conservation Strategy expresses this clearly: 'The more aid flows towards those sectors favoured by political, industrial and commercial criteria the less likely they are to arrest such environmental damage as is occurring. This is because the greatest environmental damage, and needs, tend to occur in the rural areas and amongst the urban poor of the LDCs' (WCS-UK 1983: 328).

4 I would like to thank Chuck Geisler, John Soussan, Clive Potter, David Goodman and Nanneke Redclift for their comments on earlier drafts of this paper.

REFERENCES

Bahro, R. (1982) *Socialism and Survival*, London: Heretic Books.

Batisse, M. (1985) 'Action plan for biosphere reserves', *Environmental Conservation* 12(1): 17–27.

Beck, U. (1987) 'The anthropological shock: Chernobyl and the contours of the risk society', *Berkeley Journal of Sociology* 32: 463–92.

—— (1992) 'How modern is modern society?', *Theory, Culture and Society* 9: 163–9.

Blaikie, P. (1984) *The Political Economy of Soil Erosion in Developing Countries*, London: Longman.

Blaikie, P. and Brookfield, H. (1987) *Land Degradation and Society*, London: Routledge.

Booth, D. (1985) 'Marxism and development sociology: interpreting the impasse'. *World Development* 13(7): 761–87.

Buttel, F. (1983) 'Sociology and the environment: the winding road toward human ecology'. Cornell University MS.

Commoner, B. (1971) *The Closing Circle*, New York: Knopf.

Conway, G. (1984) *Rural Resource Conflicts in the UK and Third World: Issues for Research Policy*, Papers in Science, Technology and Public Policy No. 6, London: Imperial College.

Dasmann, R. F. (1975) *The Conservation Alternative*, Chichester: John Wiley.

Diaz, Bernal (1963) *The Conquest of New Spain*, trans. J. M. Cohen, Harmondsworth: Penguin.

Durning, A. T. (1992) *How Much is Enough: The Consumer Society and the Future of the Earth*, London: Earthscan.

Ehrlich, P. (1974) *The End of Affluence*, New York: Ballantine Books.

Ekins, P. (1992) *Wealth Beyond Measure: An Atlas of the New Economics*, London: Gaia Books.

Ekins, P. and Max-Neef, M. (eds) (1992) *Real-life Economics*, London: Routledge.

Evans, M. I. (1984) 'Firewood versus alternatives: domestic fuel in Mexico', Commonwealth Forestry Institute, Occasional Paper No. 23, Oxford.

Galtung, J. (1985) 'Development theory: notes for an alternative approach', Wissenschaftszentrum, Berlin IIUG Reprints Series.

Glaeser, B. (1979) 'Labour and leisure in conflict? Needs in developing and industrial societies', IIUG preprints, Wissenschaftszentrum, Berlin.

Gonzalez, Pedredro E. (1979) *La Riqueza de la Pobreza*, Mexico City: Editorial, Joaquin Mortiz.

Goodland, R. (1983) 'Brazil's environmental progress in Amazonian development', in J. Hemming (ed.) *Change in the Amazon Basin*, Manchester: Manchester University Press.

Gorz, A. (1980) *Ecology as Politics*, London: Pluto Press.

Hardin, G. (1968) 'The tragedy of the commons', *Science* 162: 1243–8.

Holling, C. S. (ed.) (1978) *Adaptive Environmental Assessment and Management*, Chichester: John Wiley.

Humphrey, C. R. and Buttel, F. (1982) *Environment, Energy and Society*, Belmont, California: Wadsworth.

Jacobs, M. (1991) *The Green Economy*, London: Pluto Press.

King, A. D. (ed.) (1991) *Culture, Globalisation and the World System*, Basingstoke: Macmillan.

Leyshon, A. (1992) 'Regulating the global economy and environment', *Geoforum* (special issue), 23(3): 249–68.

Luxemburg, R. (1951) *The Accumulation of Capital*, London: RKP.

Martinez-Alier, J. (1987) *Ecological Economics*, Oxford: Basil Blackwell.

Marx, K. (1867) *Capital*, vol. 1. Moscow: Foreign Languages Publishing House, 1959.

McCormick, J. (1989) *The Global Environmental Movement*, London: Belhaven.

McNeely, J. and Pitt, D. (eds) (1984) *Culture and Conservation: The Human Dimension in Environmental Planning*, London: Croom Helm.

Meadows, D. C., Meadows, D. L., Randers, J. and Behrens III, W. W. (1972) *The Limits to Growth*, London: Pan Books.

Myers, N. (1979) *The Sinking Ark*, Oxford: Pergamon.

Norgaard, R. (1984) 'Coevolutionary agricultural development', *Economic Development and Cultural Change* 32(3): 382–94.

O'Riordan, T. (1981) *Environmentalism*, London: Pion.

Parkin, D. and Croll, E. (1992) *Bush Baby. Forest Farm*, London: Routledge.

Pepper, D. (1984) *The Roots of Modern Environmentalism*, London: Croom Helm.

Potter, C. (1985) 'Agricultural decision-making: the farmer as an enabled and constrained subject', paper delivered to RESG Study Group Conference, Oxford, 23–5 January 1985.

Redclift, M. R. (1984) *Development and the Environmental Crisis: Red or Green Alternatives*, London: Methuen.

—— (1986) 'Mexico's Green Movement', *The Ecologist* 19(5): 177–83.

—— (1987) *Substainable Development: Exporing the Contradictions*, London: Methuen.

—— (1992a) 'Sustainable development and global environmental change: implications of a changing agenda', *Global Environmental Change* 2(1): 32–42.

—— (1992b) 'Throwing stones in the greenhouse', *Global Environmental Change* 2(2): 90–2.

Redclift, N. (1985) 'Bringing it all back home: women and development', paper to Development Studies Association/ESRC Meeting, London.

Riddell, R. (1981) *Ecodevelopment*, London: Gower.

Saint, W. (1982) 'Farming for energy: social options under Brazil's National Alcohol Programme', *World Development* 10(3): 632–51.

Sanchez de Carmona, J. (1984) 'Ecological studies for regional planning in the Valley of Mexico', in F. di Castri, F. Baker and M. Hadley (eds) *Ecology in Practice*, Paris: UNESCO.

Smith, N. (1984) *Uneven Development: Nature, Capital and the Production of Space*, Oxford: Blackwell.

Sylvan, R. (1985a) 'A critique of deep ecology', *Radical Philosophy* 40: 2–12.

—— (1985b) 'A critique of deep ecology', *Radical Philosophy* 41: 10–22.

Toledo, A. (1984) *Como Destruir el Paraiso*, Mexico City: Centro de Ecodesarrollo.

Vitale, L. (1983) *Hacia una historia del ambiente en America Latina*, Mexico: Nueva Imagen.

WCS-UK (1983) *The Conservation and Development Programme for the United Kingdom*, London: Kogan Page.

Williams, R. (1984) *Towards 2000*, Harmondsworth: Penguin.

Wolf, E. (1982) *Europe and the People without History*, Berkeley, California: University of California Press.

8

CAPITALISM, GLOBAL HUMANE DEVELOPMENT AND THE OTHER UNDERDEVELOPMENT

Mahmoud Dhaouadi

DEVELOPMENT STATE IN THE THIRD WORLD

The development experiences of most Third World countries in the last three decades or so have been unimpressive if not disastrous and tragic at times. The burden of underdevelopment, in Ali Mazrui's terms, is probably *most* felt and experienced in today's Black Africa (Mazrui 1992). The human *misery* of some of this continent's countries like Somalia, Ethiopia and Sudan has become very familiar, especially through television news reports, to the citizens of the whole world. Drought, internal conflicts and the AIDS epidemic have certainly contributed to the deteriorated state of other African countries. But those factors are hardly adequate to account for that ugly state of affairs that has prevailed in several African countries in the last few years. Their grim situation could have surely been otherwise, in spite of the odds of internal conflicts, AIDS and droughts, had they scored average or better on the development achievement scale. In other words, those natural, political and health negative forces have come *to unveil* that development and nation-building have been far from being a success story in those societies. None the less, the pessimist image of development in Somalia, Ethiopia and Sudan constitutes obviously the extreme negative case of failure in development projects in today's Third World.

At the other extreme, there are a few developing countries which have a brighter profile on development performance. They are geographically situated in Southeast Asia. These are South Korea, Taiwan, Hong Kong, Indonesia and Thailand. They have embarked on serious economic and industrial growth. As such, they are expected in the near future to become real rivals for Japan in the Pacific.

When a general assessment of the state of development is made of today's Third World, the picture is far from being impressive. Those who have academically studied development in developing countries are of the

140

opinion that development experiences in those societies have been largely *less than a success.*

In the early 1990s, the community of scholars devoted to the study of Third World development resembles in many respects its 1960s counterpart. The decade of the sixties began thirty years ago with a pervasive sense of optimism that in the new and modernizing nations of Asia, Africa and Latin America, the processes of enlightenment and democratization will have their inevitable way . . . but it gave way increasingly to disillusionment and *loss of theoretical direction* [my emphasis]. Coups d'état, once thought of as Latin American phenomenon, become regular occurrences in other parts of the world, particularly Africa and the Middle-East. Rates of economic growth in many countries were unimpressive despite foreign aid, and even in rapidly industrializing states such as Brazil, South Africa and Iran, long-term prospects for social equality and political democracy appeared poor.

(Mano 1991: 3–4)

With the situation of Third World development achievement on the ground as briefly described has surfaced the intellectual crisis of development theorists of different social science orientations and schools. Modernization and dependency theorists have been in particular, undergoing a fundamental re-evaluation of their paradigms whose credibility face great challenge and they consequently, feel the discomforting tension created by their actual theoretical disarray (Mano 1991: 4).

CAPITALISM'S CANDIDATURE FOR GLOBAL DEVELOPMENT

The collapse of socialism as an ideology and as an economico-sociopolitical system in its place of birth (the former Soviet Union and the socialist bloc of Eastern Europe) has opened the way to western capitalist domination, throughout many societies of today's world, both as a superstructure as well as an infrastructure. The apparent immediate victory of capitalism as a liberal-socioeconomic and democratic political system has made Francis Fukuyama (1990) describe this critical historical *system shift* as the *End of History.* According to this North American author, modern western industrial capitalist liberal and democratic societies have proven now beyond any doubt, that their economico-sociopolitical system is much superior, on the global development achievement scale, than the socialist system, in Eastern Europe and the former Soviet Union. History has ended in the sense that there is no more room for large ideological battles. Liberal democracy is not merely triumphant, it is simply what there is, and all there can be: there is literally no more room for debate over fundamentals. The crystallization of the so-called New World Order has put an end to the Cold

War between the two major superpowers: the United States and the former Soviet Union. These historical worldwide transformations have favoured capitalism as an economico-sociopolitical system to become a model to be imitated and adopted not only in the former socialist Eastern European bloc but in many other of today's developing societies. In the last few years, democracy has been gaining ground in many countries of the Third World. This does not mean, however, that the democratization process has been entirely smooth in those societies. Democracy has known many setbacks here and there in the developing nations. Because of the fear of the FIS (*Le Front Islamique de Salut*) victory, the Algerian authorities cancelled (in January 1992) the second voting phase of the legislative election. This notoriously undemocratic political practice in Algeria is just one among many in the new independent nations experimenting with democracy.

On the economic front, Third World countries with socialist-oriented or state-run economies have increasingly given way to the practices of the market economy. This enhanced position that capitalism has held since the collapse of socialism requires a reassessment of the relationship between capitalism and development. This relationship could be examined in two ways: how good is capitalism as an economico-sociopolitical system for the general development of human societies? Is capitalism the ideal model that could best promote the development projects that humans and their societies really need? Could capitalism in modern western advanced societies *help* the cause of development in less developed countries? These questions add up to this question: how promising, credible and safe is capitalism as a promoter of development on a more or less worldwide scale?

CAPITALISM AND DEVELOPMENT FROM WITHIN

The term 'capitalism' refers to the economic system that has been dominant in the western world since the sixteenth century following the break-up of feudalism in Europe (Dillard 1979: 69). With the numerous sociopolitical transformations that the West had known as a result of the French and the American as well as of the industrial and scientific revolutions, capitalism has become strongly associated with *democracy* and social liberal policies. Thus, we use here the term 'capitalism' to refer specifically to the western liberal socioeconomic and democratic political system that has been in place in contemporary western advanced societies.

The more than four centuries experience with capitalism as the dominant development model in the West constitutes an adequate period of time for the evaluation of the capitalist system on the development achievement scale. As any social system, capitalism is bound to have its positive and negative accomplishments. What matters, therefore, in this assessment is how the pluses and the minuses will at the end balance out. Because of space limitation, we intend to offer only a brief portrait of these two sides of capitalist development achievement within western capitalist societies' frontiers. On the brighter side, capitalism has a great record of development achievements in the West. On the economic development front, the West has been seriously challenged only lately by Japan's growing economic muscle. An argument could be made here that Japan's great economic development was historically *more self-made* than its western capitalist economic development counterpart. The latter has often been accused since its birth of its *exploitative nature* with respect to other nations around the world (Magdoff 1978).

In the domain of industrial and technological achievements the capitalist West has indeed accomplished much. Never before were humans able to manipulate, control and transform their world as they have become able to do with the western self-made industrial and technological products. In this area, the Japanese are presently either catching up or even surpassing their western capitalist counterparts particularly in electronics and information technology like computers and robots. It remains true, however, that the capitalist West is uncontestedly the pioneer in the development of modern technology in the broader sense of the term.

In the development of the scope of knowledge and science, there is no doubt that the capitalist West stands alone in its unique role in the ignition of the scientific revolution and the formidable explosion of knowledge in modern times (Boorstin 1983). These events have brought about a radical revolution in *humans' cognition* of themselves and the world around them. With the new knowledge and science they have considerably strengthened their imposing mastership both here on earth and in space. The entire planet could not have become, in McLuhan's term, a global village, without the development of highly sophisticated information science and technology (McLuhan and Fiore 1967). Parallel to those remarkable accomplishments, western capitalism has institutionalized the practice of political democracy and guaranteed the free expression of ideas and thought. In our view, this politico-cultural development ought to be considered the *greatest* of all developments that have been associated with the rise of western capitalism. On this level, the western capitalist system is humanly far *superior* to any fading away or still existing socialist/communist system. What are scientific/technological achievements good for, if the system that has developed them is obstinate in its conviction of the need to suppress what distinguishes *most* the human species from other species? Regardless of their scientific and technological importance, the development projects of totalitarian and tyranical political regimes will always remain unimpressive, non-appealing and ultimately dehumanizing for the average human being.

As pointed out earlier, the capitalist system has its own dark points or its own contradictions as well (Bell 1976). Over four centuries of accelerating pace of capitalist development have done enough harm in the ecological system of western advanced societies and in the world at large. The pollution of the air and the environment are major concerns today in many western and non-western cities of the world. In most industrially and technologically advanced western societies, the waters of so many rivers, lakes, seas and oceans have been polluted beyond repair. Health risks from toxic chemicals are hotly debated in those societies. Deforestation, the fear of diminishing diversity of life and global warming constitute a great threat to the viability of the earth as a capable sustainer of the diversity of all forms of life on it. The Earth Summit in Rio in June 1992 bluntly warned of the pending danger. The watchword in Rio was *sustainable development.*

There are limits to the earth's resources and its capacity to absorb the waste products of industry; this must be taken into account in the process of economic development so that the legacy we leave our children is not a planet in a worse state of health than we inherited.

(*The World & I* 1992: 20)

Plainly put, the planet earth is increasingly becoming *uninhabitable.* The major role of western capitalism in the damage caused to earth's natural resources and ecology is more than obvious. The picture of our present and future planet becomes much grimmer and more desperate when we consider the ever increasing massive piles of destructive armaments of all kinds (nuclear, biochemical, etc.) that the capitalist West still *leads* in its production as well as possession. With that, the complete destruction of our planet and the entire annihilation of all living species has become indeed within easy reach. The modern capitalist West's use of its *developed* military might constitutes impending threats to the very survival of humankind. Two world wars had been already fought in this century in which capitalist-developed superpowers had played a central role. Japan had been defeated by the monopolistic development and use of nuclear weapons against it by a capitalist superpower. The building of the capitalist nuclear arsenal did not stop with the bombardment of Hiroshima or Nagasaki, rather it has continued unabated. It has become the development model to be imitated since the Second World War by big and smaller nations. It is certainly the most *terrifying* development model the capitalist West has set for itself and for others to imitate in modern times.

On the social scene capitalist societies have their adequate share of social problems. The rates of crime, divorce, suicide, alcoholic and drug addiction, AIDS victims, pre-marital pregnancy etc. . . . are considerably high by world standards. Within the fold of capitalism, individualism has run wild. De Tocqueville had already expressed his worries about young America where he observed the beginning of the weakening of collective social ties in favour of the individual's growing assertive freedom and independence. A more recent sociological study, *Habits of the Heart* (Bellah *et al.* 1985) on post-modern American society depicts a frightening portrait of its *decaying 'social ecology'.* The authors of the study argue that the harm done to Nature's ecological system under rampant expanding and exploit-ative capitalism finds its equivalent in the damage inflicted on the web of social solidarity among Americans. It is as urgent and important to save and repair 'social ecology' as it is for the environmental ecology.

This worrying pattern of capitalist development ought to call for serious reflections concerning the principal forces that stand behind today's en-dangered state, whose obvious threats are beginning to be felt by capitalist societies and the world at large. *Three* factors appear to be at work here. They are: (a) capitalism's obsession with economic/materialistic growth; (b) the capitalist person's passion for and fascination by the Conquest of Nature; and (c) the capitalist's lack of cosmic and religious frames of reference. This appears to be the result of the expanding power of the ethics of contemporary materialistic science and knowledge hostile to the Church and the religious/spiritual conceptions/ideas it stood for.

With these three forces orienting the behaviour of the contemporary capitalist western individual, it is hardly difficult to understand the state of development the West and the world at large have come to experience. Economic/materialist growth has become an end in itself for the capitalist person, even if this requires the *twisting* or the adaptation of religious sacred beliefs to fulfil that end. Weber's Protestant ethic is a good illustra-tion to this in the Rise of Captalism (Weber 1950). When economic/quantitative development becomes the target end, then all efforts and all strategies have to be used to get it. That is, *the ends justify the means.* For capitalist individuals, exploitative worldwide colonization is not something to be ashamed of. Nor is it a slander to *overuse*, exploit and pollute one's own environment and its natural resources as long as this action is done for the sake of achieving more economic/materialistic growth for societies.

This unprecedented massive collective human action in the manipu-lation and exploitation of the planet earth's resources is sanctioned by the capitalists' relation with nature. They have been known for strong passions and desire to subdue nature. This is in line with the new image the capitalist western individuals of the Enlightenment have had of themselves. They are the only masters here on earth. Everything has to submit to their will, by force if necessary. Nature's Conquest is but the fulfilment of that new perception capitalists have of themselves and the world around. Tension, hostility and conflicts are expected to prevail in relation with Mother Nature. The horrible consequences of the capitalist's interaction with Nature on planet earth's well-being are just beginning to be *graphically* and *statistically* told.

Western Renaissance, Enlightenment and Scientific Revolution have shattered the capitalist individual's cosmic vision of things. The confront-ation between the Church, on the one hand, and the men of the new science and knowledge, on the other, has *ruptured* beyond easy repair the relationship between science/knowledge and the spiritual dimension of human existence. Contemporary capitalist science cares little, if anything, about the religious/the spiritual/the cosmic manifestations that earlier scientists, from eastern civilizations in particular, had given their due attention. Heavily confined to the so-called objective and empirical research tools and method, typical contemporary western scientists do not care very much about the mysteries that lie beyond both the reach of their narrow outlook on science and the materialistic world at large.

A comparison of the place of science and knowledge in Muslim civilization and contemporary western civilization is in order. In Islam, knowledge and science are the human means of salvation *par excellence*. The ambition of the Muslim scientist and scholar is not limited to the narrow discovery of Nature's laws and their usage here on earth. The access to more knowledge and science should only make the Muslim scientists and scholars fear God more, according to the Qur'an's revelation: 'The erudiste among his bonds men fear God alone' (*Qur'an*, Surate xxv/28).

While Islamic knowledge and science enhance the closeness of the Muslim scientists and scholars to the cosmos, contemporary western knowledge and science have done practically the contrary. They have done away with the spiritual touches in the performance of human knowledge and science. The practice of the latter is far from being the means of salvation for the great majority of contemporary western scientists and scholars.

In other words, secularized western human knowledge and science have inflicted a damaging blow to the role of knowledge and science as the *most distinct* and privileged means that enable humans to communicate with the larger cosmos. Consequently, the horizons of contemporary western scientists and scholars have considerably shrunk to become eventually confined to those phenomena they can see and measure with their five senses. From an Islamic point of view, the interruption of communication between the first Spring (God) of all knowledges/sciences and the individual scientists and scholars is an aberrant state that goes against the nature of things in the acquiring processes of knowledge and science. It is as *unnatural* as putting obstacles in space in order to prevent raindrops from going back to the rivers, lakes and oceans, etc., they had evaporated from. Based on those briefly described dark points of the contemporary capitalist system, one can hardly recommend that system as the ideal model for a worldwide development. The thesis of Schumacher's *Small is Beautiful* (1976) is clearly anti-capitalist. It can be highly recommended only on the political democratic-free expression level. On the economic and technological front, capitalism's development has proven to be *very* costly to the depletion of the planet's natural resources and to the maintenance of its ecology in good standing. The development of the arsenal of destructive armaments of all sorts puts the entire survival of planet earth and everything on it at high risk. On social justice and social ecology, advanced capitalist societies' record is far from being impressive.

146

Contemporary western capitalist development of knowledge and science has been *cosmically underdeveloped*. Last, and not least, western capitalism can hardly claim its innocence from the exploitation of other societies since its birth. Its development could then be seen at least partially as the result of the underdevelopment of others.

CAPITALISM AND THE UNDERDEVELOPMENT OF OTHER SOCIETIES

The picture of capitalism as briefly outlined, adequately permits one to know in advance what to expect from this contemporary model of development when it has the opportunity to interact with other societies and civilizations. Indeed, capitalism has had the opportunity in the contemporary period to leave its place of birth and make itself present practically in all five continents. It has interacted with those societies as a dominant and powerful actor. With this unequal relation with the subdued other, the scene was set for capitalism's greater benefits from this long and continuing encounter.

The long period of contemporary western colonization of countries around the globe constitutes the peak of their exploitation by the great western capitalist powers led by Great Britain and France. This is hardly difficult to imagine. On the one hand, we have a capitalist West, strongly obsessed by the idea of achieving an ever expanding economic/materialistic growth. On the other, many of the countries which fell under capitalist colonization were quite rich in natural resources but helpless to defend themselves and protect their own wealth from an imposing powerful enemy. It is within this historical conjuncture, according to dependency theorists, that the development process of the underdevelopment of the colonized/dependent societies had begun (Frank 1969).

Arguments have been made by the opponents of the Dependency theory that the underdevelopment of contemporary Third World countries is due mainly to internal factors. The mainstream paradigm of western developmentalist social scientists asserts that the causes of Third World underdevelopment have to be primarily sought in the cultural value system and the social structures of those societies (Lerner 1964). This kind of argument remains weak as long as it denies the *colonization factor* as a crucial variable which has to be taken into account in any genuine attempt to understand the dynamics of development/underdevelopment in contemporary societies.

In the objective assessment of contemporary western capitalism's enormous development and modernization, the social scientist must indeed seriously address both the role of the spirit of capitalism and of the industrial/scientific revolutions in that process of global change that European countries have witnessed since the sixteenth century. But scientific objectivity obviously remains *lacking*. Empirically speaking it is utterly unacceptable to do away with the impact of something as concrete, as observable and as widespread as contemporary western capitalist colonization of many parts of the world.

In denying or marginalizing the effects of western capitalist colonization on Third World underdevelopment, social scientists put themselves in an unenviable situation. On the one hand, if they deny the potential impact of western colonization as an empirical social fact, they put the scientific ethics of neutrality/objectivity in real jeopardy. On the other hand, if they admit it while continuing to marginalize its role in the development of underdevelopment, then they can be accused of lacking both the ability to comprehend (*Verstehen*) and the ability to explain particularly the wide range of damaging implications that contemporary western capitalist colonization has done for the state of development in today's Third World.

Three aspects of the former western capitalist colonization to today's developing societies could be outlined. They are the political, the economic and the cultural colonizations. The act of contemporary western occupation of countries, especially in Africa and Asia means in political terms the weakening of the capacity of the occupied people fully to govern themselves independently. The ruler of colonized territories is often either a colonial national appointee or a cooperating native designated by the colonizer. Policies and decisions in the running of the affairs of people under occupation are hardly done without the consensus and the approval of the colonizers. Likewise, the sector of administration is largely run and controlled by colonial staff where the language of the colonizer and his administration culture become widely used in dealing with the local people. In legal matters the colonial authority appoints its own judges and magistrates and introduces its own law into the legal system of the societies under occupation. Furthermore, the security forces put in place like police and *garde* (Gendarmes) are in the main nationals of the foreign occupier. The same is true also for the composition of the army in colonized countries.

In social psychological terms, these aspects of western contemporary colonization mean *the political deprivation* of the occupied people of African and Asian countries from fully exercising the experience of running their own affairs. Modern researches in socialization have shown the devastating effects of social deprivation on human behaviour (Williams 1983). The colonization experience entails collective deprivation of their diverse potentials.

The dominant–dominated relation that prevails during occupation between the colonizer and the colonized creates in the latter a sense of helplessness, dependency and a feeling of inferiority before the dominant colonizer (Memmi 1960). Such a political experience can hardly claim to

148

teach the dominated party a trustful, worthy self-respect. Under coloniz-ation, political deprivation means ultimately *a collective incapacitation* that hinders people from growing towards full mature political development. In other words, political colonization experience imposes a longer period of political *childhood* for the occupied. It *underdevelops* potential for becoming their own confident masters in the reliable management of the affairs of the collectivity. The Third World's widespread behaviour of imitation of the West during and after occupation is to be accounted for, in part, by the Third World's continuing childhood in the domain of conducting success-ful independent and self-made political governance and development projects. The stage of childhood for both individuals as well as for human collectivities appears to be strongly correlated with a disproportionate tendency to imitation of those who have grown older, more mature and more developed.

Capitalist western powers' contemporary occupation of foreign terri-tories far from home was hardly an end in itself. In sociological terms, it had wider functions to accomplish in the interest of the colonizer. The British occupation of Egypt for instance, was very important for Great Britain as far as her maritime and military strategy for a worldwide effective expansion and domination. Once political and strategic colonial domination was secured, the scene was set for the exploitation of the occupied party *from within*. Economic exploitation of the colonized was bound to be high, if not the most important item, on the agenda of the contemporary western capitalist colonizers.

Dependency social science research on development/underdevelopment has amply provided many details on the various ways that capitalist eco-nomic exploitation has underdeveloped the occupied territories (Frank 1967; Baran 1957). It is not my aim here to restate them fully. It is sufficient to make reference to some of the aspects of that contemporary capitalist western economic exploitation of their former colonies. Cheap raw materials needed by the industrial revolution were shipped from these colonies to western capitalist industrial settings. Capitalist industrial de-velopment and production output depended considerably on that sort of material booty from abroad.[1] The growing in colonies of agricultural crops destined for consumption by the citizens of the colonial powers had become a common practice between the colonizer and the colonized. This exploita-tive practice could certainly endanger (underdevelop) the colonies' food self-production autonomy, if carried out widely and intensively. In con-nection with this plausible food-supply underdevelopment, one can hardly underestimate the crucial role of colonial farmers in this process of agricultural underdevelopment. Those famers were often given by the colonial authorities great areas of fertile land in order to cultivate and export much of its crops back home. The result of those diverse levels of exploitation of the occupied territories is strongly compatible with Paul

Baran's stand on capitalism and its negative impact on the underdevelopment of colonized countries. Gunder Frank sees the development of the underdevelopment of today's Third World as the outcome of what he calls the metropolis – satellite structure which 'serves as an instrument to such capital *or economic surplus* [emphasis added] out of its own satellites and to channel part of this surplus to the world metropolis of which all are satellites' (ibid.: 105). In other words, the satellite status of colonized countries during occupation and after becomes the key factor for understanding the continuing capitalist exploitation and the subsequent phenomenon of worldwide underdevelopment. In contrast to that, societies which were hardly satellites of capitalism have scored tremendously well on the development achievement scale. Frank writes: '*Japan was not satellized* either during the Tokugawa or Meiji period and therefore did not have its development structurally limited as did the countries which capitalist were so satellized' (ibid.: 109; emphasis added).

As defined here, both contemporary capitalist western political domination as well as economic exploitation of the African and the Asian colonized societies could hardly be conceivable without a concomitant *third kind* of domination of those countries. It has to do here with the phenomenon of capitalist *cultural colonial domination* of the various people who fell during the contemporary period under the occupation of capitalist western powers led by Great Britain and France. The concept of cultural domination means that once the capitalist western powers had occupied their targeted foreign territories, they had made efforts and carried out policies that helped spread, among the colonized, their *cultural symbols*. The latter refers here to such things like language, thought, religion, science/knowledge, cultural norms and values. Unlike in the economic domain, the capitalist western colonizer's export and diffusion of cultural symbols does not in any way underdevelop his ongoing development. On the contrary, cultural symbols strengthen the exporter's domination grip on his colonized and often *underdevelops* the vitality and the functioning of the colonized's own cultural symbols. The role of language in this process of cultural underdevelopment in colonized societies is most crucial and decisive. Usually, the occupying capitalist power introduces the use of its language in its colonies in many important sectors like education, administration and environment. The extent of linguistic colonization can go from a marginal use to a total use of the occupier's language in those three sectors of the colonized societies. A clear consequence of this process is a minor to a major underdevelopment of the national local language(s) of countries which fell under capitalist western colonization. Language is a living being. On the one hand, it grows and it develops its potentials with intensive use. On the other, it weakens and it underdevelops its capacities with decreased use.

With the wide diffusion of the colonizer's language, the scene was set for an extensive spread of the rest of the cultural symbols among the people under occupation. They were introduced to western ideas, science/knowledge, mores and customs. They were also exposed through Christian missions to the Christian religious beliefs which may lead to their eventual conversion. In sociological terms, a collective process of *acculturation* of the colonized population was put in place once the foreign language had gained a strong hold among them. This culturo-linguistic acculturation had led in many cases to *cultural underdevelopment* in the colonized countries. Within the capitalist western colonial educational settings pupils and students were often heavily taught western languages, history, geography, philosophy . . . ideas and, thus, their knowledge of their own language(s) and cultural heritage in these areas is frequently lacking and distorted. On the one hand this unbalanced education system taught knowledge which could only favour the development of the colonial cultural symbols in the occupied territories and the promotion of a positive and a quasi-reverent perception of the dominant colonizer (Dhaouadi 1988: 228). On the other, it was bound to lead to the underdevelopment of the colonized's own cultural symbols and the emergence of the phenomena of cultural conflicts and negative self-esteem (ibid.: 229). Cultural underdevelopment, as described above, appears to be often associated with *self-degrading* psychological manifestations (ibid.: 230) among the larger population of the world who fell victim to contemporary capitalist western occupation. It is the concept of the Other Underdevelopment that we have invented to describe that state of psycho-cultural underdevelopment which is widely experienced throughout today's Third World (ibid.: 219–34).

THE FORGOTTEN OTHER UNDERDEVELOPMENT

We were inspired by Michael Harrington's term 'the Other America' (Harrington 1963) in the invention of the label of the 'Other Underdevelopment'. On the one hand, Harrington's 'Other America' meant the *forgotten* Blacks, Hispanics and other non-white Americans by the larger white American population. On the other, our concept of the Other Underdevelopment means that kind of underdevelopment, though it is particularly widespread in today's Third World, which has been hardly studied by social scientists concerned with the issues of development/underdevelopment. That is, western liberal capitalist and Marxist social scientists alike and their followers in the Third World itself have tended to *confine* themselves to the study of the socioeconomic aspects of underdevelopment. This line of social science research and theoretical orientation on development/underdevelopment was bound to neglect and leave out the phenomenon of the Other Underdevelopment from its quantitatively impressive accumulated vast literature on the subject of development/underdevelopment. *The Other Underdevelopment*, forgotten by the mainstream of modern social sciences of development/underdevelopment constitutes in itself a phenomenon which has to be understood and explained.

The absence of modern social science literature on the Other Underdevelopment raises enough scepticism about the genuine credibility of the enormous quantity of social science articles, books, reports, etc., which have been written and published since the Second World War on the issues of development/underdevelopment. By not paying attention to the Other Underdevelopment, modern social scientists of development/underdevelopment appear to have had a rather narrowed conceptualization of underdevelopment. They do not seem to have seriously looked at development/underdevelopment as a complex social reality whose many components ultimately make up a social system. Their dealing mainly with the socioeconomic dimensions of development/underdevelopment reflects, therefore, a fragmented and a disruptive view of development/underdevelopment which is a total phenomenon whose parts are organically *interdependent.*

AN OPERATIONAL DEFINITION OF THE OTHER UNDERDEVELOPMENT

As mentioned earlier, the Other Underdevelopment has two dimensions: (a) the cultural underdevelopment dimension; and (b) the psychological underdevelopment dimension. The Other Underdevelopment is, therefore, a psycho-cultural underdevelopment whose two dimensions interact with each other and make ultimately a *psycho-cultural system.*

Cultural underdevelopment

As conceived through our concept of the Other Underdevelopment (Dhaouadi 1988) cultural underdevelopment can be measured by *three* manifestations:

1 Linguistic underdevelopment: we define it as, on the one hand, the widespread use of one or more foreign language in a given society and, on the other, the underusage (the less than full use) of society's own native language(s) (spoken/written or both).
2 Knowledge/science underdevelopment: we define this kind of underdevelopment as, on the one hand, developing countries' contemporary *acute* dependency on western science and knowledge and, on the other, as the widespread poor (*underdeveloped*) knowledge that Third World intellectuals and scientists of western educational background have of their own civilization and culture's past contributions to the fields of science and knowledge.

3 The underdevelopment of cultural value system: it is meant by this type of underdevelopment the weakening, the erosion and the breakdown of the cultural value system of dominated Third World countries as a result of their contact with the dominant West in the contemporary period.

Psychological underdevelopment

Psychological underdevelopment means here the *deterioration* of the basic foundations of the psychological well-being of the Third World's individual personality which is mainly the outcome of contemporary imperial western cultural domination. This psychological state can be measured by two major syndromes: (a) the inferiority complex: due to contemporary western domination of the Third World, the average citizen of the latter tends to manifest inferiority-complex symptoms toward the dominant West. This is often associated with a number of damaging attitudes and behaviour's to one's psychological well-being like the feeling of loss of faith in one's self, the strong desire to imitate the West, experiences of psychological alienation and stress etc.; (b) the disorganized personality: the acute state of cultural conflict between the traditional cultural value system and its modern western counterpart is bound to have certain negative side effects on the personality structure of the Third World acculturized (to western culture) individual. Znaniecki and Thomas (1958) had referred to this type of personality as 'disorganized personality'.

The other underdevelopment as a psycho-cultural system

Having operationalized our concept of the Other Underdevelopment into cultural and psychological underdevelopments, we need to show now how they interact with each other and make a system of their own. Our study has indeed shown that the *two* components of the Other Underdevelopment do mutually interact in a reciprocal manner (Dhaouadi 1988: 229–30). We have demonstrated, on the one hand, that linguistic underdevelopment and knowledge/science underdevelopment are likely to lead to the development of inferiority-complex symptoms (psychological underdevelopment) in the personality of the western-acculturized individual of the Third World. On the other hand, psychological underdevelopment predisposes the Third World individual personality to be *eager* to learn and use the language(s) and the cultures of western dominant societies. Furthermore, the inferiority-complex syndrome becomes a compelling strong force causing the development of a *negative perception* of one's national language and culture. In this sense, psychological inferiority-complex symptoms (psychological underdevelopment) appear, thus, to harden the two dimensions of cultural underdevelopment and, consequently, to contribute to the making of cultural alienation, a phenomenon which is widespread in underdeveloped countries, especially among those groups with western educational background.

To complete the description of the dynamics of the Other Underdevelopment as a psychocultural system, we need to look at the impact of the disorganized personality (psychological underdevelopment) on what we have called cultural underdevelopment or the cultural values system of the individual.

The disorganized personality seems to contribute significantly to the *breakdown* of the cultural value system. In other terms, conflicts of cultural values are likely to make the personality structure of the individual of the Third World *more vulnerable* to further breakdowns and, thus, more receptive or less resistant to the adoption of western cultural values. Ultimately, this will lead to a deepening disintegration of the personality structure and, consequently, to confusion in one's cultural identity. Figure 8.1 illustrates the main components of the phenomenon of the Other Underdevelopment as well as the nature of their interaction.

SOCIAL SCIENCES' UNDERDEVELOPMENT ON CULTURAL SYMBOLS

The long-lasting silence of modern capitalist and non-capitalist social science literature of development/underdevelopment on the Other Underdevelopment in the Third World has deprived those social sciences of a rich corpus of knowledge that could only enhance the strength of their *theoretical imagination* and their capacity to become highly applicable sciences. To put this in perspective, we focus our analysis on the component of

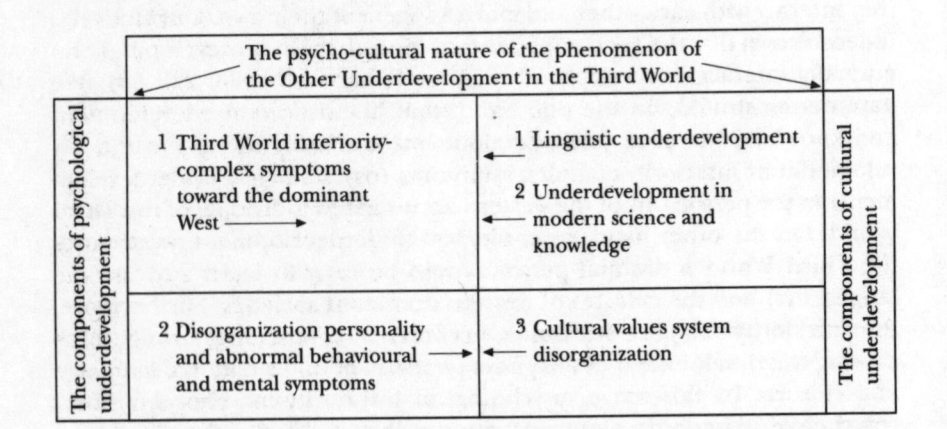

Figure 8.1 The psycho-cultural nature of the phenomenon of the Other underdevelopment in the Third World

cultural underdevelopment in the Other Underdevelopment. As defined earlier, cultural underdevelopment englobes language, knowledge/science, cultural values, etc. All human cultural symbols in Edward Tylor's (1871) sense of culture of a complex whole including knowledge, belief, art, morals, custom and other capacities and habits acquired by man as a member of society, are to be referred to in this study as *cultural symbols*. The latter are basic to the human species. It is through them that humans are most distinct from both artificial intelligence machines and other living creatures. There is a consensus among modern scholars of culture that the use of cultural symbols by human beings is the most striking feature of the entity of human culture. The symbolic abilities of humans are the yardstick by which Leslie White defines the nature of humans. He writes: 'we thus define man in terms of the abilities *to symbol* and the consequent ability to produce culture' (cited in Denisoff, Callahan and Levine 1975: 224–5). Then, White underlines *language* as the most important of all cultural symbols. 'But perhaps the best example of all is articulate speech or language; at any rate, we may well regard articulate speech as the most characteristic and the most important form of expression of the ability to symbol' (ibid.: 220).

This extreme importance of cultural symbols for the shaping and the ultimate making of the human entity and identity enables one strongly to assert that the *human species is decisively culturo-symbolic by nature*. In our own terms, cultural symbols constitute the Culturo-Symbolic Soul of human individuals (Dhaouadi 1992a). Thus, any credible scientific attempt to comprehend and explain human behaviour, be it single or collective, must give priority to the compelling weight of symbolic ability in the behavioural determination of the behaviour in question. Modern social science theories and paradigms that fail to take seriously into account the crucial role of cultural symbols are doomed to discredit themselves in their assessment of the dynamics of social action.

It is against this epistemological perspective on the nature of human cultural symbols that the silence on the issue of the Other Underdevelopment by both capitalist liberal and dependency social scientists of development/underdevelopment becomes unacceptable and it can hardly be defended on genuine solid scientific grounds. Those social scientists' disinterest in dealing with the Third World's contemporary widespread and crying Other Underdevelopment is bound to be the outcome of narrow-minded and ideologico-biased approaches to the study of development/underdevelopment in contemporary societies at large. Western capitalist liberal social scientists and their Marxist colleagues have different reasons for their lack of concern for the study of the Other Underdevelopment. The causes behind that can be classified into *two* sorts of categories:

Causes inspired by western ethnocentrism

1 Among western capitalist liberal social scientists of development/ modernization/underdevelopment there is an implicit or an explicit tendency to view the general cultural heritage (values, traditions, religions, etc.) of the Third World societies as largely representing major obstacles to the development/modernization process in those countries (Lerner 1964). This should legitimately explain why cultural under-development has hardly any place in the impressive massive quantity of academic studies produced since 1945 on development/modernization/ underdevelopment in the Third World.

2 Western capitalist liberal social scientists of development/modernization/ underdevelopment have had the tendency or the strong conviction to think of the capitalist West as the only *real maker of history* in the contemp-orary period. So the eventual success in development/modernization projects by underdeveloped societies will always need a hand from the capitalist system. So, the wide diffusion of modern western languages (English, French, etc.) as well as the cultural values into the Third World countries is expected to be endorsed or even called for especially by those modern capitalist liberal social scientists like Lerner (1964), and Inkeles and Smith (1975). For them, it is quite obvious that the diffusion of western cultural symbols in underdeveloped societies is a process which would rather help the promotion of cultural development *per se* and not a process that would lead to the Other Underdevelopment, as we have defined it.

3 As we pointed out earlier, western capitalist liberal social scientists have hardly made any direct link between the phenomenon of the Third World underdevelopment, on the one hand, and western capitalist colonialism, on the other. When that underdevelopment in all its multiple forms (economic, social psycho-cultural, etc.) is not related somehow to imperial capitalist western classical or new colonialism in the last two centuries or so, then the Other Underdevelopment, seen by us as resulting basically from capitalist western domination of the Third World, is unlikely to be recognized and, subsequently, studied by those social scientists.

4 It is only natural for western capitalist social scientists' conceptualiz-ation, understanding, paradigm and theory-building, etc. of development/ underdevelopment to be westerncentric. The social scientist, whatever his or her nationality may be, is often inclined to rely heavily on the realities of his or her own social/civilizational milieu in analysing societal phenomena as well as theorizing on them. In acting that way he or she is bound to be, at least in part, biased in going about research endeavours including his or her own choice of what dimension (economic, social, pyscho-cultural, etc.) of Third World underdevelopment has to be focused upon. In other words, contemporary advanced capitalist and

socialist societies, to which the vast majority of modern social scientists belongs, are *not* known to have *seriously* suffered, if at all, from the Other Underdevelopment syndrome as described by us here and elsewhere.[2] Consequently, the Other Underdevelopment has remained an alien phenomenon which has failed seriously to attract the scientific exploratory curiosity of those social scientists.

Causes of epistemological nature

On the whole, both western liberal capitalist and Marxist social scientists have tended to conceptualize the development/underdevelopment phenomena in *a visibly externalized* materialist/quantitative nature. If development/ underdevelopment is conceived largely in easily measurable terms of economic, social, scientific and technological indicators, then it becomes understandable why psycho-cultural underdevelopment (the Other Underdevelopment) has received practically no attention from all those social scientists. It is well known, in this regard, that Marxist social scientists have produced enormous analytical academic and scholarly works on Third World economic exploitation by the capitalist West. But in contrast to this, they have given *no more* than lip service to Third World cultural exploitation by capitalist colonial powers.[3]

By its nature, the Other Underdevelopment appears to lie beyond the reach of the mainstream of traditional contemporary sociologists and economists alike. On the one hand, what interests the latter most is the analysis of the economic forces that work for or against development/underdevelopment. On the other, it is the structures of societies that get most of the attention of traditional sociologists. Thus, it could be said that the study of the psycho-cultural dimensions of societies' underdevelopment belongs rather to the so-called 'radical sociology' (Howard and Wood 1989).

By neglecting, for epistemological, ethnocentric or other reasons, the study of the Other Underdevelopment as a principal feature of the Third World's contemporary development/underdevelopment dynamics, modern western capitalist and Marxist sociologists and economists in particular have caused *serious damage* to the integrity as well as the validity of their paradigms and theories about development/underdevelopment in the Third World.

CULTURAL SYMBOLS RESEARCH AND THE ENRICHMENT OF SOCIAL SCIENCE THEORETICAL SCOPE

The marginalization or the total disinterest in the study of the Other Underdevelopment has *impoverished* not only modern social science literature on the issues of development and underdevelopment, but has also deprived their theoretical scope of being more credible in dealing with the comprehension and the explanation of diverse societal phenomena. My own work in the last three years on cultural symbols[4] which has direct theoretical implications and concrete applications for the cultural development component of the Other Underdevelopment, has allowed us *to revitalize* the use of cultural symbols in modern social sciences. Our ultimate goal has been to put forth a *new theoretical framework* on the nature of cultural symbols. As emphasized before, cultural symbols are so central to the social actor's own identity and action. In other words, they constitute his or her Culturo-Symbolic Soul (Dhaouadi 1992a). Their impact on the behaviour of the individual and the collectivity is long lasting and so powerful that it becomes at times irresistible. Their imposing influence on social action appears to be triggered by quasi-supernatural forces. This is why the nature of cultural symbols has become to be viewed by us as being impregnated with *transcendental* dimensions.

Two examples are sufficient illustrations for this new theoretical vision of our conceptualization of the nature of cultural symbols. The two example case studies are (a) Cultural Dependency's *danger* and *longer life span*; and (b) William Ogburn's theory on the *slow* pace of cultural change (Culture Lag) in human societies.

Cultural Dependency is most dangerous

The widely quoted saying: 'The cultural conquest of people is more dangerous than its military counterpart' is almost an uncontested assertion of high credibility. One must, however, admit that there is a great deal of fuzziness and lack of precision in the use of such terms like 'Cultural Alienation', 'Cultural Imperialism', 'Cultural Dependency', etc. in the contemporary worldwide context of dominant/dominated societies. All these various terms do not offer more than a general observation of the presence of imperial foreign cultural symbols in today's dominated countries. The scientific analysis of the potential dangers of the phenomenon of cultural conquests can absolutely be unsatisfied with the mere proliferation of such general labels. A mature scientific endeavour would require *no less* than the identification of the principal foundations of the phenomenon in question. Our reference to the notion of cultural symbols in this study falls within our attempt to go beyond the philosophical and ideological levels of 'Cultural Imperialism', 'Cultural Dependency', etc. to a more scientifically grounded analysis which could ultimately help deal with the cultural symbols universe of the human species. Accordingly, the ever increasing critical complaints against the so-called 'American cultural imperialism' as claimed both by developed and developing societies[5] have to be understood through a credible scientific framework and not through a narrow demagogical/ideological oriented perspective.

The fear of those societies of 'the American cultural invasion' could only be adequately legitimized when viewed through the perspective of the thesis we have summarized, in the second part of this study, about the human cultural symbols. The propagation of foreign cultural symbols in human societies means, as we have stressed, that the impact of those cultural symbols will be of *lasting* effect once the cultural symbols are deeply implanted into the culture of the dominated societies. Thus, the task of liberating themselves from them in the future will be a difficult one indeed. Past and present evidence shows that the diffusion of language, cultural values, religious beliefs, etc. in other societies and civilizations is the best clever strategy that a society could resort to in order to secure the establishment of more permanent relations with other countries. At this level, there is no doubt that the *cultural factor* is much superior to the military, geographic, political and economic strategies. Ultimately, it is the *key* for securing other societies' easier dependency on all these fronts.

Contemporary researchers do concur that the French colonization had given more importance than its English counterpart to the cultural colonization of the occupied people in Africa and Asia (Calvet 1977: 84–5; Eudes 1982). Consequently, it could be said that today's Maghrebian societies (Algeria, Tunisia, Morocco and Mauritania) suffer *more* than their Mashrequian (Middle Eastern) counterpart societies from colonial cultural dependency (Ruf 1974: 233–79). In our own terms, cultural dependency means the dependency of one's Culturo-Symbolic Soul to the outsider, who may be one's enemy. The dependency of one's Culturo-Symbolic Soul constitutes a direct assault on the basic foundations of the cultural identity of the individual and the collectivity. In light of this line of ideas and analysis, one should have no great difficulty in seeing the degree of credibility of the statement 'The cultural conquest of people is *more* dangerous than its military counterpart.' Based on this broad analysis, the Third World countries' condemnation of modern western 'Cultural Imperialism' be it American, English, French, etc., is hardly unfounded. Today's widespread official and non-official use of English (American) and French in many African and Asian societies does not only contribute to the impoverishment (*the underdevelopment*) of those societies' native languages and dialects, but it also entails that the struggle to win their linguistico-cultural independence will not be an easy task. As stated before, Cultural Dependency's longevity takes a longer time to get rid of and this is provided that all positive appropriate conditions are present in the given society/collectivity. 'Cultural Imperialism', whatever its origin, will be perceived negatively when it triggers and amplifies the processes of the disintegration of the native culturo-symbolic systems of developing and developed societies. Third World countries that suffer from the symptoms of national (or local) Cultural Alienation, disintegration and loss of collective self-esteem are countries which are bound to be most profoundly hit in the very basic foundations of their cultural collective identity (Kisber 1982).

Ogburn's Cultural Lag

The concept of Cultural Lag of the American sociologist, William Ogburn, is another genuine case whose analysis by our own theoretical framework of cultural symbols ought to make it both more understandable and theoretically more enriching (Ogburn 1964: 86–95). Ogburn's thesis contends that the pace of cultural elements' processes of change is much *slower* than that of the material elements of society's social structure. The thesis underlined earlier in our study on the nature of cultural symbols helps explain the reason behind Ogburn's Cultural Lag on which he did not seem to have said a lot. That is, his concept of Cultural Lag remains short of an explicit explanation of the *whys* of cultural change's *slowness*. As such, his notion is rather a descriptive one. On our part, the explanation of the Cultural Lag could be framed as follows: the human beings are full-blown culturo-symbolic beings. For the latter, the culturo-symbolic dimensions constitute all that is most profound and fundamental for their identity. Furthermore, the cultural symbols often bear transcendental dimensions, as pointed out. On the one hand, the cultural symbols appear to resist change more because, as we just have mentioned, they occupy all that is *most* central and strategic in the entity of the social actors. On the other, the enormous resistance which the cultural symbols deploy in the face of change seems to draw its strong force from their transcendental aspects which are ultimately of a quasi-supernatural nature, as already underlined.

With this regard, modern sociology and anthropology have hardly explicitly identified the cause (the causes) behind the great difficulty which human societies experience *vis-à-vis* the change of their culturo-symbolic systems. Our conception of the *centrality* of the cultural symbols and their transcendental input in the making of the identity of the social factors helps, in our opinion, account for the reasons that make the pace of change of cultural components drag behind (Cultural Lag) their structuro-material counterpart. As such, we are no longer in the descriptive phase 'how' at which Ogburn seemed to have stopped. This has to be seen as an obvious shortcoming of Ogburn's thought.

It is time to call upon researchers in the behavioural social sciences to integrate *seriously* the distinct nature of cultural symbols as well as their transcendental weight not only in their analysis of cultural change but also in their general attempts to capture the underlying meanings of individual human behaviour and the dynamics of human societies.

To summarize, cultural change's slowness (Cultural Lag) can be explained by:

1 Cultural symbols constitute all that is *most* profound and central in social actors' identity;

2 Cultural symbols entail transcendental dimensions whose powerful force

of resistance to change and their long-lasting longevity are originated in a quasi-supernatural universe.

THE NEED FOR *VERSTEHEN* SOCIOLOGY OF CULTURAL SYMBOLS

It is against this broad background of analysis that one can come to grips with the kind of difficulty that positivist social scientists have to face as far as perceiving and understanding the larger implications which cultural symbols could put in place for the dynamics of human groups, communities and societies. In general, the discipline of modern sociology has rejected the idea of alliance with a subjective methodology which allows the sociologist to get much *closer* to the human dimension of social actors than to the social structure surrounding them. Our modest effort in the second half of this chapter has shown through the use of our concept of the Culturo-Symbolic Soul that it is time for sociology to reintegrate fully the subjectivo-transcendental components in its perspectives in every study which aims to achieve more credibility with regard to the comprehension as well as the explanation of the behaviour of the individual or that of the collectivity.

The study of the cultural symbols by anthropologists and sociologists can not be done adequately without *internal* comprehension and assessment of them. The need is urgent indeed for the invention and establishment of some sort of *Verstehen* sociology fit to deal with the complex maze that the human cultural symbols entail.

Figure 8.2 both summarizes some of the ideas, concepts and theories which have been partly outlined, and widens and deepens the scope of the implications of the concept of cultural symbols and ultimately that of the Other Underdevelopment in today's societies.

NOTES

1 On the one hand, modern wealth of some Arab countries is usually linked to their oil resources. On the other, early Arab imperial economic expansion after the spread of Islam outside Arabia's frontiers is explained by their military invasions of the new territories. See my book review of *The Arab Political Mind* by M. Al Jabri in a forthcoming issue of *Contemporary Sociology*. There is a good reason to consider likewise western capitalism's enormous contemporary economic growth as partially the result of the worldwide colonization and its subsequent exploitations of the colonized.

2 Our first conceptualization of the Other Underdevelopment was published in *Arabic* in the *Journal of Al-Mustaqbal Al-Arabi*; see also Dhaouadi 1986.

3 Writings on development/underdevelopment of Marxist authors such as Amin, *Le Développement inégal* (1973), Baran, *The Political Economy of Growth* (1957) and Frank, *Capitalism and Underdevelopment in Latin America* (1969) reflect their

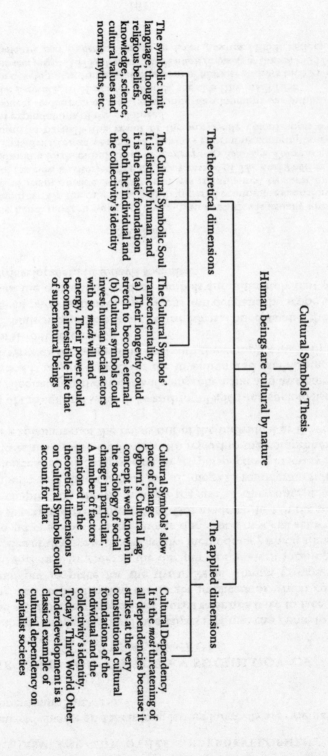

Figure 8.2 Cultural Symbols and Other Underdevelopment

Cultural Symbols Thesis

Human beings are cultural by nature

The theoretical dimensions

The applied dimensions

The symbolic unit
language, thought,
religious beliefs,
knowledge, science,
cultural values and
norms, myths, etc.

The Cultural Symbolic Soul
It is distinctly human and
it is the basic foundation
of both the individual and
the collectivity's identity

The Cultural Symbols'
transcendentality
(a) Their longevity could
stretch to become eternal.
(b) Cultural symbols could
invest human social actors
with so *much* will and
energy. Their power could
become irresistible like that
of supernatural beings

Cultural Symbols' slow
pace of change
Ogburn's Cultural Lag
concept is well known in
the sociology of social
change in particular.
A number of factors
mentioned in the
theoretical dimensions
on Cultural Symbols could
account for that

Cultural Dependency
It is the *most* threatening of
all dependencies because it
strikes at the very
constitutional cultural
foundations of the
individual and the
collectivity's identity.
Today's Third World Other
Underdevelopment is a
classical example of
cultural dependency on
capitalist societies

silence on the psycho-cultural underdevelopment as an integral of the greater phenomenon of underdevelopment in the Third World.

4 Dhaouadi 1992b. This study is expected to be published in English in a forthcoming issue of *International Sociology*. See also note 2 above. Dhaouadi 1992a.

5 The prestigious French medical journal, *Les Annales*, has adopted English as the language of its published scientific articles. This has raised a lot of protest in France. See the interview with its editor in *Le Monde* 14 April 1989: 12. See also: 'L'influence culturelle americaine en France' in *Le Monde: dossiers et documents*, May 1981.

REFERENCES

Amin, S. (1973) *Le Développement inégal*, Paris: Le Seuil.

Baran, P. (1957) *The Political Economy of Growth*, New York: Monthly Review Press.

Bell, D. (1976) *The Cultural Contradictions of Capitalism*, London: Heinemann.

Bellah, R., Sullivan, W., Swidler, A., Tipton, S. and Madsen, R. (eds) (1985) *Habits of the Heart*, Berkeley: University of California Press.

Boorstin, D. (1983) *The Discoverers*, New York: Random House.

Calvet, L. J. (1977) *Linguistique et colonialisme*, Paris: Payot.

Denisoff, R. S., Callahan, O. and Levine, M. L. (eds) (1975) *Theories and Paradigms in Contemporary Sociology*, Illinois: F. E. Peacock Publishers, Inc.

Dhaouadi, M. (1986) 'The Other Underdevelopment as a research notion both in the Arab world and the rest of the Third World', in *Toward an Arab Sociology*, Beirut: Centre for Arab Unity Studies: 163–84.

—— (1988) 'An operational analysis of the phenomenon of the Other Underdevelopment in the Arab World and the Third World', *International Sociology*, vol. 3, no. 3: 215–34.

—— (1992a) 'The culturo-symbolic soul: an Islamically inspired research concept for the behavioral and social sciences', *The American Journal of Islamic Social Sciences*, vol. 9, no. 2, Summer: 153–72.

—— (1992b) 'The other face of cultural symbols as reflected in a special sociological analysis' (in Arabic) in *Al-Wahda*, vol. 8, no. 92, May: 75–89.

Dillard, D. (1979) 'Capitalism in the political economy of development and underdevelopment', in Charles Wilber (ed.) *Capitalism in the Political Economy of Development and Underdevelopment*, 2nd edn, New York: Random House.

Eudes, Y. (1982) *La Conquête des esprits*, Paris: Maspero.

Frank, A. G. (1967) 'The sociology of development or underdevelopment of sociology', *Catalyst* 3: 2–4.

—— (1969) *Capitalism and Underdevelopment in Latin America*, New York: Monthly Review Press.

Fukuyama, F. (1990) *The End of History and the Last Man*, New York: Free Press.

Harrington, M. (1963) *The Other America*, Baltimore: Penguin Books.

Howard, J. S. and Wood, J. L. (1989) *Sociology: Traditional and Radical Perspectives*, New York: Harper and Row.

Inkeles, A. and Smith, D. (1975) *Becoming Modern*, Cambridge: Harvard University Press.

Kisber, G. (1982) *The Disorganized Personality*, London: McGraw Hill.

Lerner, D. (1964) *The Passing of Traditional Society*, New York: Free Press.

Mcluhan, M. and Fiore, F. (1967) *The Medium is the Message*, New York: Bantam.

Magdoff, H. (1978) *Imperialism: From the Colonial Age to the Present*, New York: Monthly Review Press.

Mano, K. (1991) 'Modernist discourse and the crisis of Development Theory', *Studies in Comparative Internation Development*, 26 (Summer), no. 2: 3–4.

Mazrui, A. (1992) 'The burden of underdeveloment' a radio programme by the Canadian Broadcasting Corporation (CBC). 15 October.

Memmi, A. (1960) *Portrait au Colonise*, Paris: Payot.

Ogburn, W. F. (1964) 'On cultural and social change', in O. D. Durtan (ed.) *On Cultural and Social Change*, Chicago: University of Chicago Press.

Ruf, W. K. (1974) 'Dependence et alienation culturelle', in W. K. Ruf (ed.) *Indépendence et interdépendence au Maghreb*, Paris: CNRS.

Schumacher, E. (1976) *Small is Beautiful*, New York: Harper and Row.

The World and I (1992) ed. M. A. Kaplan 'Preserving the earth: beyond ideology', July: 20.

Tylor, E. B. (1871) *Primitive Culture*, London: Murray.

Weber, M. (1950) *The Protestant Ethic and the Spirit of Capitalism*, Glencoe: Free Press.

Znanecki, F. and Thomas, W. (1958) *The Polish Peasant in Europe and America*, New York: Dover.

9

CAPITALISM AND DEVELOPMENT IN GLOBAL PERSPECTIVE

Leslie Sklair

INTRODUCTION

My argument in this chapter is that capitalism produces a distorted form of development globally, where it produces any sort of development at all. In the Third World the distortions tend to be different from those produced in the First World. The 'developmental successes' of capitalism in the Third World, therefore, mainly consist of partially solving Third World problems (like absolute material deprivations) and replacing them with First World problems (like new diseases, some gross forms of environmental degradation and ennui). My conclusion is that global capitalism cannot develop the Third World, even in terms of the relatively limited sense in which capitalists use the concept 'development'. To signal this point throughout the text I use 'development' to denote 'capitalist or distorted development' and development (without the inverted commas) to denote a different form of non-capitalist (in fact, anti-capitalist) development.[1] This is based on specific concepts of the global capitalist system and of capitalist 'development'. It is implicit in my approach that such issues as these can best be tackled within a 'globalization' framework.

All these arguments will be hopelessly confused unless a working definition of development can be agreed. Conventionally, a distinction has been made between *economic growth* (measured on such criteria as GNP per capita, proportion of the labour force engaged in manufacturing, and value added in export goods) and *development*, which has somewhat wider social and political implications. The crucial difference is that development includes everything that is already included in economic growth plus criteria of distribution of the social product, democratic politics and the elimination of class, gender and ethnic privileges.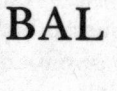

If some form of capitalist 'development', however distorted, is possible, then Third World capitalists and their affiliates could carve out niches for themselves in the crevices that the First World capitalists leave unattended, or even challenge them in certain areas. This is the conclusion that several scholars have drawn from the experiences of the NICs (see, for example, Warren 1980; Gwynne 1990). Such theories thrive on state-centrism, because it is easy to demonstrate that certain Third World states, particularly the renowned 'four dragons' of East Asia rapidly pursued by Malaysia, Indonesia, Thailand and others, and the Latin American NICs, are finding their own niches in the global system. However, a global approach suggests that it is time to refocus our attention, away from state-centrist ideas of First World countries exploiting Third World countries, and a few Third World countries managing to best First World countries, to studies of how capitalism works in the Third World through its major institutional forms, namely transnational corporations, the transnational capitalist class and the culture-ideology that persuades people of the virtues and necessity of the system.

It is important to note that not all Third World countries have been influenced to the same extent or in the same ways by global capitalism in general and the TNCs (transnational corporations) in particular. Recent research (for example, Chi 1989; Gereffi and Wyman 1990; Kim 1989/90) has documented and begun to theorize some of the differences. This chapter focuses on how TNCs influence development and underdevelopment both directly and indirectly, and how economic, political and culture-ideology practices that emanate from the TNCs interact with local practices to create certain types of 'development' and to shut off other types. In order to attack this problem properly, a specific conception of the *global* is necessary.

GLOBALIZATION

Globalization is a relatively new idea in the social sciences, though in the world of transnational corporations it is now a commonplace. Jacques Maisonrouge, one-time president of IBM World Trade, was an early exponent of the view that the future lies with global corporations which operate as if the world had no real borders rather than organizations tied to a particular country (Maisonrouge 1988). Thus, a central feature of the idea of globalization is that many contemporary problems cannot be adequately studied or solved at the level of the state.[2]

Globalization researchers have focused in particular on two new phenomena that have become significant in the last few decades: the spread of TNCs through processes such as 'the globalization of production and capital' and 'the new international division of labour' (NIDL); and transformations in the global scope of the mass media.

The largest TNCs have assets and annual sales far in excess of the gross national products of most of the countries in the world. In 1991, only about *sixty countries* had GNPs of more than $10 billion (World Bank 1993: table 3). *Fortune* magazine's 'Global 500 industrial corporations' (26 July 1993) shows *139 TNCs* with annual sales in 1992 in excess of $10 billion. Thus, more than twice as many corporations have this level of economic resources at their disposal than countries in the world. These figures prove little in themselves, they simply indicate the *gigantism* of TNCs relative to most countries. Not only have TNCs grown enormously in size in recent decades but their 'global reach' has expanded dramatically. Many major TNCs now earn more than half of their revenues from 'foreign' sales and are doing more and more of their manufacturing in 'foreign' countries (that is, countries other than those in which their headquarters are located and/or in which they are legally incorporated), including many Third World or newly industrializing countries.

The second crucial phenomenon is the global diffusion of mass media, particularly television. According to data from UNESCO (1989), the number of TVs per thousand people rose from 57 in 1965 to 145 in 1986. Even more striking is the change in geographical distribution. In 1965, only about 5 per cent of the world's TV sets were in the developing countries – by 1986, the developing countries accounted for over 20 per cent of TVs. The *total* number of TV sets (and other media) in Third World countries has grown so rapidly in recent years that a 'globalizing effect' due to the mass media is said to be taking place even in the Third World, though there is a good deal of disagreement as to its exact nature and effects (see Featherstone 1990; Sklair 1993c; Sussman and Lent 1991). The concentration in a few corporate hands of the main media of global mass communications is now well known and researched. These media, irrespective of their varying forms, are mainly dedicated to selling products (see, for example, Mattelart 1991; Schiller 1989).

While some social scientists have been aware of globalization for many years past, it is only quite recently that the idea has begun to creep towards the centre of the stage. Here, I shall elaborate one conception of the global, while acknowledging that there are others with many interesting and challenging things to say.[3]

SOCIOLOGY OF THE GLOBAL SYSTEM

The conception of the *global* elaborated here, while not ignoring the nation-state, offers in addition a conception of the global system based on *transnational practices*. Transnational practices are analytically distinguished in three spheres, economic, political and culture-ideology. In the concrete conditions of the world as it is today, a world largely structured by global capitalism in its various guises, each of these practices is typically, but not exclusively, characterized by a major institutional form. The transnational corporation is the major locus of economic transnational practices; the transnational capitalist class is the major locus of political transnational practices; and the major locus of transnational cultural-ideological practices is to be found in the culture-ideology of consumerism. (This framework is more fully elaborated in Sklair 1991, 1993c).

TNCs AND CAPITALIST 'DEVELOPMENT'

This is not the place to recapitulate in any detail the long and continuing debate over import substitution and export orientation as competing or complementary strategies of capitalist 'development' (see Gereffi and Wyman 1990). Suffice it to say that in recent decades one Third World country after another, under pressure from the World Bank, IMF, USAID and the most influential sectors of the transnational capitalist class, has adopted some form of what I have labelled 'export-led industrialization fuelled by foreign investment and technology' or ELIFFIT (Sklair 1993a). While much TNC investment in the Third World consists of well-established companies producing very much like domestic companies mainly for the local market, the emphasis since the 1960s has been on TNCs locating or relocating in the Third World to take advantage of local cheap labour for some form of export processing. Very few countries actually derive a very large proportion of their wealth from the export of manufactured goods, so ELIFFIT was often important more for its symbolic force than for its actual economic content. ELIFFIT is the way the globalizing TNCs relate to the Third World as the main 'development' strategy of the capitalist global system.

While the Third World has attracted only a small proportion of all the foreign investment that has ever taken place, the economies of many poor countries, and even some rich ones, are commonly said to be dominated by foreign capital and foreign TNCs. All of the *Fortune* 500 corporations do not have the relative economic impact on the United States, for example, that a few TNCs have had on particular Third World countries (Jenkins 1987). In research carried out to evaluate 'developmental' effects of foreign direct investment in export-oriented zones in Mexico and China (and in Egypt and Ireland) I have elaborated six criteria of 'development'. These criteria can also serve as a substantive methodology to evaluate the role of TNC investment in the Third World in general and serve as a rough guide to its overall development effects.

Criteria for the development effects of TNC investment

1 *Linkages:* linkages are the share of imports (backward) and the share of exports (forward) of TNC production that come from and go to the host economy. In general, the greater the extent of backward linkages (raw materials, components, services) and forward linkages (sales to intermediate goods industries) achieved with the host economy, then the more likely is the creation of positive 'development' effects.

2 *Foreign currency earnings*: the more value added and the higher the proportion of foreign currency retained in the host economy then the more likely the creation of positive 'development' effects.

3 *Upgrading of personnel*: the smaller the proportion of expatriate to indigenous managers, technicians and highly trained personnel, the more likely is the creation of positive 'development' effects.

4 *Technology transfer*: the greater the degree of genuine technology transfer (in contrast to mere 'technology relocation'), the more likely is the creation of positive 'development' effects.

5 *Conditions of work*: the more favourable the day-to-day conditions of work are for the labour force (wages, job security, hours, workplace facilities) in relation to prevailing conditions in the rest of the host society, the more likely is the creation of positive 'development' effects.

6 *Environment*: the more benign the environmental effects are for the workers and communities in which the TNCs are operating then the more likely is the creation of positive 'development' effects.[4]

The following discussion of each of these criteria, brief as it is, suggests that even in its own terms of export-oriented industrialization, the successes of the global capitalist project of 'development' are rather limited.

The six criteria evaluated

Linkages

Backward linkages, with very few exceptions, are very meagre in the Third World industries dominated by foreign TNCs. For example, the *maquilas* in Mexico purchase only around 2 per cent of their total inputs in Mexico, and so the *maquila* factories make almost no contribution to the growth of local industry, or indeed industry anywhere in Mexico. While there are some countries and industries with better records than this, they are atypical. The main exceptions are natural resource-based industries and the automobile industry, where local content requirements appear to create substantial backward linkages. But this is often illusory as auto-parts suppliers tend to be either affiliated with the major TNCs or locked into unequal commercial relations with them.[5] This is a particularly important issue as just-in-time inventory controls are introduced into globally competitive industries. As I have argued elsewhere (1993a: 199–202), the logic of transnational production either *forbids*, *permits* or *encourages* backward linkages. The reason why TNCs generally do not buy Third World components and materials is that they already have well-developed systems of procurement, either in-house or through subcontracting arrangements. Where no local producers will produce what is needed or where there is no access to the necessary technology, the logic of transnational production *forbids* backward linkages. As long as this situation prevails, there is little opportunity for any significant breakthroughs on a global scale by local producers in this extremely lucrative market for components and high-tech materials.

However, some Third World producers, especially in the NICs, do match and even better First World suppliers in terms of price, quality and delivery, often in business with TNCs from their own countries (see Lall 1983). In these cases, where TNCs are tempted to switch suppliers, usually for cost and logistical reasons, backward linkages are clearly *permitted*. But again, even where this does occur, local producers are usually locked into unequal commercial relationships with the TNCs. Simply put, the TNC normally has many options for buying components, while the local producers normally have few if any other customers for what they produce. An extension of this is where, under special conditions, TNCs actively *encourage* local producers to supply them or bring their own subcontractors with them when they open plants abroad.[6]

As far as forward linkages are concerned we can recall the history and practice of the import substitution path to industrialization (Hewitt, Johnson and Wield 1992). In general, TNCs will not willingly sell on components to independent local manufacturers where the products of these manufac- turers compete with TNC products in local markets. There is, however, plenty of scope for joint ventures and other forms of business alliances, but the TNC will normally retain the upper hand, globally and locally.

It is, therefore, important to look behind the crude numbers on linkages, to evaluate properly their potential for local development in global production.[7] The argument on linkages is not necessarily zero sum in the sense that although there is great competition in the Third World for TNC investment and sourcing and one location's gain is sometimes another location's loss, the general trend in the medium term is probably upward.[8] The point, however, is that the relative increase in value added that accrues in the Third World from sales of locally produced materials and components is far less than the increase in TNC economic activity as a whole. So, there is little potential for massive backward or forward linkages in the short or medium term. If this argument is correct, then there are strictly limited development prospects through linkages for the export-oriented capitalist 'development' strategy.

Foreign currency

Foreign currency earnings from TNC investment derive from two main sources: TNC purchases of local inputs; and hard currency exchanged to pay wages and salaries. The bonanza in foreign currency earnings that hopeful policy-makers predicted from TNC purchases of local materials and components, backward linkages, has not generally materialized, as indicated in the previous section, though local utility and other charges are often a good source of revenue.

What of wages and salaries? The main problem here is leakage of hard currency back to the TNCs, as employees spend their money on imported goods and services. When TNCs enter Third World countries they bring not only new factories and jobs and techniques but also new consumption needs which they are best placed to satisfy. (I return to this key issue in the section on 'Culture-ideology of consumerism' below).

The opening-up of many countries traditionally restrictive on TNC investment is likely to have considerable, if unpredictable, effects on patterns of consumer spending and foreign currency retention in the Third World (see United Nations 1988). Local retailers, with lower overheads, might benefit from freer entry of First World consumer goods and, ultimately, local consumers might enjoy lower prices as a result. The economic and social policies of most Third World governments in recent years, however, tended to widen rather than narrow the gaps in consumption between rich and poor.

The prospect of selling vast quantities of consumer goods in the Third World is an important part of the global capitalist project. As First World markets for many consumer goods become saturated (see, for example, Durning 1992: ch. 6, on cars) or consumer resistance of various types builds up against certain products, notably tobacco (see Nath 1986), TNCs are increasingly targeting Third World markets. Such practices tend to result in balance of payments crises and to intensify social inequalities as small minorities enjoy increasingly affluent life styles and the masses fall further and further behind.

Upgrading of personnel

TNCs have great incentives to employ local managers and technicians. In response to shortages of trained personnel, many TNCs have institutionalized contacts with universities, colleges and technical institutes. In general, the larger the plant size the greater the likelihood of training. The demand for local professional staff regularly outstrips the supply and salaries appear to have risen as a result.

TNC investment has had a substantial impact on upgrading of personnel in many Third World countries. In recent years, global initiatives like 'structural adjustment' and 'privatization' have increasingly 'opened up' Third World economies to global standards and practices, and the expanded influence of First World corporations, management schools, retailing, etc. deepen these processes. However, as small elite groups find new, lucrative and exciting career opportunities in and around the TNCs, the conditions of the masses have been visibly worsening as 'liberalization' facilitates the transnational practices of the TNCs.[9]

Technology transfer

The likelihood that technology relocation will result in genuine technology transfer is a conceptual as much as an empirical question and we must consider who, exactly, the technology is being transferred to when it goes to the Third World. This is a subject on which much has been written but many disagreements remain (see Hewitt and Wield 1992).

Some of the forces that lie behind this globalization epoch of capitalism – in particular the complex phenomena of the 'microelectronic revolution' and 'computer integrated manufacturing' – are already highly significant for the future of the TNCs in Third World industries and, indeed, industries all over the world. There is a substantial argument building up that new technologies will destroy the economic rationale for the new international division of labour and that as the labour component of total costs gets smaller and smaller then 'offshore' manufacturing will gradually disappear (discussed in Sklair 1993a: 255–8). The jury is still out on this issue.

Conditions of work

There has been a good deal written on the conditions of workers, especially women workers, in Third World TNC factories (see Lim 1985). Most of the research, it must be said, presents a rather negative picture of these conditions but there is agreement that most workers are glad to have the jobs even though the jobs themselves are far from ideal.

Four day-to-day conditions of work are particularly relevant in this connection: wages, job security, hours worked and workplace facilities.

Wages

There is no doubt that TNC workers in the Third World (and some salaried staff for that matter) are highly exploited compared with workers (and staff) in comparable First World factories. However, this is not necessarily the case if we compare TNC workers with workers in domestically owned industry. The methodology of such comparisons can be very uncertain: often there is no equivalent domestic industry to compare with the TNCs. It is unlikely that TNCs will have any substantial upward impact on wages in the short term for factories in the Third World will rely on their labour-cost advantages over those in the First World to survive and prosper. Former US Secretary of Labor, Ray Marshall, recently argued that under the North American Free Trade Agreement real wages in the United States would tend to fall (as they have been doing recently) towards the Mexican level rather than Mexican wages rise to US levels (in La Botz 1992: Introduction). This looks like rather a plausible proposition for the global system as a whole in the forseeable future.

172

Job security

Job security is an issue precisely because TNCs have not shaken off the image of 'runaway plants'. While there is evidence to justify this label from some parts of the world, in the long term it is unlikely that TNCs close down their plants in the Third World more than those anywhere else. To the recently redundant US or British or even Japanese car or apparel or electronics worker, industries would appear to be running away from the First World, not the Third World.

As the onslaught against trade unions gathered pace in the 1980s, often led by TNCs operating in First World countries, it became even more difficult to argue that TNC workers in the Third World were especially insecure in their jobs. In fact, few workers anywhere are particularly secure.

Hours of work

While global data on hours worked per week in TNCs is largely unavailable, it is probable that workers in indigenous firms, particularly small family-run businesses, work much longer hours than TNC workers. However, there is evidence that women shop-floor workers have been exploited in terms of being forced to work very long hours and/or compulsory overtime, especially in some export zones.[10]

Workplace facilities

Safety provisions, childcare, subsidized meals, recreation, etc. tend to be a function of plant size and sector rather than ownership. The number of studies documenting health hazards for TNC industrial workers in the Third World is growing rapidly (see Women Working Worldwide 1991, on this and related issues).

The central focus of recent analysis of the TNCs is on the wider environmental questions. In recognition of this relatively new phenomenon – that is the *visibility* as well as the actuality of TNCs as harbingers of hazardous and environmentally destructive industries – the following section will deal specifically with environmental issues.

Environment

TNCs are by no means the only source of environmental hazards in the Third World, but they have been targeted for serious and at times ferocious criticisms from their opponents. The tremendous growth of electronics assembly in the Third World suggests that the well-documented hazards of such activities for First World workers and their communities, are likely wherever they are located. Electronics is not, of course, the only industry

173

which raises health, safety and environmental problems. In his detailed study of a variety of polluting and hazardous industries, Leonard (1988) argues that neither the 'industrial flight' hypothesis (that polluting industries tend to migrate from First to Third World locations) nor the 'pollution haven' hypothesis (that Third World governments encourage them to relocate) is entirely supported by the available evidence, though many would disagree.[11]

In recent years many Third World governments have promulgated new and progressive environmental laws. However, sufficient resources are never available to permit the responsible agencies to carry out and enforce all the excellent environmental improvements that these laws dictated. Nevertheless, the increasing visibility of the TNCs in the Third World and the global environmentalist challenges to environmental irresponsibility (crystallized in the UNCED 'Earth Summit' in Rio in 1992) brought environmental issues on to the trade and production agenda in the 1990s.

There is little doubt that some TNCs have established factories in the Third World in order to escape strict First World environmental regulations, including expensive toxic-waste regulations (see Pearson 1987, for several excellent case studies). Electronic assemblers, furniture manufacturers and other industries from the United States have certainly established factories in Mexico to escape US environmental legislation, or rather its enforcement (Sklair 1993a: ch. 11).

The final balance sheet on the six criteria of development is not conclusive. The (usually unspoken) assumption on which most of the pro-capitalist case has rested is that TNCs will inevitably bring increased prosperity for all involved. The evidence appears to suggest, however, that although the TNCs have sometimes made substantial profits from their Third World operations, the overall development effects have been less than outstanding, even in terms of that (distorted) form of 'development' that they sought to create.

THE TRANSNATIONAL CAPITALIST CLASS IN THE THIRD WORLD

In my formulation, the transnational capitalist class (TCC) includes the following groups of people.

1 TNC executives and their local affiliates;
2 globalizing state bureaucrats;
3 capitalist-inspired politicians and professionals;
4 consumerist elites (merchants, media).

This class sees its mission as organizing the conditions under which the interests of its various fractions and the interests of the system as a whole (which do not always coincide) can be furthered within the context of particular countries and communities. This implies that there is one central *transnational* capitalist class that makes system-wide decisions, and that it connects with the TCC in each community, region, country, etc. There is, thus, plenty of scope for interesting research on the global features of this class and its fractions in particular localities.

TNC executives and their local affiliates

TNC executives and their local affiliates provide the backbone of the TCC. There is a vast literature on the TNCs and those who run them (for a very brief guide see Sklair 1991: 43–51). The business press dealing with TNC executives and their local affiliates now covers virtually every country in the world.[12] What Barnet and Muller (1974), in their still useful survey, called the 'global reach' of the multinational corporations is plain for all to see. However, in this huge literature there is surprisingly little substantive work on the transnationalization of TNC executives. Such research is needed to ascertain the extent to which (if at all) TNC executives and their local affiliates can be considered members of a transnational capitalist class.[13]

One interesting and significant aspect of this issue is that, while expatriate TNC top executives are still very common, increasingly they are being replaced by indigenous or third-country executives in overseas plants and operations, particularly in TNCs originating from the United States (Kobrin 1988). Indeed, the concept of the 'transnational capitalist class' implies that as TNCs are transformed from multinational (or multi-domestic) to become more genuinely transnational (global) corporations, the formal nationality of their executives matters less and less. The corporation socializes its executives into a global worldview as a result of persuading them of the necessity for a corporate global strategy. The 'corporation' needs global visionaries to start the ball rolling (see Maisonrouge 1988) and the international business press regularly features such people. While they are mainly male, North American or Western European or Japanese, the number of other 'types' is increasing.

Globalizing state bureaucrats

Globalizing state bureaucrats provide the politico-legal framework within which the TNCs are encouraged to operate. In most Third World countries there is an ongoing struggle between the economic nationalists and these globalizing state bureaucrats. While the TNCs are generally on the side of the latter this is by no means always the case as TNCs that have long-established positions in specific markets in the Third World have supported local economic nationalists to protect their own local interests (Evans 1979;

Jenkins 1987). However, global system theory predicts that as multinational give way to transnational (global) corporate strategies this will become less common. Most TNCs will ally themselves more or less wholeheartedly with the globalizing state bureaucrats against the economic nationalists and the globalizing state bureaucrats will forge closer and more extensive alliances with the TNCs.

Globalizing state bureaucrats must be seen in the context of the histories of many Third World countries characterized by protectionism, high degrees of import substitution and open hostility between government and business.[14] A central and testable consequence of global system theory is that the balance of power in many countries swung decisively from domestically oriented and internally directed to globally oriented and externally directed bureaucrats in the 1980s and will continue to do so. This was (and is) largely a result of 'structural adjustment' and concomitant export-oriented industrialization 'development' strategies. The theory predicts that in the absence of significant political change in the First World, exceptions to this rule will be few and short lived, or marginalized.

The 'foreign investment promotion' bureaucrats in cities all over the Third World have come into their own in recent decades as the economic success of export-oriented TNC-dominated industries began to show (sometimes in reality, sometimes in illusion) that competitiveness in global industries was possible in some countries outside the First World, notably in the NICs. It would be an exaggeration to suggest that the success of the export-oriented zones played a major role in the victory of the 'globalizing state bureaucrats' but when that victory was on the way, the zone bureaucrats were enthusiastic allies for the 'globalizers' in the central cities.

Capitalist-inspired politicians and professionals

Capitalist-inspired politicians and professionals make up the third fraction of the transnational capitalist class. The capitalist-inspired politicians are to be found in increasing numbers in the ruling parties all over the Third World and also in many even more 'globalizing' business-oriented opposition parties. Not all of these people are wholehearted globalizers, but advancement in such parties appears to depend more and more on toeing the line on the central issues of economic policy and the political and cultural-ideological consequences of it.

Similarly, capitalist-inspired professionals (lawyers, journalists, consultants, academics, etc.), in so far as they serve the global interests of capital, find for themselves places in the transnational capitalist class. Direct and indirect TNC employment offers attractive and well-paid employment to professionals in the Third World, whose numbers far exceed the demand for their services.

Consumerist elites

Finally, consumerist elites, merchants and those involved in media promotion of consumerism, free-market capitalism, 'modernization' in the image of First World life styles and consumption patterns, play a key role in the transnational capitalist class. I return to them in the next section.

These, then, are the component parts of the TCC. If my analysis is correct, traditional ruling classes all over the Third World are being transformed in these directions as a consequence of the changing nature of their gradual (sometimes precipitous) but inexorable insertion into the global capitalist system.[15] But every ruling class requires subordinate classes to rule. All over the Third World transnational and local industries are beginning to replace or transform the underclasses that were created by economies based on land, cattle and mines, some of which were themselves brought into being by TNCs. Industrial proletariats and quasi-industrial peasantries are being created by forces that respond not only to national development strategies but to global processes whose practical consequences are being constantly negotiated and renegotiated by local and global actors. While transnational capitalist classes dominate the system, they are not unopposed. Social movements of many kinds challenge them economically and politically in the workplace, in the domestic sphere, in places of worship and of leisure, on the streets, on street corners and in the fields. This much is well documented and thoroughly researched and needs to be constantly opposed dialectically to capitalist and neo-imperialist hegemony in theory and practice. However, at the level of culture and ideology (as Dhaouadi argues, Chapter 8 this volume) there has been less systematic research.[16] There are many plausible reasons why this should be the case, historically, but here I want to focus on what I consider to be the fundamental reason why it is the case today. Put simply, my thesis is that what I term capitalism's 'culture-ideology of consumerism' has, as yet, no serious opposition as the global value system.

THE CULTURE-IDEOLOGY OF CONSUMERISM IN THE THIRD WORLD

The concept of the culture-ideology of consumerism attempts to narrow and change the focus of 'cultural and media imperialism' research by prioritizing the exceptional place of consumption and consumerism in contemporary capitalism. Within the global system perspective, the four fractions of the transnational capitalist class all make vital contributions to the creation, sustenance and dissemination of the culture-ideology of consumerism.

A working definition of *culture-ideology of consumerism* is

A coherent set of practices, attitudes and values, based on advertising and the mass media but permeating the whole social structure, that encourages ever-expanding consumption of consumer goods and services.

(See Sklair 1991: *passim*)

Of course, not all culture is ideological. The elision of *culture-ideology* signals a specific set of practices in contemporary capitalism, namely the institutionalization of consumerism through the commodification of culture. Culture always has ideological functions for consumerism in capitalist societies, so all cultural practices in this sphere are at the same time ideological practices. Although most people would probably agree that something like a culture-ideology of consumerism is indeed established in the advanced industrial societies and in the process of formation in much of the rest of the world, a great deal of research on the question still needs to be done. Belk's argument on 'Third World consumer culture' provides a useful benchmark. He writes: 'quite unlike the evolution of consumption patterns in Europe and North America, Third World consumers are often attracted to and indulge in aspects of conspicuous consumption before they have secured adequate food, clothing, and shelter' (1988: 103–4).

The effect of the 'culture-ideology of consumerism' is to increase the range of consumption expectations and aspirations without necessarily ensuring the income to buy. At its present stage of 'development', capitalism is built on the promise that a more direct integration of local with global capitalism will lead to a better life for everyone. This has certainly been the case for most (but by no means all) people in the countries of the capitalist core, but it remains to be seen whether the goods can be delivered elsewhere. The extent to which economic, political and environmental constraints on the private accumulation of capital challenge the global capitalist project in general and its culture-ideology of consumerism, in particular, is a central issue for the global system approach to globalization.

Systematic research on global patterns of consumption and consumerism is well under way[17] and there are good prospects that this sphere, which has traditionally been rather neglected by development scholars, is finding its place in the field (see Wilk 1990). My contention here is that, while state-centrist studies of consumption and consumerism in individual countries will certainly yield useful data, theoretical progress necessitates a global approach.

An illustration of this is what may be termed the 'marginalization of local practices' hypothesis, namely that as the transnational practices of the global capitalist system become increasingly hegemonic, *then only those local (i.e. non-transnational) practices that do not threaten the global capitalist project are tolerated.* The hypothesis predicts that where local practices challenge the global capitalist system, they are either:

1 increasingly commercialized and incorporated into the system (e.g. the 'amateur' Olympics, 'hippy' culture); or

2 marginalized into obscurity (e.g. anti-consumerist environmentalism, communal forms of living); or
3 if neither of these strategies works, then global capitalism will attempt to destroy these local practices (e.g. anti-consumerist travelling people).

As will be clear by now, the culture ideology of consumerism occupies the centre ground of my analysis of globalization. The logic of this argument is clearly underconsumptionist. Capitalists in the twentieth century have the capacity to produce consumer goods at a historically unprecedented level, but capitalist relations of production tend to inhibit the level of consumption of these goods by the masses, particularly in the Third World. The cycles of boom and slump, on this view, are periods of high consumer spending followed by overproduction of goods which causes business failures, unemployment, a drop in consumer spending and, thus, underconsumption. While not wishing to become embroiled in the sometimes quite technical debate on underconsumptionism, overproductionism and the various crises of capitalism, I shall simply note that the point of the concept of the 'culture-ideology of consumerism' is precisely that, under capitalism, the masses cannot be relied upon to keep buying, obviously when they have neither spare cash nor access to credit, and less obviously when they do have spare cash and access to credit. The creation of a culture-ideology of consumerism, therefore, is bound up with the self-imposed necessity that capitalism must be ever expanding on a global scale. This expansion crucially depends on selling more and more goods and services to people whose 'basic needs' (a somewhat ideological term) have already been comfortably met as well as to those whose 'basic needs' are unmet.

This implies that the culture-ideology of consumerism serves different functions for different social groups and even for different communities. Clearly, the culture-ideology of consumerism is superfluous to an explanation of why people who are hungry or cold, eat or clothe themselves, while it does help to explain snacking or 'grazing' on food and drinks that are demonstrably unhealthy and why people go into debt to buy many sets of clothes. Even more challenging is the enigma of why poor people, in poor and rich countries, apparently defy economic rationality by purchasing relatively expensive global brands in order to forge some sense of identity with what we can only call in a rather crude sense 'symbols of modernity'.

DISTORTED 'DEVELOPMENT' AND DEVELOPMENT

The idea that capitalist 'development' is distorted will be seen by many as a rather evaluative (perhaps even emotive) claim. This chapter has tried to illustrate the ways in which capitalist 'development' is distorted. Economically, the benefits of export-oriented strategies (ELIFFIT) as measured by my six criteria, are only very weakly supported by the available evidence. While specific communities within a few Third World countries (the NICs) – though even here, as Bello and Rosenfeld (1990) show, there are many problems – have achieved some measure of 'development', it seems implausible that this experience could be reproduced on a global scale. Politically, it is unlikely that any system dominated by a transnational capitalist class will be able to deliver what is demanded by genuine development. And in the culture-ideology sphere, I am surely not alone in arguing that a system based on consumerism is bound to produce a distorted form of 'development'.

If this analysis is correct then we are left with at least two alternatives. First, while capitalist industrialization cannot succeed globally, perhaps some other form of industrialization can produce genuine development. This is my view. The second alternative is that industrialization (or 'development') is not the solution, but the problem. This is the view of a small but increasing number of theorists and practitioners (for example, contributors to the volume edited by Wolfgang Sachs in 1992). While I sympathize greatly with this point of view, I am largely unconvinced by its central arguments against industrial civilization and entirely unconvinced that a non- or anti-industrial society is likely to be more democratic and fair than an industrial one.

Nevertheless, the anti-development argument does have many strengths. Export-oriented industrialization, increasingly seen as necessary for capitalist (distorted) 'development', cannot work on a global scale. In its place some argue that a type of local needs-oriented industrialization is necessary for development. While vulnerable to the usual criticisms made of dependency theory, the work of such scholars as Thomas (1975) on appropriate industrialization for small Third World socialist countries, and Amin (1990) on the need to 'delink' in order for countries and communities to be able to set their own developmental agendas, repay close study.

Though export-oriented industrialization is not always TNC-led, it usually is. Where it is, I argue, it tends to produce distorted 'development'. Indigenous capitalist 'development' often has even worse consequences. In contrast, local producer-consumer led industrialization for development, organized around democratic relations of production (not some fictive bureaucratic state ownership on behalf of 'all the people') promises, in theory if not yet in practice, a more genuine form of development. There has been some important work done on this crucial issue, but discussion of this must be left for another occasion.[18]

In order to make the case for a different type of industrialization on a global scale the debate around 'sustainable development' has to be engaged, though not necessarily in the terms in which its major proponents dictate. As I argue elsewhere (1994) the radical thrust of 'sustainable development' has all but been blunted by an alliance between the transnational capitalist class and what I label the 'transnational environmentalist class', which has marginalized anti-capitalist and particularly anti-consumerist environmentalists.

The capitalist global project is based on a powerful vision of human needs, wants and nature, in particular moralistic views of greed (enterprise) and competition as the only reliable motivators of human effort. In this time of capitalist triumphalism, socialist alternatives, such as communitarian altruism and the force of moral and collective incentives over material and individual incentives, are said to have been 'tried but found wanting'. Despite the pathetic even if true appeals of anti-Stalinists of whatever variety that these alternatives have never genuinely been tried, it is indisputable that the verdict of recent history lays a heavy burden of proof on those who would replace capitalism. It is, after all, perfectly possible to answer the question: can capitalism develop the Third World? with the reply: no, but all the other alternatives are even worse.[19]

If we go back to basics, then we must recall Marx's insight that socialism cannot be built on scarcity, but only on plenty. While capitalism may be the only system that can produce plenty, theory and practice suggest that it cannot distribute it fairly on a global scale, that is, capitalism cannot develop the Third World.

CONCLUSION

The conclusion I am drawn to, stated rather crudely, is that as the culture-ideology of consumerism replaces local cultures and ideologies and as long as transnational corporations and transnational capitalist classes in the Third World can ensure that consumer goods and services are available to dominant groups in these communities, then the realities and illusions of capitalist 'development' will continue to appear to be the only global path to development.

One highly significant consequence of this is that radical demands for political reforms, particularly genuine 'democratization', will fail to attract mass support. My argument is that in 'reforming' societies it is not economic reforms that trigger off political change. On the contrary, it is the failure of economic reforms to satisfy consumer demands that triggers off mass movements based on the illusion that 'democratic' reforms and capitalist free markets will bring rapid improvements in standards and styles of living for everyone. On this view, the failure of capitalism (and communism) in the Third World is not so much the inability to cope with political aspirations, but the inability to offer any viable alternative to the culture-ideology of consumerism.[20]

NOTES

1 There are many versions of this, some explicitly rejecting 'industrialization' (Sachs 1992), some based on a strategy of 'delinking' from global capitalism (Amin 1990), some explicitly recommending capitalist industrialization as a necessary stage for the eventual transcendence of capitalism (Warren 1980). A brief account of my own version, 'democratic, feminist socialism', will be found in Sklair (1991: ch. 8). I would argue that major changes will have to come in the First World through a transition from social democracy to democratic socialism, before the rest of the world can embark on such a path, though social movements anywhere can accelerate this process.

2 There are several different conclusions drawn from this general thesis. The most influential currently appear to be those of the Japanese management guru Kenichi Ohmae, and Michael Porter, from the Harvard Business School. Ohmae (1990) presents a more genuinely 'globalist' vision than Porter (1990), whose analysis is more state-centrist.

3 For a discussion of these, see Sklair (1993b) and references therein. The recent rise of 'globalization' research, while naturally to some extent a creature of intellectual fashion, has much more to do with the changing nature of capitalism and the global role of the mass media.

4 See Sklair (1993a: chs 9 and 11) for extensive discussion of these criteria for the *maquila* (export-oriented in-bond) industry in Mexico. In the first edition (1989) of that book the sixth criterion was *distribution* (the more equitable the distribution of the costs and benefits between the foreign investors, the competing strata among the local populations and the host government, the more likely is the creation of positive 'development' effects). I have since come to appreciate the importance of environmental issues here, and to see that *distribution* is more adequately treated as the context within which these criteria operate than simply as one of the criteria.

5 A UN survey of 'Triad' (United States, European Community and Japan) foreign direct investment suggests that such relationships tend to cluster geographically to some extent and that Asian countries in the 'Japanese cluster' may do better on linkages than others (see United Nations 1991, especially ch. 3). As the contributors in Part II of this book document, very few Third World industries have made much progress on this.

6 Some Japanese *maquilas* in Mexico have brought their Asian suppliers with them, while some US *maquilas* have encouraged their suppliers to move to border locations, but usually on the US side of the border (see Sklair 1993a).

7 Research on commodity chains (see chapter 11, this volume and references therein) does precisely this in a very illuminating manner.

8 I am cautious on this point because, though production of goods and services continues to increase, I believe that the carrying capacity of the planet (in terms of resources and environmental damage) does place a limit on growth, eventually. The key question is the extent to which this eventuality is coped with by reductions in consumption by the rich or by the poor or both (see my 1994). This is the central issue that problematizes the very concept of *development* (see Sachs 1992).

9 While this is a rather blanket judgement on a very complex set of issues, a formidable array of research supports it. See, for example, Beneria and Feldman 1992; Ghai 1991; Woodward 1992.

10 There is a considerable literature on this. In addition to chapter 16 in this volume, see Women Working Worldwide (1991); Sklair (1991: 96–101, and 1993a: 167–80).

11 The magazine *Multinational Monitor* is an excellent source of information on this issue, as is Draffan (1993). I am grateful to Peter Robbins, who is doing a Ph.D. thesis at LSE on corporate responses to environmental challenges, for this reference.

12 A few examples will illustrate the point. In March 1993, the cover story in *Fortune International* concerned entrepreneurs and their transnational connections in the 'new' Vietnam; many new magazines for entrepreneurs are being published in China, the former Soviet Union and Africa; *Billion* magazine (published in Hong Kong) regularly features these people and their life styles. Latin America has a longer tradition of such publications.

13 The research of Zeitlin and Ratcliff (1988) is of great relevance here. In a much less systematic fashion I have begun to analyse the transnational capitalist class in the *maquilas* (1992). Alejandra Salas-Porras' forthcoming Ph.D. thesis from the LSE on the 'transnationalization of the Mexican capitalist class' promises to be a notable contribution to this literature.

14 See the volume edited by Gereffi and Wyman (1990), in which a variety of recent contributions to this debate are discussed; and the contributions of Tom Hewitt, Rhys Jenkins and Chris Edwards in Hewitt, Johnson and Wield (1992). I discuss the struggle between inner-oriented localizers and outward-oriented globalizers in Mexico in my (1993a) and in general in my (1991, especially: 117–26).

15 Notable contributions to the debate on 'ruling classes' in various parts of the Third World which, due to limitations of space, cannot be discussed here, include Becker *et al.* (1987), Evans (1979), Johnson (1984), Lubeck (1987), Shivji (1976) and Zeitlin and Ratcliff (1988).

16 This appears to be changing. See, for example, the 'subaltern studies' project of Guha and his colleagues (Guha 1982/9) and the emerging field of 'colonial discourse and post-colonial theory', well documented mainly for Africa and Asia in Williams and Chrisman (1993), and for Latin America in the 'Commentary and Debate Section' of *Latin American Research Review*, 28, 3 (1993).

17 In addition to the work of Belk cited above (Belk 1988), valuable information and useful analysis will be found in *Journal of International Consumer Marketing, Advances in International Marketing, Annals of Tourism Research, International Journal of Advertising*, and *Journal of Consumer Research*. Durning (1992) provides a wealth of examples and references.

18 I have in mind, for example, 'Critique of the Gotha Programme' of 1875 (Marx 1958) and Greater London Council (1985). As I note in the 'Preface' to this volume, the focus here is on capitalist development, not on the alternatives.

19 Compare W. Churchill's aphorism that democracy is the worst political system, except for all the others.

20 This chapter borrows and updates material from my *Sociology of the Global System* (1991) and *Assembling for Development*, 2nd edn (1993).

REFERENCES

Amin, S. (1990) *Delinking: Towards a Polycentric World*, London: Zed Press.

Barnet, R. and Muller, R. (1974) *Global Reach: The Power of the Multinational Corporations*, New York: Simon and Schuster.

Becker, D., Frieden, J., Schatz, S. and Sklar, R. (1987) *Postimperialism. International Capitalism and Development in the Late Twentieth Century*, Boulder CO: Lynne Rienner.

Belk, R. (1988) 'Third World consumer culture', *Research in Marketing,* Supplement 4: 103–27.

Bello, W. and Rosenfeld, S. (1990) *Dragons in Distress. Asia's Miracle Economies in Crisis,* San Francisco: The Institute for Food and Development Policy.

Beneria, L. and Feldman, S. (eds) (1992) *Unequal Burden: Economic Crises, Persistant Poverty and Women's Work,* Boulder CO: Westview.

Chi Huang (1989) 'The state and foreign investment: the cases of Taiwan and Singapore', *Comparative Political Studies,* 22, April: 93–121.

Draffan, G. (1993) *Wasting the Earth: A Directory of Multinational Corporate Activities,* Seattle: Institute on Trade Policy Task Force on Multinational Corporations.

Durning, A. (1992) *How Much is Enough? The Consumer Society and the Future of the Earth,* London: Earthscan.

Evans, P. (1979) *Dependent Development. The Alliance of Multinational, State and Local Capital in Brazil,* Princeton: Princeton University Press.

Featherstone, M. (ed.) (1990) *Global Culture: Nationalism, Globalization and Modernity,* London: Sage.

Gereffi, G. and Wyman, D. (eds) (1990) *Manufacturing Miracles: Development Strategies in Latin America and East Asia,* Princeton: Princeton University Press.

Ghai, D. (ed.) (1991) *The IMF and the South: The Social Impact of Crisis and Adjustment,* London: Zed Press.

Greater London Council (1985) *The London Industrial Strategy,* London: GLC.

Guha, R. (ed.) (1982/9) *Subaltern Studies: Writings on South Asian History and Society,* 6 vols, Delhi: Oxford University Press.

Gwynne, R. (1990) *New Horizons? Third World Industrialization in an International Perspective,* London: Longman.

Hewitt, T. and Wield, D. (1992) 'Technology and industrialization' in Hewitt, Johnson and Wield 1992.

Hewitt, T., Johnson, H. and Wield, D. (eds) (1992) *Industrialization and Development,* Oxford: Oxford University Press/Open University.

Jenkins, R. (1987) *Transnational Corporations and Uneven Development,* London: Methuen.

Johnson, D. (ed.) (1984) *Middle Classes in Dependent Countries,* Beverley Hills: Sage.

Kim, E.M. (1989/90) 'Foreign capital in Korea's economic development, 1960–1985', *Studies in Comparative International Development,* 24, Winter: 24–45.

Kobrin, S. (1988) 'Expatriate reduction and strategic control in American multinational corporations', *Human Resource Management,* 27, Spring: 63–75.

La Botz, D. (1992) *Mask of Democracy: Labour Suppression in Mexico Today,* Boston: South End Press.

Lall, S. (ed.) (1983) *The New Multinationals: The Spread of Third World Enterprises,* Chichester: Wiley.

Leonard, H. J. (1988) *Pollution and the Struggle for the World Product,* Cambridge: Cambridge University Press.

Lim, L. (1985) *Women Workers in Multinational Enterprises in Developing Countries,* Geneva: International Labour Organization.

Lubeck, P. (ed.) (1987) *The African Bourgeoisie. Capitalist Development in Nigeria, Kenya, and the Ivory Coast,* Boulder CO: Lynne Rienner.

Maisonrouge, J. (1988) *Inside IBM: A European's Story,* trans. Nina Rootes, London: Collins.

Marx, K. (1958) 'Critique of the Gotha Programme', in K. Marx and F. Engels *Selected Works,* vol. 2, Moscow: Foreign Languages Publishing House.

Mattelart, A. (1991) *Advertising International: The Privatisation of Public Space,* trans. M. Chanan, London: Routledge.

184

Nath, U. R. (1986) *Smoking: Third World Alert*, Oxford: Oxford University Press.

Ohmae, K. (1990) *The Borderless World*, London: Collins.

Pearson, C. (ed.) (1987) *Multinational Corporations, Environment, and the Third World*, Durham NC: Duke University Press.

Porter, M. (1990) *The Competitive Advantage of Nations*, New York: Free Press.

Sachs, W. (ed.) (1992) *The Development Dictionary*, London: Zed Press.

Schiller, H. (1989) *Culture, Inc.: The Corporate Takeover of Public Expression*, Oxford: Oxford University Press.

Shivji, I. (1976) *Class Struggles in Tanzania*, New York: Monthly Review Press.

Sklair, L. (1991) *Sociology of the Global System*, London: Harvester and Baltimore: Johns Hopkins University Press.

—— (1992) 'The Maquilas in Mexico: a global perspective', *Bulletin of Latin American Research* 11: 91–107.

—— (1993a) *Assembling for Development: The Maquila Industry in Mexico and the United States*, 2nd updated edn, San Diego: University of California, Center for U.S.–Mexican Studies.

—— (1993b) 'Going global: competing models of globalization', *Sociology Review* 3, 2: 7–10.

—— (1993c) 'Consumerism drives the global mass media system', *Media Development* XL, 2: 36–40.

—— (1994) 'Global sociology and global environmental change', in M. Redclift and T. Benton (eds) *Social Theory and Global Environment*, London: Routledge.

Sussman, G. and Lent, J. (eds) (1991) *Transnational Communications: Wiring the Third World*, London: Sage.

Thomas, C. (1975) *Dependence and Transformation*, New York: Monthly Review Press.

UNESCO (1989) *World Communication Report*, Paris: UNESCO.

United Nations (1988) *Transnational Corporations in World Development*, New York: UN Centre on Transnational Corporations.

—— (1991) *World Investment Report 1991: The Triad in Foreign Direct Investment*, New York: UN Centre on Transnational Corporations.

Warren, B. (1980) *Imperialism: Pioneer of Capitalism*, London: New Left Books.

Wilk, R. (1990) 'Consumer goods as dialogue about development', *Culture and History* 7: 79–100.

Williams, P. and Chrisman, L. (eds) (1993) *Colonial Discourse and Post-Colonial Theory: A Reader*, London: Harvester.

Women Working Worldwide (ed.) (1991) *Common Interests: Women Organizing in Global Electronics*, London: WWW.

Woodward, D. (1992) *Debt, Adjustment, and Poverty in Developing Countries*, 2 vols, London: Pinter.

World Bank (1993) *World Development Report*, New York: Oxford University Press.

Zeitlin, M. and Ratcliff, J. (1988) *Landlords and Capitalists: The Dominant Class in Chile*, Princeton: Princeton University Press.

Part II

SECTORAL STUDIES

10

UNEVEN DEVELOPMENT AND THE TEXTILES AND CLOTHING INDUSTRY

Diane Elson

INTRODUCTION

The production, distribution and consumption of textiles and clothing has epitomized the uneven development of the world economy since the very beginning of industrial capitalism in the eighteenth century, when the high-quality, handicraft-based, Indian textile industry was destroyed by the out-put of Lancashire's mills. In its turn Lancashire gave way to the United States, Germany and Japan; while today South Korea, Taiwan, Hong Kong and, latterly, China, challenge the older established locations.

The unevenness of development in the industry is not, however, simply geographical. The industry has also been characterized by technological unevenness, and by uneven development of ways of utilizing labour. At different times technological advance has been concentrated at certain points in the production process, where productivity has surged ahead, leaving bottlenecks in lagging sectors. The industry has always been char-acterized by a multiplicity of ways of utilizing labour, from huge mills employing thousands, to medium-sized family-run firms, to tiny sweat-shops, to individual outworkers (usually women) toiling in their own homes. Even within the huge mills, different segments of the workforce have typically had different types of labour contract, with some workers (typically adult males) being recognized as highly skilled and enjoying considerably greater rewards and job security than those (typically women and juveniles) categorized as semi- and unskilled. Labour flexibility, in the sense of the ability to adjust rapidly the size of the labour force, the wage bill, and the hours of work to changing conditions, is nothing new in this industry. Nor is the interconnection of firms through complex chains of subcontracting.

In addition, the international development of the industry has always been regulated in various ways by the state, from the banning of imports of chintz from India in eighteenth-century Britain to today's Multi-Fibre

Arrangement (MFA) which controls imports into developed countries from developing countries; and forms of labour utilization have also always been shaped by state policy, from the Poor Law of nineteenth-century Britain to the export processing zones of today's developing countries.

In this chapter we will examine some key features of the global capitalist textiles and clothing industry in the late twentieth century and consider the impact of this form of industrial capital on the countries of Asia, Africa and Latin America. We shall not examine the industry in Russia and Eastern Europe, as it is too soon to say how the collapse of central planning and the entry of these countries into the international capitalist market will affect the textiles and clothing sector.

The basic question with which we are concerned is the extent to which the textile and clothing industry has contributed toward the development of what we used to call the Third World, but what in the absence of a Second World, might more appropriately be called the South. This is a complex question because development is multidimensional and the countries of the South are heterogeneous. The first point to consider is the extent to which there is a modern power-machinery based textiles and clothing industry in developing countries; and the extent to which it is competitive with that based in developed countries. The second point concerns the organization of the industry – it may be located in developing countries, but to what extent do citizens of developing countries own and control it? The third point is the question of the benefits which this industry confers on those who work in it in developing countries. How significant is it as a source of employment? How do wages and working conditions compare with those in other industries in developing countries and with textile and garment workers in developed countries? How far does it contribute to increasing the capabilities of people in developing countries to undertake skilled work and make technical innovations? Finally, we need to consider the extent to which this industry has contributed to and can contribute in the future to the development of a wide range of developing countries. Can other developing countries expect to follow the path pioneered by the newly industrializing countries? Or will the way be blocked?

THE GLOBAL DISTRIBUTION OF TEXTILES AND CLOTHING PRODUCTION AND EXPORTS

Since the late 1970s there has been a substantial increase in the proportion of global production of textiles and clothing located in the South, as reported in official statistics.[1] The United Nations Industrial Development Organisation (UNIDO) has estimated that the share of the South in world output of textiles increased from 18.6 per cent in 1975 to 26.1 per cent in 1990, and expects this to reach 31.6 per cent in 1993 (UNIDO 1991: table

1.2). In clothing there has been a similar shift with the share of the South in world output estimated at 11.7 per cent in 1970 and 20.4 per cent in 1990 and predicted to be 25.9 per cent in 1993 (UNIDO 1991: table 1.2).

This shift is not simply a matter of the increasing importance of the South as a location for low-tech production. There has been a substantial expansion of capacity in the South in synthetic fibres: in 1992 the South accounted for over half the world's installed capacity for production of non-cellulosic fibres (UNIDO 1992: table V.5.6). There has been considerable diffusion of new technology in weaving to the South, especially to the Asian newly industrializing countries (NICs) where shuttleless looms accounted for about 81 per cent of weaving capacity in 1990, a greater share than in Western Europe, where the figure was about 75 per cent (Jenkins 1993: 45). In clothing, computer-aided design and cutting systems are being introduced in some of the Asian NICs (Jenkins 1993: 6). However, it is true that outside the Asian NICs the use of the latest technology remains limited, with diffusion in Latin America limited by the debt-related economic crises of the 1980s. Moreover, the production of textile machinery and computer-controlled systems remains dominated by Western Europe, Japan and the United States.

As well as an increasing share of world production of textiles and clothing being located in the South, an increasing share of world exports comes from the South, despite the restrictions imposed by the MFA. The share of the South in world exports of textiles increased in the 1980s from 22 per cent to over 25 per cent in 1989 (GATT 1991: table IV.4.5). In clothing, the share of the South is larger, amounting to over 40 per cent in 1991 (GATT 1991: table IV.5.1.).

However, although textiles and clothing production is widely distributed among a large number of developing countries, exports from the South remain concentrated among a relatively small number of countries. Table 10.1 shows the world's leading textiles-exporting countries in 1989, and table 10.2 shows the world's leading clothing-exporting countries in 1989.

It is apparent that it is only the East Asian countries (China, Hong Kong, Taiwan and South Korea) which are really challenging the dominance of the developed capitalist economies in the international market. By 1989 some of the developed capitalist economies had substantial balance of trade deficits in textiles (e.g. Australia, Canada, France, United Kingdom, United States) and clothing (e.g. Belgium, Canada, France, Germany, Japan, Netherlands, Sweden, Switzerland, United Kingdom, United States) while the East Asian countries generally recorded substantial surpluses (Dicken 1992: 239, 243).

Exports from developing countries would have been higher had it not been for trade restrictions operated by most of the developed countries. Trade in textiles and clothing between developed and developing countries is regulated by the Multi-Fibre Arrangement which was introduced in 1974.

Table 10.1 The world's leading textiles-exporting countries, 1989

Rank	Exporter	Share of world textiles exports (%)		Average annual growth (%)		
		1980	1989	1980–8	1989	1989
1	West Germany	11.5	11.5	6.5	9.0	5.0
2	Italy	7.5	8.0	7.5	2.5	6.5
3	Hong Kong[a]	3.0	7.5	17.5	12.5	19.0
4	China	4.5	7.0	12.0	11.5	8.5
5	Japan	9.0	5.5	1.0	−1.5	0.0
6	Taiwan	3.0	5.5	12.5	11.0	19.5
7	South Korea	4.0	5.5	10.5	19.0	11.0
8	Belgium–Luxembourg	6.5	5.5	4.5	8.0	6.5
9	France	6.0	5.0	4.0	9.5	7.5
10	United States	7.0	4.5	0.5	24.5	12.0
11	United Kingdom	5.5	3.5	1.5	14.0	4.5
12	Netherlands	4.0	2.5	4.0	4.0	21.5
13	Switzerland	2.5	2.0	4.5	3.5	3.5
14	Pakistan	1.5	2.0	9.5	−2.5	13.0
15	India[b]	2.0	2.0	5.5	14.5	—
	Above 15 countries	77.5	77.5			

Source: Dicken (1992: 238)

Notes: (a) Includes substantial re-exports; (b) 1978; a dash indicates no data available

The MFA permits developed countries to impose quotas which limit the quantity of specified textiles and clothing exports which specified developing countries can make to them.[2] Only Japan does not take advantage of this.

The MFA has had a particularly restrictive effect on imports into Europe, while at the same time trade barriers between European countries have been largely removed. The outcome has been a regionalization of European trade in textiles and clothing and an expansion of output from relatively high cost producers such as Germany (Moore 1991). About 80 per cent of exports of textiles and clothing from European countries are to other European countries; and about 79 per cent of textile imports into Europe, and 62 per cent of clothing imports, are supplied by other European countries. The situation is rather different in the United States, where 50 per cent of imports of textiles and 87 per cent of imports of clothing come

Table 10.2 The world's leading clothing-exporting countries, 1989

Rank	Exporter	Share of world clothing exports (%)		Average annual growth (%)		
		1980	1989	1980–8	1988	1989
1	Hong Kong[a]	12.0	14.5	11.5	10.0	18.5
2	Italy	11.0	9.5	9.0	1.0	4.0
3	South Korea	7.0	9.5	14.5	17.5	4.5
4	China	4.0	6.5	14.0	30.0	26.0
5	West Germany	7.0	5.5	8.0	7.5	5.0
6	Taiwan	6.0	5.0	8.5	−5.5	0.5
7	France	5.5	3.5	4.5	8.0	10.0
8	Turkey	0.5	3.0	43.5	7.0	18.0
9	Portugal	1.5	2.5	17.5	11.5	12.5
10	United Kingdom	4.5	2.5	3.5	7.5	−6.0
11	Thailand	0.5	2.5	27.0	21.5	28.0
12	United States	3.0	2.5	3.5	36.0	34.5
13	India	1.5	2.0	13.0	7.5	24.5
14	Netherlands	2.0	1.5	7.0	9.5	4.0
15	Greece	1.0	1.5	15.0	−16.5	22.5
Above 15 countries		67.0	72.0			

Source: Dicken (1992: 242)

Note: (a) Includes substantial re-exports

from developing countries (Moore 1991: 158).[3] If it were not for the MFA, there would almost certainly be more exports of cotton cloth and of standard items of clothing such as T-shirts, men's shirts, trousers and knitted sweaters to Europe from developing countries.

It has been suggested that underlying the global shifts in production and trade is a typical sequence of textile and clothing development through which countries have tended to pass. Dicken (1992) suggests this sequence may be pictured in terms of six stages, which are shown in table 10.3. This table is informative but, as Dicken cautions, like all sequential models, 'it should not be regarded necessarily as being predictive of what will happen in the future'. In particular, we must beware of assuming that large numbers of other developing countries will achieve the break-through in exports achieved by Hong Kong, South Korea and Taiwan. This is a question that will be considered in more detail in the last section of this chapter.

Table 10.3 A sequence of development in the textiles and clothing industries

	Type of production	Trade characteristics	Examples of countries
Stage 1	Simple fabrics and garments manufactured from natural fibres	Production oriented to domestic market. Net importers of fibre, fabric and clothing	Least developed
Stage 2	Production of clothing for export. Mostly standard items or those requiring elaborate 'craft' techniques	Export of clothing to developed country markets on basis of low price	Less advanced Asian, African, Latin American
Stage 3	Increase in quantity, quality and sophistication of domestic fabric production. Expansion of clothing sector with upgrading of quality. Development of domestic fibre manufacturing	Much increased international involvement in export of fabric, clothing and even of synthetic fibres	More advanced ASEAN and Eastern Europe. China starting to enter this stage
Stage 4	Further development and sophistication of fibre, fabric and clothing production	Full-scale participation in international trading system. Substantial trade surpluses	Taiwan, South Korea, Hong Kong
Stage 5	Output of textiles and clothing continues to increase but employment decline. Increased capital intensity and specialization	Facing increased international competition	Japan, United States, Italy
Stage 6	Substantial reduction in employment and number of production units. Decline both relative and, in some sectors, absolute	Severe problems of competition. Substantial trade deficits	United Kingdom, West Germany, France, Belgium, Netherlands

Source: Dicken (1992: 245)

THE GLOBAL ORGANIZATION OF THE TEXTILES AND CLOTHING INDUSTRY

Statistics telling us the national location of production and the origin of exports give us little clue about the global organization of the textile and clothing industry. For instance, in what sense are the textiles and clothing produced in South Korea, 'Korean'? Is it simply that the production is located in South Korea and that the workforce is South Korea? Or do South

Koreans play a substantial decision-making role in the organization of the industry; do they own and control it?

Some accounts of the growth of the share of developing countries in global production of textiles and garments emphasize the role of offshore assembly or outward processing by developed country firms, suggesting that in the 1970s and 1980s such firms have relocated their factories to developing countries, attracted by much cheaper labour costs, and use these 'offshore' locations to serve their home markets. Certainly wages in developing countries in the 1970s and early 1980s were lower, and in some cases very much lower, than in developed countries as is indicated by the figures in table 10.4. Moreover one can certainly find plenty of examples of the following kind: 'trouser material is cut in Federal Germany, sent to Tunisia for sewing into trousers, and finally shipped back, in made up form, to the home market in Germany' (Fröbel, Heinrichs and Kreye 1980: 134). However, offshore assembly for re-export is not a feature of fibre and fabric production, which cannot be fragmented in quite the same way. Nor is direct foreign investment in the textiles and clothing industry of much quantitative significance, apart from the case of Japan, as is shown by table 10.5. Though there are multinational corporations in the textiles and clothing industry, the industry is far less concentrated in the hands of multinational corporations than is, for example, the automobile industry. In 1989 only seventeen firms produced nine-tenths of world automobile output; and the two leading firms General Motors and Ford produced almost 30 per cent between them (Dicken 1992: 289). In each of the major producing countries about three or four massive corporations produced between them almost all output (Dicken 1992: 289). Even the largest textiles and clothing multinational comes nowhere near this scale of operation. For instance, an analysis of the five hundred largest multinational corporations carried out in the early 1980s found that only five textile and clothing multinationals were large enough to be included – Courtaulds and Coats Viyella (British); and Burlington, Levi Strauss and Blue Bell (American) (Stopford and Dunning 1983).

Of those five companies, three (Burlington, Courtaulds and Coats Viyella) are integrated textile producers, producing yarn, fabric, household furnishings, industrial textiles and clothing; while two (Levi Strauss and Blue Bell) are clothing producers (specializing in jeans). But these firms are not typical of the industry. Most textile firms are medium size, while clothing is an archetypal small-firm industry. However, these medium and small firms do not operate in isolation from one another. They are frequently linked by dense and complex networks involving various forms of cooperation, and the industry is better understood in terms of commodity chains than of oligopolies.

Thus although developed-country firms have played a significant role in the growth of the textiles and clothing industry in developing countries,

Table 10.4 Earnings in the textiles and clothing industry, 1980 ($ per hour)

Country	Spinning and weaving	Clothing
USA	5.29	4.57
Hong Kong	1.85	1.03
South Korea	0.78	0.59
Philippines[a]	—	0.17
Singapore	0.94	0.80
Sri Lanka[b]	—	0.12

Source: Elson (1988: 358–9)

Notes: (a) 1978; (b) 1981

this role is not primarily one of direct foreign investment in branch plants in developing countries (Elson 1988, 1989).[4] Rather it involves the internationalization of their networks of licensees and subcontractors to include developing-country firms owned by citizens of developing countries. Moreover, the developing-country firms are not by any means all small and dependent. Particularly in the Asian NICs, there are technically advanced locally owned firms, with their own networks, which they have in turn internationalized to encompass firms in other less industrially advanced Asian countries.

The complex factors at work in the global organization of the textiles and clothing industry can be illustrated through three case studies: the internationalization of the operations of a British textiles multinational, Tootal; the development of the nationally owned textiles industry in South Korea; and the development of an export-oriented clothing industry in Bangladesh – an industry in which firms owned by citizens of the Asian NICs play an extremely important role.

Table 10.5 Outward foreign direct investment in textiles, leather, clothing and footwear, 1975

Country	Value ($ million)	Share in all outward FDI %
Japan	918	22
USA	1099	2
United Kingdom	1038	7
Sweden	65	1
West Germany	469	4

Source: ILO (1984: 10)

The stereotype of multinational corporations driven by a search for export platforms with cheap labour misses much that is important about the operations of multinational corporations in the industry, in particular their concern with developing countries as markets, and not just as sources of supply (Elson 1988). Its limitations are illustrated by the case of Tootal, one of the three leading British multinationals in the industry in the 1970s and 1980s. During this time Tootal certainly internationalized its operations and ran down employment in the United Kingdom, so that by 1990 it employed less than 7,000 people in the United Kingdom, while abroad its wholly owned and associate plants employed 14,000 (Peck, Dicken and Chaudhri 1993: 1). But this was driven more by the desire to maintain and gain access to markets for industrial sewing thread in developing countries, particularly in East Asia, than by a search for cheap labour export platforms (Elson 1989; Peck, Dicken and Chaudhri 1993). Moreover, Tootal did not so much relocate its production to developing countries, as reposition itself as a service company, drastically reducing its in-house manufacturing, and emphasizing instead the provision of design, technical, marketing and financial know-how, to a range of associated joint ventures, subcontractors and licensees in Asia and the southern Mediterranean area. By the end of the 1980s Tootal was organized as a global *sourcing* company, planning its supply of thread, fabrics and garments on a global basis, but relying on many other firms to carry out their production.

Factories in developing countries were integrated in this global sourcing network – but rarely as wholly owned export-platform branch plants supplying the UK market. The case of China is an interesting example. In the 1980s Tootal made substantial investments in thread production in China, in joint ventures with publically owned Chinese enterprises, to produce basic industrial sewing thread for the Chinese market and other markets in Southeast and East Asia. More sophisticated 'flexi-mills' to 'finish' the thread to the quality requirements of the international market were located in newly industrialized countries and in Portugal and Turkey to serve the growing garment industries there. Tootal was also involved in the clothing industry, but largely through marketing and design services, with production being carried out through subcontractors, both in the United Kingdom and throughout Southeast and East Asia, to supply not just the UK market but also other developed countries such as Australia and New Zealand.

Emblematic of the kind of company Tootal had become was the operation whereby it imported into the United Kingdom 'grey cloth' from China (from mills it did not own); printed the cloth with complex and colourful batik designs at its own finishing plant near Manchester; and re-exported the finished fabric to West Africa where it was a popular item of 'traditional' (*sic*) costume.

It is worth emphasizing that Tootal's strategy of internationalization did not bring it corporate success. There is often a tendency to overestimate the powers and capacities of multinational corporations. It is worth reminding ourselves that they sometimes fail. Tootal proved vulnerable to the overvaluation of sterling in the late 1980s. This undermined the ability of Tootal's UK operations to compete with imports from East and Southeast Asia in supplying the UK market, while at the same time reducing the value in sterling the profits Tootal made overseas. In May 1990 the company announced a 15 per cent fall in pre-tax profits and subsequently proved unable to resist a takeover bid by a rival British textiles and clothing multinational, Coats Viyella (Peck, Dicken and Chaudhri 1993).

Western multinational corporations have played relatively little role in the development of the textile and clothing industry in South Korea and Bangladesh – though Japanese multinationals had a significant role in cooperating with locally owned conglomerate groups (the *chaebol*) in the build-up of the textile industry in South Korea; and firms from Hong Kong, Taiwan and South Korea have been significant in the development of clothing exports from Bangladesh.

The cases of South Korea and Bangladesh[5] also illustrate two different ways in which governments of developing countries have acted to stimulate the growth of textiles and clothing production and exports. In the case of South Korea, the government used various kinds of subsidies to foster investment by the indigenous private sector, plus penalties if they did not meet export targets. Whereas in Bangladesh, the government set up an export processing zone to attract direct foreign investment in branch plant garment factories.

The key players in the South Korea industry are fifteen locally owned firms represented by the Spinners and Weavers Association of Korea. These have cooperative agreements and ventures of various kinds with Japanese firms, but wholly foreign-owned enterprises play little role in the industry. It has been estimated that in the mid-1970s the employment share of foreign-owned enterprises in South Korea textile and clothing industry was no more than 6 per cent (Stopford and Dunning 1983: 26–7.) There are reported to be fewer multinationals in Korea than in almost any other newly industrializing country, possibly even India (Amsden 1989: 147).

The textiles and clothing industry was the leading sector in South Korea's industrialization in the 1950s and 1960s, accounting for as much as 20 per cent of GDP. By 1975, textiles and clothing accounted for 19 per cent of total value added, 25 per cent of industrial employment and 34 per cent of total exports (Majmudar 1991: 27). Since then the relative importance of the industry has declined, so that in 1989 it contributed 9 per cent of value added and 14 per cent of industrial employment; even so textile products remained the top foreign-exchange earner (Majmudar 1991: 27).

There are two interpretations of the growth of this industry and its success in competing in world markets. One stresses the role of market forces, arguing that the key factors were the 'right prices' especially low wages and an exchange rate that was not overvalued (e.g. Kreuger 1979). The other stresses the role of the state in providing subsidies and disciplining firms to meet export targets (e.g. Amsden 1989). There seems to be strong evidence to support the view that the subsidies were crucial in getting the industry going after the Korean War – cotton spinning and weaving received a substantial amount of American aid (Amsden 1989: 65); and in allowing local firms time to 'learn-by-doing' and acquire new technological capacity, for instance in the production of synthetic fibres (Amsden 1989: 78). In return for the subsidies, firms were expected to meet export targets and were disciplined by the government if they did not, by a combination of price controls, restrictions on capacity expansion, limits on market entry, prohibitions on capital flight, restraints on tax evasion and government control of the banking system (Amsden 1989: 147).

By the beginning of the 1990s the South Korean industry was beginning to experience some of the problems of success. Its ability to increase exports was restricted by the operation of the MFA under which most developed countries operated very restrictive quotas on imports from South Korea. At the same time rapid growth of employment and increasing levels of trade-union activity in the late 1980s pushed up wage levels so that costs were well above those in many other Asian countries, even though they remained below those in the developed countries. Table 10.6 shows labour costs comparisons in spinning and weaving and in clothing in 1991. It is apparent that by then spinning and weaving costs in South Korea were still about one-sixth of those in the highest cost developed countries – though about a third of those in Britain. However they were over three times the level of costs in Malaysia and Thailand and about ten times the level of costs in China and Indonesia. In the case of clothing, we can see that South Korea's costs were about a fifth of those in the highest cost developed countries, about a third of those in Britain, but about four times higher than in Malaysia and more than fifteen times higher than in Indonesia, the lowest-cost country in the table. Not surprisingly, South Korean firms began to look for other production locations in lower-cost areas of Asia which had unused MFA quotas, or faced no quotas at all. Bangladesh was one such location.

The textiles and clothing industry in Bangladesh is in itself a perfect example of uneven development. In 1989 the industry employed about one and half million people, about 50 per cent of the country's industrial employment. However much the largest sector was the hand-loom sector, employing one million people. According to a recent report by an industry specialist, the power-machine-based mill products sector suffers from low productivity, poor quality raw materials and outdated machinery (Bhuiyan 1991). It was nationalized in 1972 and subsequently denationalized in 1982, but still requires a large amount of investment and modernization if it is

Table 10.6 Labour cost comparisons[a] in spinning and weaving, and clothing, 1991 ($ per hour)

Country	Spinning and weaving	Clothing
Sweden	19.5	—
West Germany	17.0	14.81
Japan	16.4	—
USA	10.3	6.77
United Kingdom	10.2	7.99
Spain	7.7	7.11
Taiwan	5.0	3.74
South Korea	3.6	2.75
Hong Kong	3.4	3.39
Portugal	3.2	2.15
Singapore	3.2	2.72
Turkey	3.1	2.31
Tunisia	2.8	1.46
Morocco	1.4	0.94
Malaysia	1.0	0.62
Thailand	0.9	0.69
Philippines	0.7	0.46
Sri Lanka	0.4	0.39
Indonesia	0.3	0.18
China	0.3	0.24

Source: Jenkins (1993) based on Werner International and Economist Intelligence Unit

Note: (a) Includes fringe benefits and social insurance costs as well as earnings

to compete in international markets. The clothing industry presents a different picture – in the 1980s it expanded dramatically and by the early 1990s had overtaken jute products and tea to become the country's main export earner, generating more than 50 per cent of gross foreign exchange earnings (*Guardian*, 25 May 1993). In net terms, the earnings were much less because of the high import content of the clothing, reflecting the lack of development of the domestic textiles industry. One estimate suggests that Bangladesh retains only about 30 per cent of the total of fob value of exported garments, with the other 70 per cent paid out for imported fabrics – mainly to Asian textile producers (Bhuiyan 1991: 71).

The rapid expansion of clothing production and exports was stimulated by a new industrial policy based on trade liberalization and provision of generous incentives to inward investment by foreign firms; by the search for ways through the barrier of the MFA by firms from the Asian NICs, and by the availability of some of the lowest labour costs in the world (Feldman 1992). In the early 1980s the developed industrial countries placed relatively few quota restrictions on clothing exports from Bangladesh, making it an attractive location for East Asian firms that had used up all the export possibilities allowed to them in their home country under the MFA. An examination of foreign direct investments in Bangladesh in the late 1980s found that over 40 per cent of the companies involved were from the Asian NICs; and that 70 per cent of the investments were in the clothing industry (Feldman 1992). However, the expansion is now being met with increasing restrictions on exports from Bangladesh to the markets of North America and Western Europe. It is far from clear that the rapid development of clothing exports from Bangladesh will prove more than a limited boom of an 'enclave' type.

THE GLOBAL DISTRIBUTION OF EMPLOYMENT IN THE TEXTILE AND CLOTHING INDUSTRY

Textiles, and especially clothing, are relatively labour-intensive industries and in global terms are very large-scale employers of labour. Official figures put the number of textiles workers in the world at the end of the 1980s at about fifteen million; and the number of clothing workers at about eight million (Dicken 1992: 234). But, particularly in clothing, official figures are underestimates, leaving out the large numbers employed in small workshops and as outworkers in their own homes. Some official statistics of employment in the textiles and clothing industries in the 1980s are given in tables 10.7 and 10.8.

Within the developed capitalist economies there has been a massive decline in employment in the textiles and clothing industry in the last thirty years. Between 1963 and 1987 the biggest losses in the European Community were experienced by the United Kingdom (780,000 jobs), followed by West Germany (564,000) and France (520,000). The United States, although a much larger economy, had a lower level of losses – about 500,000 (Dicken 1992: 264).

It is tempting to see these job losses as the result of 'transfers' of jobs to the developing countries; and indeed this interpretation underpins the support of trade unions in the developed countries for the MFA, which they see as defending their members' jobs. But this is oversimplified. Job losses are the result of several different processes. Studies of the United States, United Kingdom and Germany have distinguished three major forces: changes in domestic demand, changes in productivity and changes in imports and exports. They have concluded that the biggest source of employment loss is productivity growth (Dicken 1992: 264). However, it must be noted that these studies suffer from a methodological weakness, in

Table 10.7 Employment in the textiles industry, 1980–1986 (thousands)

Country	1980	1981	1982	1983	1984	1985	1986
Largest producer countries: North							
United States	848	823	749	741	746	702	705
Japan	645	630	607	579	567	555	—
Italy	—	—	569	560	554	543	535
United Kingdom	418	341	315	—	284	—	—
West Germany	—	266	245	—	235	231	228
France	251	229	222	—	203	193	181
Canada	89	88	76	—	80	78	80
Largest producer countries: South							
China	—	—	—	—	4,229	—	—
India	—	1,950	1,950	—	2,010	1,765	1,712
Brazil	837	751	736	—	—	328	334
South Korea	756	729	742	736	721	725	759
Taiwan	379	410	436	438	445	485	474
Mexico	254	266	—	—	—	—	—
Egypt	—	—	—	—	—	285	290
Turkey	217	250	254	—	251	255	260
Argentina	110	—	110	—	80	80	81

Source: UNIDO (1988: 140)

that they assume the three forces operate independently of one another, whereas, in practice, import penetration is likely to stimulate changes that lead to at least some of the productivity growth.

It is tempting to assume that workers in developed countries unequivocally regret the decline in employment opportunities in the textiles and clothing industry. But that again is an oversimplification: much depends on the alternatives available. A study of employment change in the 1980s in the textiles industry of Northwest England found that very few young women today seek jobs in the mill; rather they prefer service-sector jobs in health, education, welfare and distribution – 80 per cent of women in the 1980s entered service-sector employment when they first entered employment. The study concluded that the central factor in the declining female share of textile employment in the 1980s was

an increasing perception by women in Rochdale that textile employment is undesirable when compared with new types of paid employment in the town . . . All [textile] firms report increasing difficulties in recruiting women into textile occupations traditionally

Table 10.8 Employment in the clothing industry, 1980–1986 (thousands)

Country	1980	1981	1982	1983	1984	1985	1986
EEC							
Belgium	—	—	—	32.8	31.8	30.4	30.6
Denmark	16.1	15.3	16.2	16.4	17.1	17.9	18.0
France	251.3	237.1	237.2	226.2	215.4	207.0	200.0
West Germany	248.8	230.0	209.7	193.9	191.1	188.4	185.5
Greece	—	—	—	—	—	69.0	—
Ireland	—	—	—	16.0	—	17.7	17.0
Italy	213.0	207.0	202.0	194.0	183.0	179.0	174.0
Netherlands	17.1	14.0	12.6	11.8	10.5	10.5	10.5
Portugal	73.0	69.5	66.9	66.5	67.1	67.1	67.1
United Kingdom	241.8	217.5	210.3	227.0	226.0	232.0	235.0
Other Europe							
Austria	33.2	31.9	30.3	29.2	29.0	28.6	27.8
Finland	34.6	32.0	32.0	30.8	30.6	29.4	28.5
Norway	7.1	6.4	5.7	5.2	4.6	4.7	4.3
Sweden	—	13.2	—	12.1	11.2	11.3	10.2
Switzerland	17.6	16.4	15.2	15.0	15.0	15.5	15.5
Asia and Oceania							
Australia	71.0	—	—	—	—	67.0	—
China	—	—	—	—	—	—	3,000.0
Hong Kong	—	—	—	—	—	276.3	—
Japan	399.3	387.3	398.8	415.9	418.1	417.2	418.0
South Korea	368.0	382.1	383.4	384.4	383.9	393.6	397.1
Taiwan	—	—	128.6	132.3	145.0	158.1	157.4
Turkey	—	—	—	—	—	—	—
North America							
United States	1,079.0	1,060.0	981.0	984.0	1,003.0	945.0	931.0
Africa							
South Africa	—	—	—	—	—	—	150.0

Source: UNIDO (1989: 207)

undertaken by women and increasing difficulty in retaining women in these categories of employment.

(Penn, Martin and Scattergood 1991)

The real problems come when alternative jobs are not available: an OECD study found that textiles unemployment is frequently concentrated in areas with above-average unemployment rates (OECD 1983: 76).

The question of alternatives is also important in understanding workers' reactions to the growth of employment opportunities in the textiles and clothing industry in developing countries. Women in Bangladesh have flocked to join the workforce in the clothing industry. Kabeer (1991) distinguishes several reasons for this: for the poorest women, who had to earn cash out of dire necessity in order to survive, the clothing factories offered better prospects than other alternatives, such as domestic service or prostitution; for somewhat better off married women, the factories offered an acceptable way to earn cash to improve the living standards of their families, especially to finance the education of their children; for somewhat better off unmarried women, the factories offered a way to earn cash to save for their dowries or to finance personal consumption of clothes and leisure activities – all means to acquiring more say over the choice of husband.

However, the fact that women workers in Rochdale do not protest against the loss of textile jobs, preferring work in the service sector; or that women workers in Dhaka welcome the new opportunities in the clothing factories, does not means we should be complacent about the implications of the international restructuring of the textiles and clothing industry. In particular, we need to bear in mind the fact that lack of development means that none of the options facing most of the population in a country like Bangladesh is very good. Working in a clothing factory may be just the best of a bad lot. Thus we may also want to judge employment in the textiles and clothing industry in developing countries against some more absolute standard of human welfare, including some notion of 'decent' wages and working conditions, and the opportunity to acquire more skills, and more possibilities for self-development.

What implications does the development of the textiles and clothing industry have for human development, understood broadly in terms of the quality of life and opportunities for self-development?[6] Ever since the nineteenth century outcry against the exploitation of women and children in the mills of Lancashire and the sweat-shops of London there has always been concern that the operations of the industry have been more bene-ficial to those who owned it than to those who worked in it. Particular concerns have been the employment of child labour, unhealthy working conditions, long hours of work, lack of trade-union rights, and wages that are low compared to the cost of living, or to wages available in other industries – issues which are currently being raised in relation to Bangladesh. For instance some American trade unions have alleged that there are frequent violations of the International Labour Office (ILO) convention on labour standards:

> the most shocking abuses involve young children, many of whom work in factories for 60 hours or more a week with extremely poor wages. About 40 per cent of workers are employed as helpers and they are paid wages of only TK 300–400 ($9) a month.
>
> (Bhuiyan 1991: 70)

However, others argue that despite long hours and low wages, such employment is beneficial. In particular it is suggested that it 'liberates' young Bangladeshi women. Though they may be working long hours for little pay at the age of fourteen, they are less dependent on their parents and are able to resist a forced early marriage (*Guardian*, 25 May 1993). In evaluating these claims one must bear in mind that while jobs in the clothing factories improve the terms on which young women are able to negotiate the social relations that subordinate them, the structures of gender inequality are not thereby dissolved, any more than they were in nineteenth-century Lancashire when thousands of young women went to work in textile mills.

However, it is true that net benefits of new employment opportunities in textiles and clothing are stronger in some cases than in others, and it is worth distinguishing between them. The evidence gathered by an ILO study seems to suggest that the prevalence of negative features is greater in the sweat-shop and outwork sector of the industry than in the medium- and large-scale factories; and that conditions in multinational corporations tend to be no worse, and are in many cases better, than in locally owned firms (ILO 1984). Moreover, the prevalence of negative features is also related to the general level of development of the whole economy, and the absence or availability, of supplies of surplus labour.

A study of wages and labour conditions in Southeast and East Asian NICs found that real wages in these countries have increased, and that they are not in general lower in the export sector than in sectors catering to domestic markets; indeed many workers in the export sector earn more than workers in other sectors (Addison and Demery 1988). However, the study did find that hours of work are a major problem – both in terms of the length of the working week and in terms of shift-work patterns. Labour legislation setting a 48-hour week as the norm is not enforced; and overtime premiums are frequently not paid.

In the case of South Korea, the growth in real wages in the 1980s is argued by some to have eroded competitive advantage in the textile and clothing industry; certainly in the late 1980s the industrial workforce was able to mobilize to win wage increases of 19.6 per cent in 1988 and 21.1 per cent in 1989 (Majmudar 1991). However there is a sizeable and growing 'informal' sector in the clothing industry in which women make up garments at home or in small workshops (Kim 1991). In this sector rates of pay are considerably lower than in garment factories; and labour costs even lower yet, as there is no payment of bonuses or provision for social insurance, such as pensions. Homeworkers have no guarantee of regular work; and their homes suffer from the noise and pollution of industrial processes.

But outworking and sweat-shops in the clothing industry are not confined to the developing countries – a sizeable and probably growing amount of clothing in the developed countries is produced under these conditions, often by women immigrants from developing countries (Mitter 1986).

We may summarize by saying that the benefits to workers are greatest in conditions of rapid growth and in larger-scale factories, because these are the conditions which do most to strengthen the bargaining power of workers. However, even in these conditions only a minority of workers can acquire the skills that permit them either to set up a business of their own; or to earn a relatively high salary as a technical or professional employee. New opportunities in the textiles and clothing industries are countered by new limitations, as peoples' capacities are confined by business strategies they play no part in determing, or people are displaced by machines, in a dialectic that is intrinsic to capitalist development. More general limitations stem from the very success of textiles and clothing industries in some developing countries.

SOME LIMITS TO THE DEVELOPMENT OF THE TEXTILES AND CLOTHING INDUSTRY IN DEVELOPING COUNTRIES

An obvious limit is posed by the MFA. We have seen that as the Bangladeshi clothing industry grew, restrictions began to be placed on exports from Bangladesh to the United States and Europe. A similar experience took place in Lesotho (Baylies and Wright 1993) where the share of export earnings derived from fabric, clothing and footwear increased from 9 per cent in 1981 to 21 per cent in 1985. Further rapid growth was countered in 1992 by the imposition of a quota on the export of certain garments from Lesotho to the US market.

However reform of the MFA is planned in the context of a new GATT agreement. Quotas will be phased out over a ten-year period, probably coupled with the reduction of restrictions on imports of textiles into the NICs. But it would be a mistake to think that free trade will remove all significant obstacles to the further development of the textiles and clothing industry in developing countries. Two further obstacles remain: the fact that the developed countries still have the edge in terms of development of new technology, which gives them a continuing capability to transform the parameters of competition; and the fact that the international capitalist market has entered a period of stagnation, not unconnected with the achievements of the leading Asian NICs.

Let us consider the development of new technology first. A recent UNIDO report puts spending on textiles and clothing research and development in the OECD countries at about $668 (UNIDO 1989: 216). This level of expenditure has enabled the development of new technology in textile production that has reduced labour cost as a share of total cost to quite low levels, as is shown in table 10.9. (The share is lower for developing than for developed countries because of lower wages and fringe benefits.) It has also facilitated the application of computer technology in clothing to

206

develop the 'quick response system' in which there are rapid information flows between the retailer, the clothing manufacturer, the textile mill and the fibre producer, permitting delivery of garments to the shops within a shorter of period of time, with considerable savings in the cost of holding stocks of unsold goods and 'work-in-progress'.

Some analysts suggest that these new technologies have undermined the comparative advantage of developing countries as locations for production of textiles and garments for the developed country markets. Others point to the capacity of developed country fibre producers to develop completely new fibres, such as microfibre fabrics which have filaments finer than silk. Although it is unlikely that these new technologies will lead to a reversal of the direction of change in the pattern of textiles and clothing production and trade that has been described in this chapter, it means that substantial investment in training and equipment will be required in many developing countries to ensure that their competitive position is maintained. South Korea will be able to do this and so will other Asian NICs – but will Bangladesh, or the countries of sub-Saharan Africa or Latin America? Already some developing countries find that low-cost labour does not translate into competitive advantage as lack of investment in training and equipment lead to low-quality production (Morawetz 1981).

The other problem that would-be emulators of the Asian NICs face is a slow-growing, destabilized world capitalist economy – problems that stem from the very success in the 1980s of the major Asian textile exporters. The annual average GDP growth rates in the 1980s of the major Asian exporters of textiles and clothing were as follows: South Korea (9.7 per cent); China (9.5 per cent); Taiwan (8.0 per cent); Thailand (7.6 per cent); Hong Kong (7.1 per cent); Singapore (6.4 per cent); Indonesia (5.5 per cent); and Malaysia (5.2 per cent). The gap between these rapid growth rates and the sluggish performance of the OECD countries leads credence to the idea that the world is at the beginning of the fourth great change in the relative

Table 10.9 Labour costs as a share of total costs, 1991

Country	Yarn (%)	Fabric (%)
Brazil	4	5
Germany	10	22
India	3	4
Japan	14	20
South Korea	14	6
USA	14	22

Source: Jenkins (1993: 49–50)

economic weight of countries since the industrial revolution; the first being the rise of the United Kingdom; the second the rise of the United States and Germany; and the third the rise of Japan. The second and third changes were associated with major international recessions in the period 1873–96 and in the 1930s, as the old 'rules of the game' were no longer appropriate and new 'rules of the game' did not immediately emerge (Reading 1993). The fourth great change seems on present evidence to be becoming marked by similar phenomena.

For the populations of the Asian NICs in which textiles and clothing have been the leading sector, there have been considerable benefits. But the people of other developed countries especially in sub-Saharan Africa are likely to find themselves caught in the backwash, competing for markets which are far less buoyant than in the 1970s and 1980s. The development associated with the textiles and clothing industry has always been uneven, and that seems set to continue in the foreseeable future. The problem with capitalism is not that it is incapable of leading to development, both industrial and human, in the South, but that the development to which it gives rise is unequal; and the very success of capitalist development in some locations limits the possibilities open in others.

NOTES

1 Official statistics tend to leave out small-scale workshops and outwork, and thus underreport activities in the clothing industry and the handicraft sector of the textiles industry. The underreporting of the clothing sector affects figures for both developed and developing countries; while the underreporting of the hand-loom sector of the textiles industry affects only developing countries to any significant extent.
2 Import duties are also charged, but some countries, most notably the United States, have provisions which reduce the amount of duty that has to be paid on imports of clothing that have been assembled out of fabric supplied by the importing country. This facilitates 'outward processing' or 'offshore assembly' i.e. the process by which firms in a developed country design clothes and cut out the cloth at home, send the pieces to a developing country for sewing, and reimport the finished product to serve the home market (Lall 1980; Grunwald and Flamm 1985).
3 This is probably connected with the greater use made of outward processing by American firms, facilitated by the structure of American import duties.
4 With the exception of Japanese textiles firms which have set up a considerable number of joint venture plants in Southeast Asia and Latin America (UNCTAD 1980: 183; OECD 1983: 58).
5 In 1990 the GDP per capita in South Korea was $5,400 and in Bangladesh $210; in the United Kingdom it was $16,100 (World Bank 1992: 218–19).
6 For more discussion of ways of defining and measuring human development, see UNDP (1990).

REFERENCES

Addison, T. and Demery, L. (1988) 'Wages and labour conditions in East Asia: a review of case study evidence', *Development Policy Review* 6: 371–3.

Amsden, A. (1989) *Asia's Next Giant – South Korea and Late Industrialisation*, Oxford: Oxford University Press.

Baylies, C. and Wright, C. (1993) 'Female labour in the textile and clothing industry of Lesotho', *African Affairs* 92: 577–91.

Bhuiyan, M. (1991) 'The textile and clothing industry in Bangladesh', *EIU Textile Outlook International* (March): 57–75.

Dicken, P. (1992) *Global Shift* (2nd edn), London: Chapman.

Elson, D. (1988) 'Transnational corporations and the new international division of labour: a critique of the "cheap labour" hypothesis', *Manchester Papers on Development* IV (3): 352–76.

—— (1989) 'The Cutting Edge: multinationals in textiles and clothing', in D. Elson and R. Pearson (eds) *Women's Employment and Multinationals in Europe*, London: Macmillan.

Feldman, S. (1992) 'Crisis, Islam and gender in Bangladesh: the social construction of a female labour force', in L. Beneria and S. Feldman (eds) *Unequal Burden*, Boulder CO: Westview Press.

Fröbel, F., Heinrichs, J. and Kreye, O. (1980) *The New International Division of Labour*, Cambridge: Cambridge University Press.

GATT (1991) *International Trade 1990/91*, Geneva: GATT.

Grunwald, J. and Flamm, K. (1985) *The Global Factory*, Washington DC: Brookings Institution.

ILO (1984) *Social and Labour Practices of Multinational Enterprises in the Textiles, Clothing and Footwear Industries*, Geneva: International Labour Office.

Jenkins, R. (1993) 'International competitiveness in the textile-clothing industry', report for Regional and Country Studies Branch of UNIDO, Vienna: UNIDO.

Kabeer, N. (1991) 'Cultural dopes or rational fools: women, factory employment and garment production in Bangladesh', *European Journal of Development Research* 3: 133–60.

Kim, Y. (1991) 'Women, home-based work and questions of organising: the case of South Korea', paper given at Workshop on Women Organising in the Process of Industrialisation, Institute of Social Studies, The Hague, April.

Kreuger, A.O. (1979) *The Developmental Role of the Foreign Sector and Aid*, Cambridge, MA: Harvard University Press.

Lall, S. (1980) 'Offshore assembly in developing countries', *National Westminister Bank Quarterly Review* August: 14–23.

Majmudar, D. (1991) 'South Korea's textile and clothing industry: an export perspective', *EIU Textile Outlook International* May: 22–33.

Mitter (1986) 'Industrial restructuring and manufacturing homework: immigrant women in the UK clothing industry', *Capital and Class* 27: 37–80.

Moore, L. (1991) 'International trade in textiles and clothing', *Journal of Textile Institute* 82 (2): 145–59.

Morawetz, D. (1981) *Why the Emperor's New Clothes are not Made in Colombia*, Oxford: Oxford University Press.

OECD (1983) *Textile and Clothing Industries*, Paris: OECD.

Peck, J., Dicken, P. and Chaudhri, Z. (1993) 'Losing the thread: internationalisation, corporate restructuring and "hollowing out" in the Tootal textile group', School of Geography, University of Manchester.

Penn, R., Martin, A. and Scattergood, H. (1991) 'Gender relations, technology and employment change in the contemporary textile industry', *Sociology* 25 (4): 569–87.

Reading, B. (1993) *Monthly International Review: May,* London: Lombard Street Research.

Stopford, J. M. and Dunning, J. (1983) *Multinationals: Company Performances and Global Trends,* London: Macmillan.

UNCTAD (1980) *Fibre and Textiles: Dimensions of Corporate Marketing Structures,* TD/B/C.1/219, Geneva: UNCTAD.

UNDP (1990) *Human Development Report 1990,* New York: Oxford University Press.

UNIDO (1988) *Industry and Development: Global Report 1988/89,* Vienna: UNIDO.

—— (1989) *Industry and Development: Global Report 1989/90,* Vienna: UNIDO.

—— (1991) *Industry and Development: Global Report 1990/91,* Vienna: UNIDO.

—— (1992) *Industry and Development: Global Report 1992/93,* Vienna: UNIDO.

World Bank (1992) *World Development Report 1992,* New York: Oxford University Press.

11

CAPITALISM, DEVELOPMENT AND GLOBAL COMMODITY CHAINS

Gary Gereffi

THE EMERGENCE OF A GLOBAL MANUFACTURING SYSTEM

Contemporary industrialization is the result of an integrated system of global trade and production. Open international trade has encouraged nations to specialize in different branches of manufacturing and even in different stages of production within a specific industry. This process, fuelled by the explosion of new products and new technologies since the Second World War, has led to the emergence of a 'global manufacturing system' in which production capacity is dispersed to an unprecedented number of developing as well as industrialized countries. What is novel about today's global manufacturing system is not the spread of economic activities across national boundaries *per se*, but rather the fact that international production and trade are globally organized by core corporations that represent both industrial and commercial capital.

Three specific trends in the international economy serve to illustrate the nature of the contemporary global manufacturing system in greater detail: (a) the spread of diversified industrialization to large segments of the Third World; (b) the shift toward export-oriented development strategies in peripheral nations, with an emphasis on manufactured exports; and (c) high levels of product specialization in the export profiles of most Third World countries, along with continual industrial upgrading by established exporters among the newly industrialized countries (NICs). Although these processes of change have incorporated most nations into the global manufacturing system, their roles and resources are quite different. Each Third World region is characterized by an internal division of labour involving countries at distinct levels of relative development and with unique patterns of cooperation and competition to exploit this regional potential.

211

Worldwide industrialization

Since the 1950s the gap between developed and developing countries has been narrowing in terms of industrialization. Industry as a share of gross domestic product (GDP) has increased substantially in many Third World nations, not only in absolute terms but also relative to that of the core countries. By 1990, the industrial sector in East and Southeast Asia averaged 45 per cent of GDP, and manufacturing (a subset of industry) averaged 34 per cent. Both figures are considerably above those for any of the high-income, advanced industrial economies, including Japan.[1] Thus the most 'developed' nations in the world today are no longer the most industrial ones. As core economies shift predominantly toward services, vigorous industrialization has become the hallmark of the periphery, or at least of certain parts of it. This can be seen by taking a closer look at the major Third World regions.

East Asia, Southeast Asia, Latin America, South Asia and sub-Saharan Africa have sharply contrasting development profiles. Between 1965–80 and 1980–90, East and Southeast Asia increased their GDP growth rates from an annual average of 7.3 per cent to 7.8 per cent, while South Asia also accelerated from an annual average growth rate of 3.6 per cent in the first period to 5.2 per cent in the latter. The OECD countries, sub-Saharan Africa, and Latin America and the Caribbean, on the other hand, all registered substantial declines in the growth of their economies during the past decade (World Bank 1992: 220–1).

Industry outstripped agriculture as a source of economic growth in all regions of the Third World. From 1965 to 1990, industry's share of GDP grew by 13 percentage points in East and Southeast Asia, by 10 per cent in sub-Saharan Africa, 5 per cent in South Asia, and 3 per cent in Latin America. Agriculture's share of regional GDP, on the other hand, fell by 16 percentage points in East and Southeast Asia, 11 per cent in South Asia, 8 per cent in sub-Saharan Africa, and 6 per cent in Latin America (World Bank 1992: 222–3).

Manufacturing has been the cornerstone of development in East and Southeast Asia, as well as in Latin America. In 1990, 34 per cent of the GDP of East and Southeast Asia was in the manufacturing sector, compared to 26 per cent for Latin America, 17 per cent for South Asia, and only 11 per cent for sub-Saharan Africa. The manufacturing sector's share of GDP in some developing nations, such as China (38 per cent), Taiwan (34 per cent), and South Korea (31 per cent), was even higher than Japan's manufacturing/GDP ratio of 29 per cent. These differences in performance are corroborated over time as well. The manufacturing sector exhibited much greater dynamism in East and Southeast Asia than anywhere else in the Third World. Between 1965 and 1990, manufacturing increased its share of GDP in these two regions by 10 percentage points, compared to net sectoral growth rates of 4 per cent in sub-Saharan Africa and 2 per cent in South Asia and Latin America[2] (World Bank 1992: 222–3).

Diversified, export-oriented industrialization

World trade expanded nearly thirtyfold in the three decades since 1960. Manufactured goods as a percentage of total world exports increased from 55 per cent in 1980 to 75 per cent in 1990. Furthermore, the share of the manufactured exports of the NICs that can be classified as 'high tech' soared from 2 per cent in 1964 to 25 per cent in 1985, and those embodying 'medium' levels of technological sophistication rose from 16 per cent to 22 per cent during this same period (OECD 1988: 24). This expansion in the quantity and quality of the Third World's export capacity, particularly for manufactured goods, embraces such a diverse array of countries that it appears to be part of a general restructuring in the world economy.

East and Southeast Asian nations more than doubled the advanced industrial countries' average annual export growth rate of 4.1 per cent with a sizzling standard of 9.8 per cent during the 1980s. The star performers from this region (Thailand, South Korea, Taiwan and China) nearly tripled the OECD average with export growth rates ranging from 13 to 11 per cent for the past decade. Taiwan and South Korea topped the list of individual exporters in 1990 with $67 and $65 billion in overseas sales, respectively, followed closely by China ($62 billion) and then Singapore ($53 billion). In the next tier, Hong Kong, Brazil, Mexico and several of the Southeast Asian nations (Malaysia, Indonesia and Thailand) all generated substantial exports, ranging from $31 to $23 billion. Exports accounted for 26 per cent of GDP in East and Southeast Asia, in contrast to an export/GDP ratio of 15 per cent for the OECD nations (World Bank 1992: 244–5).

In exports as in production, manufactures are the chief source of the Third World's dynamism. In 1990, manufactured items constituted well over 90 per cent of total exports in the East Asian NICs (except Singapore), and nearly three-quarters of all exports in China and India. For the major Latin American economies, the share of manufactures in total exports is between one-third and one-half, while in sub-Saharan Africa the manufacturing figure is less than 10 per cent (World Bank 1992: 248–9).

The maturity or sophistication of a country's industrial structure can be measured by the complexity of the products it exports. Here again, the East Asian NICs are the most advanced. In Singapore and South Korea, overseas sales of machinery and transport equipment, which utilize capital- and skill-intensive technology, grew by 38 and 34 per cent, respectively, from 1965 to 1990 as a share of total merchandise exports. Taiwan's exports in this category increased by 21 per cent and Hong Kong's by 16 per cent. In Southeast Asia, Malaysia (25 per cent) and Thailand (20 per cent) have been strong performers in this sector, while in Latin America, Mexico

(24 per cent) and Brazil (16 per cent) also made machinery and transport equipment a dynamic export base. In 'other' manufactures,[3] South Africa, the Philippines, India, Brazil, Thailand, Indonesia and Argentina all achieved solid export gains ranging from 42 to 20 per cent since 1965 (World Bank 1992: 248–9).

It is interesting to note that textiles and clothing, the most dynamic export sector in the East Asian NICs in the 1960s, actually shrank as a proportion of total exports in these four nations (as well as India) during the past 25 years. None the less, while the NICs in East Asia and other regions were shifting into more advanced export industries, textiles and clothing became a key growth sector for countries at lower levels of development like Pakistan, Bangladesh, Thailand and Indonesia. Despite their status as 'traditional' industries in developed countries, textiles and clothing actually represent the leading edge of economic globalization for Third World nations that seek to be incorporated into the world economy as manufactured goods exporters.

Geographical specialization and export niches

While the diversification of the NICs' exports toward non-traditional manufactured items is a clear trend, less well recognized is the tendency of the NICs to develop higher levels of specialization in their export profiles. Within a given region, such as East Asia or Latin America, nations tend to establish particular export niches within the world economy. In the footwear industry, for example, South Korea specialized in athletic footwear, Taiwan in vinyl and plastic shoes, Brazil in low-priced women's leather shoes, Spain in medium-priced women's leather shoes, and Italy in high-priced fashion shoes. Mainland China traditionally has been a major player in the low-priced end of the world footwear market especially in canvas and rubber shoes. Because of its low wages and vast production capacity, however, China now has displaced Taiwan and South Korea from many of their mid-level niches, and it is challenging Brazil, Spain and even Italy in the fashionable leather footwear market (Gereffi and Korzeniewicz 1990). Similar trends are apparent for numerous other consumer items and even intermediate goods, such as semiconductors.[4]

International competitiveness thus depends on a nation's ability to consolidate and upgrade its industrial export niches. Large, vertically integrated companies in the Third World (such as South Korea's *chaebol* and transnational corporations in Singapore) have significant advantages in forging forward and backward linkages in their production networks because of scale economies and substantial financial support from the state. However, established exporters in small-firm dominated economies like Taiwan and Hong Kong also have been successful in their efforts to move downstream by mergers and acquisitions that give them access to brand names and marketing outlets in their major overseas markets.

More generally, new production and trade patterns in the world economy tend to be coordinated by transnational capital of two types: (a) transnational manufacturing firms that shape the globalization of production by their strategic investment decisions; and (b) the foreign buyers (retailers and branded merchandisers) of consumer goods in the developed countries that use their large orders to mobilize global export networks composed of scores of overseas factories and traders. As we will see in the following sections, transnational manufacturers and foreign buyers are the main agents in producer-driven and buyer-driven global commodity chains, respectively. These contrasting patterns of international economic organization, in turn, reflect changes in labour conditions, manufacturing technologies and state policies in today's global economy.[5]

PRODUCER-DRIVEN VS. BUYER-DRIVEN COMMODITY CHAINS[6]

Global commodity chains (GCCs) are rooted in transnational production systems that give rise to particular patterns of coordinated international trade. A 'production system' links the economic activities of firms to technological and organizational networks that permit companies to develop, manufacture and market specific commodities. In the transnational production systems that characterize global capitalism, economic activity is not only *international* in scope; it also is *global* in its organization. While 'internationalization' refers simply to the geographical spread of economic activities across national boundaries, 'globalization' implies a degree of functional integration between these internationally dispersed activities. The requisite administrative coordination is carried out by diverse corporate actors in centralized as well as decentralized economic structures. The GCC perspective thus highlights the need to look not only at the geographical spread of transnational production arrangements, but also at their organizational scope (i.e. the linkages between various economic agents – raw-material suppliers, factories, traders and retailers) in order to understand their sources of both stability and change (see Gereffi and Korzeniewicz 1994).

Global commodity chains have three main dimensions: (a) an input–output structure (i.e., a set of products and services linked together in a sequence of value-adding economic activities); (b) a territoriality (i.e., spatial dispersion or concentration of production and marketing networks, comprised of enterprises of different sizes and types); and (c) a governance structure (i.e., authority and power relationships that determine how financial, material and human resources are allocated and flow within a chain). The governance structure of GCCs, which is essential to the coordination of transnational production systems, has received relatively little attention in the literature.[7] Two distinct types of governance structures for GCCs have emerged in the past two decades, which for the sake of simplicity can be called 'producer-driven' and 'buyer-driven' commodity chains[8] (see figure 11.1).

Producer-driven commodity chains refer to those industries in which transnational corporations or other large integrated industrial enterprises play the central role in controlling the production system (including its backward and forward linkages). This is most characteristic of capital- and technology-intensive industries like automobiles, computers, aircraft and electrical machinery. The geographical spread of these industries is transnational, but the number of countries in the commodity chain and their levels of development are varied. International subcontracting of components is common, especially for the most labour-intensive production processes, as are strategic alliances between international rivals. What distinguishes 'producer-driven' production systems is the control exercised by the administrative headquarters of transnational corporations.

The automobile industry offers a classic illustration of a producer-driven commodity chain. In his comparative study of Japanese and US car companies, Hill (1989) shows how both sets of firms organize manufacturing in multilayered production systems that involve thousands of firms (including parents, subsidiaries and subcontractors).[9] Florida and Kenney (1991) have found that Japanese automobile manufacturers actually reconstituted many aspects of their home-country supplier networks in North America. Doner (1991) extends this framework to highlight the complex forces that drive Japanese auto-makers to create regional production schemes for the supply of auto parts in a half-dozen nations in East and Southeast Asia. Henderson (1989) also supports the notion that producer-driven commodity chains have established an East Asian division of labour in his study of the internationalization of the US semiconductor industry.

Buyer-driven commodity chains refer to those industries in which large retailers, brand-named merchandisers, and trading companies play the pivotal role in setting up decentralized production networks in a variety of exporting countries, typically located in the Third World. This pattern of trade-led industrialization has become common in labour-intensive, consumer goods industries such as garments, footwear, toys, household goods, consumer electronics, and a wide range of hand-crafted items (e.g. furniture, ornaments). International 'specification contracting' is generally carried out by independent Third World factories that make finished goods (rather than components or parts) under original equipment manufacturer (OEM) arrangements. The specifications are supplied by the buyers and branded companies that design the goods.

One of the main characteristics of firms that fit the buyer-driven model, including athletic footwear companies like Nike (see Donaghu and Barff

1 Producer-driven commodity chains
(Industries such as automobiles, computers, aircraft and electrical machinery)

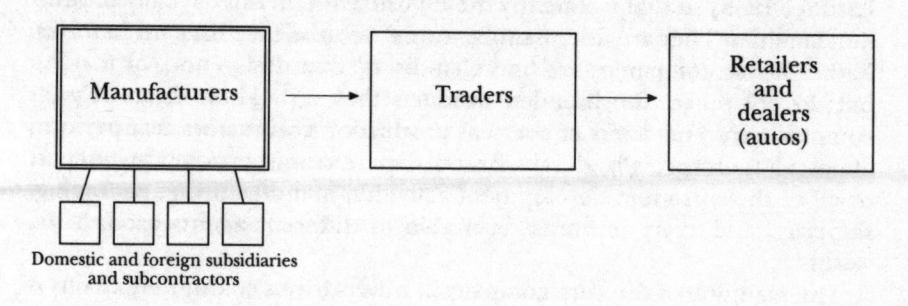

2 Buyer-driven commodity chains
(Industries such as garments, footwear, toys and housewares)

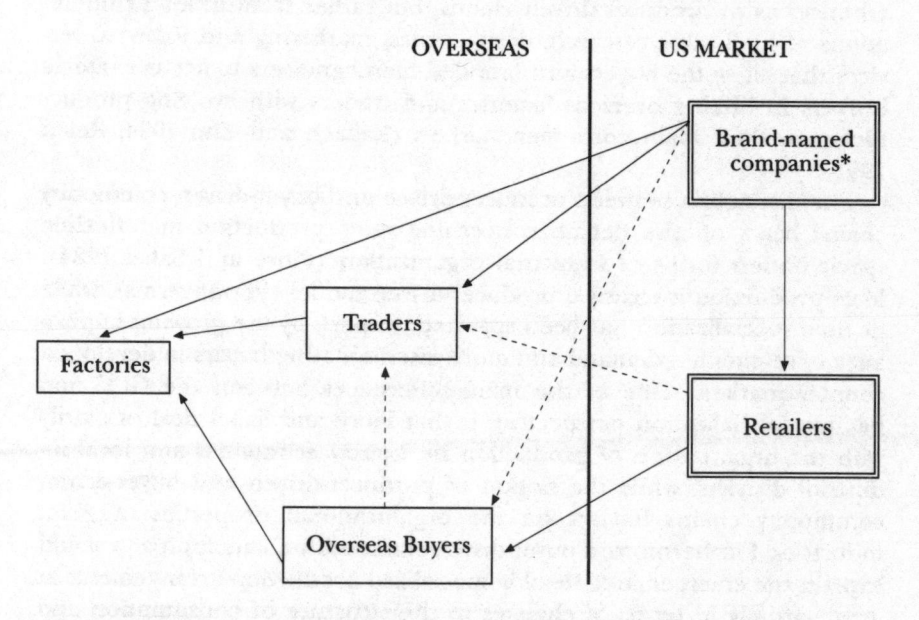

Notes: Solid arrows are primary relationships; dashed arrows are secondary relationships

* These design-orientated, national brand companies, such as Nike, Reebok and Liz Claiborne typically own no factories. Some, like The Gap and The Limited, have their own retail outlets that only sell private label products

Figure 11.1 The organization of producer-driven and buyer-driven global commodity chains

Source: Gereffi 1994: 98

1990), Reebok and L.A. Gear, and fashion-oriented clothing companies like The Limited, The Gap (see Mitchell 1992), and Liz Claiborne (see Lardner 1988), is that frequently these businesses do not own any production facilities. They are not 'manufacturers' because they have no factories. Rather, these companies are 'merchandisers' that design and/or market, but do not make, the branded products they sell. These firms rely on complex tiered networks of overseas production contractors that perform almost all their specialized tasks. Branded merchandisers may farm out part or all of their product development activities, manufacturing, packaging, shipping, and even accounts receivable to different agents around the world.

The main job of the core company in buyer-driven commodity chains is to manage these production and trade networks and to make sure all the pieces of the business come together as an integrated whole. Profits in buyer-driven chains thus derive not from scale, volume and technological advances as in producer-driven chains, but rather from unique combinations of high-value research, design, sales, marketing and financial services that allow the buyers and branded merchandisers to act as strategic brokers in linking overseas factories and traders with evolving product niches in their main consumer markets (Rabach and Kim 1994; Reich 1991).

The distinction between producer-driven and buyer-driven commodity chains bears on the debate concerning mass production and flexible specialization forms of industrial organization (Piore and Sabel 1984). Mass production is clearly a producer-driven model (in our terms), while flexible specialization has been spawned, in part, by the growing importance of segmented demand and more discriminating buyers in developed country markets. One of the main differences between the GCC and flexible specialization perspectives is that Piore and Sabel deal primarily with the organization of production in *domestic* economies and local industrial districts, while the notion of producer-driven and buyer-driven commodity chains focuses on the organizational properties of *global* industries. Furthermore, a buyer-driven commodity chain approach would explain the emergence of flexibly specialized production arrangements at least partially in terms of changes in the structure of consumption and retailing, which in turn reflect demographic shifts and new organizational imperatives. Finally, while some of the early discussions of flexible specialization implied that it is a 'superior' manufacturing system that might eventually displace or subordinate mass production, buyer-driven and supplier-driven commodity chains are viewed as contrasting (but not mutually exclusive) poles in a spectrum of industrial organization possibilities.

An explanation for the emergence of producer-driven and buyer-driven commodity chains can be derived from the barriers to entry that allow core industrial and commerical firms, respectively, to control the backward and forward linkages in the production process. Industrial organization economics tells us that profitability is greatest in the relatively concentrated segments of an industry characterized by high barriers to the entry of new firms. Producer-driven commodity chains are capital- and technology-intensive. Thus manufacturers making advanced products like aircraft, automobiles and computer systems are the key economic agents in these producer-driven chains not only in terms of their earnings, but also in their ability to exert control over backward linkages with raw-material and component suppliers, as well as forward linkages into retailing.

Buyer-driven commodity chains, on the other hand, which characterize many of today's light consumer goods industries like garments, footwear and toys, tend to be labour-intensive at the manufacturing stage. This leads to very competitive and globally decentralized factory systems. However, these same industries are also design- and marketing-intensive, which means that there are high barriers to entry at the brand-name merchandising and retail levels where companies invest considerable sums in product development, advertising and computerized store networks to create and sell these items. Therefore, whereas producer-driven commodity chains are controlled by core firms at the point of production, control over buyer-driven commodity chains is exercised at the point of consumption.

In summary, the world economy today is a 'global factory' in which the production of a single good commonly spans several countries, with each nation performing tasks in which it has a cost advantage. Even the most highly integrated company is not self-sufficient, and thus virtually all firms acquire a substantial portion of their inputs from outside suppliers. In fact, the major international buyers of consumer goods often have no 'in-house' manufacturing capability whatsoever. Unlike arm's-length purchases of ready-made parts and components from independent suppliers (or 'merchant' producers), the global sourcing of consumer items usually revolves around an agreement or contract between the buyer and the overseas factory setting out detailed specifications for the order. Once established, these buyer-supplier networks may last for years and even be extended to third-party countries through 'triangle manufacturing' arrangements that are generating new options for Third World industrialization.

The factories that produce the consumer products that flow through buyer-driven commodity chains are involved in contract manufacturing relationships with the buyers who place the orders. Contract manufacturing[10] (or specification contracting) refers to the production of finished consumer goods by local firms, where the output is distributed and marketed abroad by trading companies, branded merchandisers, retail chains, or their agents. This is the major export niche filled by the East Asian NICs in the world economy.

In 1980, for example, Hong Kong, Taiwan and South Korea accounted for 72 per cent of all finished consumer goods exported by the Third World to OECD countries, other Asian nations supplied another 19 per cent, while just 7 per cent came from Latin America and the Caribbean. The United States was the leading market for these consumer products with 46 per cent of the total (Keesing 1983: 338–9). East Asian factories, which have handled the bulk of the contract manufacturing orders from US retailers, tend to be locally owned and vary greatly in size – from the giant plants in South Korea to the myriad small family firms that account for a large proportion of the exports from Taiwan and Hong Kong.[11]

LOCATIONAL PATTERNS OF GLOBAL SOURCING

Big retailers and brand-named merchandisers have different strategies of global sourcing, which in large part are dictated by the client bases they serve (see figure 11.2 and table 11.1). Fashion-oriented retailers that cater to an exclusive clientele for 'designer' products get their expensive, nationally branded goods from an inner ring of premium-quality, high-value-added exporting countries (e.g. Italy, France, Japan). Department stores and specialty chains that emphasize 'private label' (or store brand) products as well as national brands source from the most established Third World exporters (such as the East Asian NICs, Brazil, Mexico and India), while the mass merchandisers that sell lower-priced store brands buy from more remote tiers of medium- to low-cost, mid-quality exporters (low-end producers in the NICs, plus China and the Southeast Asian countries of Thailand, Malaysia, the Philippines and Indonesia). Large-volume discount stores that sell the most inexpensive products import from the outer rings of low-cost suppliers of standardized goods (e.g. China, Indonesia, Bangladesh, Sri Lanka, Mauritius, the Dominican Republic, Guatemala). Finally, smaller importers serve as industry 'scouts'. They operate on the fringes of the international production frontier and help develop potential new sources of supply for global commodity chains (e.g. Vietnam, Myanmar, Saipan).

Several qualifications need to be mentioned concerning the schematic, purposefully oversimplified locational patterns identified in figure 11.2 and table 11.1. These production frontiers represent general trends that can vary by industry, by specific products and by time period. More detailed analyses that trace the global sourcing of particular products over time are required to explore the factors that lead to shifts in these linkages. Two examples will illustrate the complexity of these arrangements.

The first example focuses on large-volume discount stores such as Kmart and Wal-Mart. According to table 11.1, they should source primarily from the three outer rings of the production frontiers, but our direct research indicates these discounters also are prominent buyers in the second ring of East Asian NICs. Why? The reason is twofold. Apparel factories in relatively high-wage countries like Taiwan and South Korea work with anywhere from

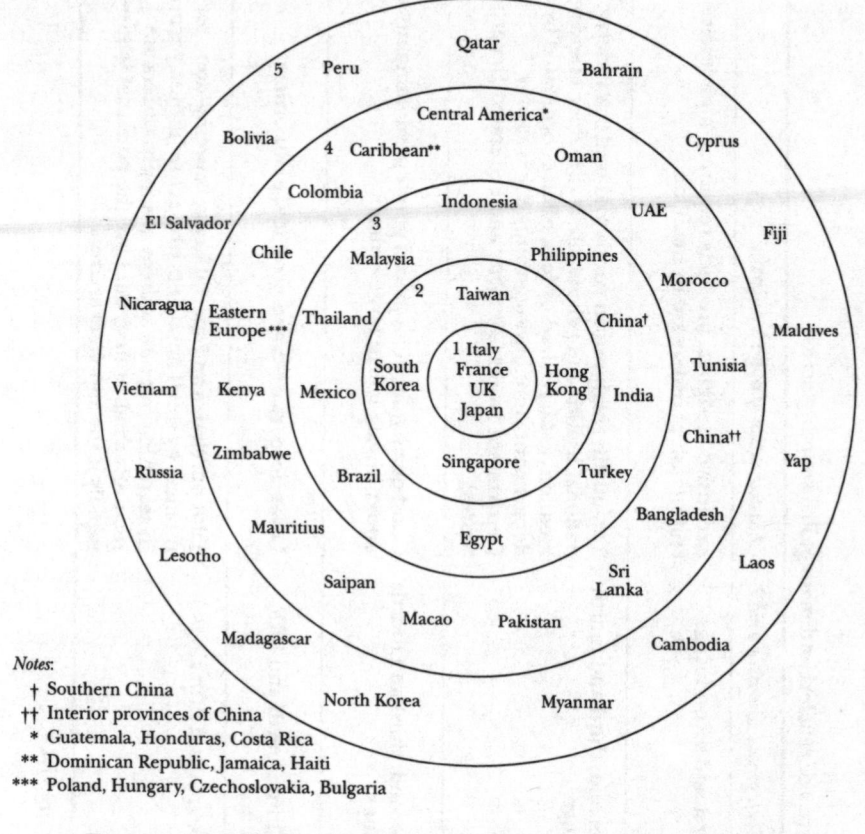

Notes:
† Southern China
†† Interior provinces of China
* Guatemala, Honduras, Costa Rica
** Dominican Republic, Jamaica, Haiti
*** Poland, Hungary, Czechoslovakia, Bulgaria

Figure 11.2 Production frontiers for global sourcing by US retailers:
the apparel industry

five to twenty clients (buyers) in a year. Although Kmart and Wal-Mart pay much less than department stores and specialty retailers like Macy's or Liz Claiborne, the factories use these discounters' large-volume orders to smooth out their production schedules so they do not have gaps or downtime. The other side of the equation is the discounter's vantage point. Kmart and Wal-Mart tend to source their most expensive, complicated items in the second-ring countries (e.g. infant's wear with a lot of embroidery). Thus they are using the more expensive and skilled workers in the NICs to produce relatively high-quality merchandise.

A second illustration deals with the upper-end retailers. Large apparel retailers like The Limited and The Gap, and brand-named companies like Phillips-Van Heusen and Levi Strauss, tend to source heavily in the second and third rings of figure 11.2, but they also buy from countries located in

Table 11.1 Types of retailers and main global sourcing areas

Type of retailer	Representative firms	Main global sourcing areas[a]	Characteristics of buyer's orders
Fashion-oriented companies	Armani, Donna Karan, Polo/Ralph Lauren, Hugo Boss, Gucci	First and second rings	Expensive 'designer' products requiring high levels of craftmanship; orders are in small lots
Department stores, specialty stores and brand-named companies	Bloomingdale's, Saks Fifth Avenue, Neiman-Marcus, Macy's, Nordstrom, J.C. Penney, The Gap, The Limited, Liz Claiborne, Calvin Klein	Second, third and fourth rings	Top-quality, high-priced goods sold under a variety of national brands and private labels (i.e. store brands); medium- to large-sized orders, often coordinated by department store buying groups (such as May Department Stores Company and Federated Department Stores)
Mass merchandisers	Sears Roebuck, Montgomery Ward, J. C. Penney, Woolworth	Second, third and fourth rings	Good-quality, medium-priced goods predominantly sold under private labels; large orders
Discount chains	Wal-Mart, Kmart, Target	Third, fourth and fifth rings	Low-priced, store-brand products; giant orders
Small importers		Fourth and fifth rings	Pilot purchases and special items; sourcing done for retailers by small importers who act as 'industry scouts' in searching out new sources of supply; orders are relatively small at first, but have the potential to grow rapidly if the suppliers are reliable

Note: (a) For the countries in each of these rings, see figure 11.2

the fourth and even the fifth rings. The reason they are positioned in the outer reaches of the production frontiers is because these companies engage in 'price averaging' across their different manufacturing sites. A company like Phillips-Van Heusen, the number-one seller of men's dress shirts in the United States, is confidant that its quality control procedures will allow it to produce identical dress shirts in its factories in the United States, Taiwan, Sri Lanka or El Salvador. This also permits these companies to keep some of their production in, or close to, the United States for quick response to unexpectedly high demand for popular items as well as to gain the good will of the consuming public.

Figure 11.2 highlights some methodological difficulties raised by the commodity chains perspective. Nation-states are not the ideal unit of analysis for establishing global sourcing patterns, since individual countries are tied to the world economy through a variety of export roles (Gereffi 1989, 1992). Production actually takes place in specific regions or industrial districts *within countries* that have very different social and economic characteristics (Porter 1990). Where commodity chains 'touch down' in a country is an important determinant of the kind of production relationships that are established with retailers. Thus there can be several forms of international sourcing within a single nation.[12]

In the People's Republic of China, for example, Guangdong Province has very substantial investments from Hong Kong and Taiwan, while Fujian Province has a natural geographical and cultural affinity for Taiwanese investors. These two provinces in China are part of a Greater China Economic Region that includes Hong Kong and Taiwan (see Chen 1994). Thus China falls within both the third and fourth rings of figure 11.2: the quality and price of the products made in southern China (third ring) in affiliation with its East Asian NIC partners tend to be higher than for the goods produced in the interior provinces of China (fourth ring) where state enterprises are more prevalent.

Despite these qualifications, several generalizations can be made about the production frontiers identified in figure 11.2. As one moves from the inner to the outer rings, the following changes are apparent: the cost of production decreases; manufacturing sophistication decreases; and the lead time needed for deliveries increases. Therefore, there is a strong tendency for the high-quality, multiple-season 'fashion' companies, as well as the more upscale department and specialty stores, to source their production from the three inner rings, while the price-conscious mass merchandisers and discount chains are willing to tolerate the lower quality and longer lead times that characterize production in the two outer rings. The 'industry scout' role played by certain importers is particularly important for this latter set of buyers, since these importers are willing to take the time needed to bring the new, low-cost production sites located in the fourth and fifth rings into global sourcing networks.

'TRIANGLE MANUFACTURING' IN GLOBAL COMMODITY CHAINS

How do the countries in the inner rings of our global sourcing chart deal with the maturing of their export industries? What mechanisms are utilized to ensure a smooth transition to higher-value added activities? One of the most important adjustment mechanisms for maturing export industries in East Asia is the process of 'triangle manufacturing', which came into being in the 1970s and 1980s.

The essence of 'triangle manufacturing' is that US (or other overseas) buyers place their orders with the NIC manufacturers they have sourced from in the past (e.g. Hong Kong or Taiwanese apparel firms), who in turn shift some or all of the requested production to affiliated offshore factories in one or more low-wage countries (e.g. China, Indonesia or Vietnam). These offshore factories may or may not have equity investments by the East Asian NIC manufacturers: they can be wholly owned subsidiaries, joint-venture partners, or simply independent overseas contractors. The triangle is completed when the finished goods are shipped directly to the overseas buyer, under the import quotas issued to the exporting nation. Payments to the non-NIC factory usually flow through the NIC inter-mediary firm.[13]

Triangle manufacturing thus changes the status of the NIC manufacturer from a primary production contractor for the US buyers to a 'middle-man' in the buyer-driven commodity chain. The key asset possessed by the East Asian NIC manufacturers is their long-standing link to the foreign buyers, which is based on the trust developed over the years in numerous successful export transactions. Since the buyer has no direct production experience, he prefers to rely on the East Asian NIC manufacturers he has done business with in the past to assure that the buyer's standards in terms of price, quality and delivery schedules will be met by new contractors in other Third World locales. As the volume of orders in new production sites like China, Indonesia or Sri Lanka increases, the pressure grows for the US buyers eventually to bypass their East Asian NIC intermediaries and deal directly with the factories that fill their large orders.[14]

The process of third-party production began in Japan in the late 1960s, which relocated numerous plants and foreign orders to the East Asian NICs (often through Japanese trading companies or *sogo shosha*).[15] Today, the East Asian NICs, in turn, are transferring many of their factories and orders to China and a variety of Southeast Asian countries. Initially, triangle manufacturing was the result of US import quotas that were imposed on Hong Kong, Taiwan, South Korea and Singapore in the 1970s. These quotas led to the search for new quota-free production sites in the region. Then in the late 1980s the move to other Asian and eventually Caribbean factories occurred because of domestic changes – increased labour costs, labour scarcity and currency appreciations – in the East Asian NICs. The shift toward 'triangle production' has been responsible for bringing many new countries into these production and export networks, including Sri Lanka, Vietnam, Laos, Mauritius, small Pacific islands (like Saipan and Yap), Central America and Caribbean nations.

The importance of 'triangle production' from a commodity chain's perspective is threefold. First, it indicates that there are repetitive cycles as the production base for an industry moves from one part of the world to another. An important hypothesis here is that the 'window of opportunity' for each new production base (Japan – East Asian NICs – Southeast Asian countries – China – Vietnam – the Caribbean) is growing progressively shorter as more new entrants are brought into these global sourcing networks. The reasons include the fact that quotas on new exporting countries in apparel are being applied more quickly by the United States,[16] and technology transfer from the East Asian NICs is becoming more efficient.

The second implication of 'triangle manufacturing' is for social embeddedness. Each of the East Asian NICs has a different set of preferred countries where they set up their new factories. Hong Kong and Taiwan have been the main investors in China (Hong Kong has taken a leading role in Chinese production of quota items like apparel made from cotton and synthetic fibres, while Taiwan is a leader for non-quota items like footwear,[17] as well as leather and silk apparel); South Korea has been especially prominent in Indonesia, Guatemala, the Dominican Republic, and now North Korea; and Singapore is a major player in Southeast Asian sites like Malaysia and Indonesia. These production networks are explained in part by social and cultural networks (e.g. ethnic or familial ties, common language), as well as by unique features of a country's historical legacy (e.g. Hong Kong's British colonial ties gave it an inside track on investments in Jamaica).

A final implication of the GCC framework is that 'triangle manufacturing' has allowed the East Asian NICs to move beyond OEM. Most of the leading Hong Kong apparel manufacturers have embarked on an ambitious programme of forward integration from apparel manufacturing into retailing. Almost all of the major Hong Kong apparel manufacturers now have their own brand names and retail chains for the clothing they make. These retail outlets started out selling in the Hong Kong market, but now there are Hong Kong-owned stores throughout East Asia (including China), North America and Europe.[18] These cycles of change for East Asian manufacturers suggest the need for more elaborated product life cycle theories of Third World industrial transformation.

CONCLUSIONS

As the centre of gravity for basic manufacturing activities has shifted to the Third World, industrialization itself is losing the key status it once had as a hallmark of national development. This observation leads to two conclusions about the impact of industrialization in the contemporary world economy. First, 'industrialization' and 'development' are not synonymous. This fact is apparent in the disparate social and economic consequence of industrial growth in the Latin American and East Asian NICs over the past couple of decades. Despite similarly high levels of industrialization in the NICs from both regions, the East Asian nations have performed significantly better than their Latin American counterparts in terms of standard indicators of development such as GNP per capita, income distribution, literacy, health and education (see Gereffi and Fonda 1992). Conversely, while the 1980s has been the 'lost decade' of development in many Latin American nations as they have suffered through the debt crisis, among other economic woes, redemocratization has been a major political trend in the region. In East Asia, however, there is little evidence of a real turn to democratic institutions and civilian rule. There are a set of paradoxes here that need to be unravelled.

Second, while industrialization may be a necessary condition for core status in the world economy, it no longer is sufficient. Mobility within the world economy should not be defined simply in terms of a country's degree of industrialization, but rather by a nation's success in upgrading its mix of economic activities toward technology – and skill-intensive products and techniques with higher levels of local value added. Continued innovations by the advanced industrial countries tend to make core status an ever receding frontier. Third World nations have to run faster just to stay in place.

The major issues for Third world nations revolve around the various modes of incorporations that define how they are linked to the world economy. These modes of incorporation are not mutually exclusive, however, and in practice most nations are tied to the world-economy in multiple ways. Each type of linkage has its advantages and disadvantages. One of the central tasks in fashioning national development strategies is to determine how to plug into transnational production systems in a way that allows nations to increase their productivity and international competitiveness, while simultaneously generating a higher standard of living for the local population. Ideally, countries should try to move up commodity chains to the highest value-added segments that generate the greatest domestic linkages and profits, and employ the most skilled workers. In practice, however, this often requires the most substantial investments in technological infrastructure and worker training, as well as control over difficult to reach marketing networks in core countries.

Buyer-driven commodity chains mark a key shift in the organization of transnational production systems that affects how countries are incorporated into the world economy. Major retail chains and brand-named companies possess concentrated buying power that has stimulated the proliferation of overseas factories (especially in Asia) in most consumer-goods industries. Big buyers also are acutely sensitive to political factors that shape global supply networks and they currently are in a position to alter overseas production patterns accordingly. For example, during the recent debate in the United States about renewing the People's Republic of China's most-favoured-nation (MFN) status, several large retailers and importers decided to diversify or curtail their purchases from China.[19] This led overseas suppliers to scramble to set up production facilities in nations perceived as relatively 'safe' in terms of domestic political stability (such as Indonesia, Thailand and Malaysia). In quota-restricted industries like garments, retailers and importers also have taken the lead in encouraging production in countries that have favourable quota arrangements with their main export markets in North America and Europe. In other words, quotas drive overseas-investment decisions and thus help shape global commodity chains.

The recent recession in the world-economy has placed a premium on low-priced goods in developed-country markets. This has strengthened the position of the large-volume, low-priced discount chains in the retail sector, and led retailers and manufacturers alike to look for new ways to cut costs. This further enhances the impact of retailers on overseas production networks. One trend we might look for in the future is the establishment of consolidated factory groups (perhaps involving linkages between manufacturers and trading companies) to counter the increased leverage of the large buying groups. These could be coordinated by manufacturers in the East Asian NICs, who continue to be the nexus for many of the orders placed by US big buyers. Exporters in the East Asian nations have accounted for much of the technology transfer to lower-cost production sites, they have access to export networks through their established contacts with the US buyers, and they still handle much of the quality control, financing and shipping needed to get goods to their destination markets in a timely fashion.

Finally, despite the fact that the East Asian NICs have managed to move beyond OEM production through forward as well as backward integration in the apparel commodity chain, the implications of triangle manufacturing for downstream exporters in Southeast Asia, Latin America and Africa are not so promising. Genuine development in these countries is likely to be truncated by the vulnerabilities implied by their export-processing role in global sourcing networks. The main assets Third World exporters possess in buyer-driven commodity chains are low-cost labour and abundant quotas. However, these are notoriously unstable sources of competitive advantage.

Few countries in the world have been able to generate the backward and forward linkages, technological infrastructure, and high levels of local value-added of the East Asian NICs. Even the obvious job-creation and foreign-exchange benefits of export-oriented industrialization for Third World nations can become liabilities when foreign buyers or their East Asian intermediaries decide because of short-term economic or political considerations to move elsewhere. Triangle manufacturing is most advantageous to the overseas buyers and their intermediaries in buyer-driven commodity chains. The long-run benefits for Third World countries occur only if exporting becomes the first step in a process of domestically integrated development.

NOTES

1 Using the World Bank's criteria, 'high-income, advanced industrial economies' which are defined as all 19 members of the Organization for Economic Cooperation and Development with per capita incomes of $7,620 or more in 1990. See World Bank (1992: 213).
2 Countries that developed their manufacturing capabilities early, such as the Latin American NICs and Hong Kong, show little or even negative growth during this period because the manufacturing sector was at a relatively high level of development in 1965.
3 These are predominantly mid-level manufactured exports in terms of technical complexity because textiles and clothing (traditional items) as well as machinery and transport equipment (advanced manufactures) are excluded from this category.
4 South Korea, for instance, has focused on the mass production of powerful memory chips, while Taiwan makes high-value designer chips that carry out special functions in toys, video games and electronic equipment. Singapore has upgraded its activities from the assembly and testing of semiconductors to the design and fabrication of silicon wafers.
5 For an analysis of these factors with a focus on the development trajectories of East Asia and Latin America, see Gereffi and Wyman 1990.
6 This section is adapted from a more complete discussion of this topic in Gereffi (1994).
7 An important exception is the insightful article by Storper and Harrison (1991).
8 These two patterns of international industrial organization are best conceptualized as ideal types, rather than as a dichotomy or a continuum.
9 The average Japanese automaker's production system, for example, comprises 171 first-layer, 4,700 second-layer and 31,600 third-layer subcontractors. See Hill (1989: 466).
10 'Contract manufacturing' is more accurate than the commonly used terms 'international subcontracting' or 'commercial subcontracting' (Holmes 1986) to describe what the East Asian NICs have excelled at. Contract manufacturing refers to the production of finished goods according to full specifications issued by the buyer, while 'subcontracting' actually means the production of components or the carrying out of specific labour processes (e.g. stitching) for a factory that makes the finished item. Asian contract manufacturers (also known as contractors or vendors) have extended their production networks to encompass domestic as well as international subcontractors.

11 Taiwan and Hong Kong have multilayered domestic subcontracting networks, including large firms that produce key intermediate inputs (like plastics and textiles), medium-sized factories that do final product assembly, and many small factories and household enterprises that make a wide variety of components.

12 In Mexico, for instance, there is a vast difference between the *maquiladora* export plants along the Mexico–US border that are engaged in labour-intensive garment and electronics assembly, and the new capital- and technology-intensive firms in the automobile and computer industries that are located further inland in Mexico's northern states. These latter factories use relatively advanced technologies to produce high-quality exports, including components and subassemblies like automotive engines. They pay better wages, hire larger percentages of skilled male workers, and use more domestic inputs than the traditional *maquiladora* plants that combine minimum wages with piecework and hire mostly unskilled women (Gereffi 1991).

13 Typically this entails back-to-back letters of credit: the overseas buyer issues a letter of credit to the NIC intermediary, who then addresses a second letter of credit to the exporting factory.

14 For a detailed analysis of triangle manufacturing and the role of overseas buying offices in Taiwan's apparel industry, see Gereffi and Pan (1994).

15 The industries that Japan transferred to the East Asian NICs are popularly known as the 'three D's': dirty, difficult and dangerous.

16 This may change if a new General Agreement on Tariffs and Trade is signed.

17 After controls were relaxed on Taiwanese investments in the People's Republic of China in the late 1980s, around 500 footwear factories were moved from Taiwan to China in less than two years. Although China recently passed Taiwan as the leading footwear exporter to the United States (in terms of pairs of shoes), it is estimated that nearly one-half of China's shoe exports comes from Taiwanese owned or managed firms recently transferred to the mainland (author's interviews with footwear industry experts in Taiwan).

18 A good example of this is the Fang Brothers, one of the principal suppliers for Liz Claiborne, who now have several different private label retail chains (Episode, Excursion, Jessica, and Jean Pierre) in a variety of countries including the United States (Cawthorne 1993).

19 During an interview in October 1991 in the Hong Kong office of one of the largest US footwear importers, I was told that the American headquarters of the company ordered 25 per cent of the importer's purchases from the People's Republic of China to be shifted to Indonesia within one year to avoid the supply disruptions that would occur if China's MFN status were denied.

REFERENCES

Cawthorne, Zelda (1993) 'Paris chapter for Episode', *South China Morning Post* (Hong Kong), 24 July.

Chen Xiangming (1994) 'The new spatial division of labor and commodity chains in the Greater South China Economic Region', in Gereffi and Korzeniewicz 1994: 165–86.

Donaghu, Michael T. and Barff, Richard (1990) 'Nike just did it: international subcontracting and flexibility in athletic footwear production', *Regional Studies* 24, 6: 537–52.

Doner, Richard F. (1991) *Driving a Bargain: Automobile Industrialization and Japanese Firms in Southeast Asia*, Berkeley CA: University of California Press.

Florida, Richard and Kenney, Martin (1991) 'Transplanted organizations: the transfer of Japanese industrial organization to the United States', *American Sociological Review* 56, 3 (June): 381–98.

Gereffi, Gary (1989) 'Rethinking Development Theory: insights from East Asia and Latin America', *Sociological Forum* 4, 4 (Fall): 505–33.

—— (1991) 'The 'old' and 'new' Maquiladora industries in Mexico: what is their contribution to national development and North American integration?', *Nuestra economía* 2, 8 (May–August): 39–63.

—— (1992) 'New realities of industrial development in East Asia and Latin America: global, regional, and national trends', in Richard P. Appelbaum and Jeffrey Henderson (eds) *States and Development in the Asian Pacific Rim*, Newbury Park, CA: Sage Publications: 85–112.

—— (1994) 'The organization of buyer-driven global commodity chains: how US retailers shape overseas production networks', in Gary Gereffi and Miguel Korzeniewicz (eds) *Commodity Chains and Global Capitalism*, Westport CT: Greenwood Press: 95–122.

Gereffi, Gary and Fonda, Stephanie (1992) 'Regional paths of development', *Annual Review of Sociology* 18: 419–48.

Gereffi, Gary and Korzeniewicz, Miguel (1990) 'Commodity chains and footwear exports in the semi-periphery', in William Martin (ed.) *Semiperipheral States in the World Economy*, Westport CT: Greenwood Press: 45–68.

—— (eds) (1994) *Commodity Chains and Global Capitalism*, Westport, CT: Greenwood Press.

Gereffi, Gary and Pan Mei-Lin (1994) 'The globalization of Taiwan's garment industry', in Edna Bonacich, Lucie Cheng, Norma Chinchilla, Nora Hamilton and Paul Ong (eds) *Global Production: The Apparel Industry in the Pacific Rim*, Philadelphia, PA: Temple University Press.

Gereffi, Gary and Wyman, Donald (eds) (1990) *Manufacturing Miracles: Paths of Industrialization in Latin America and East Asia*, Princeton, NJ: Princeton University Press.

Henderson, Jeffrey (1989) *The Globalization of High Technology Production: Society, Space and Semiconductors in the Restructuring of the Modern World*, New York: Routledge.

Hill, Richard Child (1989) 'Comparing transnational production systems: the automobile industry in the United States and Japan', *International Journal of Urban and Regional Research* 13, 3 (September): 462–80.

Holmes, John (1986) 'The organization and locational structure of production subcontracting', in Allen J. Scott and Michael Storper (eds) *Production, Work, and Territory: The Geographical Anatomy of Industrial Capitalism*, Boston: Allen & Unwin: 80–106.

Keesing, Donald B. (1983) 'Linking up to distant markets: south to north exports of manufactured consumer goods', *American Economic Review* 73: 338–42.

Lardner, James (1988) 'The sweater trade – I', *The New Yorker*, 11 January: 39–73.

Mitchell, Russell (1992) 'The Gap: can the nation's hottest retailer stay on top?', *Business Week*, 9 March: 58–64.

OECD (1988) *The Newly Industrializing Countries: Challenge and Opportunity for OECD Industries*, Paris: OECD.

Piore, Michael J. and Sabel, Charles F. (1984) *The Second Industrial Divide*, New York: Basic Books.

Porter, Michael E. (1990) *The Competitive Advantage of Nations*, New York: Free Press.

Rabach, Eileen and Kim Eun Mee (1994) 'Where is the chain in commodity chains? The service sector nexus', in Gereffi and Korzeniewicz 1994: 123–41.

Reich, Robert B. (1991) *The Work of Nations*, New York: Knopf.

Storper, Michael and Harrison, Bennett (1991) 'Flexibility, hierarchy and regional development: the changing structure of industrial production systems and their forms of governance in the 1990s', *Research Policy* 20, 5 (October): 407–22.

World Bank (1992) *World Development Report 1992*, New York: Oxford University Press.

12

TOURISM, CAPITALISM AND DEVELOPMENT IN LESS DEVELOPED COUNTRIES

David Harrison

During the nineteenth century, improved standards of living, increased leisure and more efficient forms of transport enabled the working class of Western Europe to benefit from capitalist growth. Along with altered perceptions in medical science – most notably concerning the medicinal properties of sea water and the sea air – such changes led to the rapid development of seaside holiday resorts and, more generally, of the domestic tourism industry. International tourism, especially the Grand Tour, was also affected. With increasing numbers of the bourgeoisie able to afford pursuits traditionally enjoyed by the aristocracy, the established upper classes sought alternative holiday venues. The pattern was to become common throughout the tourism industry: as the lower classes moved into the holiday resorts, their predecessors moved apart, and often away. International tourism[1] is not a new phenomenon and has been directed towards a mass market since the mid-nineteenth century, when Cook pioneered the package tour (Swinglehurst 1982). However, it was only after the Second World War that this approach was extended to air travel. Aircraft produced for the war effort became surplus to the standard requirements of civil airlines and, along with advances in aviation technology and post-war prosperity, led to the development of charter flights. As a consequence, international tourism became big business. In 1950, a little over 25 million tourists (excluding day trippers) crossed national boundaries. By 1990, this figure had increased to 425 million (WTO 1991a: 11) and numbers are expected to rise to 638 million by the year 2000 (WTO 1991a: 7). International tourism is now the third largest item in world trade, accounting for more than 7 per cent of all world exports, and involves expenditure higher than the GNP of any single country except the United States. Combined, international tourism and domestic tourism are said to account for 12 per cent of the world's GNP and 100 million jobs (Waters 1988: 4; WTO 1991b, vol. I: 24; Hall 1991a: 24).

INTERNATIONAL TOURISM AND LESS DEVELOPED COUNTRIES[2]

Although there are numerous problems involved in measuring the extent and impact of international tourism (Harrison 1992a: 2–18), it is clearly an integral feature of the world system. Like other sectors of the world economy, it is dominated by developed countries, as indicated in table 12.1. Of the top ten earners in 1986, only Mexico might arguably be defined as an LDC (less developed country), depending on the criteria for such a classification (see O'Neill 1984: 710), and it is also evident that tourism earnings are related to tourist numbers. In 1989, developed countries attracted 65 per cent of all international arrivals and 72 per cent of all tourism receipts. Europe was the main destination area and the chief source of tourists, receiving 64 per cent of all international arrivals and providing more than 60 per cent of visitors to other countries. In other words, most international tourists live in developed countries and visit other developed countries.

By contrast, in 1989 LDCs attracted 21 per cent of all international tourists and 26 per cent of the receipts from international tourism (WTO 1991b, vol. I: 37). However, this relatively low position does not imply that international tourism is unimportant to LDCs. In themselves, absolute numbers are a poor indicator of significance and, as in the West, the 'benefits' of tourism are spread disproportionately among the LDCs.

A more detailed regional survey of tourism in the LDCs has been provided elsewhere (Harrison 1992a: 4–8). However, some regions are clearly far more involved in the tourism industry than others. Latin America and the Caribbean ('the Americas') and South and Southeast Asia attract 67 per cent of all arrivals to LDCs and obtain 74 per cent of all LDC receipts from this industry. Oceania, West Asia and Africa (along with Turkey, regarded by the WTO as the only LDC in Europe) lag considerably behind, as indicated in table 12.2.

In the Americas, Mexico and Argentina are major recipients of tourists and, among islands classified by the WTO as Caribbean, the Bahamas, Puerto Rico and the Dominican Republic are dominant. Smaller Caribbean islands, too, which tend to have mono-crop economies, are especially reliant on tourism. By contrast, in East Asia and the Pacific the most successful countries in attracting tourism, especially from Japan, are also those which are most rapidly industrializing, notably Thailand, South Korea, Singapore, Hong Kong, the Philippines, Taiwan and Malaysia. China, too, is developing its tourism industry but still caters primarily for visiting Chinese from Hong Kong, Macao and Taiwan.

The Middle East, Africa and South Asia attract relatively few international tourists – a little over 5 per cent of all arrivals in 1989 (WTO 1991a: 11). In the Middle East, Egypt (as classified by the WTO) and, until the Gulf

Table 12.1 World's top tourism earners and spenders, 1989 ($ million)

Country	International tourist receipts	Rank	International tourist expenditure	Rank	Share of world total (%) Receipts	Share of world total (%) Expenditure	International tourist arrivals (000s)	Rank
United States	34,432	1	34,977	1	16.4	15.1	36,604	2
France	16,500	2	10,292	5	7.9	4.4	50,199	1
Spain	16,174	3	3,080	15	7.7	1.3	35,350	3
Italy	11,984	4	6,772	7	5.7	2.9	25,935	4
UK	11,182	5	15,111	4	5.3	6.5	17,338	6
Austria	9,317	6	5,027	9	4.5	2.2	18,202	5
Germany	8,658	7	23,727	2	4.1	10.2	14,653	8
Switzerland	5,568	8	4,907	10	2.7	2.1	12,600	10
Canada	5,014	9	7,370	6	2.4	3.2	15,111	7
Mexico	4,794	10	4,247	13	2.3	1.8	6,297	16
Hungary	738	46	800	28	0.3	0.3	14,236	9
Japan	3,143	15	22,490	3	1.5	9.7	2,676	32
Netherlands	3,002	18	6,454	8	1.4	2.8	3,542	25

Sources: WTO (1991b: 130–2); Harrison (1992a: 3)

Table 12.2 World tourism and less developed countries: international arrivals and tourism receipts, 1989

Region	% of all arrivals to LDCs	% of all LDC receipts from tourism
Americas	31.3	31.4
Africa	17.7	9.9
West Asia	12.6	12.6
S and SE Asia	35.8	42.8
Oceania	1.6	2.6
Europe	1.0	0.7
Total	100.0	100.0

Sources: WTO (1991b, vol. I: 36–7); Harrison (1992a: 8)

War, Jordan have dominated the market, and other North African countries have also developed successful tourism industries, especially Morocco, Tunisia and Algeria. To a lesser extent, this also applies to Kenya, Zimbabwe and the Republic of South Africa. In South Asia, India is utterly dominant, and from 1985 to 1989 increased its share of the region's tourists from 49 per cent to 60 per cent (WTO 1991a: 17).

The future of international tourism is likely to be along much the same lines. However, over the next decade, some 'exotic' destinations, notably the Caribbean and Southeast Asia, are expected to increase their share of the long-haul market (along with the United States), whereas the performance of Africa and South America is expected to decline (Lickorish 1988: 271; Edwards 1991).

At the most basic level, tourists have an evident physical impact on the receiving society and several measures have been used to relate numbers of tourist arrivals to the population size and area of specific countries (Hall 1991a: 17–24; Harrison 1992a: 11–13). Clearly, population size is important. In 1988, for example, tourists to the Bahamas amounted to six times that country's population. Length of stay is also a factor and, in 1988, tourists stayed on average for eleven days in Barbados, more than twice as long as in the Bahamas or Singapore. As a consequence, one method of increasing revenues from tourism is to persuade people to stay longer rather than to try and attract more tourists. If the area of the 'host' country is relatively small, pressure of numbers may be especially great. Barbados, for example, has 431 square kilometres compared to Kenya's 580,000, and it is the relatively small size of Singapore, with 1,000 square kilometres and more than 4 million tourists a year that gives it one of the highest tourist density rates in the world (Harrison 1992a: 12).

Despite such measurements, however, 'league tables' of tourist penetration and density are of limited value. They ignore seasonality and concentration of tourist facilities, both of which are major characteristics of domestic and international tourism. Equally important, they do not deal with sociocultural features, which are crucial in assessing how far tourism is contributing to 'development'. Despite high numbers of tourist arrivals relative to their land mass, the Bahamas, Barbados and Singapore, for example, may cope more easily with tourism than poorer countries, for example, Kenya and Sri Lanka. that are much lower in the rankings. And the social impact of more than 15.5 million visitors a year to a developed country with a population of 57 million (the United Kingdom) may be less than two thousand tourists to an extremely poor country of 1.4 million (Bhutan), where differences in culture and standards of living between 'host' and 'guest' are much greater.

As an industry 'without chimneys', and one that seems to require relatively low initial capital investment, tourism is an attractive option to many LDCs. Indeed, the lack of industrial development, along with 'unspoiled' natural resources and 'traditional' indigenous cultures, often regarded as indicators of economic backwardness, may be considered assets in attracting tourists from developed societies. Undoubtedly, they are marketed as such.

THE ECONOMIC IMPACT OF TOURISM

There is already a substantial literature on the economic impact of international tourism (see, for example, Harrison 1992a: 13–17; Ryan 1991: 65–94). Although quantification is difficult, tourism is generally considered to have direct and indirect effects on foreign-exchange earnings, on GDP and on employment. Meeting tourist demands involves the production of capital and consumer goods and services from a wide range of economic sectors and, where economies are diversified, the multiplier effects may be considerable.

In general, LDCs are net recipients of foreign exchange arising from tourism (Sinclair, Alizadeh and Onunga 1992: 48). Although figures must be interpreted with caution, for some island economies, especially, tourism is a major contributor to GDP and a key source of export earnings, as indicated in table 12.3, where several developed countries have been included to facilitate comparison. Indeed, by 1988, 'visitor expenditure was more than half the size of GDP in Anguilla, Antigua and Barbuda, Bahamas, Bermuda, St Kitts and Nevis, the Turks and Caicos Islands and the US Virgin Islands' (Caribbean Tourism Organisation 1990: 148). In Singapore, which is also highly export-oriented, tourism plays an important role and, by 1985, it was the island's third most important source of foreign exchange (Khan, Chou and Wong 1990: 409). The pattern is repeated elsewhere: in 1984, receipts from tourism were higher than from the main export product in Barbados, Haiti, and Bermuda and in Panama, the Philippines, Thailand and India (WTO 1988: 105).

In general, the more diversified the economy, the less importance tourism will have either for GDP or for exports. Indeed, critics argue that there is little point in accumulating tourist dollars if most are used to pay for imports to satisfy tourist demand for high standard accommodation, food, drink and entertainment. This raises the twin issues of multipliers and leakages, which are the subject of great debate in the tourism literature (Sutcliffe 1985; Harrison 1992a: 16–17; Ryan 1991: 70–94; Archer 1977, 1989). Some of these debates focus on techniques of measurement but the overall issues are clear. For as long as it remains within the 'host' country, tourists' expenditure creates income and has knock-on effects throughout the economy. By contrast, expenditure that leaves the country, as profit, dividends or wages, or to import goods and services, for example, is classified as a 'leakage' and creates incomes elsewhere. In practice, countries

Table 12.3 Volume of tourism receipts for selected countries, 1984

Country	Tourism receipts as % of	
	GDP	Exports of goods
USA	0.3	5.2
Italy	2.3	11.7
UK	1.3	6.5
Spain	4.5	32.8
Cyprus	11.3	47.0
Morocco	3.1	21.0
Tunisia	5.2	25.8
Kenya	1.6	8.9
Bermuda	36.5	819.5
Haiti (1983)	5.4	51.2
Jamaica	16.4	52.1
Costa Rica	4.0	12.0
Argentina	0.9	7.4
Mexico	2.1	14.0
Hong Kong	4.0	4.8
Malaysia	1.8	3.5
Singapore	10.0	7.7
Thailand	2.7	11.3
India	0.6	14.0
Mauritius	4.0	11.8

Source: WTO (1988: 103–4)

with few industries other than tourism, or who cannot persuade tourists to consume local produce, suffer the greatest leakages. Generally, large and highly populated 'host' countries tend to have high tourist-income multipliers, whereas small island economies, with few natural resources, have low income multipliers and a correspondingly greater 'leakage' (Fletcher 1989: 527).

How far tourism contributes to employment is also a matter of considerable debate (Harrison 1992a: 14–15), mainly because tourism covers several economic sectors in which local residents also participate. Transportation systems, entertainment complexes, restaurants and bars, shops and cultural centres, for example, cater for tourist and local residents alike. As a consequence, the extent tourism contributes to employment in these sectors is often difficult to quantify. Even hotels which cater primarily for tourists encourage local custom (of the 'right' sort), especially in the low season. Furthermore, a successful tourism industry, with high multiplier effects, will help create a buoyant economy and thus increases the overall ('induced') demand for goods and services. That said, it remains an open question whether or not the alleged benefits would have been greater if investment in some other industry had occurred.

According to the World Tourism Organisation (WTO), tourism is more labour-intensive than many other industries, provides opportunities across a wide range of skills, and is a ready source of employment for low-income groups, often attracting a relatively high proportion of women (WTO 1988: 75). Indeed, in some island societies, it is quite clear that tourism is the major employer. In Bermuda in 1985, for example, 11,000 jobs (63 per cent of the total labour force) were directly attributed to the tourism industry, which was said to contribute 59 per cent to all household incomes. It was also estimated that 75 per cent of all tourist expenditure left the country to pay for imports, and that 40 per cent of such imports went either to households which had become more affluent as a result of tourism or to businesses which had benefited from tourist expenditure (Archer 1987). In larger and more diversified economies it is more difficult to estimate tourism's contribution to employment. In 1979 in Kenya, international tourism is said to have directly or indirectly provided jobs for 57,000 people, nearly 6 per cent of all wage employees but only 0.5 per cent of the total workforce (Bachmann 1988: 186). By including the non-wage sector, much of which was devoted to subsistence agriculture, Bachmann thus presented tourism in a poorer light than portrayed by the WTO. His findings have been echoed by others who have studied tourism in Kenya (Summary 1987: 537; Rajotte 1987: 87).

Additional complications arise because, like other industries, tourism is not static. Employment requirements change at different stages in the development of a tourist region (Butler 1980). Furthermore, much depends on the type of tourism development which prevails. In Bali, for example, large international hotels generated more jobs and more foreign exchange than smaller, locally owned establishments. However, expenditure in the former was reportedly subject to a greater level of leakage and international hotels also had fewer linkages with the rest of the economy (Rodenburg 1980). By contrast, it is claimed that in the Cook Islands (Milne 1987) and in Thailand (Meyer 1988: 478) small, locally owned hotels and boarding houses have been more successful in creating income, employment and government revenue. Such differences across countries may be due, in part, to the use of different criteria in the measurement of tourism's economic impact. However, they can also be explained by the varied capacity of other economic sectors to meet tourist demand from within a country's resources. Although it would be comforting to record a consensus on the strictly economic impact of international tourism on LDCs, it is simply not possible. That some countries rely greatly on tourism is undeniable, and in so doing they increase their overseas earnings and tourism becomes a significant component of their GDP. In addition, jobs are created, directly or indirectly, and wage labour in the country is correspondingly increased. However, this does not occur in all LDCs. Tourists (in any numbers) visit only societies which have already reached certain 'acceptable' standards in their physical infrastructure, in public health and in personal safety. Unlike P. J. O'Rourke (1988), tourists do not intentionally go to the world's trouble spots and, if unrest does occur, the tourism industry is the first to suffer. In short, although they visit the exotic poor, tourists do so in relative comfort and in the expectation of continued security. Like other international investors, they avoid regions that contain the poorest of the poor.

INTERNATIONAL TOURISM AND CAPITALISM

The extent to which tourism has become internationalized was described in a far-sighted article more than a decade ago by Lanfant, who referred to 'a powerful multinational industry employing the very latest in highly developed marketing techniques' (1980: 23). Increasingly reliant on information technology, the multifaceted product of tourism is promoted by large-scale capitalism in conjunction with state authorities and international organizations (for example, the World Tourism Organisation), and 'global planning thus takes on an international dimension through the co-ordination of measures that were isolated or peculiar to a single country and their combination to produce an overall strategy that is both national and multinational' (Lanfant 1980: 30). Although the majority of tourists travel to and from developed countries, the internationalization of tourism has affected LDCs. In 1989 they attracted more than 89 million visitors, primarily from developed countries. Capitalism is crucially involved in managing and profiting from this massive, temporary and annual migration, a factor which has been noted (and often bewailed) by many commentators.

Precisely what motivates millions of people to travel for holiday purposes every year is a matter of considerable debate among social scientists. For a key figure in the early studies of tourism (MacCannell 1976), tourism was a consequence of an overriding process of modernization, especially in developed societies. In a world characterized by increasing structural differentiation, social life, especially for the middle classes, is organized around leisure rather than work, and 'modern man' and 'modern woman' become tourists in two senses: quite literally they become sightseers but, in addition, they are tourists in a spiritual sense, searching for authenticity and value whilst beset by continuous change and uncertainty. Through tourism in the latter sense, modernity is provided with its dominating ideology and tourist attractions take on the functional significance previously held by religious symbols. The tourist is thus a modern pilgrim and tourist attractions, be they objects, places, or even entire communities or societies, are shrines at which authenticity is worshipped, albeit in vain: in discovering new sources of authenticity, tourists inevitably pollute that which they seek to preserve.

The links between tourism and pilgrimage have since been stressed by many other writers (Turner and Turner 1978; Graburn 1989; Smith 1992a). However, for MacCannell, the modern pilgrim's search for authenticity and 'tradition' commences in developed societies but is soon extended to LDCs, thus fuelling the growth of international tourism. Such a neo-Durkheimian view is not without its critics (Cohen 1979: 179–81; Schudson 1979; Thompson 1981: 30–6) and the driving force behind modernization is not clear, especially as MacCannell claims (1976: 2) that it transcends socialism and capitalism, the latter of which he avowedly detests (1992: 58–60, 69, 105). In fact, modernization is probably best regarded as a feature of westernization, related to (but not synonymous with) capitalism (Harrison 1988: 154–6). Nevertheless, irrespective of which view is accepted in this matter, MacCannell's earlier writing focuses on social change in the developed parts of the world and provides insights into how they may be related, through tourism, to the LDCs, which are frequently marketed as embodying the very characteristics sought by MacCannell's hapless tourist.

The role of transnational companies provides considerable evidence of the capitalist nature of the world tourism industry. They are less important in domestic tourism which, according to the WTO (1988: 51), tends to be 'a fundamentally spontaneous phenomenon, organised by the family with the automobile constituting the most widely used means of transport'. Nevertheless, much of the accommodation may be provided by large, capitalist companies. International tourism gives greater scope for the operation of the transnationals, even though regional variations remain considerable. In the United States, Canada and Japan, most travel is organized through intermediaries, whereas in Europe it is more likely to be independent. There are strong regional differences, with UK travellers most likely, and the Italians least likely, to use travel agencies. Among tour operators, who are nearly all based in Europe, there is also increasing concentration (which is exacerbated in times of recession) but, again, with regional differences (WTO 1988: 51–4). The overall situation is complicated further by the growing privatization of tourism in Eastern Europe which, until recently, has been monopolized by state organizations.

Transnational companies normally become involved in providing accommodation during the 'consolidation stage' of a tourist region, when the influx of tourists can no longer be met by relatively small, locally owned establishments (Butler 1980). By 1975, 47 per cent of all hotels associated with transnational companies were in LDCs, primarily in countries with relatively high levels of economic development. The top eleven in this league table, with 35 per cent of the hotels and 43 per cent of hotel bedrooms, were Mexico, the Philippines, Indonesia, Hong Kong, Venezuela, the Bahamas, Puerto Rico, Morocco, Singapore, Israel and Brazil (Dunning and McQueen 1982: 76–7).

In the LDCs, as elsewhere, the internationalization of tourism is clearly the norm, and continued evidence to this effect is provided in studies of the Pacific, Malta, India, Kenya, the Gambia, the Caribbean, southern Africa and Thailand (Harrison 1992b: 23). In 1983–4, for example, '97 per cent of all tourists flying a commercially scheduled airline to ... Paradise Island [in the Bahamas] ... arrived on an American-owned airline' (Debbage 1990: 516). Once there, they enjoyed accommodation of international standard, as more than 90 per cent of all hotel beds on the island were owned or managed by one of five transnational companies (Debbage 1990: 518). In all likelihood, too, they were plied with food and drink which had been imported from developed capitalist countries.

An earlier study of another Bahamian island (La Flamme 1979), which then catered for small groups of tourists, painted a different picture in which local (white) entrepreneurs were holding their own against outside competition. However, as tourist numbers increase, such a stand is more difficult to maintain, as shown in numerous studies elsewhere, including Greece (Tsartas 1992).

Transnational companies operate at all levels of the industry, as travel agents, tour operators, hoteliers and airline operators. Indeed, the industry as a whole is characterized by considerable vertical and horizontal integration. Even in 1978, when only sixteen transnational hotel companies were linked with international airlines, they accounted for 34 per cent of all foreign hotels: 'on average, nearly three quarters of the airline-associated hotels were foreign based and, of these, three fifths were in developing countries' (Dunning and McQueen 1982: 74).

Not surprisingly, tourist-receiving countries, especially LDCs, are at a disadvantage when negotiating with transnational companies. The issue is more of control than of ownership, as Sinclair and her co-authors make clear:

> Contractual relationships between local and foreign tourism enterprises vary across different sectors of the industry. The predominant form of relationship between the airline sector and foreign tour operators, for example, is the short-term contract, whereas contractual arrangements involving the hotel sector, tour operators and other foreign firms include short-term contracts and other types of arrangements. The latter include management contracts, franchising agreements and common ownership of hotels, tour operators and, in some cases, airlines, mainly through joint ventures between local and overseas investors. In addition, different types of arrangement may overlap, so that a hotel located in a developing country may be owned by one foreign firm and managed by another.
>
> (Sinclair, Alizadeh and Onunga 1992: 61)

One response to this kind of situation is for the state to lend its support to local entrepreneurs, or even to become directly involved in the tourism industry as, for example, seems to have occurred in Thailand, where the tourism industry is dominated by an alliance involving the government, the royal family, the Chinese commercial class and the transnationals (Meyer 1988: 113–95). However, even where the state acts in their support, as in Kenya, the dice may be loaded against indigenous entrepreneurs: 'Local hoteliers, faced with competition within the country and from other developing countries, are dependent on foreign tour operators, who control the overseas marketing of the accommodation' (Sinclair, Alizadeh and Onunga 1992: 61).

The pattern tends to be repeated in other LDCs, to the extent that one critic, favouring an approach based on underdevelopment theory, considers international tourism to be dominated by metropolitan capital, supported by comprador capital in LDCs, with small, locally owned enterprises left to scratch around for any crumbs that might fall from this highly elitist table (Britton 1982: 346–7).

Finally, it is worth noting that (like any other new industry) tourism not only creates new jobs, but also brings opportunities for entrepreneurship. Exactly who takes these openings will depend very much on the existing social structure. In some cases, established elites are able to capitalize on their advantages, but opportunities may also arise for groups that are marginal to society, perhaps ethnic minorities or returning migrants, to establish a niche in the new industry. In the informal sector, too, an 'under class' may develop (or be expanded) to cater for tourist demands, some of which may be regarded as morally suspect (Harrison 1992b: 23–6).

International tourism and commoditization

The loss of 'authenticity' and the consequences of the commoditization of 'traditional' cultures are major issues in the study of tourism. For MacCannell, the process of modernization leads to the despoilation, deconstruction and reconstruction of tradition as it is increasingly integrated into the modern world. 'Tradition' has become a tourist attraction and, in the process, has been undermined, 'embedded in modernity but in a position of servitude' (MacCannell 1976: 34). More recently, he has suggested that traditional (or 'primitive') societies have completely disappeared: 'primitive' cultures have become 'ex-primitive' and, at least in theory, societies can move from 'ex-primitive' status to either 'modern' or 'post-modern' (MacCannell 1992: 302–3).

Others have taken up the theme. Focusing on the movement from 'functional traditional arts', which were developed in traditional societies primarily for use in religious rituals, to their reproduction as 'commercial' replicas for purchase by tourists, Graburn (1984) notes that this may be followed by the production of souvenirs and novelties, which owe their existence entirely to the demand of the tourist market. He suggests that such artefacts may later be incorporated into the indigenous culture, which adapts or adopts art forms from elsewhere and produces 'assimilated' arts which, although barely distinguishable from the art forms of others, may attain the status of 'popular art' within the community if purchased by members of the indigenous culture.

Implicit in Graburn's account of the movement away from traditional art forms is the idea that, with increasing acculturation, the quality of life of the community is threatened. No longer central to the indigenous culture, traditional art becomes 'museumified' and community members encounter a 'symbolically incomplete experience', themselves becoming marginalized and alienated (Graburn 1984: 406, 414).

In tourism studies there is certainly a tendency to decry the production of 'tourist art', which is accompanied by an apparent sense of superiority over the tourist, who is deemed different from and more ignorant than the social scientist who (by a process which is not entirely clear) has come to be an expert on what is and what is not 'authentic'. Fortunately, this view is not universally held (Cohen 1988; Richter 1989: 188–9) and some evidence suggests that many 'traditional' communities are quite capable of extending their production for an external market and yet retaining a sense of the intrinsic worth of the good produced (Jules-Rosette 1984). What is not in doubt, however, is that tourism, as part of a wider process of modernization, incorporates hitherto isolated communities into the world market and brings far more of the items they produce into that market. The process has frequently been associated with colonialism. Nason, for example, notes that the Caroline Islands of the Pacific were subject to a series of cultural influences, stemming mainly from colonialism, from Spain, Germany, Japan and the United States. As a consequence, there was an increase in handicraft production, especially among women, but a reduction in the goods considered by islanders to be 'worthy of special aesthetic consideration' (Nason 1984: 446). However, as with the Amish of Pennsylvania (an interesting example of a 'traditional' community having to contend with 'developed country' tourism), commoditization did not appear to have led to a decline in the quality of the goods produced (Boynton 1986: 460).

A similar but even more contentious process has occurred with what might be described as cultural products: rituals, ceremonies, festivals and the like. In many LDCs (and elsewhere), ceremonies and religious rituals practised by indigenous peoples have become tourist attractions for outsiders. That commoditization has occurred is not in dispute; however, opinions vary on the implications of such changes. Some have argued that although the 'traditional' and the 'sacred' have been monetized, the end result has been to highlight the importance of such activities to members of the host community and, as a consequence, to increase respect among host community members for the practices themselves and their practitioners. This, indeed, has been the position taken over religious dances in Bali and Indonesia (cf. Noronha 1979; Crystal 1989; McKean 1989), and other research has established a highly complex relationship between 'sacred' and 'secular' dances in this region (Picard 1990).

By contrast, seminal articles by Greenwood (1972 and 1989, first published 1978) took a different view. Focusing on the Alarde, an annual public ritual in Fuenterrabia, in northern Spain, which celebrated victory over the French in 1638, he noted that this annual and popular participatory event had for generations served to heighten community solidarity. In 1969, the municipal authorities decreed that the Alarde was a tourist attraction and, as a consequence, should be performed twice on the same day to allow for more tourist spectators: 'In service of simple pecuniary motives, it defined the *Alarde* as a *public show to be performed for outsiders* who, because of their economic importance to the town, had the *right* to see it' (Greenwood 1989: 178; emphasis in the original).

At the time, Greenwood considered this decision by the authorities to sound the death knell for the Alarde. Hitherto enthusiastic townspeople became reluctant to participate and the ritual's significance disappeared: 'what was a vital and exciting ritual had become an obligation to be avoided ... The ritual has become a performance for money. The meaning is gone' (Greenwood 1989: 178). As the title of the article implied, to sell 'Culture by the Pound' necessarily separated the ritual from the townsfolk. Once accorded a commercial value, the ritual became culturally valueless for the participants.

Tourism, social structures and value change

Inevitably, incorporation into the world system through tourism brings considerable change to LDCs. As in developed societies (Pearce 1992), formal institutions are established or expanded to organize and promote the new industry and coordinate activities of the disparate groups interested in its expansion. Banks and other financial institutions, estate agents and solicitors, quickly realize the advantages involvement in tourism may bring and the state bureaucracy is expanded, normally with the addition of a separate department or ministry to promote tourism, along with national and regional tourist boards. As tourism increases, other government agencies arise: national and regional planning authorities are established and the police force and other agencies of social control may be expanded, or reorientated, to deal with the extra pressures an influx of relatively wealthy and pleasure-seeking tourists, perhaps from an alien culture, may bring. Improvements in the infrastructure are necessitated to cope with increased pollution, demands on the electricity supply and sewage disposal. In addition, occupational groups with an interest in the promotion of tourism, or its curtailment, arise. In short, as a key feature of modernization in many LDCs, tourism brings about a radical transformation in the economic and political life of receiving societies.

Values in the 'host' society are also challenged by tourism development. The young, especially, who regard tourists as a source of income and who are more likely than their elders to interact with them on an informal basis, may be keen to adopt forms of behaviour associated with tourists. Such acculturation (commonly known as 'demonstration effects' or, more disparagingly, as 'cultural imperialism') has often been reported from tourist-receiving LDCs. In Malindi, on the Kenyan coast, for example, the authority of the traditional (Moslem) elders declined as the younger generation gained financial independence, either through office jobs in hotels or by the more dubious route to riches offered to beach boys, and with independence came a desire for western consumer goods and an increased tendency to form nuclear families (Peake 1989). Similar accounts have been provided for other parts of Kenya (Bachmann 1988: 191) and elsewhere in the world, including India, Malaysia, Swaziland and the Philippines (UNESCO 1976: 93–4; Chandrakala 1989: 15–8; Bird 1989: 51–2; Harrison 1992c: 154–6; Smith 1992b: 152–4). In the face of the pressure of modernization, 'traditional' authorities may be undermined, and western foodstuffs, fashion, forms of entertainment and consumer items may be preferred to products and pursuits hitherto emanating from within the LDC. Such acculturation is not unique to tourism and the extent it occurs will depend on a wide variety of factors. However, just as capitalism involves an increase in the cash economy, market relationships and commoditization, 'demonstration effects' might be regarded as their cultural equivalent.

The position of women, especially, has often been altered by tourism. It is commonly argued that such changes have been for the worse and, undoubtedly, female prostitution has increased, for example, in parts of Southeast Asia (Hall 1992), as a result of increased tourist numbers. However, benefits have also accrued. The earliest Cook's tours were highly popular among women, who valued the increased safety such package holidays provided (Swinglehurst 1982: 35, 43) and, more recently, women in receiving societies have been influenced by tourist visitors. In Mexico, for instance, women workers in the tourism industry reportedly admire the freedoms enjoyed by women tourists, emulate their less restrictive clothing, and generally value the independence that employment in tourism brings. As a consequence of this enhanced independence, domestic relationships for such women are more egalitarian: 'husbands tend to have greater respect for their wives and treat them accordingly, possibly recognizing that their wives can leave them if they want' (Chant 1992: 98). Of course, this independence might have resulted from other forms of employment but, by the same token, prostitution and crime might also be exacerbated by any influx of relatively wealthy visitors, for example, soldiers, construction workers or accountants.

DOES TOURISM BRING DEVELOPMENT TO LESS DEVELOPED COUNTRIES?

Since the 1950s, international tourism has developed rapidly and in many LDCs (but not the poorest) it is a major contributor to GDP and to export earnings. The industry is undoubtedly an example of advanced capitalist development, uneven though this might be. Transnational companies are important at all levels of the tourism industry but tour operators, airlines and hotels, in particular, have substantial transnational involvement. The better and more expensive the hotel room, the more likely it is to be owned or controlled by a transnational company. In addition, as tourism develops, it is characterized by the increased commoditization of goods sold to tourists, including cultural products as well as 'traditional' arts and crafts. Put differently, production is increasingly for sale rather than for use, exchange is increasingly mediated by money, and there is external control of the production process, with many important financial decisions being made outside tourist-receiving societies.

In this context, tourism within the former 'socialist' countries of the Soviet bloc may now be regarded as a subsystem of the capitalist model, perhaps best described as a form of delayed or stunted capitalism. Until recently, however, tourism in and between these countries had evolved rather differently from tourism in the West (Allcock and Przeclawski 1990; Hall 1991c); their ('social') tourism was geared to socialist goals and was collectively orientated for both production and consumption. In addition, the state held a virtual monopoly at all levels of the industry. However, although some barter arrangements facilitated foreign travel within Eastern Europe for workers or youth groups, international tourism was geared to a mass market and was promoted primarily to obtain foreign exchange. Indeed, from the 1960s, tourists from capitalist countries were an important priority and tourism in the Eastern bloc became highly segmented, with western tourists occupying (and paying more for) the best accommodation (Hall 1991c; Harrison 1993).

Since 1989, the economies of Eastern Europe and the constituent parts of the former Soviet Union have moved closer to the West. The change has been exacerbated by the absorption of the German Democratic Republic in a united Germany, the collapse of the Council for Mutual Economic Assistance (CMEA) and the disruption of travel patterns throughout the region. Consequently, the need for western tourists and their foreign currencies has intensified. Internally, 'social' tourism is increasingly being replaced by a more market-orientated approach and, throughout the region, privatization and the abolition of state power are key objectives of reform (Hall 1991a, b; Harrison 1993). The process has only just started but the focus is firmly on the extension of market relationships. If ever there was a 'socialist model' of tourism development (Hall 1991c), it is now in decline.

Clearly, the expansion of the cash economy, the spread of market relationships and the commoditization of culture are not unique to LDCs. They are the stuff of which capitalism is made. Indeed, debates about 'authenticity' continue to be aired in developed capitalist societies. In the United Kingdom, for example, such 'cultural' institutions as art galleries and museums have increasingly been forced to market their wares, and open-air museums and heritage centres are replacing the more 'traditional' (and dusty) institutions (Urry 1990: 128–34). Authenticity, or 'authentic reproduction' is the vogue, as typified by the reconstruction of a face from a genuine Viking skull at the Jorvik Centre in York. History is allegedly being 'frozen' or 'prettified' and the new emphasis on marketing has led to claims that the product inevitably deteriorates in quality:

> The commodity which is the result of the vast system of cultural production . . . is, I submit, Heritage. Those universal values in the United Nations World Heritage Convention, those values of stewardship, scholarship and cultural identity are now subservient to questions of cash flow and consumer orientation. They are threatened by the ideology that asks . . . 'Can the truth be commercially viable?'
>
> (Hewison 1989: 22)

For some critics, any kind of capitalism is undesirable. MacCannell, whose opposition to capitalism is quite explicit, (1992: 58, 74 and 105), suggests that commercial considerations lead to the destruction of local cultures:

The dividing line between structure genuine and spurious is the *realm of the commercial.* Spurious social relations and structural elements can be bought, sold, traded and distributed throughout the world. Modern economies are increasingly based on this exchange. The line is the same one between furniture and priceless antiques or between prostitution and 'true love' which is supposed to be beyond price. It is also the same as the distinction that is commonly made between a gift that has been purchased, which is thought to be inferior, as opposed to one that has been made by the giver especially for the receiver.

(MacCannell 1976: 155–6; emphasis in the original)

Graburn is somewhat less hostile and directs his criticism more at the development of a mass market. Whereas commercial traditional art depends on 'buyers who know and care enough about the traditional arts to demand "authenticity"', souvenir art requires a 'mass audience which neither knows nor particularly cares for "authentic" artefacts'; it is simply a 'mass, ignorant market' (Graburn 1984: 400).

Greenwood, by contrast, directly links commoditization and capitalism with the deterioration of tradition in Fuenterrabia. By packaging culture 'by the pound', it has (ironically) lost its value:

By ordaining that the Alarde be a public event to attract outsiders into the town to spend money, the municipal government made it one more of Fuenterrabia's assets in the competitive tourism market. But this decision directly violated the meaning of the ritual, definitively destroying its authenticity and its power for the people. They reacted with consternation and then with indifference. They can still perform the outward forms of the ritual for money, but they cannot subscribe to the meanings it once held because it is no longer being performed by them for themselves.

(Greenwood 1989: 179)

However, he later revised this view and, on returning to Fuenterrabia many years after his initial fieldwork, conceded that the public ritual he once considered on the decline because of its exposure to tourists had retained its significance: 'it has become a much more public event and is imbued now with contemporary political significance as part of the contest over regional political rights in Spain' (1989, first published 1978: 181).

When referring specifically to LDCs, it is clear that the argument about tourism and development is, in fact, a specific example of a more general debate. How far 'development' is considered to be occurring in LDCs depends, to a large extent, on the perspective being adopted. The major perspectives have been discussed elsewhere (Harrison 1988; Barnett 1988: 3–50; Hunt 1989; Hulme and Turner 1990) but they can be summarized as modernization theory (MT), with strands from bourgeois and classical Marxism, and underdevelopment theory (UDT), also known as neo-Marxism. More recently, another development 'school' has arisen, equally western and equally reliant on 'scientific' evidence, to focus on change from (real?) 'overdevelopment' to an ideal (and greener) future. Like MT and UDT, environmental perspectives involve a concept of a 'world system' and encompass a wide range of opinion (Redclift 1984, 1987; Brandon and Brandon 1992).

Many advocates of tourism, including the WTO (1988: 81–4) operate, either implicitly or explicitly, with a perspective derived from modernization theory. Here, tourism is seen as a valuable aid to national, regional and local development, with capital investment and the transfer of skills specific to tourism leading to increased employment and general prosperity through changes in the infrastructure and through the operation of various kinds of Keynesian multipliers. According to this perspective, there is no doubt that capitalism, and capitalist-run tourism, brings development.

By contrast, critics of tourism, often employing a perspective derived from UDT, are inclined to suggest that because of the domination of international capital, and the service element implicit in tourism, the industry reinforces the dependence of LDCs on western capitalism (Harrison 1992a: 8–11 and 1992b: 24). According to this view, investment is followed by 'leakage' of foreign exchange, the jobs created in tourism are menial and demeaning, and the profits made from the labour of the poor in LDCs are repatriated to the West. According to this view, capitalist-run tourism contributes to underdevelopment and not development.

Environmentalist perspectives, which have been applied to domestic and international tourism in recent years, tend to focus most on the destructive effects of tourism, especially mass tourism, on the natural environment (Mathieson and Wall 1982: 93–132; Farrell and McLellan 1987; O'Grady 1990: 30–41; Farrell and Runyan 1991; Ryan 1991: 95–130; Eber 1992; Jenner and Smith 1992; Yale 1992: 269–78). There is much evidence from developed and less developed countries to support this view. Large numbers of visitors require transport and impose a heavy burden on the local infrastructure. Pollution from vehicle emissions and from garbage and sewage is a frequent result and the more popular the 'host' region, the greater the pressure on its natural and physical capacity to absorb visitors. New roads and buildings eat into the natural habitats of plant and animal life and rare species are thus increasingly threatened. Such problems are already well known in the 'honeypots' of Europe and North America and they are surfacing in the LDCs. Ecological damage is reported to have arisen, for example, from the construction of golf courses throughout Southeast Asia, especially Thailand (Pleumarom 1992), from the over-exploitation of game parks in Africa (Jenner and Smith 1992: 70–2), from trekking in the Himalayas (Singh 1983), and from ill-judged 'development' along the coast of Malaysia (Wong 1990) and the islands of the South Pacific (Baines 1987).

There is also evidence, however, that tourism and a concern for the environment can operate in tandem. Historic sites and buildings have been rehabilitated as tourist attractions, often gaining an increased respect locally as a result, and natural resources, too (for example, wild life and their habitats) are more willingly conserved by governments once their attraction to tourists (and thus their earning potential) has been realized (Mathieson and Wall 1982: 96–101). Indeed, increased public awareness of environmental issues and self-interest on the part of the tourism industry and 'host' governments, who do not wish their assets to decline, may yet prompt a more careful approach to the environment within which tourism operates, and on which it so heavily depends (Eber 1992: 5–6, 18–9, 37–52).

Perhaps the most heated debates over the effects of tourism, however, have focused on its social impacts. Elsewhere (Harrison 1992b: 20), it has been argued that it is necessary to distinguish between social consequences and social problems. Clearly, as an aspect of modernization, international tourism may bring with it several quite evident social consequences, including capitalist organization, commoditization, changes in the social structure and value change, especially among the young. Such changes can be described, demonstrated and, in principle, explained. They may not be considered problematic and, even if they are so regarded, the problems need not have a moral dimension. Migration from outlying areas to tourist centres, for example, can create practical difficulties for local authorities, who may have to provide suitable accommodation for the newcomers without encroaching on tourist facilities. By contrast, social problems may also be defined from specific value standpoints (Yearley 1991); like beauty, social problems and 'development' are often in the eye of the beholder. It is a social consequence of tourism, for example, that many ceremonies and rituals once carried out within isolated communities are now performed for tourists for payment. However, it is not a moral problem unless it is so defined by individuals or groups who disapprove of this change. Young people in many tourist-receiving societies emulate tourists' taste and behaviour; however, there is nothing intrinsically wrong in drinking alcohol, dancing, wearing 'western' clothes or wanting to buy consumer goods, even though some members of the community, perhaps with interests to protect, regard such behaviour as morally reprehensible. The fact that some western observers may concur with such criticisms does not, in itself, make them morally correct.

To ask whether or not tourism brings 'development', then, is to seek an objective definition of development when such a definition cannot be given. However, some brief remarks may contribute to what will undoubtedly be a continuing debate. First, where direct comparison is possible, conventional economic criteria indicate that tourist-receiving societies are at least as economically successful as other LDCs. Of countries in which tourism is a significant part of their foreign-exchange earnings, only Kenya is classified by the World Bank as a low-income economy and, of societies with populations of less than 1 million, tourist-receiving societies are among the most prosperous, as defined by their per capita GNP (International Bank for Reconstruction and Development 1993: 238–9, 304). To argue that income distribution within many such countries is unequal is more a comment on government policy than an argument against tourism. Clearly, per capita income is a crude measure of prosperity; however, it does indicate that few tourist-receiving countries are among the poorest LDCs. In strictly economic terms, tourism is probably beneficial.

Second, although questions inevitably arise about who is representative of 'the locals', many studies suggest that when ordinary people in LDCs are asked their views, they tend to favour tourism development. Although Smith considers tourism development in Boracay, for example, to have created 'massive physical and social problems' (Smith 1992b: 136), she also notes that 'the tourist presence was viewed in positive terms' (1992b: 152). Why was this?

> Overall, Boracayans *like* and *want* tourism for social as well as economic reasons. Income generated directly into family enterprises has given many participating women considerable social independence as well as cash resources . . . In the traditional society, men had gone fishing and taken their catch to sell in larger communities while women stayed at home to tend hearth and garden. The new presence of outsiders has broadened the worldview. Local employment also has meant that family members could remain on the island (and few Boracayans truly want to live in Manila). The lack of electricity precluded families from buying non-essential gadgetry, and the new money was being used for permanent purposes, particularly higher education for a better future.
>
> (Smith 1992b: 153–4; emphasis in the original)

Despite the implication that, given the opportunity, families would have squandered their new resources on 'non-essential gadgetry', the message here is crystal clear: whatever the views of the visiting anthropologist, people in Boracay wanted tourism, and wanted more of it. Their views are far from unique. They are echoed in many Pacific island communities, where tourism was 'enthusiastically welcomed' (MacNaught 1982: 364) and, however flawed they might be (Ap 1990), questionnaire surveys in other countries indicate a high level of agreement that tourism has been economically, socially and culturally beneficial, for example, in Zambia (Husbands 1989), Turkey (Var, Brayley and Korsay 1989), Hawaii (Liu and Var 1986; Brayley, Var and Sheldon 1990), Malaysia (Ap, Var and Din 1991) and Argentina (Var, et al. 1989).

This is not to suggest that members of tourist-receiving societies are always enthusatic about their guests. Attitudes vary for all kinds of reasons, including the stage of development of the destination, the social class of the 'host', and the degree to which he or she benefits (or loses) as a result of tourism (Murphy 1985: 120–6). Ultimately, however, overt hostility to tourism inevitably removes the cause of the irritation: tourists simply stop coming. More established methods of dealing with tourists may be, like some indigenous Americans, to laugh at them (Evans-Pritchard 1989; Sweet 1989), to stereotype them, or secretly to call them names: in the West Country of England, for example, they are 'emmets' (ants) or 'grockles', and in Norfolk (because they often wear their boating clothing in towns) they are 'the boat people'. Generally speaking, tourists are valued for the economic benefits they are thought to bring. Sometimes they may be unpopular, yet people still seek work in the tourism industry – especially, perhaps, in transnational companies, where rates of pay and conditions are often (a little) better than in locally operated companies. Critics may talk of 'alternative' tourism, which could mean no tourism at all, or some kind of small-scale (and often more expensive) tourism which, if it became popular, would no longer be small-scale or an alternative form of tourism (Smith and Eadington 1992).

Does tourism bring development? It depends on who is the judge. As a reflective (and less judgemental) Greenwood remarked:

the evaluation of tourism cannot be accomplished by measuring the impact of tourism against a static background. Some of what we see as destruction is construction; some is the result of a lack of any other viable options; and some the result of choices that could be made differently.

(1989: 182)

In the meantime, of course, international tourism will continue to grow and there will be a corresponding increase in holidays taken in less developed countries. Undoubtedly, critics of tourism will be in that number, but among the saints rather than the sinners for, as Waterhouse so aptly remarked: 'I am a traveller, you are a tourist, he is a tripper' (1989: 18).

NOTES

1 Tourists come in all shapes and sizes and definitions which are broad enough to cover the entire range of 'touristic' activities. These tend to blur the purpose of travel and include widely differing individuals and groups. In essence, however, tourism is distinguished from other forms of migration by the temporary nature of the visits made, whether by people within the borders of their own country or to countries in which they do not normally reside, and by the fact that they do not normally obtain their income from the region or country being visited (cf. Harrison 1992a: 2; Var 1992: 590–1). Clearly, under

such a definition, holidaymakers are only one category of tourist although, except in sub-Saharan Africa, they tend to be, in the majority, air travellers.

2 For reasons discussed elsewhere (Harrison 1992a: 1), the term 'less developed countries' (LDCs) is preferred to the 'Third World' and other commonly used options. In this chapter, it refers to countries not regarded by the World Bank in 1993 as 'High Income Economies', as well as a few oil-rich states and island economies with relatively high GNP per capita (the Bank's sole criterion) but nevertheless considered by the UN or their own governments as 'developing' (International Bank for Reconstruction and Development 1993: 238–9, 304). In fact, the list of countries is likely to be much the same, irrespective of the favoured terminology, with the possible exception of countries in the former 'Eastern bloc'. Although not considered in this chapter to be LDCs, the analytical distinction between the former 'Second' and 'Third' Worlds is becoming increasingly difficult to maintain.

REFERENCES

Allcock, J. B. and Przeclawski, K. (1990) 'Introduction', in J. B. Allcock and K. Przeclawski (eds) *Tourism in Centrally Planned Economies, Annals of Tourism Research*, special issue 17, 1: 1–6.

Ap, J. (1990) 'Residents' perceptions research on the social impacts of tourism', *Annals of Tourism Research* 17, 4: 610–16.

Ap, J., Var, T. and Din, K. (1991) 'Malaysian perception of tourism', *Annals of Tourism Research* 18, 2: 321–3.

Archer, B. (1977) *Tourist Multipliers: The State of the Art*, Cardiff: University of Wales Press.

—— (1987) 'The Bermudian economy: an impact study', Bermuda: Ministry of Finance.

—— (1989) 'Tourism and island economies: impact analyses', in C. Cooper (ed.) *Progress in Tourism, Recreation and Hospitality Management*, vol. 1, London: Belhaven Press: 125–34.

Bachmann, P. (1988) *Tourism in Kenya: A Basic Need for Whom?* Berne: Peter Lang.

Baines, G. B. K. (1987) 'Manipulation of islands and men: sand-cay tourism in the South Pacific', in S. Britton and W. C. Clarke (eds) *Ambiguous Alternative: Tourism in Small Developing Countries*, Suva: University of the South Pacific.

Barnett, T. (1988) *Sociology and Development*, London: Hutchinson.

Bird, B. (1989) *Langkawi – From Mahsuri to Mahathir: Tourism for Whom?* Kuala Lumpur: Institute of Social Analysis.

Boynton, L. L. (1986) 'The effects of tourism on Amish quilting design', *Annals of Tourism Research* 13, 3: 451–65.

Brandon, K. E. and Brandon, C. (eds) (1992) *Linking Environment to Development: Problems and Possibilities, World Development*, special issue 20, 4.

Brayley, R., Var, T. and Sheldon, P. (1990) 'Perceived influence of tourism on social issues', *Annals of Tourism Research* 17, 2: 285–9.

Britton, S. G. (1982) 'The political economy of tourism in the Third World', *Annals of Tourism Research* 9, 3: 331–58.

Butler, R. W. (1980) 'The concept of a tourism area cycle of evolution: implications for management of resources', *Canadian Geographer* 24, 1: 5–12.

Caribbean Tourism Organisation (CTO) (1990) *Caribbean Tourism Statistical Report*, Christ Church, Barbados: CTO.

Chandrakala, S. (1989) 'The impact of tourism on India's environment', Bangalore: Equations.

Chant, S. (1992) 'Tourism in Latin America: perspectives from Mexico and Costa Rica', in D. Harrison (ed.) *Tourism and the Less Developed Countries*, London: Belhaven Press.

Cohen, E. (1979) 'A phenomenology of tourist experiences', *Sociology* 13, 2: 179–201.

—— (1988) 'Authenticity and commoditisation in tourism', *Annals of Tourism Research* 15, 3: 371–86.

Crystal, E. (1989) 'Tourism in Toraja (Sulawesi, Indonesia)', in V. L. Smith (ed.) *Hosts and Guests: The Anthropology of Tourism*, 2nd edn, Philadelphia: University of Pennsylvania Press.

Debbage, K. G. (1990) 'Oligopoly and the resort cycle in the Bahamas', *Annals of Tourism Research* 17, 4: 513–27.

Dunning, J. H. and McQueen, M. (1982) 'Multinational corporations in the international hotel industry', *Annals of Tourism Research* 9, 1: 69–90.

Eber, S. (ed.) (1992) *Beyond the Green Horizon: Principles for Sustainable Tourism*, London: Worldwide Fund for Nature/Tourism Concern.

Edwards, A. (1991) *European Long Haul Travel Market: Forecasts to 2,000*, London: Economist Intelligence Unit.

Evans-Pritchard, D. (1989) 'How "they" see "us": native American images of tourists', *Annals of Tourism Research* 16, 1: 89–105.

Farrell, B. H. and McLellan, R. W. (eds) (1987) 'Tourism and the physical environment', Annals of Tourism Research, special issue 14, 1.

Farrell, B. H. and Runyan, D. (1991) 'Ecology and tourism', *Annals of Tourism Research* 18, 1: 26–40.

Fletcher, J. E. (1989) 'Input–output analysis and tourism impact studies', *Annals of Tourism Research* 16, 4: 515–29.

Graburn, N. H. H. (1984) 'The evolution of tourist arts', *Annals of Tourism Research* 11, 3: 393–419.

—— (1989) 'Tourism: the sacred journey', in V. L. Smith (ed.) *Hosts and Guests: The Anthropology of Tourism*, 2nd edn, Philadelphia: University of Pennsylvania Press.

Greenwood, D. (1972) 'Tourism as an agent of change: a Spanish-Basque case', *Ethnology* XI(1): 80–91.

—— (1989) 'Culture by the pound: an anthropological perspective on tourism as cultural commoditization', in V. L. Smith (ed.) *Hosts and Guests: The Anthropology of Tourism*, 2nd edn, Philadelphia: University of Pennsylvania Press.

Hall, C. M. (1992) 'Sex tourism in south-east Asia', in D. Harrison (ed.) *Tourism and the Less Developed Countries*, London: Belhaven Press.

Hall, D. R. (1991a) 'Introduction', in D. R. Hall (ed.) *Tourism and Economic Development in Eastern Europe and the Soviet Union*, London: Belhaven Press.

—— (1991b) 'Eastern Europe and the Soviet Union: overcoming tourism constraints', in D. R. Hall (ed.) *Tourism and Economic Development in Eastern Europe and the Soviet Union*, London: Belhaven Press.

—— (1991c) 'Evolutionary pattern of tourism development in Eastern Europe and the Soviet Union', in D. R. Hall (ed.) *Tourism and Economic Development in Eastern Europe and the Soviet Union*, London: Belhaven Press.

Harrison, D. (1988) *The Sociology of Modernization and Development*, London: Routledge.

—— (1992a) 'International tourism and the less developed countries: the background', in D. Harrison (ed.) *Tourism and the Less Developed Countries*, London: Belhaven Press.

—— (1992b) 'Tourism to less developed countries: the social consequences', in D. Harrison (ed.) *Tourism and the Less Developed Countries*, London: Belhaven Press.

—— (1992c) 'Tradition, modernity and tourism in Swaziland', in D. Harrison (ed.) *Tourism and the Less Developed Countries*, London: Belhaven Press.

—— (1993) 'Bulgarian tourism: a state of uncertainty', *Annals of Tourism Research* 20, 3: 519–34.

Hewison, R. (1989) 'Heritage: an interpretation', in D. Uzzell (ed.) *Heritage Interpretation*, vol. I, *The Natural and Built Environment*, London: Belhaven Press.

Hulme, D. and Turner, M. (1990) *Sociology and Development: Theories, Policies and Practices*, New York and London: Harvester Wheatsheaf.

Hunt, D. (1989) *Economic Theories of Development: An Analysis of Competing Paradigms*, New York and London: Harvester Wheatsheaf.

Husbands, W. (1989) 'Social status and perception of tourism in Zambia', *Annals of Tourism Research* 16, 2: 237–53.

International Bank for Reconstruction and Development (World Bank) (1993) *World Development Report 1993*, Oxford: Oxford University Press.

Jenner, P. and Smith, C. (1992) *The Tourism Industry and the Environment*, Special Report No. 2453, London: The Economist Intelligence Unit.

Jules-Rosette, B. (1984) *The Messages of Tourist Art: An African Semiotic System in Comparative Perspective*, New York and London: Plenum Press.

Khan, H., Chou, F. S. and Wong, E. C. (1990) 'Tourism multiplier effects on Singapore', *Annals of Tourism Research* 17, 3: 408–18.

La Flamme, A. G. (1979) 'The impact of tourism: a case from the Bahama Islands', *Annals of Tourism Research* 6, 2: 137–48.

Lanfant, M.-F. (1980) 'Tourism in the process of internationalisation', *International Social Science Journal* 32, 1: 14–43.

Lickorish, L. J. (1988) 'Travel megatrends in Europe to the year 2,000', *Annals of Tourism Research* 15, 2: 270–1.

Liu, J. C. and Var, T. (1986) 'Resident attitudes towards tourism impacts in Hawaii', *Annals of Tourism Research* 13, 2: 193–214.

MacCannell, D. (1976) *The Tourist: A New Theory of the Leisure Class*, London: Macmillan.

—— (1992) *Empty Meeting Grounds*, London: Routledge.

McKean, P. F. (1989) 'Towards a theoretical analysis of tourism: economic dualism and cultural involution in Bali', in V. L. Smith (ed.) *Hosts and Guests: The Anthropology of Tourism*, 2nd edn, Philadelphia: University of Pennsylvania Press.

MacNaught, T. J. (1982) 'Mass tourism and the dilemmas of modernization in Pacific island communities', *Annals of Tourism Research* 9, 3: 359–81.

Mathieson, A. and Wall, G. (1982) *Tourism: Economic, Physical and Social Impacts*, Burnt Mill, Harlow: Longman.

Meyer, W. (1988) *Beyond the Mask*, Saarbrücken and Fort Lauderdale: Verlag breitenbach.

Milne, S. S. (1987) 'Differential multipliers', *Annals of Tourism Research* 14, 4: 499–515.

Murphy, P. E. (1985) *Tourism: A Community Approach*, New York and London: Methuen.

Nason, J. D. (1984) 'Tourism, handicrafts and ethnic identity in Micronesia', *Annals of Tourism Research* 11, 3: 421–49.

Noronha, R. (1979) 'Paradise revisited: tourism in Bali', in E. de Kadt (ed.) *Tourism: Passport to Development?* Oxford and London: Oxford University Press.

O'Grady, A. (ed.) (1990) *The Challenge of Tourism*, Bangkok: Ecumenical Coalition on Third World Tourism.

O'Neill, H. (1984) 'HICs, MICs, NICs and LICs: some elements in the political economy of graduation and differentiation', *World Development* 12, 7: 693–712.

O'Rourke, P. J. (1988) *Holidays in Hell*, London: Pan Books.

Peake, R. (1989) 'Swahili stratification and tourism in Malindi Old Town, Kenya', *Africa* 59, 2: 209–20.

Pearce, D. (1992) *Tourist Organizations*, Harlow: Longman.

Picard, M. (1990) '"Cultural tourism" in Bali: cultural performances as tourist attractions', *Indonesia* 49: 37–74.

Pleumarom, A. (1992) 'The golf war', *Tourism in Focus* 5: 2–4.

Rajotte, F. (1987) 'Safari and beach resort tourism: the costs to Kenya', in S. Britton and W. C. Clarke (eds) *Ambiguous Alternative: Tourism in Small Developing Countries*, Suva: University of the South Pacific.

Redclift, M. (1984) *Development and the Environmental Crisis: Red or Green Alternatives?* London and New York: Methuen.

—— (1987) *Sustainable Development: Exploring the Contradictions*, London: Routledge.

Richter, L. K. (1989) *The Politics of Tourism in Asia*, Honolulu: University of Hawaii Press.

Rodenburg, E. E. (1980) 'The effects of scale in economic development: tourism in Bali', *Annals of Tourism Research* 7, 2: 177–96.

Ryan, C. (1991) *Recreational Tourism: A Social Science Perspective*, London: Routledge.

Schudson, M. S. (1979) 'Review essay: on tourism and modern culture', *American Journal of Sociology* 84, 5: 1249–59.

Sinclair, M. T., Alizadeh, P. K. and Onunga, E. A. A. (1992) 'The structure of international tourism and tourism development in Kenya', in D. Harrison (ed.) *Tourism and the Less Developed Countries*, London: Belhaven Press.

Singh, T. V. (1983) 'Tourism in the Himalaya: how much is not too much', in T. V. Singh and J. Kaur (eds) *Studies in Eco-Development: Himalayas, Mountains and Men*, Lucknow: Print House.

Smith, V. L. (ed.) (1992a) 'Pilgrimage and tourism: the quest in guest', Annals of Tourism Research, special issue 19, 1.

—— (1992b) 'Boracay, Philippines: a case study in "alternative" tourism', in V. L. Smith and W. R. Eadington (eds) *Tourism Alternatives*, Philadelphia: University of Pennsylvania Press.

Smith, V. L. and Eadington, W. R. (eds) (1992) *Tourism Alternatives: Potentials and Problems in the Development of Tourism*, Philadelphia: University of Pennsylvania Press.

Summary, R. M. (1987) 'Tourism's contributions to the economy of Kenya', *Annals of Tourism Research* 14, 4: 531–40.

Sutcliffe, C. (1985) 'Measuring the economic effects of tourism on an underdeveloped region', in G. J. Ashworth and B. Goodall (eds) *The Impact of Tourism on Disadvantaged Regions*, Groningen: Geografisch Instituut, Rijksuniversiteit.

Sweet, J. D. (1989) 'Burlesquing "the other" in Pueblo performance', *Annals of Tourism Research* 16, 1: 62–75.

Swinglehurst, E. (1982) *Cook's Tours: The Story of Popular Travel*, Poole: Blandford Press.

Thompson, G. (1981) 'Holidays', in Open University, *Popular Culture and Everyday Life*, Walton Hall, Milton Keynes: Open University Press.

Tsartas, P. (1992) 'Socioeconomic impacts of tourism on two Greek isles', *Annals of Tourism Research* 19, 3: 516–33.

Turner, V. and Turner, E. (1978) *Image and Pilgrimage in Christian Culture*, Oxford: Basil Blackwell.

UNESCO (1976) 'The effects of tourism on socio-cultural values', *Annals of Tourism Research* 4, 2: 74–105.

Urry, J. (1990) *The Tourist Gaze: Leisure and Travel in Contemporary Societies*, London: Sage.

Var, T. (1992) 'Travel and tourism statistics', *Annals of Tourism, Research* 19 3: 589–92.

Var, T., Brayley, R. and Korsay, M. (1989) 'Tourism and world peace: case of Turkey', *Annals of Tourism Research* 16, 2: 282–6.

Var, T., Schlüter, R., Ankomah, P. and Tae-Hee, L. (1989) 'Tourism and world peace: the case of Argentina', *Annals of Tourism Research* 16, 3: 431–4.

Waterhouse, K. (1989) *Theory and Practice of Travel,* London: Hodder and Stoughton.

Waters, S. (1988) *The Travel Industry Yearbook,* New York: Child and Waters.

Wong, P.-P. (1990) 'Coastal resources management: tourism in peninsula Malaysia', *ASEAN Economic Bulletin* 7, 2: 213–21.

WTO (1988) *Economic Review of World Tourism: Tourism in the Context of Economic Crisis and the Dominance of the Service Economy,* Madrid: WTO.

—— (1991a) *Current Travel and Tourism Indicators,* Madrid: WTO.

—— (1991b) *Yearbook of Tourism Statistics,* vols I and II, Madrid: WTO.

Yale, P. (1992) *Tourism in the U.K.,* Kings Ripton, Huntingdon: ELM Publications.

Yearley, S. (1991) *The Green Case: A Sociology of Environmental Issues, Arguments and Politics,* London: Harper Collins.

13

ELECTRONICS INDUSTRIES AND THE DEVELOPING WORLD

Uneven contributions and uncertain prospects

Jeffrey Henderson

The story of industrialization in the developing world in large measure has been a story of the emergence and expansion of two sectors: textiles and garments; and electronics. Of these it has been electronics industries that have caught the public imagination and become a prime focus for the attention of government economic planners. The reasons for this are not hard to discern. Since the 1960s the idea that investment in 'high technology' was the fastest route to dynamic companies and prosperous economies, has been a commonplace in boardrooms, cabinet offices and in the popular consciousness. The image of Silicon Valley (California) and Route 128 (Massachusetts) as concentrations of scientists and engineers busily creating the next generation of machines destined to transform further our lives, pay packets and the profits of a few, has been particularly potent. At its extremities this imagery has been little more than media hype; but beneath this has been the reality that for some economies, investment in electronics production has delivered enormous benefits. While these benefits have accrued substantially to the developed economies, where the critical mass of scientific knowledge and technical expertise central to such a technology-driven industry historically has been located, some have been delivered to parts of the developing world.

While electronics industries have been second only to textiles and garments in providing manufacturing employment to Third World labour forces, arguably they have been much more significant in other ways. First, because of the higher technology content of their products and production processes, they have the capability to deliver higher productivity and value added, and hence rapid economic growth coupled with faster increases in general prosperity. Second, because they tend to be capital- and knowledge-intensive industries, they stimulate domestic demand for scientists and engineers and hence exert pressure on governments to upgrade their education systems. Third, rather like automobile industries, they generate substantial demands for specialized supplies, components and services and

258

hence provide opportunities for the development of production linkages with myriad other companies. In other words electronics industries offer the possibility of substantial add-on effects in terms of further employment, and increasing capital and knowledge intensity in related industries. Add to this the image that electronics industries are relatively non-polluting, provide pleasant places to work and deliver high incomes relative to the 'sweat-shops' of the garment industry, and their attractiveness as a basis for industrialization becomes clear.

The problem with all this, however, is that while the potential for electronics industries to make a massive contribution to development is clearly there, the realization of this potential has been very uneven, both in terms of the geographic spread of the industries, their levels of technological intensity and their contribution to a pollution-free, prosperous environment (Ernst and O'Connor 1992; Bello and Rosenfeld 1992; Siegel and Markoff 1985). When one speaks of electronics production in the developing world, we are talking of really only seven countries: the East Asian newly industrialized countries (NICs) – South Korea (hereafter, Korea), Taiwan, Hong Kong and Singapore; the East Asian near-NICs – principally Malaysia; the Latin American NICs, principally Brazil; and the less economically developed economies of Asia, particularly China. Four things are of additional note, however: India, Thailand and Mexico may develop significant electronics industries as we approach the twenty-first century; the Philippines, though previously significant as a labour-intensive assembly base, is now much less so; Vietnam could become an important location for electronics production, particularly once the problem of the US trade embargo is resolved; and in comparison with the output of the leading developed industrial economies, the electronics industries of the developing world, with the exception of that of Korea, remain relatively minor players (table 13.1).

Within the developing world's electronics industries there are enormous variations. The East Asian NICs – particularly Korea and Taiwan – have the largest and most technologically sophisticated industries which in some product areas (semiconductors and consumer electronics in Korea, microcomputers in Taiwan) are beginning to compete directly with the dominant Japanese, US and European producers. There and only there at present is there any possibility of firms moving to the innovation-led forms of competition necessary to become major players in the world electronics industry. Singapore is probably at a higher level technologically, but its industry is overwhelmingly foreign-owned and its domestic firms, with a few exceptions, remain underdeveloped. Malaysia and increasingly Thailand have significant industries but, like Singapore, these are largely foreign-owned and in spite of some recent upgrading (particularly in Malaysia) generally do not contain the most capital- and knowledge-intensive parts of the production system which are capable of delivering the higher levels of

Table 13.1 Electronics production and exports (in $ million), 1990: selected producer economies

	Office automation equipment		Industrial controls		Communications equipment		Consumer electronics		Electronic components		Totals	
	Production	Exports	Production	Exports	Production	Exports	Production	Exports	Production	Exports	Production	Exports
USA	54,050	22,711	34,374	9,255	66,107	5,815	6,518	1,263	41,376	11,172	202,425	50,216
Japan	58,373	22,206	11,765	4,820	23,779	7,359	32,069	20,200	58,641	21,614	184,627	76,199
Germany	11,623	8,740	12,692	6,527	8,644	2,620	4,510	3,634	11,015	9,150	48,484	30,671
France	8,269	5,155	3,704	1,911	12,155	3,166	1,841	1,552	4,944	4,297	30,913	16,081
Britain	9,393	10,319[a]	5,148	2,681	7,182	2,468	2,127	1,807	4,895	5,324[a]	28,745	22,671
Italy	6,928	4,275	3,532	1,379	7,646	871	1,128	644	2,640	2,256	21,874	9,425
Netherlands	3,568	6,690[a]	1,945	1,321	1,693	688	160	995[a]	1,792	2,927[a]	9,158	12,621[a]
Switzerland	644	501	2,411	1,713	932	478	2,489	2,620[a]	868	963[a]	7,344	6,275
Spain	1,795	1,075	461	202	3,521	199	1,003	393	871	641	7,651	2,510
Canada	2,749	2,425	1,308	540	3,418	1,414	429	152	653	2,609[a]	8,557	7,140
Korea	3,446	2,560	368	259	2,453	948	6,305	4,491	10,539	7,424[a]	23,111	15,682
Singapore	7,177	9,029[a]	256	433[a]	498	662[a]	2,117	3,659[a]	4,777	5,991[a]	14,885	19,774[a]
Taiwan	5,247	5,796[a]	273	259	1,907	1,260	1,824	1,554	4,948	4,593	14,199	13,462
Hong Kong	2,142	3,437	208	405[a]	1,032	1,772[a]	2,485	6,576[a]	2,253	5,396[a]	8,120	17,586
Malaysia	484	672[a]	139	79	930	618	1,947	1,914	4,056	5,010[a]	7,556	8,293[a]
China	1,223	531	460	120	1,327	626	6,207	3,227	3,446	1,050	12,663	5,554
India	800	211	425	46	1,240	8	1,440	33	832	72	4,737	370
Thailand	1,622	1,546	70	17	322	215	738	596	1,234	1,332[a]	3,986	3,706
Philippines	108	71	40	1	324	184	144	39	1,434	1,279	2,050	1,574
Indonesia	125	1	84	1	322	38	492	49	246	68	1,269	157
Brazil	4,949	120	810	45	2,196	77	2,170	347	2,082	136	12,207	725
Mexico	1,214	700	612	536	689	323	1,701	1,680	2,140	2,124	6,356	5,363

Source: *Yearbook of World Electronics Data 1992*, volumes 1, 2, 3, Oxford: Elsevier Advanced Technology, 1992

Note: (a) Excess of exports over production reflects the re-export of products originally imported as semi-finished manufactures. In the case of Hong Kong and Taiwan these largely originated in China value added and are essential to innovation. The others still have limited capacity, or operate overwhelmingly at the labour-intensive, low value-added end of the spectrum. The partial exception here is Brazil which has a significant presence in computers, communications equipment, certain consumer products and components (though not semiconductors) (see table 13.1). The development of the Brazilian computer industry has been particularly significant in that it is one of the cases which highlights the important role of state intervention in the technological and skill upgrading of electronics industries (Schmitz and Hewitt 1992; Hewitt 1992). This is a general issue – in as far as it also has been relevant to some of the East Asian cases – to which we shall return later.

The potential benefits of electronics industries, then, have largely bypassed the vast majority of the developing world. Given that most Third World countries do not have the pools of engineering and technical personnel required even for assembly operations, because of foreign indebtedness do not have the huge sums now necessary to induce production, have underdeveloped telecommunications and transport infrastructures, do not themselves possess significant market potential, and that the tendency of capital on a global scale anyway is to gravitate towards those locations that already have concentrations of capital in its money, technological or human forms, suggests that those benefits are likely to remain elusive for a very long time to come.

The emergence of electronics industries as a motor force of industrialization encapsulates many of the issues that have been central to debates about the relation of capitalism to development for most of the past thirty years. Such issues include the role of foreign direct investment (FDI) by transnational corporations (TNCs); the relation of state intervention to development trajectories; the role of increasing global competition in the context of contracting markets; the nature and effects of transformations in the global organization of production systems; the spatial organization of production in the context of the emergence of international and regional divisions of labour; the nature of the labour process and its consequences for various sorts of workers and particularly women; and at a more abstract, though still vital level, the prospects for developing countries to achieve core economy status. As it is impossible to do justice to all these issues in one chapter, in what follows some selectivity will be necessary. We will begin with an account of the emergence of electronics production in the developing world and with its dispersal and restructuring over time. In this context we will broach the issue of FDI and its relation to domestic production as well as discussing the role of state policy and influence. Additionally we will raise the question of the changing international organization of production and show how this has both provided opportunities for 'latecomer' electronics industries as well as saddled them with new forms of dependency. In the following section we will turn in detail to the role of FDI and advance a preliminary assessment of its consequences for economic and social development in those societies in which it has been a central, indeed dominant feature of electronics production. In the final section we will supplement the foregoing discussion with an assessment of the current state of electronics industries in the developing world and use our findings to bear on the central question of whether these industries are likely to form a basis for continued development such that we can expect some of the economies in which they are embedded to attain the 'big league' in the first decades of the next century.

Before proceeding further it is necessary to identify the types of electronics industries on which our discussion will focus. The generic term covers a vast array of processes, technologies and products; from components such as semiconductors to consumer electronics, computers of various sizes and capacities, industrial control systems, office automation and telecommunications equipment. In addition to the hardware the production of software such as computer programs is beginning to become important in a small number of developing country locations, as is the emergence of certain design functions such as electronic circuitry. From table 13.1 it can be seen that the principal concentrations of electronics activity in the developing world are in three broad product areas: components, principally semiconductors; consumer electronics; and office automation equipment, principally microcomputers. Consequently these are the industries that will provide the empirical focus of our discussion. While software engineering is beginning to develop a strong presence in countries such as Singapore, India and Taiwan, there is as yet insufficient information available on this phenomenon to ground an argument about its likely consequences for economic and social development (Ernst and O'Connor 1992).

ORIGINS AND TRAJECTORIES

Modern electronics industries originate with the development of semiconductor technology at AT&T's Bell Laboratories in 1947 and its first commercial manufacture by AT&T's Western Electric in 1951 (Braun and MacDonald 1982). Federal government anti-trust suits forced AT&T and other major producers such as General Electric and RCA to license the technology and as a consequence from the early 1950s it began to be acquired by European and Japanese companies. Japanese companies – particularly Sony and Toshiba – were quick to use the new technology as a basis for radio production and soon began to overtake US and European companies who initially remained wedded to traditional vacuum-tube technology. It was in fact radio production that was the first electronics industry to become established in the developing world. In an effort to reduce costs (and hence boost its competitive edge) by tapping even cheaper supplies of labour than those which existed in Japan, Sony developed a joint venture operation in Korea to assemble transistor radios in 1958, and the following year began producing on a subcontract basis in Hong Kong (Chen 1971).

Though radios were the first electronic products to emerge from what were then peripheries of the world economy, it was semiconductors themselves which through to the early 1980s were to become the leading edge of the developing world's electronics industries and remain a central, and in some cases – notably Malaysia – a dominant feature through to the present day (see table 13.1).

Semiconductor production was the vehicle for the first major – and still significant – wave of electronics FDI in the developing world. Originating in Hong Kong in 1961 with the establishment of an assembly plant by the US producer, Fairchild, semiconductor FDI spread throughout the following two decades to six other locations in East Asia and to a number in Latin America and the Caribbean also. In its wake the largely US and more recently Japanese companies responsible for the FDI, developed a global production system which until the late 1970s was perhaps the supreme example of an industry organized according to the principles of the new international division of labour thesis (Fröbel, Heinrichs and Kreye 1980; Henderson 1989). Specifically, global managerial control and the knowledge-intensive parts of the system such as R&D, which were largely responsible for the companies' competitive advantage, remained firmly locked into the home-country locations. While much of the more capital- and technology-intensive parts of the production process such as mask-making and wafer fabrication also remained inside of the home base, some of it had been dispersed to other industrial economies such as the European Community (EC) and (for US companies) Japan where it was necessary to supply major, but protected markets, by investment in production facilities rather than through exports. Additionally some circuit design functions had also been established in these societies. Developing societies on the other hand were recipients largely of low-value-added, low-skill and labour-intensive assembly operations (Henderson 1987, 1989).

A regional division of labour

By the mid to late 1980s the international division of labour as represented by semiconductor production had already been transformed.[1] Specifically in two East Asian locations – Hong Kong and Singapore – US, Japanese and European TNCs had invested in more technology- and skill-intensive processes such as computer-controlled testing operations, circuit design, and in Singapore wafer fabrication. Investment in these higher value-added processes was contingent on the ability of these locations to supply high-quality engineering and technical labour at costs far below those available in the core economies (Henderson 1989; Lim and Pang 1991: 123–34).

In the context of Singapore it was also a response to the government's strategy of forcing up labour costs, thus encouraging TNCs to restructure their operations to emphasize technology rather than labour-intensive operations (Castells, Goh and Kwok 1990: part II). For many of the TNCs involved, these developments also were associated with the emergence of Asian regional headquarter operations in Hong Kong and Singapore consistent with the growing significance of East Asian semiconductor markets.[2]

These transformations in the global operations of TNCs pointed to a distinct regional division of labour within their East Asian operations. The peripheries of the division of labour such as Malaysia, Thailand, the Philippines and Indonesia had begun to become subjected to new and specifically regional forms of dependency. In addition to the decision-making controls and technological dependency which emanated from the core economy bases of the respective transnationals, the peripheries were now subject to a secondary layer of managerial and technical control which originated in Hong Kong and Singapore (Henderson 1989; see also Henderson and Scott 1987, and Scott 1987).

While some of the more technology-intensive operations such as testing and wafer fabrication (though generally for less sophisticated semi-conductors) have now been dispersed to Malaysia (Henderson 1989: 70–1; Lim and Pang 1991: 107–18) it is now clear that this regional division of labour, and its implications for development, has been supplemented and strengthened from two quarters: massive intraregional flows of investment by Japanese semiconductor and consumer electronics companies (now by far the largest source of electronics FDI in the region); and an increasing integration of the peripheral economies into the production systems of electronics companies from the East Asian NICs themselves.

In the former case, the period since the late 1970s has seen the location in East Asia of about 70 per cent of Japanese offshore production facilities for semiconductors and other components. The favoured locations have been Taiwan, Korea, Singapore, Malaysia and more recently, Thailand. While most of this investment has gone into assembly and test operations, wafer fabrication plants have emerged in Singapore and Malaysia (Lim and Pang 1991). Though the drive to reduce labour costs (including on engineering and technical labour) has been partly responsible for this development, it has also been associated with the demands created by the subsidiaries of Japanese consumer electronics companies that have emerged in various parts of the region (Dicken 1992: 333–4). As some of these subsidiaries have the same parent companies as the semiconductor plants (Hitachi and Matsushita for instance), it is likely that their just-in-time (JIT) manufacturing systems have contributed to increasing investments in localized component production.

The growth of Japanese consumer electronics subsidiaries in the developing world has been more widespread than with semiconductor production, with plants emerging in Latin America as well as in East Asia. In the East Asian context where the investment has been in televisions, VCRs, airconditioners and microwave ovens, Taiwan, Malaysia, Singapore and Thailand have been the principal recipients of investment, with Taiwan receiving the dragon's share in both semiconductors and consumer products.[3] While one of the reasons for this internationalization of consumer electronics assembly has been the drive for lower manual-labour costs, an equally important reason has been the need to circumvent import quota restrictions in the US market (Dicken 1992: 339).

Consistent with rapidly rising labour costs at home, and a seeming reluctance to increase productivity by investing in technologically upgraded production processes, Korean and Taiwanese consumer electronics and computer manufacturers have developed assembly operations on a subsidiary or joint-venture basis in a number of ASEAN countries and increasingly in China. Since 1988 Taiwan, for instance, has been the second most important source of new manufacturing FDI in Malaysia. Some of this has been in electronics and has included a recent investment by Acer in PC assembly.[4] Similarly, the major Korean electronics producers, Samsung and Goldstar, now have manufacturing operations in Thailand, Indonesia, the Philippines and China as well as Mexico (Bloom 1992: 109–12, table 12). While much of the electronics assembly by Hong Kong companies has shifted to China in recent years – helping to add to growing unemployment among the colony's manufacturing workers (Fong 1989) – some of it has relocated to parts of Southeast Asia where there are well-developed business networks among the local Chinese populations and constitute the preferred conduit for internationalization in these cases (Baring Securities 1989; Redding 1990).

The emergence of these flows of FDI and managerial controls and decision-making associated with them, are but part of a more general process of economic integration taking place within East Asia. In addition to the regionalization of NIC electronics industries, considerable investment by other NIC manufacturing industries is taking place, particularly in garments, footwear and certain forms of engineering, and particularly between Hong Kong and Taiwan on the one hand and China on the other. Central to these developments, as well as some of those in electronics are production systems organized in the form of 'commodity chains' (Gereffi 1992; Gereffi and Korzeniewicz 1990) which as we shall see later, are creating yet other forms of dependency, not merely for the regional peripheries, but in some cases for the East Asian NICs themselves.

Home-grown industries

While investment by TNCs has been the primary factor responsible for the emergence of electronics production in most industrializing societies, including Singapore, Malaysia and Thailand, this has not been true to the same extent in Hong Kong, Taiwan and Korea (or, indeed, Brazil). Though FDI has certainly been significant in semiconductor production in all three Asian economies since the 1960s and more recently, as we have seen, Taiwan in particular has been a recipient of substantial investment by Japanese consumer electronics companies, a notable feature of these economies is that they have developed substantial domestically owned industries. As early as 1959, for instance, the Korean *chaebol* (conglomerate), Goldstar, started producing radios from imported components (Bloom 1992: 27). These efforts, however, remained very limited until the 1970s when subsidiaries of the Samsung, Hyundai and Daewoo *chaebol*, as well as Goldstar, began to move into the production of TVs and audio products and in the 1980s, VCRs, microwave ovens, microcomputers, compact disc players and semiconductors. The share of electronics in Korea's total manufacturing output rose from 2 per cent in 1970 to 6 per cent in 1980 and to nearly 18 per cent in 1988. By that year electronics production accounted for nearly 15 per cent of GNP and exports had reached around 25 per cent of the total, overtaking textiles and garments as the largest contributor to manufactured exports. Korea now ranks sixth in the world in terms of total electronics production and third (after Japan and the United States) in consumer electronics (table 13.1). In recent years growth in output has been close to 30 per cent per annum, with exports rising at a stunning 43 per cent per annum between 1986 and 1989 (Hobday 1992; Bello and Rosenfeld 1992: 145).

Product sophistication had also increased in some areas, with Samsung, for instance, capable of fabricating 4 and 16 megabit DRAM semiconductors, and Korea becoming the second-largest producer of memory devices in the world (Hobday 1992). By the late 1980s, domestic companies had become the dominant force in the Korean electronics industry. In 1987, for instance, domestic companies were responsible for 65 per cent of total Korean electronics output, with joint-venture companies responsible for another 24 per cent and wholly foreign-owned companies only 11 per cent of which the bulk were semiconductors. Similarly with regard to employment provision, domestic companies in 1987 were responsible for 72 per cent of total employment, or about 271,000 jobs (Bloom 1992: 72).

As with other NIC electronics industries those of Taiwan began with foreign (overwhelmingly US) investment in semiconductor assembly in the mid-1960s which diversified in the 1970s into investment in TV and other consumer products by companies such as RCA, Philips and Matsushita. Taiwanese companies emerged initially to supply the TNCs with simple components such as capacitors, resistors and transformers, but soon began to assemble radios and TVs of their own. By the 1980s firms began to move into the production of semiconductors, VCRs, colour TV monitors and particularly, microcomputers. By 1988, for instance, Taiwanese firms were exporting more than two million personal computers which accounted for about 10 per cent of world PC production (Bello and Rosenfeld 1992: 266). By 1987 electronics industries were contributing over 5 per cent of Taiwan's GNP and about 20 per cent of its exports, becoming the largest export sector (Hobday 1992). Consistent with the growth of consumer electronics and microcomputer production, Taiwan has evolved its own semiconductor production capacity. Recently this capacity has been boosted by joint ventures between the country's largest computer manufacturers Acer and Mitac and the US producers, Texas Instruments and Intel respectively. Both joint ventures are angled towards the domestic market for which the former produces advanced memory devices and the latter microprocessors (Bello and Rosenfeld 1992: 271; Hobday 1992).

I have indicated already that Hong Kong's electronics industry began with the assembly of transistor radios for Japanese producers in the late 1950s and was expanded by the attraction of US and other foreign investment in semiconductor production. Since then, Hong Kong's electronics industries, as with their counterparts in Korea and Taiwan, have come to be dominated by local producers. Although even the biggest Hong Kong firms such as Video Technology, Semi Tech, Wong Industrial, Tomei and Conic are very small by Taiwanese and particularly Korean standards, they have helped to contribute to the 23 per cent share of manufactured exports which electronics held in 1987 (Henderson 1989: 85, table 5.3 Hobday 1992). These firms and their smaller counterparts produce such things as personal computers, electronic games, TVs, audio products and watches. Although electronics industries contributed a high of over 106,000 jobs in 1984 (Henderson 1989: 86, table 5.4), since then employment in this as in other manufacturing industries has declined drastically. Rather than invest in more capital- and technology-intensive processes as labour costs in the colony rose, Hong Kong's manufacturers have sought to relocate much of their productive capacity to China's neighbouring Guangdong Province where Hong Kong-invested factories now employ over three million people. The consequence is that manufacturing employment in the colony is now down to about 600,000, a decline of one-third since 1987.[5]

This survey of the growth of indigenous electronics production in three of the East Asian NICs, though brief, has been sufficient to indicate that with the recent exception of Hong Kong, the presence of electronics industries has made a significant contribution to output, exports, employment, etc., and that there is some evidence that in certain areas manufacturers have been able to move into higher value-added operations. While this contribution to development will be examined in more detail and in a different light in the final section of this chapter, two issues that have been central to the growth of indigenous electronics capacities in these countries need to be highlighted here. These are the organizational arrangements under which much of their electronics production continues to take place and the interventionist roles of their national states.

From the beginning of their emergence as electronics producers through to the present day, the indigenous firms of the East Asian NICs have continued to operate substantially under original equipment manufacturer (OEM) arrangements with foreign companies. Under such an arrangement the purchaser supplies the designs, many of the components, oversees production quality and markets under their own brand name. The OEM tends merely to assemble the final product. The benefits to the purchaser lie largely in the cost reductions (both labour costs and overheads) while for the OEM they lie in the relatively easy and cheap access to overseas markets and in theory represent a useful conduit for technology transfer. Hong Kong's electronics firms are the ones that remain most thoroughly absorbed into OEM arrangements. There is hardly a single electronics manufacturer there that does not produce the vast majority of output under an OEM arrangement with a Japanese, US or EC firm.

Even with the more technologically sophisticated producers of Taiwan and Korea, the incidence of OEM arrangements remains high. In the case of Taiwanese computers and related goods, for instance, OEM accounted for around 43 per cent of production in 1989 with the principal buyers being IBM, Philips, NEC, EPSON, Hewlett Packard and NCR. Taiwan's largest electronics manufacturer, Tatung, for instance exports about half its PCs and colour TVs under OEM arrangements, and TECO sells about 65 per cent of its TV monitors on the same basis. Leading computer manufacturer, Acer, continues to produce a substantial proportion of its PC output for AT&T, Unysis and Siemens (Hobday 1992). The situation of Korean firms is much like their Taiwanese counterparts if not more so. By 1988, for instance, OEM arrangements still accounted for 60 to 70 per cent of local firm output (and 30 per cent of all manufactured exports). That same year nearly all the sales of 256K DRAM ICs by Hyundai Semiconductor to Texas Instruments were on an OEM basis. In 1987 OEM sales constituted 50 per cent of the exports of TVs by the main Korean manufacturers (Samsung, Goldstar and Daewoo), while half of Samsung's sales of VCRs to the United States were on an OEM basis and for Goldstar the proportion was considerably higher (Hobday 1992; Bloom 1992: 32). It is necessary to temper the discussion at this point, however, by adding that sales of own brand name microcomputers by Taiwanese producers such as Acer, Tatung and Mitac, have risen in recent years. In 1988 the share of Taiwan's own brand name PCs stood at 28 per cent of the total but by 1989 had reached 40 per cent (Ernst and O'Connor 1992: 153). The significance of own brand name sales lies in the fact that the higher their proportion of the total, the higher the value added that is likely to be retained by the manufacturer and hence the domestic economy.

There are two other issues that bear on the significance of OEM arrangements for East Asian NIC electronics manufacturers. First, much of the production in Taiwan and Hong Kong – though not to anywhere near the same extent in the other NICs – arises out of dense, socially embedded networks of small and medium enterprises but also including some of the larger firms. Many of these small and medium enterprises operate within the informal economy and hence largely beyond state control (Cheng and Gereffi 1994). Second, and more importantly for our current purposes, many of these OEM arrangements reflect international production systems organized on the basis of commodity chains. While for electronic products these commodity chains can be either 'producer' or 'buyer' driven (Gereffi, this volume) depending on the product in question, they now link many manufacturing operations in Korea, Taiwan and Hong Kong not only to the US, Japanese and EC manufacturers and buyers, but in the case of a growing number of Taiwanese and Hong Kong firms, to downstream producers and subcontractors in China (Gereffi 1992). Given that this is a production system in which value accrues according to the particular nodes of the commodity chain one controls, then it is a system that potentially has very important implications for development prospects, not only in Taiwan and Hong Kong, but increasingly in China and other peripheral economies (such as Vietnam) that are being incorporated into the world economy partly on the basis of this version of an international division of labour. We will return to the developmental significance of these arrangements in the final part of the chapter.

The second substantive issue that arises here is the fact that many of the electronics industries of the developing world, such as in Brazil and India but particularly in the East Asian NICs, owe their origins, technological trajectories and (in the latter cases) competitive advantage in large measure to state industrial policy. In stark contrast to the ideologically loaded and empirically distorted accounts of East Asian industrialization that have emerged from the pens and word processors of neo-classical economists (cf. Little, Scitovsky and Scott 1970; and in a more sophisticated vein, Balassa 1991), it is now clear that though these economies have benefited from vigorously functioning markets, state orchestration of their development projects has been a *sine qua non* of their success (Amsden 1989; Wade 1990; Rodan 1989; Appelbaum and Henderson 1992; Henderson 1993a, b). Even in the supposed free-market paradise of Hong Kong, state ownership of land and provision of the means of collective consumption have been decisive features of economic growth and redistribution (Castells, Goh and Kwok 1990; Schiffer 1991). As part of their general attempts to induce and upgrade their industrial bases, the governments of the East Asian NICs have at various moments acquired foreign technology under license for dissemination to favoured companies, encouraged joint-venture arrangements with foreign partners, protected the domestic market from foreign competition, delivered subsidized credit through nationalized or heavily regulated banking systems (Korea and Taiwan) for approved projects and invested in their own R&D facilities to help boost the technological capabilities of the private-sector manufacturers. Beginning in 1969 with the 'Basic Plan for Electronics Industry Promotion' the Korean government has been particularly active in encouraging the development of the electronics sector. Identified as a strategic industry (in both commercial and military senses) the government has invested heavily in research institutes to help ensure that the competitive edge of companies such as Samsung and Goldstar is enhanced through product (i.e. more technology intensive) and not merely price competition associated with low costs. The Korean Institute of Electronics Technology (KIET), for instance, was set up in 1976 to ensure that research into IC design and wafer fabrication was undertaken. In other electronics industries, such as telecommunications, the Electronics and Telecommunications Research Institute (ETRI) partly formed from KIET in 1985, has operated to ensure that foreign technologies, sometimes by means of 'reverse engineering'[6] are more rapidly absorbed by local companies than would have been the case had they been left to their own devices (Bloom 1992: 28–58).

The story of the Taiwan government's relation with the country's electronics companies is much the same as in the Korean case. Arguably in Taiwan, however, state initiatives have been even more important owing to the relatively small size of the companies, and hence their lack of capital compared with their Korean counterparts. Additionally in Taiwan, as in Hong Kong, there probably has been an overriding interest in quick profits among manufacturers and therefore a tendency to boost productivity by squeezing the labour process rather than by investing in more technology-intensive (and higher value-added) processes and products. In this context state R&D expenditures have been particularly important. Central here has been the way in which state research institutes have acquired foreign technologies, adapted them and encouraged their absorption by Taiwanese companies. With wages rising by 20 per cent per annum in the late 1970s it became clear to state economic planners that companies had to be encouraged to upgrade technologically their operations. It was in this context that the state instituted the Electronics Research and Service Organization (ERSO) which via a technology transfer arrangement with the US producer, RCA, became Taiwan's first designer and fabricator of ICs and effectively laid the foundations for the country's electronics industry. In 1979 ERSO developed a state-owned semiconductor industry when it 'spun-off' United Microelectronics, subsequently privatizing the company in 1985. More recently ESRO has played a central role in the acquisition and subsequent transfer of 16 bit microcomputer technology to what are now leading producers such as Acer and TECO (Henderson 1989: 67; Chen 1993).

The experience of state involvement with electronics production in Hong Kong and Singapore has differed significantly from that of the other East Asian NICs. In the case of Hong Kong the colonial government's commitment to free-market ideology has resulted in its woeful neglect of manufacturing industry. Companies have been allowed to exploit the abundant opportunities for the creation of absolute surplus value that exists across the border in southern China, and hence have disinvested in the colony rather than having been encouraged – or pressured – to invest in more technology-intensive processes and higher value-added products. In addition the government's own contribution to R&D compared with other East Asian NICs has been derisory. The consequence has been that value added by electronics companies in Hong Kong remains low and there must now be some doubt as to whether Hong Kong will retain much of a presence in electronics manufacturing beyond the 1990s (Whitla 1991; Henderson 1991: 177–8).

Though Singapore's electronics industry, in common with the rest of its manufacturing base, has been far from 'home grown', state policies have been fundamental to its technological trajectory. Singapore has the most corporatist of Asian governments in that it has successfully engineered a triadic relation between organized labour (which has been absorbed into the ruling People's Action Party since the mid-1960s) and transnational capital. On the one hand it has neutralized labour and legitimated its rule by delivering Asia's most advanced welfare state, and on the other it has encouraged the upgrading of TNC investments which are responsible for over 70 per cent of manufacturing output by value (Mirza 1986). Recognizing that cheap labour was a declining competitive advantage and having invested heavily in education and skill enhancement in previous years – including software training institutes such as the IBM-assisted Institute of Systems Analysis (Ernst 1983) – state planners began to force up labour costs in order to squeeze low-skill assembly work out of the economy and encourage the TNCs to invest in more technology-intensive processes and products. The means to this end, beginning in 1979, was to increase the compulsory employer contributions to the Central Provident Fund so as to double labour costs by the late 1980s. The government's gamble was that rather than disinvest, the TNCs would convert Singapore into their principal Asian location for high technology processes and products. The gamble seems to have paid off (Castells, Goh and Kwok 1990: part II).[7]

Brazil has been another case in which state intervention in the electronics industry has led to significant benefits, particularly with regard to mini- and microcomputers. Prior to 1975 the Brazilian computer market was supplied either through foreign imports, or in the case of mainframes from local assembly by IBM and Burroughs (now Unisys) which involved a high import content. This situation was perceived as restricting technological development and the creation of skilled employment. In 1977 the

Brazilian government created a 'reserved market' for Brazilian-owned firms in certain product areas, including mini- and microcomputers. Partly as a consequence of pressure on the domestic banking sector, which became heavily involved in equity participation and the encouragement of strong internal competition, the number of Brazilian-owned computer firms expanded from 4 in 1977 to 310 in 1986, and by the latter year had captured 51 per cent of the total domestic market for computers (Evans 1986; Schmitz and Hewitt 1992).

At the same time, employment also had expanded significantly from 4,000 in 1979 to 55,000 in 1988 (Hewitt 1992: 189). While a free market for computers would have had few or possibly negative implications for employment, it is likely that pursuing a reserved market for domestic firms had no greater consequences for employment generation than would the more usual import substitution policy regime (allowing foreign firms to participate in the domestic market). A significant contribution of this strategy, however, is that in spite of a persistent technological backwardness of the Brazilian computer industry (Ernst and O'Connor 1992), it seems to have had positive consequences for skill upgrading, over and above those that could have been expected from either of the other market strategies. As a measure of this, Schmitz and Hewitt (1992: 35) report that whereas 8 per cent of workers in foreign-owned computer firms are employed in R&D, 25 per cent of workers in their locally owned equivalents are so employed.

GENUINE DEVELOPMENT?

From the discussion so far it should be clear that the contribution made by electronics industries to economic growth and development has been substantial in the East Asian NICs, and has been important also in Malaysia, Thailand (particularly since 1987) and Brazil. In other locations such as the Philippines and Indonesia, however, the persistence of a TNC presence that remains locked into low-skill and labour-intensive assembly processes with few possibilities of transformation in sight, suggests that the contribution of electronics to development has been more limited. But these judgements are fairly superficial. Consequently before we can proceed further with our investigations we need some means of distinguishing between different forms of development; specifically between processes that tend to produce development *in* a society rather than development *of* that society; or to put it another way, between 'mere' development and 'genuine' development.

In his analysis of the foreign-invested *maquila* industries of northern Mexico, Leslie Sklair (1993: 18–21) has proposed a number of dimensions along which the contribution of FDI to development can be assessed. Given that FDI in some form was centrally important to the emergence of electronics industries everywhere in the developing world and in East Asia continues to dominate in all locations except Korea, Taiwan and Hong Kong, it seems appropriate at this point to allow Sklair's schema to guide our discussion. Where the categories are relevant we shall comment also on their significance for those economies in which domestic companies dominate. The criteria – in fact a set of continua – that Sklair proposes as a means of assessing the development contribution of FDI is as follows:

1 *Production linkages*: this is a measure of the TNC's embeddedness in the local economy. The extent to which the subsidiary establishes backward (raw materials, supplies, components, services) and forward (sales to producers of finished products) linkages significantly influence the benefit the local economy is likely to derive from the TNC presence. Specifically the extent to which the TNC subsidiary develops linkages with locally owned firms (rather than subsidiaries of other TNCs) and pressures them to move over time into higher value-added operations is particularly important for maximizing the benefit to the local economy.

2 *Retention of foreign exchange*: the higher the value added by the TNC within the local economy – both directly by its own efforts and indirectly by its linkages with local firms – and the greater the amount of foreign currency retained locally, the more positive the development implications.

3 *Employment and upgrading of personnel*: the greater the proportion of indigenous senior managers, engineers and technical personnel employed by the subsidiary, and the greater its commitment to upgrading the skills of all personnel, the greater the benefits are likely to be for the local economy. This is the case because significant proportions of skilled local employees are likely to lead to (a) a higher potential for technological and managerial learning and hence a greater possibility for successful local firm 'spin-offs'; (b) a stimulus to upgrade local educational systems to meet demands for higher skilled personnel; and (c) the possibility that local senior managers will have a higher propensity to develop local production linkages.

4 *Genuine technology transfer*: the closer the technology transferred by the TNC is to the state of the art, rather than merely being technology that is out-moded or unproductive in the context of developed economies, and the more it becomes diffused among local firms, the greater the benefit to the local economy.

5 *Working conditions*: the better the working conditions and the higher the wages paid by the TNC relative to those prevailing in the host society, the greater the contribution to development.

6 *Wealth distribution*: the more equal the distribution of profits and income generated by the TNC subsidiary as between corporate HQ and foreign shareholders on the one hand and local social classes and governments on the other (as for instance through joint-venture operations), the

greater the benefit to the local economy. (In the second edition of *Assembling for Development* Sklair replaces 'distribution' with 'environment'.)

For some of these criteria it is difficult to generate the data necessary to draw empirically grounded conclusions (as for instance with the retention of foreign exchange), though logical extrapolations from what we know of the features of the industry in each case are usually possible. For this reason, as well as space restrictions, the following discussion will concentrate on selected criteria only.

Linkages

Whether a TNC subsidiary becomes embedded in a host economy by virtue of its linkages with local firms depends on a number of factors. The global strategy and production system of the TNC concerned is one. Major Japanese companies, for instance, because of their systems of relational subcontracting with firms from their respective *keiretsu* (enterprise groups) often tend to continue those arrangements when they internationalize their operations. Even where local companies are capable of supplying components in required quantities and qualities, then, production linkages are not developed to the extent that could have been expected. As Japanese electronics FDI is now the most significant worldwide, this clearly presents a problem for economies such as Thailand, but particularly for Malaysia and Singapore whose FDI-driven electronics industries are their largest manufacturing sector. Other factors that can inhibit linkage formation include the nature of the product itself and whether the TNC is segregated from the domestic economy by virtue of its location in an export processing zone (EPZ). Semiconductors, for instance, because of the proprietory nature of their embodied technology, tend not to be good candidates for linkage formation. Similarly, where TNCs as a result of government policy are located in EPZs, local firms in search of linkages, must themselves locate in the EPZs. Consequently they must be prepared to relinquish an interest in the domestic market and weld their fortunes to a small number of firms and export markets only. Countries such as Malaysia whose electronics industry remains dominated by semiconductor production organized in EPZs (although with growing investment in consumer electronics) seem particularly exposed in these senses.

Among the developing countries with FDI-driven electronics industries, it is indeed Malaysia that presents the greatest paradox when it comes to linkage formation. Not only does the economy suffer from the sort of problems indicated above, but the development of a local electronics industry capable to linking with the TNCs seems to have been stillborn. In spite of over two decades of foreign investment in electronics, linkage formation is still very limited when compared, for instance, with Taiwan,

Hong Kong and recently Singapore. Part of the problem is associated with the regional division of labour, or at least the Southeast Asian sub-region which has already been addressed. Specifically, the emergence of Singapore as the high-tech fulcrum of the sub-region has meant that TNCs have preferred to link with their affiliates or local firms there, rather than in Malaysia. This having been said, however, there is still a Malaysian domestic problem and its roots lie in the fact that on the one hand the Malay-dominated state has systematically discriminated against Malaysian–Chinese business, when the fastest route to an indigenous manufacturing industry in the short to medium term, is Chinese entrepreneurship. On the other hand state policies have encouraged the growth of a rentier bourgoisie amongst Malays and Chinese and hence diverted investment and energies into unproductive activities that otherwise could have been channelled into manufacturing (Salih 1988; Jesudason 1989; Lubeck 1992).

In spite of these structural problems, the most recent research suggests that linkage formation is beginning to emerge. Ismail (1993a), for instance, reports that for a selection of US and Japanese electronics companies, many of them now source a wide variety of machinery, components, cables, etc. from locally owned companies. The US producer, Harris Semiconductor, for instance, sources its entire requirement for basic tools and machinery from Malaysian companies. Additionally some US TNCs have worked with local companies to upgrade the quality and add value to their supplies and components. This has been particularly true of Intel and National Semiconductor who have worked with local firms such as Eng Hardware and Loh Kim Teow Engineering for some years. Furthermore at least four Malaysian manufacturers are now producing PCs for the domestic market, one of them, Techtrans, on the basis of a technology-transfer arrangement with a Taiwanese firm (Lim and Pang 1991: 116). Although these are hopeful signs, the continued weakness of the local manufacturing sector in Malaysia is a problem that could seriously limit the benefits that could otherwise accrue from that country's industrialization process.

With regard to linkage formation with electronics TNCs in other Southeast Asian countries, with the sole exception of Singapore, the situation is more problematic than in Malaysia. In Thailand although a number of joint ventures have been formed – including with Korean companies Goldstar and Samsung – the local electronics manufacturing base is still very underdeveloped (Lim and Pang 1991: 118–23). As the bulk of FDI in electronics dates only from 1987, however, it would be premature to draw conclusions about the possibilities for linkage formation. In the Philippines and Indonesia the prospects for higher value-added linkage formation look particularly bleak, though there is some evidence that local firms capable of performing certain specialized functions, including circuit design, have arisen in the former in recent years (Scott 1987).

The Southeast Asian 'star' when it comes to linkage formation, as with so much to do with electronics production, is Singapore. After an inauspicious start in the 1970s when state policy worked against manufacturing SMEs and hence linkages with TNCs (Lim and Pang 1982), the 1980s witnessed a re-think of state priorities and a consequent upsurge in SME activity. In recent years local firms have moved into such areas as circuit boards and other subassemblies; membrane switches to replace keyboards on computers, calculators, microwave ovens, etc.; computer software and circuit design; microcomputers – including one firm, Wearnes Technology, which together with its US subsidiary (Advanced Logic Research) designs and produces a highly regarded PC for the US market; and electronic health-care products such as equipment for monitoring blood pressure and diagnosing AIDS (Lim and Pang 1991: 130–2).

For the other East Asian producers, Hong Kong, Taiwan and Korea, the earlier significance of linkages with TNCs has given way to domestically owned producers which for some time have been the dominant force in their respective electronics sectors. While OEM arrangements with foreign companies remain important for these producers, in the case of Taiwan and Hong Kong the linkage issue has been transformed into one of linkages between domestic companies in the context of dense interfirm networks. As I have already mentioned, and will return to later, these networks now extend to encompass linkages with firms in the Peoples Republic of China.

Korean companies are the deviant cases when it comes to linkage formation with other local firms. As Korean electronics production is heavily concentrated, with Samsung and Goldstar alone responsible for over 46 per cent of sales in 1988 (Bloom 1992: 41, table 3), the opportunities for linkages with SMEs tend to be limited. The *chaebol* seem to prefer to produce in-house, or source their components and supplies from overseas.

Personnel

I have already indicated the reasons why the employment and upgrading of indigenous managerial and technical personnel can deliver significant benefits for the domestic economy. While the record on this is far from complete, there are a number of discernable features of significance to developing economies. First, it appears that Japanese companies in common with some European and probably other East Asian companies, generally are less willing to localize managerial, if not technical responsibility, than are US companies. While the reasons for this may be a product of a series of factors from the nature of global control mechanisms (headquarter-subsidiary information flows and decision-making, for instance) at one polarity to racial discrimination at the other, available evidence suggests that even where highly skilled and competent managerial personnel are available – including even in other industrial economies such as Britain –

276

they tend to be underutilized by Japanese companies in senior managerial positions. The contrast between the localization policies of US electronics companies on the one hand and their Japanese and European equivalents on the other, is especially clear in Malaysia. Among the sixteen firms that are members of the Malaysian–American Electronics Association, for instance, nine of them have no expatriate managers, whereas for the others, National Semiconductor has only one expatriate, and Motorola and Texas Instruments – with a combined workforce of nearly 7,000 – have only three between them. Matsushita, on the other hand, with eight plants the largest Japanese electronics investor in Malaysia, has no Malaysians at the most senior levels, though the most recent evidence suggests that in one of their plants at least, the situation may be changing (Ismail 1993b).

Technology transfer

The extent of genuine technology transfer by TNCs and upgrading by indigenous companies themselves is again very uneven. With regard to the transfer of more advanced semiconductor technologies I have discussed already the situation which pertained by the mid to late 1980s. Specifically in the context of an evolving regional division of labour in East Asia, Hong Kong and Singapore emerged as the technological hubs. Certain inter-mediate technologies and design functions had been transferred there rendering other locations within the region dependent on their capabilities. Since then this situation, if anything, has been compounded. The peripheries (Philippines, Indonesia, Thailand and to some extent Malaysia) continue to be the major recipients of investments in assembly facilities, though test facilities are becoming more prevalent. While some technology-intensive investments have been made in Malaysia (with National Semiconductor building a diffusion plant, Motorola a wafer-fabrication facility for transistors, and Hitachi likely to follow suit), these remain fairly limited and in any case are designed to produce less technologically sophisticated products. Investment in the most advanced processes has continued to flow to the 'hubs', but with Singapore now becoming the favoured location rather than Hong Kong. Thus the nineteen semicon-ductor TNCs that produce in Singapore (e.g. AT&T, Texas Instruments, National Semiconductor, Philips, Matsushita, NEC) tend to focus on the more advanced products (1, 4 and 16 megabit DRAMs and some microprocessors). While most of these companies still concentrate on assembly and test, their plants tend to be highly automated. Additionally, SGS-Thompson has upgraded its wafer-fabrication plant (the first in the developing world, instituted in 1985) and Chartered Semiconductor, a government joint venture with two US companies, has recently opened its own wafer-fabrication facility (Lim and Pang 1991: 113–14, 127).

In other electronics industries, the picture is much the same. The bulk of investment in assembly processes continues to flow into the peripheral economies, which in the case of consumer products now include China. Again only in Malaysia is there evidence of some investment in higher value-added and skill-intensive processes. The Japanese producer, Sharp, for instance, is currently developing a training centre intended in part to transfer certain design skills (Ismail 1993b). Singapore, however, is once again the primary focus for investment in the higher value-added processes and products. In addition to the examples cited previously, Singapore since the early 1980s has become a major centre for disk-drive production, which now accounts for almost 10 per cent of domestic exports. In recent years most of the principal producers with plants in Singapore (Seagate, Control Data, Unisys, etc.), in response to government-induced labour-cost increases have pushed their lower-end products to other Southeast Asian locations, while upgrading in terms of processes and products, their Singapore plants. There disk-drive production is highly automated and concentrates on the more technology-intensive 3.5-inch drives. At least two of the companies – Seagate and Maxtor – have developed R&D facilities in Singapore (Lim and Pang 1991: 123–4).

As I have suggested already, Taiwan and Korea have the most technologically advanced semiconductor, consumer electronics and probably microcomputer industries in the developing world. The fact that a number of their leading companies now possess high-quality production facilities and technical personnel is reflected in the technological alliances and OEM arrangements they are able to forge with leading-edge foreign producers. In the Korean case, for instance, Samsung currently has 61 'technology transfer' agreements with North American, Japanese and European producers; Goldstar has 79, Hyundai 33 and Daewoo 20 (Bloom 1992: 127–33). While there are problems in many of these arrangements for the future development and continued upgrading of the Korean and Taiwanese industries (which we address below), it is unquestionably the case that on this and most of the other criteria, electronics production in these societies has made an enormous contribution to genuine development.

Much the same can be said for Singapore. There, technological upgrading in the electronics industries can be clearly seen in value-added data. Between 1980 and 1987, for instance, value added per worker increased by over 150 per cent, approaching in some instances US levels.[8] In Hong Kong, however, its earlier prominence in electronics technologies and products seems to be in decline. For the reasons identified above, it seems that though value added has continued to increase in the industry, this is occurring more slowly than in its NIC competitors (Whitla 1991).

Working conditions

Considerable attention has been paid to working conditions in the developing world. With regard to assembly operations where the vast majority of the work is done by women, the research consensus is that these generally have been particularly oppressive. In terms of wage rates, hours of work, compulsory overtime, supervisory control, health hazards, sexual harassment, limited paid holidays and dismissal without redundancy payment, the record has often been one of unremitting exploitation (Grossman 1979; Elson and Pearson 1981; Arrigo 1984; Heyzer 1986; Ong 1987; Women Working Worldwide 1991). Against this general background, however, subsidiaries of electronics TNCs tend to have a better record than their locally owned equivalents, particularly where the latter are relatively small enterprises (Chiang 1984). Thus there is evidence of semi-militaristic factory discipline in the Korean *chaebol* (Deyo 1989), the persistence the long working weeks (an average 56 hours in Hong Kong for instance), and from the new foreign invested (mainly by Hong Kong and Taiwanese capital) factories in China, child labour and forced overtime sometimes extending to 72 hour shifts![9]

Against this record, and especially for TNC electronics subsidiaries, must be set the facts that for the women involved standards of living have improved and with their rising significance for household income they have acquired more personal freedom than otherwise would have been the case. Add to this the evidence that the women who work for the TNCs are beginning to constitute a working class (Lin 1987) and it would appear that on the criteria of working conditions and wages, electronics FDI has made a positive contribution to development, at least in East Asia.

Wealth distribution

The issue of wealth distribution bears on the actions of many more parties than TNCs or local companies. While economic and organizational cultures are important (for instance, the extent to which social integration is sought partly through the minimization of payment differentials between workers and executives), state policy and the mobilization of popular forces are sometimes crucial. In the East Asian NICs the influence of the first two factors (though not especially the third) has produced in three of them (the exception is Hong Kong) some of the most egalitarian income distributions in the world. In as far as electronics production is a central component of their economies, then it is reasonable to assume that it has made an important contribution. The fact that income distributions remain much more unequal in Malaysia and Thailand, but especially in the other Asian and Latin American countries where electronics production has emerged, serves to emphasize the fact that there is much more to the question of income distribution than the configuration of the industrial base.

On most of the criteria discussed here it is clear that investment in electronics production, be it FDI or domestic, has made an enormous contribution to economic and social development, especially in the East Asian NICs and the 'near-NICs' – particularly Malaysia – as well. While it is clear that in the other locations, development, partly driven by electronics production, is taking place, what is unclear is the extent to which it is delivering genuine development as defined here. Perhaps of particular concern in this sense is China where FDI and the growth of private enterprise in the context of 'market Stalinism' seems to be creating an exploitative industrial capitalism the like of which the world economy has not seen in over a century. In sum, the contribution of electronics industries to development has been uneven. The question that remains for those societies where electronics clearly has contributed, is how much further down the development path is that contribution likely to take them. It is to that question that we now turn.

FUTURE PROSPECTS

The history of industrial capitalism in the developing world has shown that a small number of economies, most of them in East Asia, have been able to catch up with the developed economies in certain product areas and to have competed successfully against them. This has been the case, for instance, in textiles and garments, footwear, toys, steel, shipbuilding and some types of engineering such as certain machine tools. In electronics a competitive edge has been achieved in semiconductors (memory devices only), microcomputers, disk drives and certain consumer products such as TVs, audio equipment and VCRs. In electronics industries, however, and for our purposes particularly in locally owned ones, most of the output has been of less technologically advanced products. While electronics producers in some parts of the developing world have travelled a great distance economically and technologically – and in a very short period of time – it is not clear that their progress will be as rapid, or as effective, as they try to compete with the leading Japanese, US and European producers at the 'technological frontier'. This, however, is the competitive arena into which they will have to move if their respective economies are ever to make it into the 'big league'. While they have competed effectively thus far on the basis of their capacity to combine factor advantages (particularly cheap but skilled labour) with considerable technology-learning capabilities and efficient manufacturing systems, it is unclear whether they are capable of moving to innovation-driven production regimes which from Schumpeter onwards have been regarded as essential to the most dynamic and prosperous economies.[10]

Major problems lie ahead for the electronics industries of the developing world, including for the most advanced amongst them. These problems include the following.

Changing market conditions and competitive dynamics

Developing economy producers, particularly those of the NICs, achieved their expansion of output and movement into higher value-added products in the context of unprecedented growth in world markets. That period now appears to be over. Indeed declining demand in the world's principal markets for developing country manufactured commodities – the United States and the European Community – may well be structural rather than cyclical. There are two issues which arise here. First, the declining demand is disproportionately for standardized commodities, and these are the products in which East Asian manufacturers have concentrated their efforts. Second, declining demand and growing economic crisis in the principal industrial societies is likely to produce fierce responses from the market leaders. While producing for niche markets may be a way round the problem – and Taiwanese companies have been particularly active in this sense – the difficulty is that once niche markets become major markets, the principal producers tend to move into them. Given their far greater technological, financial and marketing capabilities, the costs for developing country producers of continuing to compete in these markets, tend to increase drastically.

The second major problem here is that in the absence of a viable international framework to regulate world market competition, economic crisis in the core economies can only call forward further protectionist impulses, particularly in the United States and the European Community. As Japan currently forms only 8 per cent of the world market for developing country manufactured commodities, neither it nor the expanding market in East Asia generally is likely to compensate for the relative loss of these markets (Ernst and O'Connor 1990).

Technological upgrading

The technological capabilities that developing country electronics firms now possess have been acquired by absorbing and learning from foreign technologies. In order to move into the first rank of world producers, these firms and their respective economies must develop indigenous technology-generating capacities. In spite of considerable and increasing sums committed by the private and public sectors in Korea and Taiwan to R&D, and the occasional acquisition of core economy R&D facilities (usually in the United States, never in Japan), there is still little evidence that even the leading Korean and Taiwanese producers have been able to transform themselves from price competitive to product (i.e. technology) competitive manufacturers. This, however, is one of the routes they must follow if they are to increase significantly the value added embodied in their products.

A precondition of moving into the production of higher value added, more technology-intensive products in the electronics sector, is the ability to acquire and apply advanced manufacturing technologies. Evidence here suggests that the NICs lag far behind the developed economies. With industrial robots, for instance, the NICs together had only 400 in use in 1985, while the OECD countries had over 100,000. In the case of computer aided design systems, the United States, Germany, Japan, Britain and Sweden combined had more than 90,000 'seats' in 1985, while the NICs combined had roughly 2,100. With numerical control machine tools the data for that same year suggests that only 2,700 units were in use in all the NICs as against 120,000 in Japan alone (Ernst and O'Connor 1992: 104). Clearly continued underinvestment in such process technologies poses major problems for the competitiveness of NIC electronics firms as they try to move into higher value-added products. Given the enormous implications for fixed costs of these technologies and the fact that they are most productive where economies of scale and scope can be achieved, suggests that it is likely that only the largest capital-rich firms will be able to acquire them and maximize their productive capabilities. This suggests that unless the Taiwanese government is prepared to use its vast reserves, the Korean industry, concentrated as it is under the control of huge conglomerates, may well be much better placed than its Taiwanese counterpart.

The third issue of relevance here is that it is not at all clear that developing country electronics firms will be able to continue to acquire the foreign technologies that are clearly still necessary to their development efforts. There are a number of reasons for this. First, the closer NIC companies get to the possibility of producing at the 'technological frontier', the less willing the leading edge producers will be to transfer their technology. This can already be seen in the increasing reluctance of major Japanese producers to license their technology to Korean counterparts who could soon become their direct competitors (Bello and Rosenfeld 1992: 154). Given the continued dependence of Korean and Taiwanese producers on foreign – often Japanese – components and technology[11] these developments could become very problematic indeed for NIC manufacturers.

The question of NIC access to foreign technologies, however, is no longer merely a matter of inter-firm relations driven by increasingly cut-throat competition. It is also a matter of state intervention to protect the proprietary technologies of manufacturers. OECD governments have attempted to force stricter intellectual property regimes on the NICs and there has been a determined effort by the US government to introduce these issues to the GATT negotiations (Ernst and O'Connor 1990).

Dependent production systems

I have emphasized already that much of the production of microcomputers and consumer products by Korean and Taiwanese manufacturers is under-taken on the basis of OEM arrangements. Indeed in 1988 some 60 to 70 per cent of Korean electronics exports were under OEM arrangements, which included 80 per cent of computer exports. In Taiwan in 1987 about two-thirds of computer and related exports were on an OEM basis, as were 78 per cent of disk drives (Hobday 1992; Ernst and O'Connor 1992: 153). While the production and distribution systems out of which OEM arrange-ments arise have positive implications for NIC producers, not least of which are the access to process technologies and skills from the foreign partner and the ability to enter major world markets without incurring the massive fixed costs associated with marketing and distribution networks, there are also considerable penalties. Prominent amongst these is the inability to gain control of the principal value-adding nodes in the international production and distribution system. As I have suggested already, many commodities are now manufactured on the basis of commodity chains (Gereffi, this volume; Gereffi and Korzeniewicz 1990). In the case of micro-computers, these chains connect major buyers and distributors in the United States (e.g. IBM) and the European Community (e.g. Olivetti) with manufacturers and their subcontractors in Taiwan and increasingly China. While little of the value is added in China, some is added in Taiwan, but the bulk accrues to the buyers and distributors in the United States and the European Community.

What we have with production systems organized in the form of com-modity chains are new types of dependency rooted in the configuration of inter-firm relations, rather than in the global organization of TNCs which gave rise to the international and regional divisions of labour which were discussed earlier. As with the TNC-driven regional division of labour, however, the peripheries (in our example, China) are subject to the technological and managerial control of the intermediaries (in this case Taiwanese firms) as well as that of the core economy firms. The impli-cations of commodity chain arrangements for development, then, are quite negative for the peripheries, and create serious limitations for the inter-mediary, or semi-peripheral, economies. The way forward for intermediary firms is obviously to break free from the commodity chains and distribute in the principal markets under their own brand names, thus capturing much more of the value added. As has been mentioned already, however, the fixed costs involved in making this transition are enormous, and given their relatively small size, way beyond the resources of the vast majority of Taiwanese and other East Asian NIC companies, with the principal exception of the Korean *chaebol*.

While this section has concentrated on the future prospects of those developing countries that have electronics industries, we conclude with a comment on those that do not. FDI remains the principal driving force of all developing country electronics industries with the exception of Korea,

Taiwan, Hong Kong and to a lesser extent, Brazil and India. Unfortunately for governments and firms of countries wishing to break into electronics production, FDI to the developing world has all but collapsed. While FDI flowing to the developed economies has increased, from 76 per cent of the total in 1983 to 83 per cent in 1988, the share going to the developing world has dropped from 24 to 17 per cent over the same period, and the vast majority of this has been destined for the East Asian NICs, the 'near NICs' and China (Ernst and O'Connor 1990). On this basis, then, the possibility of any other developing country creating a viable electronics industry in the forseeable future, seems remote.

CONCLUSION

This chapter has surveyed the emergence and expansion of electronics industries in the developing world. It has suggested that in terms of the criteria that bear on the capacity of any manufacturing industry to assist in the genuine development of an economy and society, the influence of electronics has been uneven. This uneven contribution has ranged from the almost total exclusion of the majority of the developing world from its potential benefits at one polarity to the strong, technologically advanced, world-competitive industries of some of the East Asian NICs at the other. Among the elements that have been decisive in arranging electronics industries on this continuum, interventionist states have been high on the list.

Additionally I have charted the emerging TNC and network-based organizational forms which the electronics sector has taken within the East Asian region and argued that in the context of world economic crisis and intensified competition, these forms are giving rise to new relations of dependency. It is in this context that there must remain a question mark over the possibility of even the most advanced firms – those from Korea and Taiwan – becoming first rank world players. In as far as electronics industries are likely to remain central to the development efforts of these countries, the question is raised as to whether there are general structural limits to economic transformation in the world economy. The history of last forty years has shown that it is possible for a few societies to move from the periphery to the semi-periphery of the world economy. In the coming decades we may know – largely from the case of Britain – whether it is possible to move from the core to the semi-periphery. Only in the unique circumstances of Japan have we witnessed movement from the semi-periphery to the core. Arrighi and Drangel (1986) have asked what happens to the semi-periphery. After detailed historical investigation, their answer is: it remains the semi-periphery. My discussion of electronics production and its likely future contribution to development, seems to point to the same conclusion.[12]

NOTES

1 For critiques of the new international division of labour thesis see Jenkins (1984), Cohen (1987: 220–53) and Henderson (1989:16–24, 156–62) among others.

2 For a diagramatic summary of the changing international division of labour among selected US semiconductor producers, see Henderson (1989: 46–7, figure 3.2 and 56–7, figure 4.2.

3 The relative underinvestment by Japanese consumer electronics firms in Korea may be a reflection partly of the Korean government's attempts to protect the domestic market from foreign competition, and partly a concern by the companies to check technology seepage to their Korean competitors.

4 Author's interviews in Malaysia, July 1992. See also Baring Securities (1989) and Ernst and O'Connor (1992: 190).

5 Author's interviews in Hong Kong, September–December 1991. See also Fong (1989).

6 Reverse engineering is a process of technology acquisition that involves taking apart the product, its components and embodied processes and tracing them to their basic elements. It is a labourious and time-consuming process that often can result in mistakes leading to poor-quality products.

7 The consequence of rising labour costs was that small and medium enterprises (SMEs) also were squeezed. This has been one of the factors underlying limited, but growing dissatisfaction with PAP rule. The government is trying to compensate for high labour costs in Singapore by giving SMEs access to cheap labour in Malaysia and Indonesia via its promotion of the 'Growth Triangle'. The export of capital to cheap-labour sites is seen by the government as preferable to importing non-Chinese labour into Singapore (Parsonage 1992).

8 Calculated from the data presented by Lim and Pang (1991: 133, table 18).

9 Author's interviews in Hong Kong, September–December 1991. On the situation in China, Leung's (1988) work is indispensable. For information on Korea and the trade-union response see Asia Monitor Resources Center (1988).

10 For a major account of the significance of institutionalized innovation to corporate success and national prosperity, see the recent work of business economist, Michael Porter (1990).

11 Bloom (1992: 15) reports that over 60 per cent of all components used in the Korean electronics industries are imported.

12 This is a substantially revised version of a paper presented to the symposium on New Trends in the Internationalisation of the Economy at the International Sociological Association's XIIth World Congress, Madrid, July 1990. I am grateful to Peter Evans for inviting me to prepare the original paper.

REFERENCES

Amsden, A. H. (1989) *Asia's Next Giant: South Korea and Late Industrialization*, New York: Oxford University Press

Appelbaum, R. P. and Henderson, J. (1992) (eds) *States and Development in the Asian Pacific Rim*, Newbury Park: Sage Publications.

Arrighi, G. and Drangel, J. (1986) 'The stratification of the world economy: an exploration of the semiperipheral zone', *Review* 10(1): 9–74.

Arrigo, L. G. (1984) 'Taiwan electronics workers', in M. Sheridan and J. W. Salaff (eds) *Lives: Chinese Working Women*, Bloomington: Indiana University Press: 123–45.

285

Asia Monitor Resources Center (1988) *Min-Ju No-Jo: South Korea's New Trade Unions*, Hong Kong: Asia Monitor Resources Center.

Balassa, B. (1991) *Economic Policies in the Pacific Area Developing Countries*, London: Macmillan.

Baring Securities (1989) *Foreign Investment in Malaysia: Economy in Transition*, Hong Kong: Baring Securities.

Bello, W. and Rosenfeld, S. (1992) *Dragons in Distress: Asia's Miracle Economies in Crisis*, London: Penguin Books.

Bloom, M. (1992) *Technological Change in the Korean Electronics Industry*, Paris: OECD Development Centre.

Braun, E. and Macdonald, S. (1982) *Revolution in Miniature: The History and Impact of Semiconductor Electronics*, Cambridge: Cambridge University Press.

Castells, M., Goh, L. and Kwok, R. Y. (1990) *The Shek Kip Mei Syndrome: Economic Development and Public Housing in Hong Kong and Singapore*, London: Pion.

Chen, E. K. Y. (1971) 'The electronics industry of Hong Kong: an analysis of its growth', unpublished M. Soc. Sc. thesis, University of Hong Kong.

Chen, S. Y. (1993) 'The historical development of technology transfer in Taiwan', unpublished MBA dissertation, Manchester Business School.

Cheng, L. L. and Gereffi, G. (1994) 'The informal economy in East Asian development', *International Journal of Urban and Regional Research* 18(2) (in press).

Chiang, S. N. C. (1984) 'Women and work: case studies of two Hong Kong factories', unpublished M. Phil. thesis, University of Hong Kong.

Cohen, R. (1987) *The New Helots: Migrants in the International Division of Labour*, Aldershot: Gower.

Deyo, F. C. (1989) *Beneath the Miracle: Labor Subordination in the New Asian Industrialism*, University of California Press: Berkeley and Los Angeles.

Dicken, P. (1992) *Global Shift: The Internationalisation of Economic Activity*, London: Paul Chapman.

Elson, D. and Pearson, R. (1981) 'Nimble fingers make cheap workers: an analysis of women's employment in Third World export manufacturing', *Feminist Review* 7: 87–107.

Ernst, D. (1983) *The Global Race in Microelectronics*, Frankfurt: Campus Verlag.

Ernst, D. and O'Connor, D. (1990) 'New technology, latecomer industrialisation and development today', *Background Report for the Technology/Economy Programme*, Paris: OECD Development Centre.

—— (1992) *Competing in the Electronics Industry: The Experience of Newly Industrialising Economies*, Paris: OECD Development Centre.

Evans, P. (1986) 'State, capital and the transformation of dependence: the Brazilian computer case', *World Development* 14(7): 791–808.

Fong, M. Y. (1989) 'Hong Kong manufacturing investment in China: social and spatial implications', unpublished M. Soc. Sc. dissertation, University of Hong Kong.

Fröbel, F., Heinrichs, J. and Kreye, O. (1980) *The New International Division of Labour*, Cambridge: Cambridge University Press.

Gereffi, G. (1992) 'New realities of industrial development in East Asia and Latin America: global, regional and national trends', in R. P. Appelbaum and J. Henderson (eds) *States and Development in the Asian Pacific Rim*, Newbury Park: Sage Publications: 85–112.

Gereffi, G. and Korzeniewicz, M. (1990) 'Commodity chains and footware exports in the semi-periphery', in W. Martin (ed.) *Semiperipheral States in the World Economy*, Westport CT: Greenwood Press: 45–68.

Grossman, R. (1979) 'Women's place in the integrated circuit', *Southeast Asia Chronicle* 66: 2–17.

Henderson, J. (1987) 'Semiconductors, Scotland and the international division of labour', *Urban Studies* 24(5): 389–408.

—— (1989) *The Globalisation of High Technology Production: Society, Space and Semi-conductors in the Restructuring of the Modern World*, London: Routledge.

—— (1991) 'Urbanisation in the Hong Kong–South China region: an introduction to dynamics and dilemmas', *International Journal of Urban and Regional Research* 15(2): 169–79.

—— (1993a) 'The role of the state in the economic transformation of East Asia', in C. Dixon and D. Drakakis-Smith (eds) *Economic and Social Development in Pacific Asia*, London: Routledge: 85–114.

—— (1993b) 'Against the economic orthodoxy: on the making of the East Asian miracle', *Economy and Society* 22(2): 200–17.

Henderson, J. and Scott, A. J. (1987) 'The growth and internationalisation of the American semiconductor industry: labour processes and the changing spatial organisation of production', in M. Breheny and R. McQuaid (eds) *The Development of High Technology Industries: An International Survey*, London: Croom Helm: 37–79.

Hewitt, T. (1992) 'Employment and skills in the Brazilian electronics industry', in H. Schmitz and J. Cassiolato (eds) *Hi-Tech for Industrial Development: Lessons from the Brazilian Experience in Electronics and Automation*, London: Routledge: 180–205.

Heyzer, N. (1986) *Working Women in Southeast Asia*, Milton Keynes: Open University Press.

Hobday, M. (1992) 'Foreign investment, exports and technology development in the four dragons', paper to the conference on 'Global Trends in Foreign Direct Investment and Strategies of Transnational Corporations in Brazil', University of Campinas, Brazil, 3–6 November.

Ismail, M. N. (1993a) 'Linkages between foreign electronics multinationals and local firms in Malaysia', unpublished paper, Manchester Business School.

—— (1993b) 'Manpower upgrading and integration in Malaysia', unpublished paper, Manchester Business School.

Jenkins, R. (1984) 'Divisions over the international division of labour', *Capital and Class* 22: 28–57.

Jesudason, J. (1989) *Ethnicity and the Economy: The State, Chinese Business and Multinationals in Malaysia*, Singapore: Oxford University Press.

Leung, W. Y. (1988) *Smashing the Iron Rice Pot: Workers and Unions in China's Market Socialism*, Hong Kong: Asia Monitor Resources Center.

Lim, L. Y. C. and Pang, E. F. (1982) 'Vertical linkages and multinational enterprises in developing countries', *World Development* 10(6): 585–95.

—— (1991) *Foreign Direct Investment and Industrialisation in Malaysia, Singapore, Taiwan and Thailand*, Paris: OECD Development Centre.

Lin, V. (1987) 'Women electronic workers in Southeast Asia: the emergence of a working class', in J. Henderson and M. Castells (eds) *Global Restructuring and Territorial Development*, London: Sage Publications.

Little, I., Scitovsky, T. and Scott, M. (1970) *Industry and Trade in Some Developing Countries*, London: Oxford University Press.

Lubeck, P. (1992) 'Malaysian industrialisation, ethnic divisions and the NIC model: the limits to replication', in R. P. Appelbaum and J. Henderson (eds) *States and Development in the Asian Pacific Rim*, Newbury Park: Sage Publications: 176–98.

Mirza, H. (1986) *Multinationals and the Growth of the Singapore Economy*, New York: St Martins Press.

Ong, A. (1987) *Spirits of Resistance and Capitalist Discipline: Factory Women in Malaysia*, Albany: State University of New York Press.

Parsonage, J. (1992) 'Southeast Asia's "Growth Triangle": a subregional response to global transformation', *International Journal of Urban and Regional Research* 16(2): 307–17.

Porter, M. E. (1990) *The Competitive Advantage of Nations*, London: Macmillan.

Redding, S. G. (1990) *The Spirit of Chinese Capitalism*, Berlin: de Gruyter.

Rodan, G. (1989) *The Political Economy of Singapore's Industrialisation: National State and Transnational Capital*, London: Macmillan.

Salih, K. (1988) 'The new economic policy after 1990', *MIER Discussion Paper*, 21, Kuala Lumpur: Malaysian Institute of Economic Research.

Schiffer, J. (1991) 'State policy and economic growth: a note on the Hong Kong model', *International Journal of Urban and Regional Research* 15(2): 180–96.

Schmitz, H. and Hewitt, T. (1992) 'An assessment of the market reserve for the Brazilian computer industry', in H. Schmitz and J. Cassiolato (eds) *Hi-Tech for Industrial Development: Lessons from the Brazilian Experience in Electronics and Automation*, London: Routledge: 21–52.

Scott, A. J. (1987) 'The semiconductor industry in Southeast Asia: organisation, location and the international division of labour', *Regional Studies* 21(2): 143–60.

Siegel, L. and Markoff, J. (1985) *The High Cost of High Tech: The Dark Side of the Chip*, New York: Harper and Row.

Sklair, L. (1993) *Assembling for Development: The Maquila Industry in Mexico and the United States*, 2nd updated edn, San Diego: University of California Center for US-Mexican Studies.

Wade, R. (1990) *Governing the Market: Economic Theory and the Role of Government in East Asian Industrialisation*, Princeton NJ: Princeton University Press.

Whitla, P. (1991) 'The competitive position of Hong Kong', unpublished MBA. dissertation, Manchester Business School.

Women Working Worldwide (1991) *Common Interests: Women Organising in Global Electronics*, London: Women Working Worldwide.

14

JAPANESE MULTINATIONALS AND EAST ASIAN DEVELOPMENT

The case of the automobile industry

Richard Child Hill and Yong Joo Lee

INTRODUCTION

The editor of this collection has challenged contributors to address some knotty questions. Can capitalism develop the Third World? If not, why not? If so, to what extent and in what institutional areas? In this chapter we explore these issues in relation to the changing structure of the world automobile industry.

A few hundred manufacturing corporations control a large fraction of the world's productive resources. Automobile companies are prominent amongst them. The extent to which producers in developing countries can build their own motor vehicle industries depends upon the relations they establish with these transnational automotive giants. Those relations in turn are influenced by the competitive environment facing transnational corporations *and* the local political-economic structures, market potential and strategic policies of the developing countries, themselves.

We will focus our attention upon relations among the auto-producing nations of East Asia: Japan, the Asian NIEs (principally South Korea and Taiwan), and the ASEAN Four (Thailand, Malaysia, the Philippines and Indonesia).[1] Why Japan? First, because Japanese industrial organization is driving transformations in the world automobile industry today. Automobile companies worldwide are emulating Japanese technology, management, labour and supplier relations (Hoffman and Kaplinsky 1988; Womack, Jones and Roos 1990).

Second, because Japan accounted for a substantial share of global growth in direct foreign investment (DFI) during the 1980s (Hill and Lee 1992). Between 1980 and 1988, Japanese DFI stocks increased nearly sixfold. One-tenth the America level in 1980, Japanese DFI flows were two-thirds higher than the American in 1989 (UNCTNC 1991). Japanese TNCs have come to play a correspondingly powerful role in shaping the world industrial economy (Emmott 1992).

Why the Asian NIEs and ASEAN countries? Because a large share of total Japanese DFI during the 1980s and virtually all of Japanese DFI in developing countries flowed into the Asian NIEs and ASEAN nations. Asian NIEs and the ASEAN nations are experiencing high economic growth rates in comparison to other nations of the world. Some analysts have concluded that the economic dynamism experienced by individual East Asian nations is rooted in a broader, Japan-centred regional division of labour (Cumings 1984). A critical issue, therefore, is whether a Japan-influenced global restructuring of industry is altering the politics and economics of industrial location and development.

CONCEPTS

As conceived here, divisions of labour in manufacturing occur within production systems. A production system is a collection of business operations linked by technology and organization into the manufacture of final products. Enterprises become linked into production systems as they develop, manufacture and market specific commodities. A transnational auto production system interlinks firms of various sizes in value added chains over regional, national and international space with varying degrees of logistical precision and efficiency (Hill 1989).

The thousands of parts and subassemblies that flow into a completed motor vehicle can be arranged on a value added continuum. Lower-value parts are more standardized and require less technological sophistication, skill and capital to manufacture; brake linings, clutchplates and wire harnesses are examples. Higher-value parts are less routine to produce and require more advanced technologies, skills and capital; transmissions, drive trains, electrical systems and engines are examples. Firms that manufacture lower-value parts tend to pay workers lower wages and make lower profits than companies manufacturing and assembling higher-value components.

High start-up costs and the difficulty of auto design and manufacturing virtually require new auto companies to affiliate with existing transnational corporations (TNCs). Therefore, Third World nations intent on constructing their own auto industries become enmeshed in transnational production systems. One can think of a ladder of national incorporation into the global division of labour that parallels the value added production hierarchy discussed above. On the lowest value added rung, Third World firms, be they subsidiaries, indigenously owned companies, or joint TNC/local ventures, import vehicles in their entirety in completely knocked down kits (CKD), and merely assemble them on local soil.

Companies on the next rung, in addition to assembling parts made elsewhere, are able to manufacture their own lower value, more standardized and less skill-intensive components. This enables indigenous firms to substitute some local production for imports and eliminate an equivalent part of the import bill. Third World manufacturers move up another notch when they are able to bring local production up to international competitive standards. Now they may be able to export lower-value parts to affiliated assembly facilities in other nations thereby earning foreign exchange to help pay for the materials, equipment and components they are not yet able to manufacture at home. Companies further up the production hierarchy, are capable of producing bigger ticket, higher technology intermediate and final products for domestic assembly and export.

This kind of value added production ladder is sometimes referred to as 'process specialization' since each step is part of the overall process of manufacturing a specific product. On the top rung of the transnational ladder is the corporate headquarters which controls and coordinates the whole process. 'Product specialization' is a second way in which a developing country can be incorporated into a transnational production system. In this case, the division of labour is horizontal rather than vertical. Producers in developed and developing nations divide up responsibilities for the manufacture of different products rather than dividing up pieces or phases in the manufacture of the same product. For example, producers in a less developed country specialize in the manufacture of standardized, lower priced, economy vehicles for domestic consumption and sale on the world market while their affiliated counterparts in an industrially advanced country manufacture higher tech, more luxurious and higher priced vehicles for their own domestic market and for international consumption.

Horizontal incorporation is a relatively advanced stage of specialization since it requires local command over the manufacture of much of the inner workings of a vehicle. The next step along the horizontal, product specialization continuum comes with the ability to manufacture a product line; not just one, but a range of small car and truck models. By this point on the development continuum, companies have acquired the research and design capabilities necessary to generate new products.

A Third World country setting out to develop an indigenous automobile industry will most likely begin at the bottom of the vertical process division of labour, by assembling CKDs and producing lower-value parts for local assembly and export. The national development objective, of course, is to move up the value added ladder to the manufacture of complete vehicles, parts and vehicle lines, and ultimately, indigenously designed brand-name products, assuming the nation wants to compete in world markets. Each step up the vertical, value added hierarchy and each step along the horizontal continuum raises the local content of production, that is, the percentage of the total value of the vehicle that is produced indigenously. As local content rises, so does the growth of enterprises knitted together in local production systems which in turn generates local employment and industrial development. Industrial investment will boost a nation's standard of living to the degree that local producers can improve their share of a production system's forward and backward linkages, high value added intermediate goods, services and components, and professional, technical and scientific expertise.

Developing countries adopt various strategies as they pursue automotive industrialization. To make the initial transition from importing whole vehicles to assembling them from CKD kits, they may place high tariffs on finished-vehicle imports and sometimes ban them altogether. In an effort to maintain indigenous control over their fledgling industry, they may set ceilings on foreign ownership and require TNCs to enter joint-venture relationships with local companies. They may legislate and incrementally raise local content levels to stimulate technology diffusion and expand the local manufacturing base. And they may offer financial incentives to encourage local firms to export locally made parts and vehicles so as to earn foreign exchange and maintain a positive trade balance.

Transnational corporations incorporate developing country trade and investment policies into their production and location decisions. But TNCs take into account other considerations as well. Chief among them are unit costs – combined wage and productivity levels that determine a nation's competitive location on the global competitive spectrum for parts, sub- and final assemblies. TNC expectations about a developing nation's market potential also play a critical role. International trade relations among the advanced industrial states are important, too. Currency-rate fluctuations, which can have a dramatic effect on production costs in various parts of the world, often reflect core country conflicts over world-trade imbalances.

CONTRASTING PRODUCTION SYSTEMS

World manufacturing was largely an American inspired phenomenon after the Second World War. Giant US companies employed legions of semi-skilled workers who mass produced standardized goods with product specific machines. The large American corporation was powerful enough to create mass demand through sophisticated marketing strategies. A high and predictable rate of profit allowed the firm to reinvest in new products, labour-saving technology and a network of large assembly plants and parts production centres exploiting economies of scale (Piore and Sable 1984).

The US centred product cycle

Researchers attempting to explain the international division of labour emerging after the Second World War often rely on Raymond Vernon's (1971, 1979) theory of the product cycle. According to Vernon, the trade and investment patterns of US corporations followed a predictable sequence determined by the manufacturing cycle of a product: innovation, imitation, standardization and diffusion. Product cycles originating in the

United States resulted in an 'industrialized pecking order' among nations (Vernon 1979).

In the first phase of the product cycle, the industrially advanced country *exports* the high-value, innovative product. Exports of the product continue to grow as long as there is a technological gap between the country of origin and importing nations. As the product stimulates foreign demand, foreign firms acquire an incentive to enter the market and are often assisted in doing so by their national governments.

As foreign firms imitate the product and begin producing it, the advanced country's exports slow down. In the second, *import-substituting* phase, corporations from the advanced nation set up their own manu-facturing plants in foreign countries to protect market share. In the third, *overseas-sourcing* phase, technology has become standardized and widely disseminated and the limit of scale economies has been reached. Trade based on wage costs begins. TNCs adopt a global outlook and set up production in locations around the world where costs are lowest. By now they are importing the product back home (Morris-Suzuki 1991).

Vernon's product cycle hypothesis relied upon the special circumstances enjoyed by the American economy following the Second World War: huge oligopolistic corporations capable of mass-producing standardized goods, scarce and well-paid labour, high per capita income, large internal markets, and war devastated competitor nations. Under these circumstances, the US market generated innovations that people in other countries would come to desire as their own nations grew closer to American income levels and market conditions.

Even as he formulated the theory, Vernon noted that market conver-gence and the global multiplication of TNC production sites would likely erode the product-cycle sequence among industrially advanced nations.[2] But he was convinced of the theory's longer term applicability to relations among developed and less developed countries where a wide gap in tech-nological know-how and living conditions was likely to persist. So long as firms in less developed countries continued to absorb innovations their TNC parents and affiliates in developed countries had earlier introduced, less developed countries would continue to lag behind the industrialized nations.[3]

The product cycle is a trade-based theory of the international division of labour among nations. But as the American corporation grew, it absorbed the activities formerly performed by many independent firms. Trade rela-tions were progressively internalized within the administrative apparatus of the firm. As that happened, students of the international division of labour began to shift their attention from trade relations among independent firms to the organization of production inside the global corporation (Hymer 1971).

The new international division of labour

Post-war US industrial relations also evinced the logic of mass production. Management viewed labour abstractly, as a factor of production to be allocated efficiently. Like machines, workers performed best when they were interchangeable, replaceable and closely supervised (Braverman 1974). Workers organized in opposition to that view. Labour and management worked out a compromise over time (Serrin 1970). Workers protected themselves from abuses of authority and managers assured tasks were carried out through a minutely defined and mutually agreed upon system of job classifications, task assignments, work rules and supervision.

As the American corporation extended its territorial reach, it extended the division between those who conceptualize and those who execute production, and between skilled and unskilled work; first, within national boundaries, and then, with advances in transportation and communication, across different workforces in different countries. Conception and skilled labour were concentrated in the advanced industrial countries, a mix of skilled and unskilled in the NIEs, and mainly unskilled in the least industrialized nations.

Students of this global factory model of the world industrial economy – also known as the 'new international division of labour' (NIDL) – argue that transnational production chains severely constrain Third World development possibilities (Fröbel, Heinrichs and Kreye 1980; Lipietz 1987). TNCs control technology, design, delivery logistics and marketing channels. Vertical specialization in low-value production creates economic enclaves with few forward and backward linkages to regional and national economies. Job growth is limited, as are skills and managerial expertise. Low wages, poor working conditions and meagre social benefits are the lot of an often predominantly female labour force.

Paradoxically, the movement of standardized branch plants to the less developed nations can boomerang and inflict economic damage on the developed countries, themselves (Bluestone and Harrison 1983; Morris-Suzuki 1991). TNC direct foreign investment in Third World production complexes reverses the direction of manufacturing imports – from developing to developed countries. As companies in the developed countries diversify out of mobile manufacturing industries, they undermine their nation's industrial base. Rising unemployment causes expenditure demands on government to rise as tax revenues are falling. Disinvestment, unemployment and fiscal crisis erode the post-war social contract between business and labour (Jenkins 1984).

Raymond Vernon pinpointed the auto industry in the late 1960s as a mature industry destined to spread to the developing countries. Engines, chassis and components became standardized over the first half of the century. The technical design of an automobile had not changed for

294

decades. According to product-cycle theory, the industry was ripe for import substitution production and developing countries were in fact pressing TNCs for more export-oriented production (Doner 1991).

Developments in the auto industry during the 1970s seemed to fit comfortably with the NIDL perspective, too. Transnational auto corporations were racing to create a world car: a small, energy-efficient vehicle with standardized, interchangeable components, designed to be manufactured and marketed throughout the world. The world car was a strategy to lower the expenses of design and engineering, realize economies of scale, and enhance manufacturing flexibility by allowing the auto giants to multiply their production locations for various kinds of components. The world car would likely shift standardized production facilities to the less industrialized countries as manufacturers sought lower wages to reduce costs. The result would be more concentrated ownership and control over auto TNCs in the developed countries and greater dispersion of auto production facilities in the rest of the world (Hainer and Koslofsky 1979; Hill 1984).

However, neither product-cycle nor NIDL theory anticipated what the world auto industry would actually be like by the end of the 1980s. Far from reaching maturity, every aspect of the industry underwent transformation. Energy crises at the beginning and end of the 1970s and environmental awareness generated a myriad of product and process innovations, including fuel efficiency, safety, emissions and use of new materials. Technological innovations in microelectronics and information processing fundamentally altered the way work was performed. The fragmentation of world markets blunted the world car strategy by discounting the utility of scale economies, long product life cycles and global sourcing. Instead, transnational auto companies were engaged in fierce competition to innovate new products and reduce the time required to bring new products to the market.

The wholesale restructuring of global car manufacturing has variously been theorized as a movement from Fordism to post-Fordism (Holmes 1986), from machinofacture to systemofacture (Hoffman and Kaplinsky 1988), from mass production to flexible specialization (Piore and Sabel 1984), and from mass to lean production (Womack, Jones and Roos 1990). These abstract models are often insightful but they should not detract from a concrete point: Japanese production organization has been generating this epochal transformation in world manufacturing and has brought the postwar era of US industrial dominion to an end.

The Japanese production system

Japan's auto companies initiated production in the 1930s, then again in the 1950s, with technical assistance from the United States. But Japanese industrialists soon realized they could not be competitive in world markets simply by following in US footsteps. Manufacturing volume and output per model in Japan were too low to compete against the economies of scale and productivity accruing to the US mass-production system. With Toyota Motor Corporation in the lead, Japanese car manufacturers responded to US industrial hegemony by constructing a different kind of production system.

The Japanese became masters at manufacturing a variety of high-quality models in relatively low volumes. US mass-production methods lowered costs by minimizing product diversity and maximizing economies of scale. Toyota, on the other hand, achieved efficiencies through flexible specialization, spatial agglomeration, and just-in-time (JIT) delivery logistics (Cusumano 1988). Greater flexibility in the deployment of equipment and labour improved quality. JIT synchronization of delivery to the assembly line enhanced productivity by reducing inventories, waste, plant size and energy costs (Friedman 1983; Cusumano 1988).

Toyota's efforts to combine the advantages of craft flexibility with the most advanced information technology required considerable cooperation among managers, workers and suppliers. In the 1950s, Toyota managers forged a cooperative relationship with workers through a mixture of threat, persuasion and collaboration. Toyota officials, in association with other industrialists, undercut Japan's national industrial unions and set up their own enterprise unions. The company fired a large number of workers, offered lifetime employment to a core group of employees in return for cooperation, and began a policy of promoting union officials to managerial positions.

Japanese manufacturers also promoted a system of worker participation and self-inspection and reduced the number of job categories in order to shift workers easily across job routines (Cusumano 1985: ch. 5). Corporate welfare programmes and an enterprise as community ideology dampened labour strife. Rising wage costs were countered by reducing labour content through automated production methods and by a tiered wage system among a regional network of suppliers based upon firm size and value added to the final product (Luria 1986).

Product diversity, short product cycles and JIT delivery in small batches also required close, cooperative contact among parent firms and subcontractors (Shimogawa 1986). Suppliers had to be expert in design and production technology if they were to deliver sophisticated parts for rapidly changing products just-in-time to the assembly line. This encouraged close social and spatial relations among assemblers and parts firms. Companies organized into Toyota style production systems possessed the capacity to respond to economic problems and market uncertainties by continuously reshaping productive processes through the rearrangement of component activities (Womack, Jones and Roos 1990).

The higher productivity, product diversity and quality generated by

Japanese flexible manufacturing methods gradually translated into global competitive power. Computer-based machines reduced the need for manufacturing scale economies allowing firms to shorten product life cycles. Customers experienced, then came to demand more product variety. Markets fragmented, severely taxing the mass production model. By the early 1980s, Toyota and Nissan, insignificant companies in the 1950s, had become the world's second and third largest car makers (Cusumano 1985). And Japanese market penetration had thoroughly shaken western assumptions about production organization.

JAPAN AND THE INTERNATIONAL DIVISION OF LABOUR

What does the Japanese production system imply about foreign direct investment, the international division of labour and export-oriented industrialization in the developing world? Researchers studying these questions in the early 1980s concluded that Japanese production organization does not encourage the pursuit of cheap labour in nations with a weak technology base. Developing countries pursuing low-wage strategies to secure a presence in the international auto industry were not likely to succeed (Hoffman and Kaplinsky 1988).

Reluctant multinationals

Japanese firms are highly capital intensive even by auto manufacturing standards. They make extensive use of advanced product and production technology: modular design, electronics and new materials in products and flexible automation in production. In the early 1980s, Japanese car companies needed only 65 per cent of the labour required in the United States to produce a comparable product and 30 per cent fewer hours than West Germans (Altshuler *et al.* 1984: 159). Moreover, because Japanese assemblers and suppliers collaborate on product design, quality control, flexible production and JIT delivery schedules, they tend to cluster close together in space and time. Consequently, Japanese industrialists prefer to export vehicles from plants in Japan rather than manufacture them abroad.

In 1980, the US Big 3 automakers produced about 35 per cent of their output abroad, and European firms 19 per cent. The combined average for Toyota and Nissan was only 1 per cent. The small number of offshore Japanese auto plants were not exporting back to Japan or to third countries. Ninety per cent of their sales went to local markets (Doner 1991: 64).

Japanese auto firms are reluctant multinationals due to the character of their production systems: capital-intensive manufacturing, a lifetime employment commitment to core workers; and tight relations with parts suppliers. From the Japanese perspective, overseas auto manufacture reduces competitiveness, efficiency and quality while raising costs. Close links between parent automakers, a skilled and flexible workforce and high quality parts firms are difficult to reproduce outside of Japan. Developing country parts firms tend to be technologically weak. Poor infrastructure impedes JIT manufacturing.[4] A case in point: engines produced in Japanese plants in Southeast Asia in the mid-1980s were three times the cost and car bodies twice as expensive as those produced in Japan (Doner 1991: 85).

Countervailing forces

During the 1970s, Japanese auto companies used Japan as a manufacturing base and drew upon the networks of giant trading companies to penetrate world markets. Direct foreign investment was insubstantial and mostly went into overseas financial services, trade and distribution outlets to buttress the export strategy. Japanese firms' global strategy was based on three principles: high productivity, domestically developed technology and expanded reproduction through exports (Yamada 1990).

But as Japan's market strength grew during the 1980s, so did her trade surplus with the rest of the world.[5] Japan's trading partners reacted with protective measures, including import restrictions and foreign exchange balancing policies. Developing countries raised local content requirements. The United States and countries in Western European set import quotas and began law suits against Japanese firms for allegedly 'dumping' underpriced vehicles in their markets. The Plaza Accord, reached by the 'G5' industrial countries in 1985, attempted to curtail Japanese exports, increase Japan's imports from the West, and stabilize exchange rates by steeply increasing the value of the yen against the dollar.

The yen doubled in value between 1985 and 1988.[6] Japanese production and labour costs shot up commensurately forcing companies to reduce sharply outlays to remain competitive in international markets. Avoiding trade restrictions abroad, reducing costs at home, and taking advantage of a powerfully enhanced yen combined into an irresistible rationale for direct foreign investment. Between 1985 and the end of 1990, Japanese companies invested an astounding $596.2 billion in auto and electronics transplants and a host of other projects in Asia, North America and the European Community (Sterngold 1992).

The big jump in Japanese DFI indexed a reorientation in Japan's growth strategy prompted by the 1985 yen appreciation and friction with trading partners. Following the 1985 G5 meeting, Japan's prime minister commissioned a blue ribbon study to recommend a course of action that would reduce Japan's trade surplus while guaranteeing continued economic growth. The 'Maekawa Report', as the commission's proposals came to be called, urged the government to facilitate transplant production abroad and spur consumption at home.[7] Japan's Ministry of International Trade and Industry (MITI) began simultaneously championing the domestic development of high-value products at home and the transfer of routine production overseas.

Japanese auto companies initially responded to the strong yen with a *cost-competitiveness strategy*. They developed technology that dramatically increased productivity in their domestic plants and they stepped up the transfer of parts manufacturing to low-cost suppliers in Korea, Taiwan and other nations along the Pacific Rim (Takeuchi 1987; Fujita and Hill 1989). To circumvent trade restrictions, Japanese TNCs exported from their subsidiaries in the Asian NIEs and ASEAN countries to their affiliates in third countries, like the United States, which were raising barriers against imports from Japan; they also exported back to the home market to reduce Japan's trade surplus. Japan's cost-containment and export-platform policies dovetailed with the development strategies of the Asian NIEs and ASEAN countries seeking to create an export-oriented industrial base (Morris-Suzuki 1991).

In the 1960s, Toyota Motor Corporation's production overseas was largely limited to CKD assembly plants. The company manufactured parts and components in Toyota City and exported them to host countries for assembly. Many first-tier suppliers followed Toyota abroad in the 1970s when the parent company built parts-manufacturing facilities in Indonesia, Thailand, Australia and Brazil in response to national car-development programmes.[8] Some Toyota suppliers produced low value added products, such as batteries, tires, glass and wire harnesses, to meet local content requirements, but most limited their activities to technical assistance and sales operations.

Toyota greatly extended the global reach of its production system after the yen appreciation in 1985. Taking advantage of its foothold in the Asian NIEs and ASEAN countries, Toyota upgraded its subsidiaries, expanded its production facilities and encouraged more of its suppliers to go offshore. The Toyota family of overseas suppliers began earnestly using East Asian countries as export platforms for markets in Japan, the United States and other parts of the world. Toyota suppliers joined with Taiwanese partners to produce engine valves for the Japanese market as well as airconditioners, auto electric equipment, auto bodies, interior equipment, plastic and rubber products for locally assembled vehicles. Toyota began exporting metal moulds manufactured in Thailand to Indonesia, Taiwan, Malaysia and Australia where they were used in the production of inexpensive pressed parts for export to Japan and the United States. And Toyota suppliers joined with Indonesian firms to produce batteries for the Japanese market as well as tyres, shock absorbers and piston rings (Fujita and Hill 1989).

The post-1985 flow of Japanese capital to Third World production sites conformed to the NIDL model for a time. Japanese TNCs fashioned a vertical, global factory division of labour to reduce yen-inflated domestic production costs by tapping overseas reserves of cheap labour. But they did not stop with the transfer of individual, low value added production processes; instead, they continued to transfer more phases in the production of low-cost, high-volume vehicles. Japanese companies are now constructing a horizontal as well as a vertical division of labour between Japan and less developed East Asian nations.

The success of Japan's cost competitiveness strategy had further aggravated trade conflicts. Overseas subsidiaries continued to rely on Japan for the dies, parts and capital equipment local industries could not provide. As local vehicle assembly expanded, local trade balances with Japan worsened, leading to confrontations over local content levels. Asian NIE and ASEAN governments demanded local production for domestic markets, technology transfer, research and development sharing and improved coordination between Japanese manufacturers and indigenous firms.

Japanese TNCs have shifted strategy in response to trade conflicts and offshore local content demands: from an emphasis on cost competitiveness to a broader strategy of *global localization*. Global localization implies that core manufacturing is governed by a global outlook but attention is also paid to growth of the host economy (Morita 1992). Several factors lie behind Japan's new global production strategy.

Developing country market considerations

Saturated demand and surplus capacity in industrially advanced countries give developing countries with expanding markets added bargaining leverage with transnational corporations. Competition among Japanese auto companies in their glutted home market spills over into rivalry for shares in developing country markets. Southeast Asia is the growth market for autos in Asia. Taken together, ASEAN countries constitute a regional market of 320 million people with an annual economic growth rate averaging 7.25 per cent between 1990 and 1992 (Branigin 1992). The Southeast Asia motor industry doubled from 1981 to 1990 (Vines 1992); regional demand is nearly 1 million units today and expected to grow to 5 million by 2000 (Maskery 1990).

To gain and retain East Asian market share, Japanese companies have been more willing than US firms to accept minority equity restrictions and invest in ways compatible with developing countries' industrial strategies (Doner 1991: 79). Escalating trade disputes between Japan and the United States, and rising North American and European trade barriers to Japanese goods elevate the value of the East Asian market even more in Japanese eyes. The Japanese government has been encouraging firms to manufacture in Southeast Asia since the mid-1970s. MITI is promoting technological cooperation with Asian NIEs and ASEAN countries. The

Japan Export/Import Bank makes loans to indigenous East Asian parts firms, assemblers and dealers. Japanese trading companies and auto firms also assist local businesses. Japanese joint ventures with local manufacturers are plugged into an information network with Japanese banks and state-backed research and development planning organizations.

Production-system consideration

The internal logic of Japan's production system reinforces the global localization strategy. The same production-system principles that made Japanese firms reluctant multinationals – capital-intensive production, collaboration among firms in product design, quality control, flexible production and JIT delivery, and spatial concentration in production complexes – predispose Japanese companies to transplant their integrated production systems abroad once exports give way to DFI (Emmott 1992).[9]

While American and European TNCs have concentrated almost exclusively on the largest developing country markets, Japanese TNCs have employed flexible manufacturing processes to meet localization requirements even in smaller, fragmented markets like those in ASEAN. Japanese companies appear to be transferring their ability to manufacture small batches of different makes and models efficiently through just-in-time delivery and rapid modification of jigs and dies. For example, Toyota assembly workers in Thailand can now change a welding jig for main body construction in 25 to 30 minutes and they can change stamping dies which press flat metal into body parts in 10 to 15 minutes, almost as quickly as their counterparts in Toyota City plants. Toyota's Thai workforce can consequently change models every 20 units (Doner 1991: 83).

Product-cycle considerations

Finally, the product cycle in Japan now also dovetails with a global localization strategy. In the 1930s, a Japanese economist, Kaname Akamatsu, formulated a product-cycle model of industrial development from the perspective of a follower country, as Japan was at the time. The time-series curve for a developing country's product cycle – imports of a product followed by domestic production and later by exports – suggested to Akamatsu a pattern like 'wild geese flying in orderly ranks forming an inverse V just as airplanes fly in formation' (Kojima 1977: 15). Such a product cycle took place only for standardized, rather than new products and in developing rather than in industrialized countries. Japanese officialdom consciously translated this 'flying geese' product-cycle model into strategic industrial practice to achieve upward mobility in the world economy (Cumings 1984; Genther 1990; Morris-Suzuki 1991).

Japan's early relations with the Asian NIEs and ASEAN countries conformed to product cycle descriptions of a 'middle country' – one that imported from developed countries and exported to developing countries (Morris-Suzuki 1991).[10] Taiwan and Korea have historically been receptacles for declining Japanese industries, and have followed Japan in the flying geese formation just as Japan has followed the lead geese in the West (Cumings 1984).

Japan's product cycle moved more in line with developed countries during the 1970s. Today, as Japanese industry moves away from traditional production for export to a new structure stressing high-value end products and high-tech parts, an innovation-centred product-development cycle is increasingly evident (Yamada 1990: 4–5; Kiyonari 1993). Factories are networking automation equipment for efficient, small-lot production to create high value added products for a diversified domestic marketplace. Vast funds are being expended on research to strengthen technological capabilities (Buderi et al. 1992).

Technological advances have stimulated consumer demand by creating products differentiated by higher utility and quality.[11] Firms that develop new products shift production capacity to the higher value added innovations to maintain a leading market position and obtain a quicker return on investment. Japanese parent companies have traditionally shifted production of more standardized but still viable product lines to their subcontractors. But as manufacturing cost differences among segments of the workforce and regions have narrowed in Japan, companies have been moving more routine manufacturing to overseas consumer markets with lower production costs.

The Japanese auto industry became increasingly crowded and competitive following the Korean War. In 1993, Japan had 11 automakers, more than any other country in the world.[12] Some specialize in trucks (Hino, Isuzu, Nissan Diesel), others in small cars (Suzuki, Daihatsu); and subgroups engage in some coordination of production and joint research through keiretsu networks (e.g. Toyota with Hino and Daihatsu). But the Japanese motor-vehicle market remains intensely competitive, none the less.

Japanese automakers spend twice the national average on R&D, roughly 6 per cent of revenues. Between 1982 and 1990, Japanese auto companies almost doubled their product line to 84 separate models. In 1991 they produced 111 models. During the same period, US companies went from 36 to 53 models while European models actually declined from 49 to 43 (Maskery 1991). Toyota alone produces 36 domestic models and 23 models for export and any one model can have as many as 50 variations (Toyota Motor Corporation 1992: 6).[13]

As Japanese firms develop new technology, they are transferring mature technologies to the Asian NIEs and the ASEAN countries. The willingness to transfer old technology is all the greater when the new technology is highly advanced, requires a large investment and has a limited life cycle (Yamada 1990). Japan's domestic demand for the products of the transferred technology can be met by imports. This kind of division of labour is promoting industrialization in the Asian NIEs and ASEAN while enabling Japan to maintain a leading goose position in the regional development formation.

THE EAST ASIAN GROWTH DYNAMIC

The changing division of labour in East Asia cannot be explained by theories, like the NIDL, that emphasize business pursuit of cheap, unskilled labour. The regional market in East Asia is growing rapidly and now weighs more heavily in Japanese investment strategies. Technology tie-ups between Japanese, Asian NIE and ASEAN firms are becoming more common. Headquarter control remains in Japan, but Japanese TNCs are locating more sophisticated products and activities in the Asian NIEs as the technological capacities of these nations increases. Local sourcing of components has become a more compelling Japanese concern because the high value of the yen makes reliance on imports from Japan costly and because the negative effect of such imports on East Asian trade balances weakens Japan's political influence in the region.[14]

Japanese officials, with the flying geese model in mind, see the Asian NIEs in the same product-cycle relation with Japan that Japan had with the United States in the 1960s, and they see the ASEAN Four in the same product-cycle relation with the Asian NIES that the Asian NIEs had with Japan three decades ago. Japanese auto assemblers and suppliers have in fact been yielding market-entry niches and transferring high value added technology to South Korea and Taiwan.[15]

The Asian NIEs

South Korea entered the world motor-vehicle arena in the early 1980s as a low-cost production site for American TNCs who had lost the compact car market to more productive and higher quality Japanese automakers. At that time, labour productivity in the South Korean auto industry was 90 per cent that in the United States and wage costs were only one-tenth as high.[16] Infrastructure for auto production – particularly steel and machinery industries transferred earlier from Japan – was also well established. Korean automakers were organized into giant conglomerates (*chaebol*) capable of making massive investments in capital-intensive production facilities. The Korean government subsidized the auto industry and repressed workers' movements to keep wages low (Amsden 1989).

Today, South Korean national assemblers use a variety of foreign technologies to manufacture and export their own vehicles. Hyundai, the nation's biggest automaker, is allied with Japan's Mitsubishi Motors. Hyundai manufactures the Pony Excel and the Sonata with core components imported or licensed from Mitsubishi and exports both cars to the US market. Hyundai also produces compact cars under Mitsubishi's Precis label for sale in the Japanese market. Mitsubishi and Hyundai jointly make the Grandeur, the best known, domestically manufactured, luxury car in South Korea. Mitsubishi designs the Grandeur and provides high-value components while Hyundai makes relatively labour-intensive parts (Berger 1990). Mitsubishi benefits from Hyundai's low unit costs, while Hyundai is acquiring Mitsubishi's technological know-how and sophisticated components it cannot yet build on its own.

Since Hyundai depends upon Mitsubishi Motors for advanced technology, a sizeable portion of Hyundai's potential profits leak to the Japanese company by way of royalties and the purchase of high-value components. Still, the Korean automaker has maintained control over its own operations. No Korean motor company allows majority foreign ownership. Hyundai's 14 per cent equity relationship with Mitsubishi came after the Korean firm rejected offers from Volkswagen, Renault and Ford. Mitsubishi offered lower royalty payments and was the only auto TNC not to demand managerial participation in Hyundai. The agreement allows Hyundai to compete directly in Mitsubishi's own markets and to import technology and parts from Mitsubishi's competitors.

Kia Motors, Korea's number two producer, is also reaching for technological independence. Kia has investment ties with Mazda and Ford. It makes the Mazda-designed Pride and Ford Festiva. Kia is preparing to launch independently its own line of lower priced cars in the United States: the Sephia (a sedan) and the Sportage (a sports utility vehicle) (Gadacz 1992a: 6).

Taiwan has 11 local assemblers. All are joint ventures with foreign makers. Ford Lio Ho is the island's largest; Yue Loong, 25 per cent owned by Nissan, is number two. Together, Ford Lio Ho and Yue Loong produce over half of the Taiwanese made vehicles sold in the domestic market (Smith 1990). Taiwan's attempt to become a major motor-vehicle exporter has foundered on rising labour and real-estate costs and the appreciation of the Taiwan dollar. Taiwan's production costs are second only to Japan in East Asia and far higher than in South Korea. Taiwanese TNC subsidiaries now see themselves becoming niche producers for relatively low volumes of expensive models made by skilled workers for sale throughout the world (Johnson 1992).

But the real lure of Taiwan is the mainland China market. The PRC has 1.2 billion people with only an estimated 40–50,000 privately owned cars, including taxis. Eighty per cent of China's current 4.4 million vehicles are trucks and buses. There is a 273:1 people per vehicle ratio, one of the highest in the world (Johnson 1992: 3, 2). Taiwanese auto companies are conducting feasibility studies for mainland joint ventures. Japanese subsidiaries in Taiwan would like to provide high-tech components for PRC-made vehicles and exchange built up Taiwan vehicles for low-tech mainland work; like castings, which require lots of labour, land and raw materials, all of which are scarce in Taiwan. Taiwanese industrialists dream of a China development triangle, made up of Taiwan, Hong Kong and the PRC. Potentially the world's largest market, a China triangle would serve as a counterweight to protectionist trends in North America and Europe.

The Asian NIEs send almost half their exports to the United States and depend on Japan for imports of parts and machinery.[17] However, trade conflicts with the United States are inhibiting export expansion and Japanese imports have increased in price due to appreciation of the yen. As a result, TNC subsidiaries in the Asian NIEs are increasingly sourcing parts from affiliates in other Asian NIEs. Asian NIE governments are also re-evaluating each other as purchasers of exports and providers of raw materials. Trade among the four Asian NIEs is booming: imports and exports increased by 50 per cent annually during the late 1980s and stood at approximately $20 billion in 1990 (UNCTNC 1991: 52). Asian NIEs are also investing heavily in the ASEAN countries and China. In 1990, DFI outflows from Taiwan were 4 times as great as DFI flowing into the country (UNCTNC 1991: 52).

As Japanese TNCs turn over market entry production niches to Asian NIE companies, the possibility opens up for ASEAN producers to supply parts for the more standardized vehicles being made in the Asian NIEs. And as Asian NIE auto manufacturers ascend the value added ladder, they are supplying ASEAN producers with less complex motor-vehicle technologies. Hyundai Motor Company is now assembling the Excel in Thailand in a joint venture with United Auto Sales, Ltd of Bangkok. Kia Motors is assembling the Pride in the Philippines and supplying truck and van kits to Indonesia's Udatinada Group. Kia's Indonesia operations will soon include the Pride and Capital passenger cars and light-truck production with the Humpuss Group (Branigin 1992; Gadacz 1992b).

In short, as Japan develops a horizontal division of labour with the Asian NIEs, the Asian NIEs are in turn developing a vertical division of labour with ASEAN nations. This process is likely to speed up as the Japanese move upmarket, and relinquish production of downmarket vehicles to the Asian NIEs (Doner 1991: 88).

The ASEAN nations

Japan's direct foreign investment in East Asia has traditionally focused on the Asian NIEs. But the Japanese began favouring the ASEAN nations, particularly Thailand and Malaysia, from the mid-1980s on, due to currency realignments, ASEAN trade barriers and rising Asian NIEs labour costs.

Intense competition among Japanese producers and the growth potential of the Southeast Asia regional market have boosted ASEAN bargaining power with Japanese TNCs and helped the ASEAN Four make progress toward their auto manufacturing goals, including higher local content, technological upgrading, controlling ownership and exports. Product differentiation in the Japanese market has also facilitated the diffusion of standardized parts and capital equipment to ASEAN firms. Production technology has been supplied by Japanese and Asian NIE assemblers and suppliers and through cooperation agreements with the Japanese government.

Japanese TNCs are employing various strategies to reduce the cost increases associated with producing in less developed ASEAN countries. They are using the ASEAN Four as production sites for standardized parts usable across different models (e.g. brake drums, radiators) while manufacturing more customized parts designed for specific models in Japan. They are producing major parts for older models (e.g. older engine types) in Southeast Asia and some bottom-end market-entry models (e.g. basic utility vehicles). ASEAN Four companies are also manufacturing machinery for local production (e.g. dies and jigs) that is expensive to produce in small quantities in Japan (Doner 1991).

Still, small markets and weak technological capabilities preclude the development of a full-scale auto industry in any one Southeast Asian country. Thailand produces 300,000, Indonesia 300,000, Malaysia 200,000, and the Philippines 50,000 new vehicles a year as compared to 10–11 million in the United States (Branigin 1992). The Southeast Asia region as a whole is the attractive site for auto TNCs, not any one individual country. As a consequence, Japanese TNCs have joined with ASEAN governments in a 'complementation programme'. Japanese TNC affiliates, many of which are joint ventures with local firms, are producing parts in each ASEAN country and then exporting them to other association countries for local assembly. This strategy allows for plant specialization, regional economies of scale and furthers economic integration among the ASEAN nations.

ASEAN initiated a 'brand to brand complementation' policy in 1988. States cut tariffs by at least 50 per cent for car components made by one of the participating members. Parts imported from other ASEAN countries also count toward local content requirements in the importing nation. A year earlier, Mitsubishi had begun shipping transmissions made by its Manila-based unit to its 48 per cent owned, Thai affiliate, Sittipol. Sittipol was importing stamped metal parts and electronic components from Malaysia's Proton Saga plant near Kuala Lumpur, which is 30 per cent owned by Mitsubishi (the remainder is owned by a Malaysian state enterprise). The 1988 complementation policy actually grew out of a Mitsubishi proposal to the governments of the four ASEAN states where Mitsubishi had established manufacturing operations (Goldstein 1990).

Following Mitsubishi's lead, Toyota Motor Corporation knitted its ASEAN manufacturing subsidiaries into a supply network and placed them under a coordinating regional headquarters in Singapore in 1989. In 1990, Manila's Board of Investment approved Toyota's application for a $55 million, car transmission plant to produce 100,000 units a year, the magnitude required to reach economies of scale. This is far more than the Philippine market alone could absorb. Toyota produced less than 13,000 cars and trucks in the Philippines in 1989. But Toyota affiliates in Thailand and Malaysia produced about 70,000 vehicles. Even without the participation of Toyota's 49 per cent owned Indonesian operation which turned out 59,000 vehicles a year, the projected doubling of the ASEAN car market over the next five years suggested the merits of the complementation strategy. Toyota followed with diesel engines from Thailand, steering linkages from Malaysia and a management service centre in Singapore to oversee total production in the area.[18]

Nissan began trading components among plants in Thailand, Malaysia and the Philippines in spring 1992. Each of these countries assembles a version of Nissan's Sunny/Sentra. Nissan's Thailand plant sends 12 parts to Malaysia, including tool sets and cables, and its Malaysia plant reciprocates with 12 items. Thailand now ships 9 parts to the Philippines, including fuel tanks and front floor panels while Nissan's operations in the Philippines is sending rear floor panels, wheel housings and 11 other items to Thailand. Taiwan will be brought into the loop in 1993 when Nissan's local affiliate begins building the car there (Johnson 1992).

The complementary production scheme indicates that taken together Japanese TNC strategies and the industrial policies of developing countries are promoting a process of regional integration in East Asia. Another sign: Japanese TNCs are building East Asian *parts procurement centres* oriented toward the Japanese and world markets; *product development centres* oriented toward local needs; and regional *headquarters facilities* coordinating production among Asian NIEs and ASEAN subsidiaries (Yamada 1990). As Japan, the Asian NIEs and the ASEAN Four specialize in different processes and products, mutual trade and direct foreign investment among them is growing. The East Asian economies are thus moving toward a multilayered divison of labour based upon vertical and horizontal specialization and deepening mutual interdependence (Yamada 1990: 53; Scott 1987).

CONCLUDING ISSUES

The increasing linkages among Japan, the Asian NIEs and ASEAN nations are part of a larger reshaping of the world economy into a system of regional blocs. Regionalization is also visible in the EC move to dismantle impediments to the free flow of goods, services, capital and labour among member states and efforts by the United States, Canada and Mexico to hammer out a North American Free Trade Agreement (NAFTA).

Today, Japanese TNCs are building regionally integrated independently sustainable networks of overseas production facilities centred on Asia, the United States and the European Community. This 'Triad' (Ohmae 1985) or 'regional core network' (UNCTNC 1991) or 'global localization' (Morita 1992) strategy forecasts a global economic structure in which developing countries located in the same geographical region will tend to cluster around the dominant Triad member in that region. As conceptualized by Kenichi Ohmae (1985: 122), each Triad member participates in the world's three major markets and emphasizes one developing region. Japan looks to Asia, the Europeans make use of historical ties in Africa and the Middle East; the United States focuses upon her continental neighbours in the Americas.[19]

We have focused upon Japan and East Asia in this chapter. But auto industrialization differs among regions of the world, as the following contrasts between East Asia and the Americas make clear.[20] In contrast to East Asia:

1 Latin American nations, save for Mexico, have experienced declining auto production, sales and employment over the past decade (Zola 1991; Fitzpatrick 1991);

2 The relative gap in hourly compensation between auto workers in the Latin America NIEs (Mexico, Brazil) and workers in the United States is twice as high as that between auto workers in the East Asian NIEs (Korea and Taiwan) and workers in Japan and is not narrowing over time as it is in East Asia ('Hourly compensation for motor vehicle production workers 1975, 1979–1989' 1991: 70).

3 Uneven development among the auto-producing countries of Latin America is growing; in particular between the NIEs (Mexico and Brazil), on the one hand, and the less industrialized Andean Pact countries (Bolivia, Columbia, Ecuador, Peru and Venezuela) on the other (Jenkins 1987: 212).

Explanations for differences in East Asian and Latin American development performance usually rely on differences in the relative autonomy of states, the organization of state bureaucracies and the resulting effectiveness of national industrial strategies. State structures and policies are usually linked in turn to domestic class relations and the timing of a nation's entry in to the world economy (Jenkins 1991).

In this chapter we draw attention to regional differences in political-economic relations among developed and developing nations. We think differences in industrial development between East Asian and Latin American nations also derive from a different pattern of TNC and state relations among Japan, the Asian NIEs and the ASEAN Four in contrast to that characterizing past US and European relations with Latin America. We have emphasized differences in the organization of transnational production systems, product cycles, and product-cycle modelled restructuring policies in Japan and East Asian developing economies. In contrast to western capitalists, the late-industrializing Japanese have been more willing to accept minority equity relations, to transfer appropriate technology, and to generally work within the framework of developing country industrial policies.

The contrasting experiences of the Andean Pact auto-producing countries in Latin America and the ASEAN Four in Southeast Asia provide a case in point. Nations in both regions suffer inefficiencies from small markets divided up among many producers. Nations in both regions framed their import substitution policies in regional terms to achieve economies of scale. The Andean Pact was initiated by member states in 1971 and required TNCs to cooperate with one another in the cross-border exchange of locally produced components within a regional division of labour. The Andean Pact strategy failed because the regional import substitution strategy initiated by the Andean states clashed with the global-integration strategies preferred by US and European TNCs to the detriment of the region (Jenkins 1987: 198–204).

The ASEAN complementary-production scheme, on the other hand, was initiated by a Japanese TNC, Mitsubishi Motor Corporation. Mitsubishi has also worked in a minority equity relationship with Hyundai in South Korea, and with the Malaysian government on its national car programme, the Saga Proton. ASEAN's regional production policy was encouraged by the Japanese Ministry of International Trade and Industry (MITI), and followed in suit by Toyota and Nissan. Because the ASEAN regional division of labour is organized within each TNC's production system, it does not depend upon the kind of cooperation that proved fatal in the Andean Pact case.

Because Japanese investment in East Asian production networks continues to create demand for Japanese goods and services, Japan's DFI and international trade are mutually reinforcing. Japan's high technology supplier relationship with the Asian NIEs and ASEAN Four sustains employment at home and therefore has garnered labour's support. But since Japan's role as a supplier of inputs to East Asia still far exceeds Japan's role as a market for East Asian goods, the continued success of this strategy is contingent upon Asian NIE and ASEAN access to North American and European markets.[21]

Continued reliance on Japan for critical components underlines the relative weakness of Asian NIEs and ASEAN parts and components industries. Developing country producers with aspirations to compete in the world market must find the wherewithal for huge investments in research and development and the basic technologies required to make vehicles differentiated by design and engineering from those produced by leading TNCs.

Japan's manufacturing imports from East Asia are increasing but remain small in comparison to domestic production. There is some doubt, moreover, that Japan will sustain a high growth of Asian imports despite the comparative cost advantages enjoyed by the Asian NIEs and ASEAN Four due to the strong yen. The Japanese market is already saturated. Companies have compensated for the appreciation of the yen by reducing production costs for the high quality, advanced function products desired by Japanese consumers. And competition among Japanese auto firms is becoming even more intense as they depend less on exports and more on the domestic market (Yamada 1990).

Whether Japan's DFI-led wave of internationalization will sustain itself in the face of a weakening domestic economy also remains to be seen. In 1991, Japan brought home $36.6 billion more than it invested overseas. It was the first time since 1980 that Japan imported more long-term capital than it sent abroad (Sterngold 1992).

National ambitions continually threaten to undermine the cooperative relations among ASEAN nations that seem a prerequisite to each nation's development. For example, Thailand, Malaysia and the Philippines signed on to the complementary production plan in 1988 but Indonesia decided to go it alone. With the largest market in the region, Indonesia feared it would be the target of other nation's exports. And there are frequent conflicts between local efforts to promote national industries and TNC efforts to exploit regional economies of scale. Trade officials in each nation want to rule on tariff cuts for imported components case by case to ensure each decision fits with their own national development plans. Thai and Malaysian officials, for example, have refused to allow Nissan to import Philippine-made headlamps, arguing these parts already were available locally (Goldstein 1990).

East Asian regional industrialization is neither a harmonious and egalitarian nor a uniformly divisive and zero sum process. Rather, the flying geese or escalator model seems to fit the current process best. As individual East Asian nations vie with one another to improve their position in a stratified regional economy, increasing specialization is interlinking all of them – Japan, the Asian NIEs, the ASEAN Four (and the PRC) – into a mechanism for combined and uneven regional economic growth.

NOTES

1 ASEAN refers to the Association of Southeast Asian Nations and includes Brunei, which does not produce motor vehicles, as well as the four auto-producing nations treated in this study.
2 Vernon (1971) noted that some TNCs were evolving into organizations with a 'global scanning capacity and global habit of mind' that could respond to foreign opportunities and foreign threats by developing complex logistical networks among their affiliates. Under these circumstances, stimulation of the

system could come from the exposure of any element in the system to its local environment and response could come from any part of the system that was appropriate for the purpose. This anticipates the Japanese global-localization strategy discussed below.

3 Vernon (1979) also saw the performance of firms in some developing countries conforming to the product cycle in a different way. Firms in more rapidly industrializing countries like Mexico, Brazil, India and Korea were beginning to produce innovations in accord with the special conditions of their own economies. Having done so they would be in a position to initiate their own export and eventual direct-investment cycle. Their target, according to Vernon's hypothesis, would be the markets of developing countries that were lagging a bit behind them in the industrialized pecking order. More will be said on this below.

4 Increased local content makes it difficult to engage in the rapid model changes necessary to survive in the Japanese marketplace. Doner's research (1991: 85) on Toyota's operations in Thailand suggests that at 20 per cent local content Thai manufacturing could follow major model changes in Japan by one or two months. At 45 per cent localization the time lag increased to a year because of the need for longer trial runs guided by technical staff sent from Japan.

5 From $35 billion in 1983 to $53 billion in 1985 (Hill and Lee 1992).

6 From 265 to the dollar in summer 1985, to 130 in summer 1988.

7 To spur domestic consumption, the report emphasized new land-use and housing-construction policies, shortened working hours and modifications in food-import controls. New forms of international cooperation to facilitate transplant production were also recommended. The state backed the Maekawa recommendations with a six-trillion-yen emergency expenditure package, including five trillion in public works and one trillion in individual tax reductions (Fujita and Hill 1989).

8 Toyota suppliers also began offshore production of electric auto parts, piping and casting products in Thailand, Taiwan and Indonesia in response to the first dollar/yen 'shock' in the early 1970s (Fujita and Hill 1989).

9 Please note that we are talking about a system governed not by the pure working out of a logic but by tendencies and counter-tendencies, preferences and compromises. All things equal, Toyota would prefer to organize abroad in concentrated production complexes as it has in Toyota City. And the company may manage to do so in the long run. But the company has to accommodate its production system to the social circumstances of each production location. Toyota's new assembly plant in Derbyshire, England, for example, is drawing upon suppliers located in Western Europe to counteract Western European fears that Toyota is using England as a Trojan Horse to penetrate the EC market. Toyota can manage to organize its production system in this way so long as its competitors in the EC market are similarly dispersed; that is, so long as Toyota does not face competition from a Toyota-style production system in the European market!

10 During the 1960s and early 1970s, Japanese firms emphasized the production of heavy duty trucks and small, durable passenger cars. These were also the vehicles needed most in Southeast Asia after the Second World War. Southeast Asia became a testing ground for Japan's efforts at penetrating advanced country markets (Doner 1991).

11 However, if new products arising from basic research are not accompanied by advances in production technology – a not frequent situation in the West, supplies will be limited and there will be little growth in the market. When advances in product and production technology go together, technological

innovation can expand markets. Japanese companies have used their electronic and process technologies to improve continuously production organization. Rising productivity reduces prices and spurs demand. Product diversification broadens the range of consumer choices, stimulates domestic demand and promotes new export markets (Yamada 1990).

12 Japan's automakers include Toyota and Nissan (largest), Mazda, Honda, Mitsubishi (medium sized), Suzuki, Subaru, Hino, Daihatsu, Isuzu and Fuji Heavy Industries (smallest).

13 The competitive, flexibly specialized and technologically dynamic characteristics of the Japanese automobile industry depart considerably from the static technology, standardized mass production and collusive, 'monopolistic' pricing assumptions underlying NIDL theory.

14 As investment on production for domestic consumption and DFI for overseas markets has expanded, Japan's overall export ratio, that is, exports as a percentage of total production, has been falling. The motor vehicle export ratio now stands at 43 per cent down (Toyota Motor Corporation 1992: 45). Japanese DFI in Asia has grown exponentially from $700 million between 1961 and 1970, to $9.1 billion between 1971 and 1980, to $12 billion between 1981 and 1986, to $10.5 billion between 1987 and 1988 (Yamada 1990: 9).

15 Recent examples include agreements between Japan's FANUC Ltd with South Korea's Daewoo Heavy Industry for welding robot technology; and a Hitachi–Daewoo electronics agreement for automotive audio production technology. Toshiba is transferring all prototyping, development and production of low-end products to its Korean partner, Samsung Electronics, so the Japanese company can concentrate resources on high-end models. This takes both firms a step closer to sharing product development (Yamada 1990).

16 In 1982, the relative productivity index of the Korean automobile industry was 0.90 as compared to 1.4 in Japan and 1.0 in the United States (Economist Intelligence Unit 1983). In 1985 Korean auto workers earned $2.50 an hour, while their Japanese counterparts earned $15 an hour and American workers earned $25 an hour (Russel 1986).

17 Seventy-five per cent of South Korea's motor vehicle exports go to the US market.

18 Toyota is promoting models based upon its Hi-Lux pick-up truck as a regional vehicle that can benefit from common parts (e.g. a 'regional truck' mini-version of the global-car model). The barrier now is that some markets emphasize trucks and others stress passenger cars (Maskery 1990).

19 This global strategy serves several objectives. It assures Japan proximity to the world's wealthiest and technologically most dynamic markets. It helps insulate Japanese TNCs from US and EC protectionist threats against exports from Japan. It allows Japanese TNCs to draw comparative locational advantages (e.g. wages, skills, transport costs) in each region to increase trade with other markets, including Japan's. And it has the added advantage of reducing Japan's trade surplus with its major trading partners (UNCTNC 1991).

20 Auto manufacturing has barely begun in Africa. South Africa is the only significant auto-producing country on the continent. South Africa's market is about the size of Taiwan's (334,779 vehicles in 1990) and is divided up among twelve transnational corporations (MVMA-USA 1992: 39).

21 In contrast to the United States, Japanese manufacturing DFI has not 'boomeranged' to weaken the competitiveness of its own manufacturing base. Rather, Japanese DFI led to a growth of manufacturing exports from the Asian NIEs and ASEAN Four to other industrial countries. Between 1982 and 1987, for example, the US trade deficit with Asian NIEs increased 4.6 times while the

deficit with ASEAN rose 3.2 times (Morris-Suzuki 1991: 149). A high percentage
of NIE and ASEAN exports are produced by Japanese TNC subsidiaries. The
boomerang thus has been deflected to strike other less adaptive, industrial
economies, like the United States. The North American Free Trade Agreement
is, among other things, meant to counter the deflected boomerang effect.

REFERENCES

Altshuler, A., Anderson, M., Jones, D., Roos, D. and Womack, J. (1984) *The Future
of the Automobile*, Cambridge, MA: MIT Press.
Amsden, A. (1989) *Asia's Next Giant: South Korea and Late Industrialization*, New York:
Oxford.
Berger, M. (1990) 'Strategic alliances', *Billion* June.
Bluestone, B. and Harrison, B. (1983) *The Deindustrialization of America*, New York:
Basic Books.
Brangin, W. (1992) 'Forgotten drivers in southeast Asia: since Detroit didn't care,
Japanese stepped in', *International Herald Tribune* 21–22 March.
Braverman, H. (1974) *Labor and Monopoly Capital*, New York: Monthly Review
Press.
Buderi, R., Carey, J., Gross, N. and Miller, K. L. (1992) 'Global innovation: who's in
the lead?' *Business Week*, 3 August: 68–73.
Cumings, B. (1984) 'The origins and development of the northeast Asian political
economy: industrial sectors, product cycles, and political consequences', *International Organization* 38, 1: 1–40.
Cusumano, M. (1985) *The Japanese Automobile Industry*, Cambridge, MA: Harvard
University Press.
—— (1988) *Manufacturing Innovation and Competitive Advantage: Reflections on the
Japanese Automobile Industry*, Cambridge, MA: Sloan School of Management.
Doner, R. F. (1991) *Driving a Bargain: Automobile Industrialization and Japanese Firms
in Southeast Asia*, Berkeley: University of California Press.
Economist Intelligence Unit (1983) *Special Report, No. 154*, London: Economist
Magazine.
Emmott, B. (1992) *Japan's Global Reach*, London: Century.
Fitzpatrick, K. (1991) 'Booming Mexico industry awaits decision on free trade',
Ward's Automotive Yearbook: 112–14.
Friedman, D. (1983) 'Beyond the age of Ford; the strategic basis of the Japanese
success in automobiles', in J. Zysman and L. Tyson (eds) *American Industry in
International Competition*, Ithaca, NY: Cornell University Press.
Fröbel, F., Heinrichs, J. and Kreye, O. (1980) *The New International Division of Labor*,
Cambridge: Cambridge University Press.
Fujita, K. and Hill, R. C. (1989) 'Global production and regional "Hollowing Out"
in Japan', *Comparative Urban and Community Research* 2: 200–28.
Gadacz, O. (1992a) 'Hyundai ties up with Thai assembler', *Automotive News* 7
December.
—— (1992b) 'Kia, Indonesian firm ok kit assembly deal', *Automotive News* 1 June.
Genther, P. A. (1990) *A History of Japan's Government–Business Relationship: The
Passenger Car Industry*, Ann Arbor: Center for Japanese Studies, University of
Michigan, Michigan Papers in Japanese Studies No. 20.
Goldstein, C. (1990) 'Japanese car makers forge ASEAN component links', *Far
Eastern Economic Review* 15 February: 67.
Hainer, M. and Koslofsky, J. (1979) 'The world car: shifting into overdrive', *NACLA
Report on the Americas* 13, 4 (July–August).

Hill, R. C. (1984) 'Transnational capitalism and urban crisis: the case of the auto industry and Detroit', in I. Szeleyni (ed.) *Cities in Recession*, London: Sage.

—— (1989) 'Comparing transnational production systems: the automobile industry in the United States and Japan', *International Journal of Urban and Regional Research* 13, 3: 462–80.

Hill, R. C. and Lee, Y. J. (1992) 'Japan and the triad: the regional restructuring of the world economy', paper given at conference on A New Urban and Regional Hierarchy, University of California, Los Angeles, April.

Hoffman, K. and Kaplinsky, R. (1988) *Driving Force*, Boulder, CO: Westview.

Holmes, J. (1986) 'The organization and locational structure of production sub-contracting', in A. J. Scott and M. Storper (eds) *Production, Work, Territory*, Boston: Allen & Unwin.

'Hourly compensation for motor vehicle production workers 1975, 1979-1989' (1991) *Wards Automotive Yearbook*: 70.

Hymer, S. (1971) 'The multinational corporation and the law of uneven development', in J. W. Bhagwati (ed.) *Economics and World Order*, New York: Macmillan.

Jenkins, R. (1984) 'Divisions over the international division of labor', *Capital and Class* 2: 28–57.

—— (1987) *Transnational Corporations and the Latin American Automobile Industry*, Pittsburgh: University of Pittsburgh Press.

—— (1991) 'The political economy of industrialization: a comparison of Latin American and East Asian newly industrializing countries', *Development and Change* 22: 197–231.

Johnson, R. (1992) 'Nissan plants in Asia begin sharing parts', *Automotive News* 26 June.

Kiyonari, T. (1993) 'Restructuring urban-industrial links in Greater Tokyo: small producers' responses to changing world markets', in K. Fujita and R.C. Hill (eds) *Japanese Cities in the World Economy*, Philadelphia: Temple.

Kojima, K. (1977) *Japan and a New World Economic Order*, Boulder CO: Westview Press.

Lipietz, A. (1987) *Mirages and Miracles: The Crises of Global Fordism*, London: Verso.

Luria, D. (1986) 'New labor-management models from Detroit?' *Harvard Business Review* September–October: 22–9.

Maskery, M. (1990) 'Backyard boom: Southeast Asia prospers with Japan's investment', *Automotive News* 9 July: 26.

—— (1991) 'Fast-paced Japanese hit the expansion redline', *Automotive News* 2 September: 1, 34.

Morita, A. (1992) 'A critical moment for Japanese management', *Economic Eye* Autumn: 4–10.

Morris-Suzuki, T. (1991) 'Reshaping the international division of labor: Japanese manufacturing investment in Southeast Asia', in J. Morris (ed.) *Japan and the Global Economy*, London: Routledge.

MVMA-USA (1992) *World Motor Vehicle Data*, Detroit: Motor Vehicle Manu-facturers' Association of the United States.

Ohmae, K. (1985) *Triad Power: The Coming Shape of Global Competition*, New York: Macmillan.

Piore, M. J. and Sabel, C. (1984) *The Second Industrial Divide*, New York: Basic Books.

Russel, G. (1986) 'Big three get in gear', *Time* 24 November.

Scott, A. J. (1987) 'The semiconductor industry in Southeast Asia: organization, location and the international division of labour', *Regional Studies* 21, 2: 143–60.

Serrin, W. (1970) *The Company and the Union*, New York: Vintage.

Shimogawa, K. (1986) 'Product and labour strategies in Japan', in S. Tolliday and

J. Zeitlin (eds) *The Automobile Industry and its Workers: Between Fordism and Flexibility*, Cambridge: Polity Press.

Smith, G. (1990) 'Taiwan dawns as Shangri-La for big 3, U.S. parts makers', *Automotive News* 18 June: 20.

Sterngold, J. (1992) 'Japanese shifting investment flow back home', *New York Times* 22 March.

Takeuchi, H. (1987) 'Japan fuels rocketing economies of Asian NICs', *Japan Economic Journal* 25 July.

Toyota Motor Corporation (1992) *The Automobile Industry: Toyota and Japan, 1992 Edition*, Toyota City: Toyota Motor Corporation, International Affairs Division.

United Nations Centre on Transnational Corporations (1991) *World Investment Report 1991: The Triad in Foreign Direct Investment*, New York: United Nations.

Vernon, R. (1971) *Sovereignty at Bay: The Multinational Spread of U.S. Enterprises*, New York: Basic Books.

—— (1979) 'The product cycle hypothesis in a new international environment', *Oxford Bulletin of Economics and Statistics* 41, 4: 255–69.

Vines, S. (1992) 'Japan to gain from SE Asia boom', *Automotive News* 17 February.

Womack, J., Jones, D. and Roos, D. (1990) *The Machine That Changed The World*, New York: Rawson Associates.

Yamada, B. (1990) *Internationalization Strategies of Japanese Electronics Companies: Implications for Asian Newly Industrializing Economies*, Paris: OECD.

Zola, D. (1991) 'Focus: South America', *Wards Automotive Yearbook*: 103–4.

15

CAPITALISM, AGRICULTURE AND WORLD ECONOMY

Philip McMichael and Laura T. Raynolds

INTRODUCTION

Since the onset of the colonial era, food and agricultural systems across the world have undergone continual reorganization as they have been incorporated into capitalist market relationships. Central to this reorganizing process has been the global division of labour, based originally in an exchange of metropolitan manufactures for colonial primary products. The specialization in extractive raw material and agricultural commodity production imposed on the colonies integrated rural social systems within the broader market and political relations of the world economy. Peasants and labourers in the colonies subsidized metropolitan expansion through their labour and products. Producing regions and their communities of support thus became participants in a global dynamic. The state of Third World agricultures today cannot be understood outside of this world-historical context.

While the legacy of this global division of labour continued into the post-colonial mid-twentieth century, Third World agricultural organization and markets have become more differentiated and complex. Post-colonial governments have universally adopted policies of national industrialization which have in turn imposed new demands on domestic agricultures. Such demands include the promotion of traditional and, recently, non-traditional agro-exports to bolster foreign exchange earnings and pay off international loans, technological intensification to increase yields through the adoption of the Green Revolution, and increased production of new food crops and agricultural inputs to service affluent consumers and agro-industries. As new social diets have emerged through the process of urbanization and industrialization, governments (whose legitimacy concerns include food delivery to urban populations) and agribusinesses alike have reorganized agricultural production. Already weakened peasant agricultures have experienced further marginalization and deterioration as

316

market forces have claimed rural resources such as land, labour and government subsidies.

Within this scenario, the question of capitalism's impact on Third World agricultures is linked to the changing political configuration of the world economy, within which the growing reach of agribusiness must be assessed. Current development strategies of Third World governments, for example, often subsidize the inroads of agribusiness. Such policies must be situated within prevailing world-economic orthodoxy which subordinates the agricultural sector to industrialization and the domestic economy to foreign currency requirements.

We maintain that the construction and reconstruction of the Third World and its agricultures over time has been a global process, though differential policy conditions across Third World states can be identified. This has been a global process in a double sense. First, as governed by the historic division of labour on a world scale, tropical agricultures have been incorporated into evolving metropolitan consumption patterns. Second, metropolitan agro-food models have been transferred to the Third World to sustain the global division of labour (now organized by food corporations), as well as to embrace modern production and consumption relations. The internationalization of agriculture has accelerated in the last quarter of a century, especially with the widespread adoption of Green Revolution technology and the development of global sourcing of food products by transnational corporations. This consolidated the post-war trend of de-peasantization. After the Second World War, large populations still lived by agriculture, even in countries like Germany and the United States. Yet between 1950 and 1975 peasants became the minority in Europe, in the Americas, and in the western Islamic world – in fact everywhere except continental South and East Asia and sub-Saharan Africa (Hobsbawm 1992: 56).

The historic fact of de-peasantization guides our analysis of the impact of capitalism on Third World agriculture. It signals the general destabilizing character of this process, at the same time as it records the elimination of centuries-old agricultural practices that only now are we beginning to recognize as a serious ecological, cultural and demographic consequence of the fetishism of industrialism and its associated consumerism. In order to understand the long-term impact of capitalism, we need to distinguish its historical phases of development as they relate to the construction and reconstruction of Third World agriculture. We begin with a summary of the colonial period up to the Second World War, and then focus on agro-industrial developments in the post-war era, differentiating forms of agricultural capitalism and their impact on different world regions.

THE COLONIAL ERA

The central historical fact of the colonial era was the violent incorporation

317

of colonial lands and peoples into an expanding world capitalist economy driven by the process of commodification. The global division of labour that emerged was the result of separate, and rival, colonial systems established by the metropolitan powers to service their growing needs for tropical products, and to enrich their merchants who organized the associated trade in slave labour and manufactured goods to facilitate colonization. Colonial administrations were extensions of metropolitan bureaucracies, organized to extract profits and materials through exclusive trading monopolies geared to metropolitan requirements. Vast plantations, estates and small-farming schemes developed around the production of tropical export crops ranging from rubber to bananas to groundnuts, depending on local agro-ecologies. The cumulative effect of colonialism was to generate a pattern of world-economic specialization whereby agriculture, and agricultural exports, became the defining specialty of the region that became known as the 'Third World'.

Third World agro-exports complemented metropolitan agriculture and the colonial world became identified with providing the raw materials of capitalist civilization. The non-European world became associated with labour-intensive production of tropical products and labour forces throughout the colonies were uprooted and reconstituted in the service of large-scale commodity production (Baran 1967; Stoler 1985). The fate of Third World economy thus came to depend on this imposed specialization and the complementary relation with the First World via agricultural exports. This condition continues today, although the content of the complementarity has changed, as we shall see below.

Over the course of the nineteenth century, with the trade liberalization associated with British global power, agro-exports from the colonies changed from supplying luxury markets, such as for spices and silks, towards commodities destined for consumption in Europe by the new industrial proletariat (such as sugar, coffee, tea, cocoa, vegetable oils) and the expanding factories (such as cotton, timber, rubber and jute) (Woodruff 1967: 264–8). As this colonial complementarity deepened, another pattern of trade with the ex-colonial settler states (the United States, Australia, New Zealand, Canada) emerged which would transform the shape of world agriculture in the twentieth century. Exports from these countries of temperate products (e.g. grains, meat) supplemented, and then competed with, metropolitan agriculture, becoming the staple provisions for European labour forces (Friedmann 1987). Whereas the colonial trade was founded in the particular ecology of tropical production, the settler trade was based in the replication of metropolitan production, but at lower cost given the new agricultural frontier and the flexibility of family farming (Friedmann 1978).

Settler farming became the new agricultural core within the world economy, fuelling industrialization in Europe as well as in the settler states.

Given the relatively low person-to-land ratio on the frontier, this strategic provisioning role encouraged the development of a highly productive energy- and capital-intensive agriculture (Goodman, Sorj and Wilkinson 1987). In fact, this form of industrial agriculture became the model for agricultural development in the twentieth century, first in Europe and then in the post-colonial world (Friedmann and McMichael 1989; Burbach and Flynn 1980; George 1984). The nature of this model is significant. To begin with, it required continual external inputs provided through the market (such as inorganic fertilizers, hybrid seeds, machinery, pesticides, etc.). Its near universal adoption after the Second World War, with US encouragement, meant greater integration of the capitalist world as agribusiness established upstream and downstream industries servicing farming on a transnational scale. And its industrial dimension meant that it became a key vehicle of articulation of farming with industry as the basis for national economic growth. These two opposite tendencies – toward transnational and national integration – have shaped the process of world agricultural transformation over the past half century.

THE FORDIST AGRO-FOOD SYSTEM

Metropolitan agriculture in global perspective

In the post-war years, responding to the social and political weight of industrial classes, metropolitan states adopted political management of national economies as the key to reviving capital accumulation. National regulation introduced new social structures of accumulation legitimized by the Keynesian prescription of counter-cyclical fiscal public expenditure and sustained by the Fordist practice of raising wages to deepen commodity purchasing. Full employment and continuously rising consumer expectations were the goals, and, for a time, the outcome in metropolitan countries. The stable exchange controls and multilateral lending facility of the Bretton Woods institutions (World Bank, IMF), underwritten by the US dollar as the international reserve currency, anchored this pattern of political economy.

Within this post-war arrangement, US government farm subsidies consolidated a 'Fordist' industrial agro-food system based in the oil economy and the high-input technology of hybrid maize (Kenney *et al.* 1989). The agro-food system found its profitable core in the animal-protein complex built around growing, and nutritionally complementary, hybrid maize and soybean animal feeds. Meat became the central component of the post-war American Fordist diet. Since then, meat has been promoted globally as a symbol of affluence, even while it has declined in the US due to the growing health consciousness of local consumers.

Building on the historic development of an American agro-industrial complex in the late nineteenth century, a farm subsidy system barring agricultural imports developed in the United States in the early 1900s (Bovard 1991: 159). This institutionalized a national articulation of agriculture and industry. As the basis of post-war national economic planning, this system was then exported via the Marshall Plan to Europe, where, with the aid of US agribusiness, national agricultures were reconstructed as complements to industry (Cleaver 1977). The combination of industry and agriculture and its public subsidization laid the long-term foundations of European agricultural overproduction, matching that of the United States. This system has in turn been responsible for current US and European cycles of dumping of farm surpluses on world markets. In the meantime, the Fordist agro-food system reshaped Third World agricultures by restructuring international trade.

The Fordist expansion of industrial production and consumption in the post-war period intensified the global division of labour associated with colonialism. While industrial uses of rubber, fibres and some vegetable oils (for soaps, lubricants and paint) had expanded since the late nineteenth century, in the mid-twentieth century diets based in processed foods expanded dramatically, deepening the demand for certain tropical products, such as vegetable oils and sugar. Fats and sweeteners were the key ingredients of what Friedmann (1991a) has termed 'durable foods', the analogue of manufactured consumer durables associated with the Fordist period of manufacturing. Following metropolitan substitution of rubber and fibres (Mann 1987), the search for substitutes for tropical food products began as the agribusiness complex matured and corporations sought to use by-products of metropolitan agriculture as alternatives to Third World food products. While food substitutes appeared during the Fordist period, they did not seriously affect trade volumes until the 1970s and beyond, as discussed below.

The first 'by-products' of metropolitan agriculture were the excess supplies of grain and milk produced under the combined momentum of farm subsidies and improving farm technologies. Farm supports actually institutionalized overproduction by stabilizing prices under conditions of rising costs and new technological inputs (Wessel 1983: 22–3). These government-managed agricultural surpluses were initially disposed of through the US food aid programme, which tied foreign policy to the American agro-food system (Wallerstein 1980). By 1965 food aid accounted for more than 80 per cent of American wheat exports, and around one-quarter of the total world wheat trade (Friedmann 1992: 373).

Food aid established new patterns of food dependency in many Third World countries, as shipments rose from 8 million tons in 1974–5 to 12 million tons in 1984–5 (World Bank 1987). Most Third World countries were eager to accept food aid since it provided substantial financial support for state institutions and government policies. Under the US PL480 programme, concessional imports could be purchased using local currencies and soft credit terms, thus placing limited demand on typically scarce foreign exchange. Income generated from commodity sales provided an important source of government revenue, often surpassing local tax returns (Garst and Barry 1990: 17–39).

Concessional exports allowed the United States a certain political leverage over Third World states while providing a convenient mechanism for displacing the problem of government-managed surpluses. US diplomatic and business communities abroad gained economic leverage through their influence over the use of local currencies generated by the sale of food aid commodities, leverage often used to promote foreign policy goals such as internal stability and American agribusiness interests (Wessel 1983). The production of agricultural surpluses behind tariff walls compelled the US government to facilitate their disposal overseas. In this way, a profound link was established between the national organization of metropolitan agriculture (note that the European Community adopted a similar farm subsidy programme to that of the United States, resulting in surpluses for commercial export) and the international reorganization of agricultural trade and peripheral food systems. The long-term consequence of protected metropolitan farm sectors was to compromise similar Third World endeavours to establish national food self-sufficiency, to which we now turn.

The reorganization of Third World agro-food systems and class relations

The restructuring of the international grain trade around large-scale shipments of surplus US wheat has had dramatic, and quite contradictory, effects on the traditional agro-food systems and corresponding class relations of the Third World. On the one hand, access to cheap food underwrote the process of nation-state building in the former colonies and recent patterns of urban industrialization (Friedmann 1982). On the other hand, massive imports of subsidized grains undermined local peasant production and threatened Third World food self-sufficiency (Garst and Barry 1990; Lappe and Collins 1978).

In pursuing widely accepted industrially based development strategies, most Third World governments utilized inexpensive imported grains to underwrite a set of cheap food policies. From the early 1950s to the late 1970s, 'per capita consumption of wheat increased by 63 per cent in the market economies of the Third World, but not at all in the advanced capitalist countries,' while during the same period 'per capita consumption of all cereals except wheat in the Third World increased only 20 percent, and per capita consumption of root crops actually declined by more than 20 percent' (Friedmann 1992: 372). The availability of cheap imported agricultural commodities greatly increased Third World state intervention in the pricing and marketing of food, and in many cases, government food distribution programmes were established which passed the international subsidies on to local urban consumers (Knudsen and Nash 1990: 58–60). In addition to its social welfare function, cheap food promoted the expansion of the national urban industrial economy by (a) supporting the purchasing power of consumers, thus increasing their capacity to buy locally produced non-food items; and (b) supplementing the wages of the industrial workforce, thus subsidizing the cost of labour for industry and stimulating private investment and economic growth (de Janvry 1981: 148–52).

Cheap food policies fuelled the rise of new consumption patterns among the growing urban population of Third World countries. The availability of subsidized wheat stimulated international demand for western foods, such as bread and pasta, even in countries where wheat was not part of the traditional diet. Wheat products were increasingly defined by Third World governments and by the escalating numbers of urban working- and middle-class consumers as basic staple foods. In Asian and Latin American urban social diets, wheat progressively replaced rice and corn (Friedmann 1982: 254). As a result of changing consumption patterns, wheat (and rice) imports displaced corn in Central America and parts of the Middle East, and millet and sorghum in West Africa (Tubiana 1989: 27). Subsidized grain imports undercut the prices of traditional starches and undermined Third World production of cereals, as well as traditional root and tuber crops – including potatoes, cassava, yams and taro. Imported cereals have also subsidized the expansion of grain-fed beef and poultry sectors and, by encouraging the consumption of animal proteins, have weakened the market for traditional proteinaceous pulses (Barkin, Batt and DeWalt 1990).

First World dumping of inexpensive agricultural commodities has encouraged Third World countries to increase their reliance on imported foodstuffs at the expense of local food production. Since importing food has been cheaper than producing it locally, most Third World governments have neglected domestic production, diverting scarce resources to higher priority industrial projects. Africa has witnessed by far the greatest deterioration in local food production, with the continent's food self-sufficiency ratio falling from 98 per cent in 1961 to 78 per cent in 1978 (Bradley and Carter 1989: 104). While per capita production of cereal declined precipitously, African cereal imports increased fourfold between 1961 and 1978 (UNFAO 1961: 112, 1980: 108). Over recent decades, food self-sufficiency has declined in many parts of the Third World – even in areas such as Central America which have abundant natural resources (Barkin 1987; Garst and Barry 1990). Since many Third World countries rely on imports for their staple foods, the nutritional well-being of their populations has become increasingly dependent on shifting First World farm policies and volatile international market conditions (Raikes 1988; Sanderson 1989).

Though the import substitution policies adopted by most Third World countries in recent decades were aimed largely at strengthening national industry (Hirschman 1968), certain segments of agriculture were also strengthened by domestic market protections (Gomez and Goldfrank 1991). These policies most directly stimulated the local production of agro-industrial luxury foods oriented toward expanding middle- and upper-class consumer markets. In industrializing Third World countries with large consumer populations – like Mexico, Argentina, Brazil, Hong Kong and Singapore – foreign-owned transnational corporations took a leading role in developing these new agro-industrial sectors as a way of accessing lucrative protected markets (Rama 1992; Teubal 1987; Whiting 1985). Locally owned agro-industries also became important in (a) wealthier countries, such as Brazil and Korea, where tax exemptions and credit programmes were provided (Goodman and Redclift 1982: 142–50; Burmeister 1988); and (b) smaller countries with less profitable internal markets, such as the Dominican Republic (Raynolds 1993).

The state-supported growth of processed food sectors in the Third World greatly increased the demand for local agro-industrial inputs. Mexico, for example, has seen a dramatic increase since the 1950s in the production of new oilseeds and forage crops destined for booming beef, pork and poultry industries (Rama 1985; DeWalt 1985). State and agribusiness pressures reoriented agriculture towards the demands of privileged consumers, thereby shifting land away from alternative crops, undermining the profits of peasant producers, and shaping a new class of agrarian capitalists (Barkin 1990; Sanderson 1986b; Yotopoulos 1985).

The production of wage foods, as well as luxury items, has risen impressively in recent decades in Third World countries where (a) state protections and investments were high; (b) yield-increasing technologies were available; (c) fertile land was sufficient; and (d) local demand was strong (de Janvry 1981: 167–9). Increases in Third World grain production were largely derived from the state-sponsored adoption of the high-input US agro-industrial model described earlier which was most clearly extended to the Third World via the 'Green Revolution' (George 1984). The Green Revolution involved the adoption of internationally developed rice and wheat varieties which, with adequate fertilizer, pesticides and water, produce substantially higher yields than older varieties. Collaborating with international funding agencies, most Third World governments promoted this new production system through extension programmes and by subsidizing agricultural chemicals, tractors, irrigation and credit (Griffin 1974).

Yield increases from the green revolutions have been dramatic, but highly concentrated in a few ecologically advantaged regions of the Third World. Asia, and to a much lesser degree Latin America, have captured the benefits from the new grain varieties, while Africa has experienced few gains. The major Third World wheat producing countries – India, Argentina, Pakistan, Turkey, Mexico and Brazil – have planted the vast majority of their wheat acreage in the new varieties and account for fully 86 per cent of the total Green Revolution wheat area (Dalrymple 1985: 1069). The production of high yielding rice varieties is even more concentrated, with six Asian countries – India, Indonesia, Philippines, Bangladesh, Burma and Vietnam – accounting for over 87 per cent of Green Revolution rice acreage (Dalrymple 1985: 1069). In countries benefiting from the new technologies, yield disparities between irrigated and non-irrigated districts has increased, undermining the production of rain-fed grains and pulses (Griffin 1974). Since little commercial wheat or rice is grown in much of Africa, the Green Revolution has largely bypassed the continent. Stagnant food production in many African countries has stimulated soaring wheat imports, destined largely for the growing urban middle class (Raikes 1988).

Where the Green Revolution and the introduction of high-input agriculture has increased yields, it has also tended to increase rural income inequalities and promote the differentiation of Third World social classes. This production system privileges large landowners able to secure critical agricultural inputs and government services (Knudsen and Nash 1990: 84–94). In parts of Latin America, such as Mexico, Argentina, Brazil and Venezuela (Llambi 1990; Sanderson 1986b), and Asia (Byers 1981), this state supported agricultural system permitted the formation of a class of capitalist grain producers. While prosperous farmers were able to profit from higher yields, poorer producers lacked the political and economic resources to take full advantage of these new technologies (Griffin 1974). In fact, peasants were often left worse off by this pattern of agricultural modernization since their access to land was restricted by rising land prices and their employment opportunities curtailed by farm mechanization (Pearse 1980; Raikes 1988).

The combination of state neglect and national and international competition has fuelled the long-term historical decline in Third World peasant agriculture. Though many Latin American and Asian countries initiated agrarian reform programmes during the 1950s and 1960s, giving peasants title to their plots, opportunities to settle new agricultural areas, and/or access to redistributed land, these programmes typically did little to halt the deterioration of peasant economy (de Janvry 1981). The commercialization of agriculture has undermined the viability of household food production as a livelihood strategy for peasant populations and a subsistence base for the rural poor (Barkin 1987). Increasing land pressures and related processes of environmental degradation have further curtailed peasant productivity in many Third World countries. In recent decades, we have witnessed an unprecedented rise in rural proletarianization and growing streams of peasants migrating to the overcrowded metropolitan centres of Latin America, Africa and Asia. Due to the restricted

324

employment options and resultant poverty of displaced peasants, this process of de-peasantization has in most parts of the world been associated with growing immiseration and hunger (Griffin 1987; de Janvry, Sadoulet and Young 1989).

CRISIS IN FORDISM AND IMPLICATIONS FOR THIRD WORLD AGRICULTURE

Metropolitan crisis and restructuring of the world (food) economy

The early 1970s crisis in Fordism included both a profitability crisis for metropolitan industry, parts of which relocated to low-cost production sites in the Third World (Lipietz 1987), and the collapse of the institutional supports of the international regime associated with post-war 'managed capitalism' (Ruggie 1982). When the US dollar was uncoupled from gold in 1972 the Bretton Woods system of stable currency exchanges unravelled, ushering in an era of unstable trade and volatile exchange rates. This instability was exacerbated by the rise of an international capital market beyond the regulatory capacity of national governments. Meanwhile, the nationally based mass-production system associated with metropolitan Fordism was confronted with increasing competition based on the international sourcing of product markets. Production in Third World locations, cheapened by low wages and often by subsidies from the new global banks, mounted (Daly and Logan 1989). The crisis in the Fordist system has not ended mass production, rather new forms of 'flexible' labour force organization and new, specialty marketing now compete with, or complement, the mass economies established within the political framework of the post-war Keynesian state. This is true for agriculture, industry and services alike.

In the 1970s, the United States established an export-expansion strategy aimed at softening the balance of payments crisis and defraying the rising costs of empire, in which agriculture played a key role (Wessel 1983: 162–3). Farm policy shifted from domestic-supply management, which used food aid to dispose of surpluses, to global-demand management. The US government provided farmers with export incentives, favouring commercial, rather than concessional sales and espoused trade liberalization to maximize US 'comparative advantage' and reduce production costs (Tubiana 1989: 38; Revel and Riboud 1986: 91–8). In the first half of the 1970s, US wheat exports rose by 90 per cent, and grain prices by 400 per cent (Wessel 1983: 163); through the decade the US share of world trade in grains doubled to about 60 per cent in 1980–1 (Insel 1985: 897; Johnson 1989: 178). The international grain trade shifted significantly, with rising imports to the developing countries, including China, in addition to the Eastern European bloc (Hathaway 1987: 13). Meanwhile, Soviet grain imports accounted for 60 per cent of the increase in world grain imports, marking the conjunction of the merging of the Cold War blocs and the end of the stable world food prices upon which the post-war international food order depended (Friedmann 1991a, b).

The demise of the Bretton Woods system of stable currency exchanges and the instabilities of world financial and agricultural markets brought disorder to the world economy. Economic restructuring defined the process whereby states reorganized their political economies to improve competitive status in burgeoning global markets. Capital mobility accelerated as international capital markets mushroomed (recycling oil revenues and offshore dollars) and manufacturing processes were relocated to the Third World in a bid to regain the profit levels of the Fordist period through wage cutting. Within this context the regulated high-wage economy was no longer either possible or adequate, encouraging new corporate strategies geared to global and regional, rather than national, markets.

The exception to this trend remained metropolitan agriculture, which retained its expensive farm support structure. By 1980–1 the European Community had become a net exporter of 4 million tons of grain, signalling the maturation in Europe of the US model of government-managed surpluses. Corporate strategies in the grain trade had become more global, responding to the transformation of the world grain market: in 1980–1 developing countries imported 73 million tons of grain, the Soviet Union 39 million tons and Eastern Europe 12 million tons (Hathaway 1987: 13). The surplus/deficit pattern in the international grain trade was now quite pronounced, with the Third World accounting for 57 per cent of all wheat imports in 1980, up from only 10 per cent in the 1950s (Grigg 1986: 248).

The protectionist model in metropolitan agriculture has encouraged the use of industrial substitutes for tropical products. Protectionism has fuelled developments in food manufacturing and the corporate search for (subsidized and stable supplies of) substitutes for the key ingredients, sweeteners and oils, in the production of 'durable foods' (Friedmann 1992). High fructose corn syrup (HFCS) and soyoils, both by-products of the animal protein complex, symbolized the displacement of tropical imports. Substitutionism reinforced the historical decline in the terms of trade for tropical agro-exports, given that 'industrial substitution of tropical products was simultaneously import substitution of tropical exports' (Friedmann 1992: 374–5).

In 1974, the world's largest sugar importer, the United States, began displacing sugar imports, first, by removing domestic production controls on sugar. However, under protection of the high domestic sweetener price, HCFS quickly displaced cane sugar. Sugar's share of the domestic sweetener market in the United States declined from 72 per cent to 43 per cent between 1978 and 1985. Over the same period US sugar imports fell by half, and by 1985 all US soft-drink sweeteners were supplied by sugar substitutes. Meanwhile, protection of domestic sugar production in Europe's Common Agricultural Policy (CAP) expanded from 1967, making the European Community the world's largest exporter of sugar. The impact of these policies on the world sugar market has been most detrimental to producers in Brazil, India, the Philippines, Thailand and several poor African and Caribbean countries (Hathaway 1987: 40–1).

The decline of markets for tropical exports associated with metropolitan substitutionism and the growing food dependency of Third World countries coincided with a dramatic restructuring of economic activity across the world, hastened by (a) capital decentralization as mass production subsided; and (b) 1980s monetarist policies, which accelerated the de-regulation of markets and national welfare systems across the world. This restructuring fuelled widespread income and class polarization patterns in metropolitan and newly industrializing countries (NICs) such as South Korea, Taiwan, Singapore, Hong Kong, Brazil and Mexico (Clarke 1988: 349). Meanwhile, the international credit crunch produced a debt crisis for overcommitted Third World states, and their financial disciplining by the newly empowered multilateral institutions led by the International Monetary Fund (MacEwan 1990).

Two trends (elaborated in the following section) emerged out of this conjunction of decline and discipline. First, new class consumption patterns centred in metropolitan countries stimulated niche (rather than mass) markets for specialty products, including food. Health-conscious and/or luxury consumption of fresh, exotic and ethnic foods has differentiated markets between mass/durable and specialty foods with both markets being supplied by agribusinesses engaged in cost-reducing global sourcing operations. Second, Third World states, under intense pressure to earn foreign currency, increased production of new agro-exports. These 'non-traditional' exports were promoted to compensate for declining markets and world prices for the tropical products associated with the colonial era (Raynolds 1994).

These trends have shaped a new global division of labour in agriculture in the 1980s between low-value and high-value products. Low-value temperate cereals and oilseeds are the predominant metropolitan exports, while Third World exports concentrate in high-value products. For example, in 1986 Mexico's exports to the United States exceeded $2 billion, dominated by fruits and vegetables and beef, while imports from the US totalled $1.5 billion, largely made up of grains and oilseed (George 1988: 143).

The difference between these two trades on a world scale is that due to their political and market power, metropolitan exporters have considerably more access to Third World markets than their Third World counterparts have to metropolitan markets. For example, in raising export subsidies and driving down the price of corn in 1986, the US government expanded foreign markets for American corn. At the same time, responding to food-company pressure to intensify the substitution of corn in sweetener production, the US government reduced the sugar import quota by 60 per cent (Danaher 1989: 37). A similar protective dynamic has occurred in Europe in the highly competitive industrial sweetener complex (Goodman 1991: 53). Protection against Third World exports of agricultural and manufactured goods has accelerated as metropolitan economic growth has subsided (Gilpin 1987) and metropolitan producer groups have clamoured for increasing barriers to cheap imports. Metropolitan agriculture is sheltered by high tariff barriers and a plethora of non-tariff barriers to trade (such as quotas, embargoes, and health and quality standards) that constitute the arsenal of government commercial agricultural policies (Llambi 1994b). As the World Bank stated in its *Development Report*:

> The industrial countries have erected high barriers to imports of temperate-zone products from developing countries and then have subsidised their own exports. The special trade preference schemes they have extended to many developing countries have not been a significant offset to their trade restrictions.
>
> (1986: 11)

Third World crisis and constraints on agro-industrial development

The imported agricultural/agro-industrial development model established after the Second World War in much of the Third World has been undermined over the past two decades by shifting national and international commodity prices and policy priorities. The 1970s world oil-price hikes vastly increased critical import costs and launched escalating trade deficits in most Third World countries. Paradoxically, modernization and import substitution policies had created local production systems dependent on increasingly costly imported petroleum and industrial inputs. While the international liquidity of the 1960s and early 1970s had encouraged Third World governments to finance import-dependent growth using foreign loans, rising interest rates undercut this national economic strategy. By the start of the 1980s, most Third World countries were experiencing balance of payment problems which, particularly in Latin America and Africa, engendered a ruinous debt crisis (Weeks 1989).

During the 1980s, Third World trade deficits were exacerbated by the global recession and declining export earnings. While the prices of imported goods rose, those for traditional exports (such as sugar, coffee, tea and cocoa) plummeted (ECLA 1989). The historical decline in the international terms of trade for tropical products has been greatly aggravated in recent years by (a) rising tariff and non-tariff barriers to trade in tropical products in major First World markets (World Bank 1986: 22); (b) shifting metropolitan consumption patterns and the substitution of tropical agro-industrial inputs with chemical alternatives (Goodman, Sorj and Wilkinson 1987); and (c) the failure of Third World producer countries to organize effectively to control global surpluses (Llambi 1994a).

In most Third World countries, foreign exchange and debt problems were tied to a state fiscal crisis with important roots in the agro-food sector. Food import bills rose dramatically in the early 1970s due to a substantial drop in US concessional wheat exports and a corresponding rise in world food prices (Friedmann 1982: S271). The cost of food subsidization programmes soared, threatening fiscal stability in countries such as Bangladesh, Korea, Morocco, Pakistan, Sri Lanka and Tanzania (World Bank 1986: 91). While state food expenditures rose, agro-food related revenues generally declined. In addition to reducing foreign exchange, the collapse of traditional agricultural exports significantly curtailed government budgets, since heavy taxes on these commodities have historically generated a large share of Third World domestic receipts (Knudsen and Nash 1990: 63).

Responding to the crisis, most Third World governments were forced to institute severe austerity measures. State spending on rural development infrastructure, extension services and agricultural credit declined as increasingly scarce public resources were concentrated in the external financial sector (Canak 1989). At the same time, Third World governments found themselves increasingly unable to afford to maintain subsidies on the imported inputs required by the new high-input agricultural system. Without these subsidies, agricultural production costs spiralled with rising world gasoline, machinery and chemical-input prices.

The tenuous balancing of agricultural subsidies with food price controls, which had supported the activities of local wage-food producers in some Third World countries, was shattered by escalating input costs. The profitability of domestic agriculture declined sharply, even in countries such as Mexico which had established strong national food sectors (Raynolds et al. 1993). Local wage-food producers suffered most in countries which, in order to stem urban protests over rising living costs, were able to postpone food price increases (Walton 1989).

Over the past two decades, the contraction in Third World economies has been the most severe in those debt-ridden countries which have been forced by international financial institutions to impose stabilization and structural adjustment programmes reorienting local economic activity toward international debt repayment (Wood 1986). Domestic agricultures have been severely weakened by the application of neo-liberal monetarist policies. Exchange-rate reforms and devaluations have accentuated the rising costs of imported agricultural inputs, putting them out of reach of most peasant producers. Fiscal restraints have limited credit access and concentrated resources in the most profitable portions of the agro-food sector. While wage-food segments have been decapitalized, agro-industries have sometimes flourished due to their monopolization of available credit and their access to substantial private investments (Raynolds 1993). Adjustment policies have reduced the purchasing power and food budgets of lower- and middle-income populations in much of Latin America and Africa (Tokman and Wurgaft 1987; Aboagye and Gozo 1987), decreasing local demand for wage-foods. This contraction hurt domestic producers except where declining incomes have forced consumers to substitute cheaper locally produced commodities for imported luxury items.

Internationally sponsored adjustment programmes have attempted to decrease direct state involvement in Third World economies via privatization measures. While government agricultural services and institutions have been dismantled, private agro-industrial investments have been promoted and publicly subsidized. Weakened state regulation of national agriculture has encouraged the unhampered pursuit of private profits by local, and more commonly transnational, corporations (Bonat and Abdullahi 1989). In regions such as Central America, where agricultural production has been intensified in the search for short-term profits, it has led to potentially irreparable ecological harm (Murray and Hoppin 1992). Unregulated agricultural exploitation and the 'mining' of local environmental resources has seriously jeopardized food production and export earnings in some Third World countries (Raynolds 1994b).

The new neo-liberal monetarist orthodoxy champions 'opening' Third World economies to international investment and trade. Liberalization policies intended to increase direct foreign investment and rationalize production have replaced previously popular import substitution policies. Despite these measures, foreign capital in the agro-food sector has remained concentrated in a few newly industrialized Asian and Latin American countries, with new agricultural investments in other Third World countries proving limited and often highly transient (Mackintosh 1989; Rama 1992). Trade barriers protecting Third World agriculture have been widely lifted in the name of 'free trade'. Yet, since the subsidization of domestic producers has been curtailed, trade liberalization policies place Third World producers in direct competition with First World farmers who, as we have noted above, remain highly subsidized.

Most Third World governments have replaced earlier nationally oriented growth strategies with export-led development strategies espoused by the international financial community. Under structural adjustment programmes, debtor countries have been forced to shift public resources away from domestic spending toward the subsidization of exports. Since traditional Third World products have been on the decline, this new strategy has entailed the promotion of non-traditional export commodities. For countries which have historically relied heavily on overseas earnings, the current political project is one of export substitution; for historically more articulated economies, it represents a break from nationally integrated growth (Raynolds *et al.* 1993).

The promotion of non-traditional agricultural and agro-industrial exports has typically played a central role in new outward-oriented development strategies. With the encouragement and often financial backing of international organizations, Third World states have stimulated production in this sector by subsidizing credit and other inputs, and providing substantial tax and tariff exemptions. New agricultural commodities – such as specialty horticultural crops, off-season fruits and vegetables, and ornamental plants – have been introduced in many Third World locations to take advantage of growing fresh-food and luxury-good markets in metropolitan centres (Llambi 1994b; Raynolds 1994b). At the same time, Third World shipments of processed foods – such as fruit juices, frozen vegetables, boxed beef, and chicken – for mass consumer markets in Europe, North America, Japan and (increasingly) the Near East and the newly industrialized countries of Asia have expanded rapidly (Constance and Heffernan 1991; Mackintosh 1977; Williams 1986).

The rise of Third World non-traditional agricultural and agro-industrial exports is partially rooted in the international corporate relocation of production in search of cheap labour, government subsidies, and limited environmental regulations. Since the 1960s, improvements in transportation and communication systems and biochemical changes in plant requirements and storage capacities have vastly increased the potential geographic separation of agricultural production from major markets (Friedland 1994). These changes have encouraged the establishment of large-scale plantation-style enterprises in new commodity areas and new regions of the Third World. Central America, for example, has experienced a boom in large-scale beef export production, largely under the aegis of foreign agribusiness (Sanderson 1986; Williams 1986). Since labour makes up a large share of variable costs, transnational agro-food corporations tend to locate where labour is cheapest, often taking advantage of the depressed wages of women and children (Mackintosh 1989). In order to further limit costs and production risks, many fruit and vegetable corporations contract out production to Third World peasants (Little and Watts forthcoming; Raynolds 1994b).

Despite the apparent boom in non-traditional agricultural and agro-industrial exports, the long-term benefits for Third World trade balances and populations are uncertain. These new exports enter highly volatile and competitive international markets. Since non-traditional exports are at the core of the international financial community's economic revitalization formula, many Third World countries are being propelled into the very same commodity markets (Barham *et al.* 1992). World prices for fresh and processed agricultural goods are very volatile and new exports are restricted by high, and politically changeable, tariff and non-tariff barriers to trade (Islam 1990). While Third World states have been required to provide substantial subsidies to attract foreign investments in this sector, the expansion of non-traditional agricultural exports may bring only poorly paid jobs and exploitative contracts to rural populations. The growth of new agro-industrial exports brings fewer jobs and no necessary boost to local commodity markets (Rama 1992). Only in rare cases, such as Chile, where state support has been sufficient and local agrarian capitalists powerful enough, have Third World producers been able to take the lead in the recent non-traditional export boom (Gomez and Goldfrank 1991).

CONCLUSION

Food and agricultural systems around the world have undergone continual reorganization as a result of their dynamic encounter with capitalist market forces. This reorganization entails substantive changes which go far beyond the simple subjection of agriculture and food production to market principles. Clearly, the development of capitalism cannot be understood historically outside of the wider political and institutional relations within which capitalist markets operate. This is particularly evident in the case of agriculture, which is at once an important segment of the economy and the source of food – a basic requirement of all people and a concern of all governments.

As outlined above, the incorporation of Third World agricultures into the capitalist economy has been shaped by the specific political and institutional relations prevailing during a given historical period. The introduction of capitalist market forces was originally a political act, institutionalized in the international division of labour associated with the colonial system. Within this framework, the Third World emerged as a region dependent upon primary-product exports which were exchanged for more expensive metropolitan manufactured goods and financial services. Tropical products from the colonies fuelled capitalist industrial development in metropolitan states, providing complementary foods for the growing urban workforce and raw materials for the expanding factories. Temperate products from the settler states, meanwhile, supplied an increasing share of European staple foods, leading to the intensified production of these goods within a high-input system of industrial agriculture.

During the post-colonial era, the existing international division of labour was initially reinforced by the Fordist system of mass consumption which augmented the role of tropical exports as inputs in metropolitan agro-food industries. Yet, at the same time, this nationally oriented system worked to reverse world agricultural trade flows by subsidizing metropolitan farm sectors and shipping surplus commodities to the Third World. Cheap grain imports undermined local peasant production, fostered urbanization, and transformed diets throughout the Third World. In many cases national food self-sufficiency was seriously compromised. Where basic food production was maintained via the adoption of the high-input agricultural model, class-based inequalities were exacerbated, leading to increased rural proletarianization and growing peasant immiseration.

Since the early 1970s, traditional Third World agricultural export markets have contracted due to widespread substitution of tropical products and mounting protectionism in metropolitan states. Despite attempts to promote non-traditional agricultural exports aimed at expanding luxury markets, balance of payments problems have deepened throughout most of the Third World. During this period of economic upheaval, Third World food access has been weakened by the shift from concessional to commercial grain sales and by rising input costs which undermine the viability of high-input agriculture. As the nationally oriented model of capitalist development is replaced by the export-oriented model fostered by multilateral lending agencies, national food security and local agricultures are increasingly threatened. Within the growing corporate-dominated liberal market regime, purchasing power, rather than government policy, dictates what is grown and where it is consumed. While Third World countries perhaps suffer the most from the current unequal application of market liberalization measures which exempt metropolitan states, the more widespread extension of these measures will not automatically benefit Third World populations.

Current General Agreement on Tariff and Trade (GATT) proposals claim to benefit Third World agro-exporters by decreasing metropolitan trade barriers and liberalizing agricultural policies across the world. Yet, the implications of these negotiations for Third World countries appear more complex and potentially contradictory. For one thing, trade liberalization is the goal of most transnational corporations, who stand to gain from a free trade regime through the reduction of price supports, expansion of global markets, and broader access to differential labour costs across the world. This would intensify the subordination of Third World states to world market conditions and the global organizing capacity of large corporations (McMichael 1992, 1993). For another, while a number of studies trying to legitimize the GATT negotiations have argued that the reduction of metropolitan protection would expand world trade to the advantage of Third World producers (see Raikes 1988: 156–60), these projections focus only on aggregate exchange values. By failing to recognize the critical use value of food, such reified models ignore distribution and sovereignty issues so important in determining food production and consumption relations (Raikes 1988: 160–1).

In fact, recent research (UNCTAD 1990: 47) suggests that liberalization would raise basic foodstuff prices in the short run to the benefit of temperate commodity producers supplying now food-dependent Third World countries. Improved market access will not result in higher world prices for most tropical products exported from the Third World, so 'For this class of countries gains from trade liberalisation will be much smaller than losses in higher import costs' (Raghavan 1990: 174). Third World food dependency is thus likely to deepen alongside of the large-scale conversion of Third World land to agro-export cropping.

In short, the historical sweep of capitalism reveals not only a wholesale transformation of world agriculture, but also the centralization of political power in the hands of food corporations and metropolitan governments that control access to food. Such power is disguised by the rhetoric of market forces. However, as we have argued here, market forces are embedded in concrete social structures with profound political impact, rather than being invisible mechanisms that allocate resources on the basis of abstract efficiencies.

REFERENCES

Aboagye, A. and Gozo, K. (1987) 'Sub-Saharan Africa', in World Employment Programme (ed.) *Recession and Global Interdependence: Effects on Employment Poverty and Policy Formation in Developing Countries*, Geneva: International Labour Office.

Baran, P. (1967) *The Political Economy of Growth*, New York: Monthly Review Press.

Barham, B., Clark, M., Katz, E. and Schurman, R. (1992) 'Non-traditional agricultural exports in Latin America: toward an appraisal', *Latin American Research Review* 27, 2: 43–82.

Barkin, D. (1987) 'The end to food self-sufficiency in Mexico', *Latin American Perspectives* 14: 271–97.

—— (1990) *Distorted Development: Mexico in the World Economy*, Boulder, CO: Westview Press.

Barkin, D., Batt, R. L. and DeWalt, B. R. (1990) *Food Crops Vs. Feed Crops: Global Substitution of Grains in Production*, Boulder, CO: Lynne Rienner Publishers.

Bonat, Z. and Abdullahi, Y. (1989) 'The World Bank, IMF and Nigeria's agricultural and rural economy', in B. Onimode (ed.) *The IMF, The World Bank and the African Debt: The Social and Political Impact*, London: Zed Books Ltd.

Bovard, J. (1991) *The Farm Fiasco*, San Francisco: Institute for Contemporary Studies.

Bradley, P. N. and Carter, S. E. (1989) 'Food production and distribution – and hunger', in R. J. Johnston and P. J. Taylor (eds) *A World in Crisis? Geographical Perspectives*, Oxford: Basil Blackwell.

Burbach, R. and Flynn: (1980) *Agribusiness in the Americas*, New York: Monthly Review Press.

Burmeister, L. (1988) *Research, Realpolitik and Development in Korea: The State and the Green Revolution*, Boulder, CO: Westview Press.

Byres, T. J. (1981) 'The new technology, class formation and class action in the Indian countryside', *Journal of Peasant Studies* 8, 4: 405–54.

Canak, W. L. (1989) 'Debt, austerity, and Latin America in the new international division of labor', in W. L. Canak (ed.) *Lost Promises: Debt, Austerity, and Development in Latin America*, Boulder, CO: Westview Press.

Clarke, S. (1988) *Keynesianism, Monetarism and the Crisis of the State*, Aldershot: Edward Elgar.

Cleaver, H. (1977) 'Food, famine and the international crisis', *Zerowork* 2: 7–70.

Constance, D. H. and Heffernan, W. (1991) 'The global poultry agro/food complex', *International Journal of Sociology of Agriculture and Food* 1: 126–42.

Daly, M. T. and Logan, M. I. (1989) *The Brittle Rim: Finance, Business and the Pacific Region*, Ringwood, Victoria: Penguin.

Danaher, K. (1989) 'US food power in the 1990s', *Race and Class* 30, 3: 31–46.

Dalrymple, D. (1985) 'The development and adoption of high-yielding varieties of wheat and rice in developing countries', *American Journal of Agricultural Economics* 67: 1067–73.

DeWalt, Billie (1985) 'Mexico's second Green Revolution: food for feed', *Mexican Studies/Estudios Mexicanos* 1: 29–60.

de Janvry, A. (1981) *The Agrarian Question and Reformism in Latin America*, Baltimore: John Hopkins University Press.

de Janvry, A., Sadoulet, E., and Young, L. (1989) 'Land and labour in Latin American agriculture from the 1950s to the 1980s', *Journal of Peasant Studies* 16, 3: 396–424.

ECLA (United Nations Economic Commission for Latin America) (1989) 'Ronda Uruguay: hacia una posicion Latino-Americana sobre los productos agricolas', *Comercio Exterior* 39, 6: 458–84.

Friedland, W. (1994) 'The global fresh fruit and vegetable system: an industrial organization analysis', in P. McMichael (ed.) *The Global Restructuring of Agro-Food Systems*, Ithaca, NY: Cornell University Press.

Friedmann, H. (1978) 'World market, state and family farm: social bases of household production in an era of wage labor', *Comparative Studies in Society and History* 20, 4: 545–86.

—— (1982) 'The political economy of food: the rise and fall of the post-war international food order', *American Journal of Sociology* 88: S248–86.

—— (1987) 'Family farms and international food regimes', in T. Shanin (ed.) *Peasants and Peasant Societies*, Oxford: Basil Blackwell.

—— (1991a) 'Changes in the international division of labor: agri-food complexes and export agriculture', in W. Friedland, L. Busch, F. H. Buttel and A. Rudy (eds) *Towards a New Political Economy of Agriculture*, Boulder, CO: Westview Press.

—— (1991b) 'Regulating capital on a global scale', *Studies in Political Economy* 36: 9–42.

—— (1992) 'Distance and durability: shaky foundations for the world food economy', *Third World Quarterly* 13, 2: 371–83.

Friedmann, H. and McMichael, P. (1989) 'Agriculture and the state system: the rise and decline of national agricultures, 1870 to the present', *Sociologia Ruralis* 29, 2: 93–117.

Garst, R. and Barry, T. (1990) *Feeding the Crisis: US Food Aid and Farm Policy in Central America*, Lincoln: University of Nebraska Press.

George, S. (1984) 'Culture, economics, politics and food systems', in S. George (ed.) *Ill Fares the Land: Essays on Food, Hunger, and Power*, Washington DC: Institute for Policy Studies.

—— (1988) *A Fate Worse than Debt*, New York: Grove Press.

Gilpin, R. (1987) *The Political Economy of International Relations*, Princeton NJ: Princeton University Press.

Gomez, S. and Goldfrank, W. L. (1991) 'World market and agrarian transformation: the case of neo-liberal Chile', *International Journal of Sociology of Agriculture and Food* 1: 143–50.

Goodman, D. (1991) 'Some recent tendencies in the industrial organization of the agri-food system', in W. Friedland, L. Busch, F. H. Buttel and A. Rudy (eds) *Towards a New Political Economy of Agriculture*, Boulder, CO: Westview Press.

Goodman, D. and Redclift, M. (1982) *From Peasant to Proletarian: Capitalist Development and Agrarian Transitions*, New York: St Martin's Press.

Goodman, D., Sorj, B. and Wilkinson, J. (1987) *From Farming to Biotechnology: A Theory of Agro-Industrial Development*, Oxford: Basil Blackwell.

Griffin, K. B. (1974) *The Political Economy of Agrarian Change: An Essay on the Green Revolution*, Cambridge: Harvard University Press.

—— (1987) 'World hunger and the world economy', in W. L. Hollist and F. L. Tullis (eds) *Pursuing Food Security. Strategies and Obstacles in Africa, Asia, Latin America and the Middle East*, Boulder, CO: Lynne Rienner.

Grigg, D. (1986) *The World Food Problem*, Oxford: Basil Blackwell.

Hathaway, D. E. (1987) *Agriculture and the GATT: Rewriting the Rules*, Washington DC: Institute for International Economics.

Hirschman, A. O. (1968) 'The political economy of import-substituting industrialization in Latin America', *The Quarterly Journal of Economics* 82, 1: 1–32.

Hobsbawm, E. (1992) 'The crisis of today's ideologies', *New Left Review* 192 (March/April): 55–64.

Insel, B. (1985) 'A world awash in grain', *Foreign Affairs* 63: 892–911.

Islam, N. (1990) 'Horticultural exports of developing countries: past performances, future prospects, and policy issues', Washington DC: International Food Policy Research Institute, Research Report No. 80.

Johnson, D. G. (1989) 'The current setting of US agriculture', in G. Horwick and G. J. Lynch (eds) *Food, Policy and Politics. A Perspective on Agriculture and Development*, Boulder, CO: Westview Press.

Kenney, M., Lobao, L. M., Curry, J. and Goe, W. R. (1989) 'Midwestern agriculture in US fordism: from the New Deal to economic restructuring', *Sociologia Ruralis* 29, 2: 131–48.

Knudsen, O. and Nash, J. (1990) *Redefining Government's Role in Agriculture in the Nineties*, Washington DC: The World Bank.

Lappe, F.M. and Collins, J. (1978) *Food First: Beyond the Myth of Scarcity*, New York: Ballantine Books.

Lipietz, A. (1987) *Mirages and Miracles. The Crisis of Global Fordism*, London: Verso.

Little, P. D. and Watts, M. (forthcoming) *Peasants Under Contract: Contract Farming and Agrarian Transformation in Sub-Saharan Africa*, Madison: University of Wisconsin Press.

Llambi, L. (1990) 'Transitions to and within capitalism: agrarian transitions in Latin America', *Sociologia Ruralis* 30, 2: 174–96.

—— (1994a) 'Opening economies and closing markets: the difficult insertion of Latin American agriculture in the emerging world order', in A. Bonnano, L. Busch, W. Friedland, L. Gouveja and E. Mingione (eds) *From Columbus to Conagra: The Globalization of Agriculture and Food*, Lawrence: University Press of Kansas.

—— (1994b) 'Back to the future? Comparative advantages and disadvantages in Latin American non-traditional fruit and vegetable exports', in P. McMichael (ed.) *The Global Restructing of Agro-Food Systems*, Ithaca, NY: Cornell University Press.

MacEwan, A. (1990) *Debt and Disorder*, New York: Monthly Review Press.

Mackintosh, M. (1977) 'Fruit and vegetables as an international commodity: the relocation of horticulture production and its implications for the producers', *Food Policy* 2: 277–92.

—— (1989) *Gender, Class and Rural Transition*, London: Zed Books Ltd.

Mann, S. (1987) 'The rise of wage labor in the cotton South: a global analysis', *Journal of Peasant Studies* 14: 412–29.

McMichael, P. (1992) 'Tensions between national and international control of the

world food order: contours of a new food regime', *Sociological Perspectives* 35, 2: 343–65.
—— (1993) 'World food system restructuring under a GATT regime', *Political Geography* 12, 3: 198–214.
Murray, D. and Hoppin, P. (1992) 'Recurring contradictions in agrarian development: pesticide problems in Caribbean Basin nontraditional agriculture', *World Development* 20, 4: 597–608.
Pearse, A. (1980) *Seeds of Plenty, Seeds of Want*, Oxford: Clarendon Press.
Raghavan, C. (1990) *Recolonization. GATT, the Uruguay Round and the Third World*, Penang, Malaysia: Third World Network.
Raikes, P. (1988) *Modernising Hunger. Famine, Food Surplus and Farm Policy in the EEC and Africa*, London: Catholic Institute for International Affairs.
Rama, R. (1985) 'Some effects of the internationalization of agriculture on the Mexican agricultural crisis', in S. Sanderson (ed.) *The Americas in the New International Division of Labor*, New York: Holmes and Meier.
—— (1992) *Investing in Food*, Paris: OECD.
Raynolds, L. T. (1993) 'Agrarian restructuring: internationalization and the reconfiguration of production and labor forces in the Dominican Republic', unpublished Ph.D. dissertation, Cornell University.
—— (1994b) 'The restructuring of export agriculture in the Dominican Republic: changing agrarian production relations and the state', in P. McMichael (ed.) *The Global Restructuring of Agro-food Systems*, Ithaca, NY: Cornell University Press.
Raynolds, L. T., Myhre, D., McMichael, P., Carro-Figueroa, V. and Buttel, F. H. (1993) 'The "new" internationalization of agriculture: a reformulation', *World Development* 21, 7: 1101–21.
Revel, A. and Riboud, C. (1986) *American Green Power*, Baltimore: Johns Hopkins University Press.
Ruggie, J. G. (1982) 'International regimes, transactions and change: embedded liberalism in the post-war economic order', *International Organization* 36: 397–415.
Sanderson, S. (1986a) 'The emergence of the "world steer": internationalization and foreign domination in Latin American cattle production', in F. L. Tullis and W. L. Hollist (eds) *Food, the State and International Political Economy*, Lincoln: University of Nebraska Press.
—— (1986b) *The Transformation of Mexican Agriculture: International Structure and the Politics of Rural Change*, Princeton, NJ: Princeton University Press.
—— (1989) 'Mexican agricultural policy in the shadow of the US farm crisis', in D. Goodman and M. Redclift (eds) *The International Farm Crisis*, London: Macmillan Press.
Stoler, A. L. (1985) *Capitalism and Confrontation in Sumatra's Plantation Belt, 1870–1979*, New Haven: Yale University Press.
Teubal, M. (1987) 'Internationalization of capital and agroindustrial complexes: their impact on Latin American agriculture', *Latin American Perspectives* 14: 316–64.
Tokman, V. and Wurgaft, J. (1987) 'The recession and the workers of Latin America', in *World Recession and Global Interdependence*, Geneva: International Labour Office.
Tubiana, L. (1989) 'World trade in agricultural products: from global regulation to market fragmentation', in D. Goodman and M. Redclift (eds) *The International Farm Crisis*, New York: St Martin's Press.
UNFAO (United Nations Food and Agriculture Organization) (1961) *Trade Yearbook*, Rome: FAO.
—— (1980) *Trade Yearbook*, Rome: FAO.

UNCTAD (1990) *Agricultural Trade Liberalisation in the Uruguay Round: Implications for Developing Countries*, New York: United Nations.

Wallerstein, M. B. (1980) *Food for War – Food for Peace*, Cambridge, MA: MIT Press.

Walton, J. (1989) 'Debt, protest, and the state in Latin America', in S. Eckstein (ed.) *Power and Popular Protest*, Berkeley: University of California Press.

Weeks, J. F. (1989) 'Losers pay reparations, or how the Third World lost the lending war', in J. F. Weeks (ed.) *Debt Disaster?*, New York: New York University Press.

Wessel, R. (1983) *Trading the Future. Farm Exports and the Concentration of Economic Power in our Food System*, San Francisco: Institute for Food and Development Policy.

Whiting, V. R. Jr (1985) 'Transnational enterprise in the food processing industry', in R. Newfarmer (ed.) *Profits, Progress, and Poverty*, Notre Dame, IN: University of Notre Dame Press.

Williams, R. G. (1986) *Export Agriculture and the Crisis in Central America*, Chapel Hill: University of North Carolina.

Wood, R. E. (1986) *From Marshall Plan to Debt Crisis: Foreign Aid and Development Choices in the World Economy*, Berkeley: University of California Press.

Woodruff, W. (1967) *Impact of Western Man. A Study of Europe's Role in the World Economy 1850-1960*, New York: St Martin's Press.

World Bank (1986) *World Development Report 1986*, New York: Oxford University Press.

—— (1987) *World Development Report 1987*, New York: Oxford University Press.

Yotopoulos, P. (1985) 'Middle-income classes and food crises: The "new" food-feed competition', *Economic Development and Cultural Change* 33, 2: 463–83.

16

GENDER RELATIONS, CAPITALISM AND THIRD WORLD INDUSTRIALIZATION

Ruth Pearson

There are two ways of interrogating the relationship between capitalism and gender; the first is to analysis the growth of waged labour, particularly in the transition to industrialization that has formed the context in which capitalism has rooted itself in many economies both of the already industrialized countries of the North and in the newly industrialized countries in East Asia and elsewhere. This approach involves an understanding of the different dynamics of industrial accumulation in different time periods and locations, different industrialization strategies and the ways in which their labour forces were selected and managed. Most analyses of this type restrict their understanding of gender to a discussion of the sexual division of labour in the industrial workforce and the implications for women of exclusion and inclusion in such work.

This approach is very much linked to the Marxist tradition and particularly the writings of Engels which saw women's incorporation into the waged labour force as a key element in the undermining of women's oppression within capitalist society. The stress 'socialist' regimes laid on women's employment in the formal economy and the links made between such employment and formal declarations of women's emancipation enshrined in political manifestos and national constitution was also heralded as a feature that distinguished women's oppression under capitalism from their liberation under socialism.

The second approach takes a broader conceptualization of both capitalism and gender. If capitalism is understood as a system which extends beyond formal factory-type workplaces as sites of appropriation of surplus to the wide range of productive activities which form part of the national and international systems of capitalist accumulation then attention must be paid to organization and conditions of work far beyond the factory gate. A fuller understanding of gender would also incorporate the gendered structures of social relations both in work and outside it – in political structures, intra-household relations and in a wide range of social interactions in

339

which gender is an important, if not determinant factor, in determining the relative power and autonomy of different individuals to determine outcomes. Such an approach of necessity questions the automatic linkage often made between wage employment and women's liberation, substituting a framework in which changes in economic systems and women's roles within them can be examined in order to understand how such changes affect the nature of gender relations, rather than assuming a causal and unidirectional linkage.

This chapter will attempt to use both approaches in order to analyse the relationship between gender and industrialization. The first section will review the major trends in global industrialization and the changing gender division of labour which is associated with different phases. The second section will take a broader view of both gender and industrialization and discuss how different kinds of work – not necessarily within the formal waged labour force – are associated with industrialization. This section will also question the relationship between women's work and emancipation and show how gender relations are present in all aspects of economic and social relations in diverse industrial societies.

INDUSTRIALIZATION AND THE GENDERING OF THE LABOUR FORCE

Whether or not women form part of the waged labour force in industrializing or industrialized countries is one of the most visible – if the least stable – aspect of industrial change. It is perhaps pertinent that the first so-called industrial revolution – that in the United Kingdom in the eighteenth and nineteenth centuries was also characterized by changing sexual or gender divisions of labour. Prior to factory production, proto-industrialization whereby consumption goods were produced by household-based work groups were also characterized by a social division of labour whereby certain tasks were allocated to men and others to women. During the industrial revolution changes in the technology and organization of production were accompanied by changes in the sexual division of labour, and a new social order emerged in which very often women and children were increasingly confined to certain low-technology sectors of the economy whilst being progressively excluded from sectors using mechanical or steam power, extractive industries such as coal mining, or those based on metalworking (Berg 1985). The expansion of the so-called 'new industries' in the 1920s and 1930s in Britain, also brought significant changes in the types of products produced, the organization and technology of production. Again some dynamic sectors – such as steelworks and motor-car or aerospace manufactures continued to exclude women, but dynamic sectors producing electrical goods for the expanding consumer markets were based on women's factory labour (Glucksmann 1986).

340

The changing place and visibility of women in the British industry serves as a warning against making any unitary predictions about the implications of industrialization for women's employment. In spite of this it was widely predicted that women would be marginalized from the workforce when modern industry began to be established in Third World countries, as capitalist relations of production and employment were extended.

Ester Boserup, who pioneered the study of women in the process of economic development, focused her attention on the absence of women in the new factories and waged workplaces of modern industry. From a perspective which echoes historians lamenting the transition from cottage-based proto-industries of the seventeenth and eighteenth centuries to the new factories of the industrial revolution, she argued that women were marginalized or excluded from employment in industry (Boserup 1987).

The theoretical perspective of Boserup's analysis was one of industrialization as a linear progression from pre-factory artisan production to modern large-scale industry. Her observations on the process of industrialization view it as a process involving the social and technical division of labour, the transference of production from household-based enterprises to firms and factories, and the increasing skills demarcation and hierarchization of the labour force. Conceptually her view of the ways in which modern industrial production is organized is not dissimilar to that of Marx's analysis in Volume 1 of *Capital* and includes like Marx, the view that this kind of organization will be generalized to all sectors and all kinds of production. This implies a total separation of households – which now have become the site of reproduction only – and factories – which is where production (other than agricultural) is centred.

Boserup's analysis, first published in 1970, was robustly supported by available evidence. International employment data from the 1960s indicated that women's share in industrial employment declines as the importance of industry within the economy grows.

At a time when industry was considered to be the apotheosis of capitalist development, women's share of industrial employment was important not for the reasons that Engels and others stated – that it was the basis for the dissolution of gender oppression endemic in bourgeois households and society – but because employment in modern industry represented sharing in the benefits of progress and development. To be excluded from the waged labour force of the dynamic sectors of capital accumulation was to be deprived of the benefits of progress and technological change which the expansion of capitalist industry offered to societies as a whole and to individuals able to take advantage of new opportunities.

Since Boserup was writing from within a modernization perspective she did not question the unilinearity view of capitalist development exemplified by large-scale capital-intensive production; her concern was with measures which would increase women's participation in paid employment. She attributed womens' relative exclusion from industrial work to both supply and demand factors; on the _demand_ side, regulations concerning the employment of women workers, including maternity benefits, childcare provision, exemption from night work and equal-pay legislation were held to increase the cost of hiring women workers (although such legislation rarely applied to any but the largest employers, and in most post-colonial and other states, was honoured more in the breech) (Boserup 1987: 113); on the _supply_ side she argued that the inflexibility of modern industrial disci- pline, with fixed working hours in discrete locations made factory work incompatible with the domestic duties of women, especially mòthers. Struc- tural factors, such as lack of educational and skills training opportunities also make women unsuitable candidates for the skills and discipline required of workers in modern factories.

The separation of production from reproduction is also an important theme in Marxist explanations of women's lesser role in the European and North American industrial workforces of the nineteenth and twentieth centuries. Jane Humphries (1977) and Brenner and Ramas (1984) lay much stress on the physical separation of production from the household, and the incompatibility of factory work with nursing infants and other aspects of mothering and housekeeping.

A similar analysis is used, this time from a dependency perspective, to explain women's marginalization from the growing industrial workforce in Latin America as a consequence of accelerated industrialization, particu- larly in the post-Second World War period. Women retained a substantial share of industrial employment as enterprises grew to supply wage goods to the growing urban populations of the region. But the marginalization of women was particularly marked in the fast growing new industries which formed part of the import substitution industrialization strategies which were adopted in the larger Latin American countries such as Brazil, Mexico and Argentina from the 1950s onwards. In sectors of Latin American industry which were still in the phase of simple accumulation such as textiles and chemicals, where increases in production and productivity were achieved by increasing absolute surplus value, women's share in employment remained large. But when industrial expansion focused on the capital-intensive sectors such as automobiles, domestic appliances and steel and metal working, women's share in industrial employment dropped dramatically (Humphrey 1987).

The dependency argument is that this exclusion of women as industrial- ization deepens is attributable to various factors. The nature of industrial growth in peripheral economies reduces the overall demand for labour, since, first, it is based on imported technology overscaled for the markets and relative factor costs of peripheral economies; and second, because the transition from pre-capitalist industrial production where women were central to household-based petty commodity production (as family not

342

waged labour) 'into a fully fledged capitalist system of production accelerated the expulsion of women from directly economic roles' (Saffioti
1978: 188).

This rather overstates the case since the figures indicate in fact that
women's relative marginalization is the result of the faster growth of total
industrial employment in comparison with women's employment, resulting
in a lower female share of industrial employment rather than direct 'expulsion' and/or substitution of men in jobs and occupations previously
filled by women. However, the effect of these two factors combine to
produce a situation where demand for women workers is less strong
because they lack the education and skills required for modern industry;
either way, it can be argued, the nature of capitalist production in the
periphery is the primary cause of women's marginalization:

> The special situation of the peripheral economies in the world capitalist
> system has hindered a greater utilisation of the labour force in general
> by virtue of labour-saving technology. The limited dissemination of
> birth control techniques or the incorporation of medical and
> paramedical techniques for health care, at least in urban areas, ac-
> centuates even more the problem of unemployment. This does not
> mean that a country that develops along the path of capitalism is able
> to absorb the whole of its available labour force. In such countries the
> labour power factor is gradually replaced by technology, that is, it
> diminishes as the use of machinery increases the productivity of
> labour. Even this phase of increased employment, however, which
> permits a more rapid accumulation of capital and enables income to
> be distributed to segments of the population that will later be mar-
> ginalised from the system of production, does not occur in countries
> with dependent economies. International purchase of machinery
> considered obsolete in the country of origin makes it difficult to
> maintain employment levels in countries on the periphery. Quite
> apart from the effects of such commercial transactions on the balance
> of payments and the repercussions this has on the domestic economy,
> the importation of machinery drives labour from the secondary
> sector, but because domestic production of such machinery is almost
> out of the question. For this reason, the problem of unemployment,
> both apparent and concealed is much more serious in countries with
> dependent economies than in the centre of the international capit-
> alist system. This marginalisation of female labour, which is often
> explained almost exclusively in terms of prejudice, the vestiges of
> 'traditional society' and the low level of economic development turns
> out to be a consequence of the full development of capitalist
> production.

(Saffioti 1978: 188)

It is interesting to find these three distinct theoretical perspectives on industrialization – modernization, Marxist and dependency – all concur on two aspects; (a) that women are systematically excluded from, or left out of the waged labour force as industrialization results from the extension of capitalist relations of production and accumulation in world economy; and (b) that the central theme for discussion in terms of the interplay of gender and capital under industrialization concerns the presence or absence of women in the industrial waged labour force.[1]

To the extent that these analyses are correct in agreeing that capitalist industrialization tends to exclude women from waged employment, they are also clearly bound by the historical and geographical circumstances which they describe. The attempts to generalize the relationship between women's work and industrialization were premature.

First, as noted above there is the experience from Britain in the interwar period. Unlike the situation in Brazil and Latin America in the import substituting industrialization period when men were the preferred labour force in the extension of industrialization to consumer durables which had previously been imported from the West, Britain's new industries relied on female labour. Women were targeted as the workforce in these industries not just because of their much heralded 'nimble fingers' but also because a disciplined and docile workforce was required to adapt to the new order of assembly-line production. In terms very similar to those used by management in Third World manufacturing plants, the superiority of young women who commanded the lowest wage rates and 'who might submit more willingly to the harsh discipline . . . was frequently rationalised by the argument that the younger the hands, the more nimble the fingers' (Glucksmann 1990: 217).

Second, there is the experience of the changing geography and sociology of international industrial production. Since the 1960s there has been a sharp upturn in women's share of industrial employment in less developed countries, a trend which is particularly marked in particular countries such as Hong Kong, Phillipines, Mexico, Singapore, Taiwan, South Korea in the 1970s. This trend was continued into the 1980s and 1990s in a growing raft of countries including Mauritius, Bangladesh, Jamaica and Indonesia as they initiated the production of manufactured goods for export (Pearson 1992).

Women's employment in manufacturing industry in less developed countries grew both in absolute and relative terms. The explanation for this lies in the increasing adoption of exporting manufactured goods and components to international markets as the basis of LDCs' strategies for industrialization and development. Unlike the import substituting industrialization strategies of the 1950s and 1960s, export-oriented industrialization was aimed at international markets, producing wage goods or components which required relatively high proportions of direct labour in their production or

344

processing. The so-called 'new' international division of labour was seen by some to herald a new era in the international economy in which more and more of the world's manufacturing industry would shift to less developed countries because of their comparative advantage of 'cheap labour' which would give their products a competetive edge in international markets (Fröbel, Heinrichs and Kreye 1980).

In fact the relocation of industrial production to Third World countries from the 1970s was more limited and largely concentrated in a narrow range of goods, and in specified countries and regions. Two kinds of manufactured products featured very significantly in the surge of industrial production and exports, particularly from East and Southeast Asia and Latin America; first textiles and garments, particularly those produced for the mass-consumer markets of the West were sectors where production could easily be transferred to low-waged economies. A range of goods from T-shirts, to ladies' underwear to training shoes were produced, often to specifications and designs carried out in the West, with minimal technology or investment, relying primarily on the cheap labour of the local factory workers who were recruited and trained for this purpose (Elson and Pearson 1981).

The second kind of products was electronic components and assembly of consumer electronics goods for the burgeoning product ranges which developed on the basis of the microchip. Many of these processes carried out in Third World countries were in fact partial processing and assembly of components manufactured in the West. Conditions were suitable for the relocation of just the labour-intensive part of the production process, assembling lightweight components which could be flown or shipped out to dedicated factories, sometimes together with American or European management whose task it was to maximize productivity and minimize local value added cost.

The rise in women's share of manufacturing employment in Third World countries parallels the rise in manufactured exports of the kind described above – to such an extent that one writer commented that 'Exports of manufactures from developing countries have been made up in the main of the kind of goods normally produced by female labour: industrialisation in the post war period has been as much female-led as export-led' (Joekes 1987: 81).

The presence of a growing number of women employed in Third World factories was frequently explained by reference to traditonal patterns of employment in industry, although this argument is slightly dubious given that the second category of goods comprises new kinds of processes and products for which very little tradition pre-dated their establishment and growth in less developed countries. The point is rather, that the manufacturing processes on which such industrialization is based – that is labour intensive repetitive work requiring high levels of accuracy and application (such as sewing with industrial machines, or assembling electronic circuits under microscope magnification), to be carried out at high speed with good quality control – require the kind of jobs traditionally carried out by women, who have generally been the preferred employees on factory assembly lines requiring manual dexterity and continued application over time. Contemporary commentators were fond of rationalizing the preference for women workers in these so-called 'world market' factories by likening their work on the assembly line to domestic skills, which they assumed were innate qualities possessed by all women:

> manual dexterity of a high order may be required in typical sub-contracted operations, but nevertheless the operation is usually one that can be learned quickly on the basis of traditional skills. Thus in Morocco, in six weeks, girls, (who may not be literate) are taught the assembly under magnification of memory planes for computers – this is virtually darning with copper wire and sewing is a traditonal Moroccan skill. In the electrical field the equivalent of sewing is putting together wiring harnesses and in metal-working one finds parallels in some forms of soldering and welding.
>
> (Sharpston 1976: 334)

The recruitment of women followed economic rationality rather than essential or traditional women's skills. First, in most recorded situations women's wage levels are lower than those of men employed in comparable occupations, either because basic hourly rates are lower – which is the case over a range of agricultural, construction and production jobs – or because women do not have access to overtime and special piece rates which enhance men's earnings. In countries where export processing played an important role in industrialization in recent decades women's earnings in 1980 ranged from 45 per cent of male earnings in South Korea, to 62 per cent in Hong Kong, compared with 44 per cent in Japan and 69 per cent in the United Kingdom.[2] So although it is correct to argue that (some) manufacturing production tended to relocate in Third World countries because of their lower wage rates, it is important to remember that for labour intensive production processes, the preferred labour force is likely to be women because they combine both lowest cost with highest level of output.

The achievement of maximum productivity also depends on what the workforce does, rather than the efficiency and capacity of machinery; in the production lines of export processing factories this often means the ability to carry out detailed tasks such as etching electronic circuits or sewing in zip fasteners or sleeves. Women have often proved to be more efficient and reliable workers for these kinds of tasks, not because they are born wielding a needle and thread, but because they are socialized, through various kinds of productive and domestic work – including food preparation and weeding and harvesting – to carry out detailed work over sustained periods. At the same time the gendering of factory jobs (that is, the way the organization of work is designed for men or women – see Humphrey 1987) and the gendered nature of social relations makes it more likely that women are willing to submit to quite intrusive and directive discipline from male management without becoming militant or sabotaging production.[5]

There is a clear contrast between this kind of industrialization process in which women formed up to 90 per cent of the manufacturing labour force in some situations, and the exclusion, or minimal participation of women in the workforce of the import substituting industrialization of previous years. Whilst the relative presence or absence of women in the industrial labour force in either situation can be explained with reference to the type of production process involved, it tells us little about the ways in which industrialization affected the nature of gender relations – or the oppression of women, as the classical Marxists would have it. Perversely many later writers have since declared that the heavy presence of women in Third World industrial labour forces are evidence of how capitalist industrialization *exploits* Third World women who are defenceless in the face of international capitalism.

There are problems with any of these conclusions. First, although it is clear that the exclusion from or incorporation of women in the industrial labour force is related to the nature of different industrialization strategies, this in itself tells us nothing about the ways in which women's subordination – or oppression – is changed or modified by the process of industrialization. Within the perspectives cited above we can find quite contradictory positions. Modernization theorists – and dependency theorists – would insist that women are excluded from the benefits of capitalist industrialization by being excluded from employment. Others would argue the opposite – that women's presence in export processing factories constitutes exploitation and degradation of Third World women who are bearing the brunt of working conditions which are characterized by low pay, insecurity, exposure to health hazards, lack of social benefits, dead-end jobs with no prospect of training or promotion (Edgren 1982), an example of how industrialization within the world economy as presently constituted, brings benefits to international capital rather than local economic agents, be they enterprise, labour or the state.

The argument is further complicated by the fact that the dynamics of capital accumulation and technological change means that the situation regarding the employment of women in Third World industry is not static. Since the 1970s there have been various different tendencies observable in the world economy which demonstrate diverse trends concerning the gender compostion of the labour force, and the location of manufacturing industry. In some LDCs the percentage of women in the manufacturing labour force has in fact diminished. Whilst women's share of industrial employment has continued to rise in South Korea, Malaysia, Thailand and the Philippines, it has started to decline in Singapore, Taiwan and Hong Kong.

Changes in women's share of manufacturing employment reflect two different tendencies. The first tendency is the maintenance of export processing in an increasingly competitive international economy in which 'new' countries, such as Bangladesh, Thailand and Mauritius achieve an ever more firm foothold in the global share of the export processing market on the basis of even lower labour costs, Taylorist labour intensive production methods, and rigid control of the labour force. The markets in which they are competing are also the lowest cost markets, the markets for cheap wage goods which retail in high street stores and market stalls all over Western Europe and North America. The extent to which more women in more countries are drawn into this industrial labour force will be reflected in growing female shares of industrial employment in the regions where such employment is growing.

There is also a second tendency. In the countries which piloted export processing as a strategy for ongoing industrialization there has been a retreat from the reliance on low cost female labour. Countries such as Taiwan, Hong Kong, Singapore and Malaysia have moved up the technology and quality ladders, focusing their resources on the up-market end of the garments and footwear market and on transforming their capacity in the electronics sector, particularly in the consumer and industrial branches of the electronics industry so that instead of just assembly they manufacture components and final products. These processes are increasingly based on skilled (that is trained and qualified) labour and technically sophisticated manufacturing processes. In such circumstances the rate of increase of women in the industrial labour force is halted as expansion is no longer based on the incorporation of more (young) women into factories. The labour output ratio of this post-export-processing form of industrialization is much lower, so that whilst women continue to occupy the majority of the 'unskilled' assembly and operator jobs, new technically skilled or multi-skilled jobs are created to meet the demands of a more technologically sophisticated manufacturing environment. Many women will continue to find employment opportunities throughout this transformation in some situations such as Singapore, where a very tight labour market made the government introduce policies such as state supported childcare which allowed women to combine a long-term commitment to training and employment with parenting. In other countries such as South Korea, the abundance of trained (male) labour in addition to gendered norms which required married women to devote themselves to the care of the children and elders has effectively begun to reverse the upward trend of women's share of industrial employment recorded since the 1960s (Phongpaichit 1988).

If we are to take women's share of industrial employment as a measure of women's emancipation or as an indicator of progress towards equity with men, the story of Third World industrialization is highly conjunctural. Rather than exhibiting long term linear trends of a move towards equity, it is clear that the ways in which different Third World economies are integrated in the world economy have an immediate effect on women's share of industrial employment. As long as a country's place in the world system is on the basis of producing low-cost goods, based on low-wage, labour-intensive factories, for export then women's share of industrial employment will increase dramatically. But in this situation women are not of course achieving equity alongside men. The construction of this labour force is – as ever – gendered – and women are the targeted group because social relations and socially constructed characteristics and skills make women the most profitable workers (Pearson 1988). Undoubtedly the opportunity for waged employment in factories increases women's opportunities to gain income, to establish an identity outside of the household – and even to socialize with other women leading potentially to greater political consciousness and militancy, and in many cases these have been the outcomes of incorporating women into the industrial labour force. But the interesting question goes beyond that asked by Lim (1990) within the Marx-Engels tradition of whether or not women workers are 'unambiguously better off than they would be without those (industrial) jobs' (ibid.: 112). We need to pose a more comprehensive and open-ended question – which is: given that women have been incorporated rapidly and in large numbers into the industrial labour force of many developing countries, what does this mean for gender relations, and thus for the women themselves?

In posing this question we are not contesting the indisputable fact that where export processing industrialization has been successful and sustained it has generally been accompanied by economic growth. The labour-intensive nature of the waged employment on which it is based means that the benefits of the growth in industrial employment has probably been more widely distributed than the benefits from export-led agriculture dominated by rural oligarchies, or even the piece rate seasonal employment which characterizes the export of fruit and flowers which is part of the contemporary pattern of international trade. And, given that women have formed the major part of the employed labour force in export processing industrialization, it is indisputable that there are economic benefits to women as the result of their ability to earn factory wages.

Indeed, as Warren (1973) argued a generation earlier, there are always economic benefits for those involved in capitalist industrialization in terms of increases in monetarized flows within the market. But it is necessary to examine the changes in social relations to understand fully the sharpening of contradictions inherent in the capitalist industrialization project. Warren was of course, addressing another debate – the so-called 'dependency

349

debate' in which anglophone academics accused dependency writers of denying that capitalism brought any benefits in terms of economic development.

The problem about this debate was that the original dependency writers, who wrote in Spanish, had based their analysis on looking at what happened to inter- and transnational class relations as the result of integration into the world economy for the purpose of capitalist industrialization (Cardoso 1977). A parallel misreading of the original argument is taking place over the impact of industrial employment for Third World women. Whilst acknowledging the importance for women workers of access to wage-earning opportunities, and to the wages themselves, it is also crucial to examine the contradictions these changes give rise to in order to deepen our understanding of the relationship between gender and industrialization.

We shall extend our analysis by looking at three separate but connected issues: the diversity and changing nature of women's work in Third World industrialization; the gendering of work itself and the implications for women while they are part of the industrial labour force; and the relationship between women's employment experience and gender relations in the household and the wider society.

WOMEN AND INDUSTRIALIZATION: DIVERSITY AND CHANGE

As we indicated above the demand for women to work in Third World manufacturing factories is neither uniform nor constant. First, there has been an extension of the number of countries where export processing has been established and expanded. In the 1960s export-based industrialization, backed by a range of policy instruments to encourage foreign investment and promote the growth of export industries was confined to a handful of countries, the most important being the Mexican border industries and what came to be known as the four Asian 'tigers' – Hong Kong, South Korea, Taiwan and Singapore. Throughout the 1970s the strategy was adopted by a growing number of countries including Malaysia, Philippines, Sri Lanka, Mauritius, Indonesia and a number of Caribbean and Central American countries; and in the 1980s a further tranche of countries entered the market, most notably Bangladesh, Thailand and the Dominican Republic.

The diversity in the place and timing of the expansion of industrial employment in export factories is also matched by a diversity of strategies for constructing a female labour force. Many of the earlier analyses recycled a stereotype of the Third World woman worker – that she was young – recruited from an age cohort ranging from 15 to 25, concentrated in the 18 to 21 age group; that she was single, that she was childless and that she had no previous experience of industrial employment. Typically it was thought that workers were rural urban migrants seeking wage employment in the cities, and that they would retain their factory jobs only for a brief period before they left the labour force to concentrate on marriage and motherhood.

History and more extensive research has revealed the myopia of this stereotype, although even in the 1970s it was hardly accurate. While it was clear that it was most profitable for employers to hire women who were not heavily committed to reproductive roles outside the factory, this does not exclusively mean young single women. In the Mexican border industries, for example where there is a high rate of single motherhood, employers routinely required pregnancy tests rather than marriage certificates to reassure themselves that they would not be landed with costs of maternity pay (Pearson 1991). In the Caribbean, where the fertility patterns mean that women tend to complete their families at relatively young ages, the average age of garments and electronics workers tends to be some ten years older than those in South Asia (Pearson 1988).

When export processing first establishes itself in a country, it does generally target young unmarried women. But where there is a relatively limited supply of these 'ideal' women workers, employers soon settle for older/married women, even arguing that they are more productive (Hein 1986). Whilst many industrial recruits are drawn from rural areas, especially where factories are located in 'export processing zones' located far from major conurbations, employers can be quite discriminating about who they prefer to hire. In some cases inexperienced and uneducated women from the villages are recruited, often via an intermediary who has status in those rural communities; in others, particular training and experience is stipulated such as secondary-school education, English language proficiency or even certain physical characteristics are stipulated, both as forms of rationing and control.

Earlier analyses predicted that factories would exhaust a particular labour force and move on to a new green-field site where a fresh supply of young women would be available; foreign-owned export processing factories were termed offshore factories and runaway shops to denote their assumed instability and temporary nature. Whilst some factories did migrate from one location to another, fluctuations in employment were more often caused by the cyclical nature of demand for their products caused by reduction in international trade following the recessions which characterized western economies in the 1970s and 1980s. The threat of relocation to a country where the workforce was cheaper, more cooperative, less militant, and had higher productivity is now seen more as a bargaining position taken by management seeking to improve the profitability of the workforce or seeking improvements in the incentive packages offered by host governments.

Ironically in several countries including Mexico, Malaysia, Taiwan, South Korea and Singapore export production has continued for up to and over twenty years. Although there have been high levels of turnover amongst large sections of the labour force it is also the case that a sizeable minority of women working in export factories has been there for many years – sometimes because they have not married or had children, sometimes because they have managed to continue their employment throughout their reproductive years, and sometimes because they have re-entered the labour market after an interval for child-rearing, a pattern which mirrors that in western countries.

The changing technological and skills base of the industry also can require the hiring and/or retention of workers who have the experience and the ability to adapt to changing production circumstances. While upgrading the technological sophistication of production can, as we argued above, lead to a reduction in women's share of employment, women are not eliminated altogether. In Scotland's Silicon Glen for example the share of women in the electronics factories in the 1980s was about 50 per cent (Goldstein 1989). These were automated assembly plants where the labour/output ratio was much lower than the non-automated plants in Malaysia and elsewhere. The work the women did was also different, requiring high levels of concentration to maintain the correct level of quality control and production conditions, rather than relying on their manual skills. The same situation can be seen in Mexico's border industries in the 1990s. Technological change, including the introduction of programmable machinery and equipment requires the still predominantly women operators to exercise analytical skills and judgement. Although still a minority, a new type of woman worker is emerging who has combined factory work with reproductive duties over a number of years, whose wages are the basis for the household's support and subsistence, and whose 10 to 15 years experience in electronics production makes her crucial to the companies' ability to upgrade their production processes and products to meet changing market requirements (Barajas Escamilla and Rodriquez Ramirez 1991).

Equally important is the fact that the effect on women of industrialization is not confined to wage employment in factories. A whole range of products, and parts of production processes are subcontracted outside the factory either to small sweat-shops or to individual women working in their own homes, in much the same way as home-work has been carried out for decades in western countries. For example the hand embroidery of factory-made blouses and shirts is subcontracted to rural workshops in the Philippines (Pineda Ofreneo 1984); trainers are finished by hand in South Korea, often by women who previously were employed in factories (Kim 1991); hammock fringes are sent out in Brazil (Schmitz 1982); and springs for automobile parts are assembled at home in Malaysia (Open University/

BBC 1992). Whilst it is generally adult women who are prevented from seeking factory work by the demands of domestic work, childcare and/or care of elderly relatives who are the principle subcontractors, small children, particulary pre-adolescent girls often carry out a large share of home-based work subcontacted from export factories even though there is little recognition and no reward for their labour (Salaff 1990).

Subcontracting and home-based production are usually seen as part of the informal sector, although as these examples demonstrate they can be directly connected with export processing factories. Other women who are excluded from regular wage employment in factories maintain their income earning and economic activity by preparing and selling food or clothes to factory workers, and by doing domestic work of various kinds for other households. Although they may have limited prospects of continued factory employment through export industrialization the alternatives are often forms of income generation which are indirectly linked to factory work rather than being re-absorbed into the reproductive sphere of the economy.

THE GENDERING OF INDUSTRIAL WORK

The focus on women's share of industrial employment often assumes – implicitly or openly – that if women and men have equal access to industrial jobs women are incorporated on an equitable basis into the industrialization process.

There are problems with this assumption. First, the conditions on which women are recruited into the industrial labour force are often very heavily gendered. Certain skills associated with women such as manual dexterity, conscientiousness and the ability to work accurately at speed are demanded of women wanting 'unskilled' factory work, even by highly paid men who are totally incapable of doing such work themselves (Konig 1975). While, as we argued before, the skills women bring to the production process are deemed to be 'natural' gender attributes they are neither recognized as skills nor rewarded as such. This situation has not changed even though, as we have argued above, the technology of production is frequently much more sophisticated than it was 10 to 20 years ago. Women electronics operators, now required to carry out tasks which have been transformed by technological development and which require the exercise of analytical and judgemental faculties are still deemed unskilled and semi-skilled and paid accordingly. In spite of the transition to more capital- and technology-intensive processes, there is still a flat and sexualized hierarchy in most export factories, which means not only that women continue to fill the vast majority of unskilled posts, although recruitment of young men has increased in some locations, but that there remains very little prospect of women being promoted to either technical or management posts.

353

In Malaysia this is reflected by the falling share of female employment in the electronics sector where women's employment has fallen from over 80 per cent in the 1970s to 67 per cent in 1986. Retrenchment needed to cut production because of global recession and technological change primarily reduced women's employment, whereas the job opportunities created by automation were largely for men (Narayanan and Rasiah 1992).

The sexual division within the production process – with the women as operators and the men as management and technical personnel – enabled (particularly) American firms to promote management methods which manipulated the women's gendered position, introducing models of western femininity and sexuality to control and divide the workforce and to try and pre-empt the development of workers' conciousness and mili- tancy amongst the women (Grossman 1978/9). Such strategies have long since lost their efficacy, not least because cultural and political changes in many Third World countries have reshaped prevailing images of femininity in opposition to western values. In Malaysia, for example, factory workers in the past were subject to western management manipulation. But young women have used the revival of Islam in the context of a religiousized if not fundamentalist political project, to construct a new and respectable image of the factory worker – as a woman who is true to Islamic values, working in a segregated workplace, wearing modest clothing including veils and tradi- tional dress, who is devout and uses factory-provided prayer rooms and times, and who lives in supervised hostels for young women (Scott 1989). By contrast women factory workers in Bangladesh, who remain a small minority of working women in that populous country in spite of a rapid growth in their employment have been caught between the government's drive to industrialize and the increasing political power of fundamentalist Islamic movements who seek to impose strict constraints on women's movements and access to the public sphere. Bangladeshi women workers have been subject to increasing levels of harassment and violence as they seek to adapt their new working roles to the changing and contradictory nature of cultural norms (Feldman 1992).

The ways in which women are incorporated into the industrial workforce – from the hiring criteria and procedure, the techniques of management and control of work, the lack of promotion opportunities, inferior pay and conditions, and lack of job security and retraining opportunities – are all plainly gendered. Although women retain an important if not major share of industrial employment they have not achieved equity with men in the labour force; on the contrary gendered relations are not only exploited at the workplace in order to increase the profitability of women workers, but are continually reinforced or adapted to ensure that the subordination of women workers is not diluted as the result of their working experience.

WOMEN'S INDUSTRIAL EMPLOYMENT AND GENDER RELATIONS IN THE HOUSEHOLD AND THE COMMUNITY

The assumption that women who earn wages increase both their autonomy over decisions about their own lives, and their status and power within the household also needs to be examined in the light of available evidence.

First, we cannot assume automatically that women choose to take factory jobs and that this is their preferred option. Whilst economic necessity dictates that most low-income households will seek to take advantage of any income-earning opportunity that arises, the interests and preferences of the individuals within the household will not necessarily coincide and the employment decisions, particularly of those who are daughters in their households will conflict. Wolf (1992) found that in Java young women sought factory work in defiance of their parent's wishes, whilst in Taiwan and Hong Kong young women are frequently pressured to seek and remain in factory employment in order to meet family goals such as the education of sons, rather than to follow their own choices in obtaining education or leaving the workforce to get married (Salaf 1990).

Even when there is not conflict between the decision made by the women factory worker and the strategy of the household as a whole, we should be cautious about interpreting this as an increase in women's autonomy and control over decision-making. Sen (1990) points out that although women's status and bargaining position within the household is affected by the contribution others perceive she is making to the household, there are various well-charted strategies which ideologically invisibilize the importance of women's earnings to household survival and well-being (Whitehead 1984). It is possible for women's wages to be the central economic support of the household whilst at the same time for control over the women to be intensified in order to maintain that income without any concomitant improvement in women's status within the household or in their power to influence decision-making about the allocation of household resources, labour and opportunities. Again, the nature of perception of contribution and the correlation between economic contribution and social power is a gendered relation and is not necessarily amenable to economic linear logic.

As far as the wider community is concerned there is a range of attitudes which range from respect and protection of women factory workers where their visible participation in the economy is matched by a social legitimation of their new status, to public ideological pressure – in the media and elsewhere – which denigrates women who seek factory work, labelling them as dishonourable if they are breaking codes of purdah and segregation; as unnatural if they are mothers who seek waged work rather than remaining at home to care for their children; as promiscuous and unvirtuous if they are single women who live and travel separately from their parents; or undutiful wives if they disregard their husband's pride and prioritize income earning for their children and household needs, all of which have been documented in various case studies of women workers in different parts of the world.

It is important therefore to be aware of these contradictory attitudes in the public sphere which also affect how women are treated by the factory management, by trade unions and by other members of the household before we can unequivocally conclude that women's experience of factory employment necessarily empowers them, decreases their oppression and subordination and improves their status within the household and the community. In fact, the implications for women of industrial employment and the larger question of the relationship between industrialization and gender needs to be subjected to quite careful inquiry. It needs to go beyond a simple calculation of women's share of industrial employment to take into account women's experience of that employment, and the ways in which both the organization of their work, the prospects for their working lives, their opportunities and choices within the household and community are patterned not only by the fact that they are able to work for wages but also by the ways in which decisions about the work and reactions to them as workers interact with other patterns of gender relations within their communities. It is much more complicated than many would have us believe.

NOTES

1 Folbre (1986) has observed the coincidence of approach of Marxists and neo-classical writers to the domestic division of labour within the household.
2 These figures are taken from ILO (1988). The figures are not strictly comparable as those for South Korea are for monthly earnings, and those for the other countries for weekly earnings.
3 This is not to say that there are not many instances of women workers in export processing factories organizing within and outside trade unions, and/or of resisting management control by absenteeism, going slow and other strategies. The argument is that the nature of gender relations in most societies constructs women as more docile and reliable than men in the same class and occupation. See Elson and Pearson (1981) for an elaboration of this argument.

REFERENCES

Barajas Escamilla, Rocio and Rodriguez Ramirez, C. (1991) 'La mujer ante la reconversion productivc: el caso de la maquila electronica', in *Subcontraccion y empresas transnacionales*, Tijuana: Colegio de la Frontera Norée.
Berg, Maxine (1985) *The Age of Manufactures: 1700–1820*, London: Fontana.
Boserup, Ester (1987) *Women's Role in Economic Development*, Aldershot: Gower Press.
Brenner, Johanna and Ramas, Maria (1984) 'Rethinking Women's Oppression', *New Left Review* 144: 33–71.

Cardoso, F. H. (1977) 'The consumption of dependency theory in the United States', *Latin American Research Review* vol. 12, no. 3.: 7–240.

Edgren, G. (1982) 'Spearheads of industrialisation or sweatshops in the sun?' in E. Lee (ed.) *Export Processing Zones and Industrial Employment in Asia*, Bankok: ILO.

Elson, Diane and Pearson, Ruth (1981) 'Nimble fingers make cheap workers: an analysis of women's employment in Third World export manufacturing', *Feminist Review* no. 7: 87–107.

Feldman, Shelley (1992) 'Crisis, Islam and gender in Bangladesh: the social construction of a female labour force', in Lourdes Beneria and Shelley Feldman (eds) *Unequal Burden: Economic Crises, Persistent Poverty and Women's Work*, Boulder CO: Westview Press.

Folbre, Nancy (1986) 'Hearts and spades: paradigms of household economics', *World Development* vol. 14, no. 2: 245–55.

Fröbel, F., Heinrichs, J. and Kreye, O. (1980) *The New International Division of Labour*, Cambridge: Cambridge University Press.

Glucksmann, Miriam (1986) 'In a class of their own: women workers in the new industries in inter-war Britain', *Feminist Review* no. 24, Autumn: 7–37.

—— (1990) *Women Assemble: Women Workers in the New Industries in Inter-War Britain* London: Routledge.

Goldstein, Nance (1989) 'Silicon Glen: women and semi-conductor multinationals', in Diane Elson, and Ruth Pearson (eds) *Women's Employment and Multinationals in Europe*, Basingstoke: Macmillan.

Grossman, Rachel (1978/9) 'Women's place in the integrated circuit', *Southeast Asia Chronicle* no. 66.

Hein, Catherine (1986) 'The feminisation of industrial employment in Mauritius: a case of sex segregation', in Richard Anker and Catherine Hein (eds) *Sex Inequalities in Urban Employment in the Third World*, Basingstoke: Macmillan.

Hewitt, Tom, Johnson, Hazel and Wield, David (eds) (1992) *Industrialisation and Development*, Oxford: Oxford University Press.

Humphrey, John (1987) *Gender and Work in the Third World: Sexual Divisions in Brazilian Industry*, London: Tavistock.

Humphries, Jane (1977) 'Class struggle and the persistence of the working class family', *Cambridge Journal of Economics* vol. 1, no. 3: 241–58.

ILO (1988) *Yearbook of Labour Statistics*, Geneva: ILO.

Joekes, Susan (1987) *Women in the World Economy*, Oxford: Oxford University Press.

Kim, Y. (1991) 'Women, home-based work and questions of organisation: the case of South Korea', paper presented at the International Workshop on Women Organising in the Process of Industrialisation, Institute of Social Studies, The Hague, Netherlands.

Konig, W. (1975) 'Towards an evaluation of international sub-contracting activities in developing countries: report on "Maquiladoras" in Mexico', Mexico City: UNECLA.

Lim, Linda (1990) 'Women's work in export factories: the politics of a cause', in Tinker 1990.

Narayanan, S. and Rasiah, N. (1992) 'Malaysian electronics: the changing prospects of employment and restructuring', *Development and change* vol. 23, no. 4: 75–99.

Open University/BBC (1992) 'I used to work in the fields' video programme made for course on Third World Development.

Pearson, Ruth (1988) 'Female workers in the First and Third Worlds: the "Greening" of women's labour', in Ray Pahl (ed.) *On Work*, Oxford: Blackwell.

—— (1991) 'Male bias and women's work in Mexico's border industries', in Diane Elson (ed.) *Male Bias in the Development Process*, Manchester: Manchester University Press.

—— (1992) 'Gender issues in industrialisation', in Hewitt, Johnson and Wield 1992.

Phongpaichit, P. (1988) 'Two roads to the factory: industrialisation strategies and women's employment in South East Asia', in B. Agarwal *Structures of Patriarchy: the State, the Community and the Household*, London: Zed Press.

Pineda-Ofreneo, R. (1984) 'Subcontracting in export-oriented industries; the impact of Filipino women', in I. Norland *et al. Industrialisation and the Labour Process in Southeast Asia*, Copenhagen: Institute of Cultural Sociology, University of Copenhagen.

Saffioti, Helieth (1978) *Women in Class Society*, New York and London: Monthly Review Press.

Salaff, Janet (1990) 'Women, the family and the state: Hong Kong, Taiwan and Singapore – newly industrialised countries in Asia', in Sharon Stichter and Jane Parpart (eds) *Women, Employment and the Family*, Basingstoke: Macmillan.

Schmitz, Hubert (1982) *Manufacturing in the Back Yard*, London: Pinter.

Scott, M. (1989) 'Brave new world', *Far Eastern Economic Review* 21 December 1989.

Sen, Amartya K. (1990) 'Gender and cooperative conflicts', in Tinker 1990.

Sharpston, Michael (1976) 'International subcontracting', *World Development* vol. 4, no. 4: 333–7.

Tinker, Irene (ed.) (1990) *Persistent Inequalities: Women and World Development*, New York and Oxford: Oxford University Press.

Warren, Bill (1973) 'Imperialism and capitalist industrialisation', *New Left Review* no. 81: 3–44.

Whitehead, Ann (1984) '"I'm hungry Mum": the politics of domestic budgeting', in K. Young, C. Wolkowitz and R. McCullagh (eds) *Of Marriage and the Market*, London: Routledge and Kegan Paul: 93–116.

Wolf, Diane (1992) *Factory Daughters: Gender, Household Dynamics and Rural Industrialization in Java*, Berkeley, Los Angeles and London: University of California Press.

AUTHOR INDEX

SUBJECT INDEX